SHELLEY'S ESSAYS AND LETTERS.

ESSAYS AND LETTERS

BY

PERCY BYSSHE SHELLEY.

EDITED, WITH INTRODUCTORY NOTE,

BY

ERNEST RHYS.

———◆———

BOOKS FOR LIBRARIES PRESS
FREEPORT, NEW YORK

First Published 1886

Reprinted 1971

INTERNATIONAL STANDARD BOOK NUMBER:
0-8369-5778-4

LIBRARY OF CONGRESS CATALOG CARD NUMBER:
75-154162

PRINTED IN THE UNITED STATES OF AMERICA

CONTENTS.

———◆———

PERCY BYSSHE SHELLEY.

COR CORDIUM.

NATUS IV. AUG. MDCCXCII.
OBIIT VIII. JUL. MDCCCXXII.

" Nothing of him that doth fade
But doth suffer a sea-change
Into something rich and strange."

[Inscription upon Shelley's Grave at Rome.]

SHELLEY'S PROSE WRITINGS.

T is impossible to turn to Shelley's prose with the untroubled interest and judgment that we summon in the case of most authors, especially those who are only, or mainly, prose-writers. Shelley's mark as a poet, in the narrower sense, that is, of a writer of verse, is so well-known, that almost everyone who turns to his prose will bring to it a set opinion, implying more or less of enthusiasm or uninterest, or even perhaps antagonism, based upon the already familiar grounds of his verse and the story of his life. The first interest of the book will therefore be a relative one, to be referred to previous ideas of its author's genius and personality ; and knowing what warmth of discussion these have constantly called forth, it will be well for us to approach any new signs of their quality, such as are offered here, in the urbanest and most reasonable temper we can bring to bear. Fortunately, judged for themselves alone, these prose-writings of Shelley are not hard to judge. Their literary setting is so perfect and delightful, that, if they had no other interest, they could not fail to be sought at last simply for artistic quality, and placed high among masterpieces of style accordingly. But the interest they bear is higher still, and having regard to it we should be mistaken in not profiting by the zest already created in us by the poet's grace for anything further coming from him and helping to interpret the fine and deep secrets of his nature.

These secrets, as we think them over, easily resolve themselves into one, the secret of Shelley's personal fascination for
so many of us, in especial at a certain period of our growth. It
would be useless to try and account very exactly for so subtle
an influence. The ideal atmosphere that fills the poems, that
seems to linger in the very collocation of their syllables, affects
us, we hardly know how or why, and creates the feeling which
is more than any reasoned theory of appreciation. Against this
feeling, once created, with its chivalrous faith and boundless
enthusiasm, scientific analysis, equally with matter-of-fact de-
traction, is powerless. It is a feeling akin to all that is ideal
and heroic in us when the hopes of youth most irradiate the
surroundings and direction of life.

> " The world's great age begins anew,
>   The golden years return,
> The earth doth like a snake renew
>   Her winter weeds outworn.
> Heaven smiles, and faiths and empires gleam
> Like wrecks of a dissolving dream."

In this music we have its very tone and echo. Vague it
may be, but most magical and strong nevertheless, and of
the ideal enterprise it inspires, Shelley is the spirit incarnate.
He inhabits with a princely if somewhat translunar splendour a
tower of his own on the mount of vision which is peculiarly
dedicated to his century. There we have known how to
picture him, gazing out upon what ideal vistas of the land of
promise, imagined after the half-realised accounts of the Italy he
loved. There, with him in spirit, looking out with his eyes, we
have seen the mystic vision of the future, as in a sunset whose
cloud-veil unclosing a moment has permitted a glimpse of perfect radiance within. That glimpse, once caught, leaves for
ever afterwards a restless longing to fully see what was so
nearly revealed; for within, we felt, were it but throughly
penetrated, lay the secret of the great progression through space
and time, in which the stars move so serenely, and men with
such tragic endeavour and disruption. It is the old story

of the Quest of the Grail, and many another since ; and its glimpse of the perfect, and its after-longing and spiritual unrest, are all centred in the feeling which is associated with the very name of Shelley. So much of this feeling as it is well for us to keep, perhaps, in a world that is material as well as ideal, these *Essays and Letters* will help to embody and make sure. The proof they give of their author's humanity is a capital antidote to anything extreme in our worship of him as an accession to the saints. So, having before endangered his right fame by hailing him as of the gods, we shall establish him more surely now, let us hope, by discovering how thoroughly, in virtue and default, he was a man.

The ideal Shelley has long been known to us, and lately we have been presented with a so-called " Real Shelley," for counterblast, as much painted as ever was the first, seeing that it has only been a matter of painting black what was before a somewhat too unrelieved white. This method of disillusioning is highly characteristic of the downright British temper of mind, which does so like to deal absolute judgments ; but it is peculiarly inapplicable in the case of a nature like Shelley's. The same method applied to a series of heroes and poets of much more definite quality than his could not fail to utterly destroy all right knowledge and love of them. Conceive the aspect of, let us suggest, Sir Philip Sidney, or to be bolder, Saint Francis of Assisi, or others more spiritually eminent still, under such malevolent treatment. The judgment upon Shelley, in truth, will always be very much a matter of standpoint. Those to whom the conventionalities are more than the ideal principles of which they are the often worn-out clothes, will necessarily fail in sympathy for such a nature as his, with its insistent relation of everything to the ideal, in a way, let it be admitted, a little oblivious apparently, at times, to the warm touch of human dependency. But the growth of humanity in his nature was as strong and sure as his literary growth ; there is an intimate relation between the two in all true natures. It may well be, therefore, that the *Essays and Letters* in which this is so clearly shewn may form an opening to appreciation by those who from

one cause or another have not been hitherto greatly attracted
by the poet or his writings. Studying the simpler evidence of
prose, they will find that neither angels nor evil spirits claim
him away from the difficult human mean, where he existed with
our everyday susceptibilities, only heightened and modified by
the poet's ten-fold greater liability to the drawings of pleasure
and of pain. The *real* " Real Shelley," neither selfish dreamer
nor untempted saint, but one like ourselves, with added qualities
of genius which bear their appointed defects, is clearly seen in a
hundred passages of his letters ; and how much more interesting in this reality of broad sunshine than, as often before shown,
under haze of moonshine or eldritch smoke.

Here is scarcely the place and time, however, for lengthy
analysis of Shelley's life and individuality. This has already
been admirably done in memoirs by Mrs. Shelley and Lady
Shelley, by Mr. William M. Rossetti and Mr. J. Addington
Symonds, and in quite a number of shorter essays by other
writers, with one or the other of which we are all well familiar.
It will be best perhaps, then, to touch only upon one or two
points which have special significance in the light of these prose
writings, and having so far rested a claim for Shelley's fund of
everyday humanity, we ought first of all to turn to the broad
basis of his character. One of the first things that occur to us
in reading the Letters, one laid stress upon by several writers, is
their absolute consistency with the poetry formally prepared by
Shelley with an eye to the public during his lifetime. This is
most important, for it touches upon the question of Shelley's
main sincerity, which, called in question, has formed the turning
point of more than one elaborated attack upon him. But in his
prose we are taken behind the scenes of his poet's theatre
to find, wonderful to tell, that all there really is what it artis-
tically gave itself out to be. The corroboration by the letters of
his deliberate verse utterance is indeed remarkable, and a
sufficient argument in itself for Shelley's utter thoroughness
and honesty of purpose. For, as another poet, whose
dignified loyalty to Shelley through a long life must have been
cause enough in itself for belief to many, has conclusively

asked :—" How shall we help believing in him when we find even his carnal speech to agree faithfully with the tone and rhythm of his most oracular utterances ? " With this quality is closely allied another which did more than anything to wreck the happiness of Shelley's life, his " egregious practical energy," as it has been well called by Mr. H. Buxton Forman. We all know how disastrously it resulted, lacking the higher prudence which could alone make such a tendency nobly valuable ; but at the same time it is by no means a common or a base quality, the unhalting readiness to act out one's theories, and Shelley had this innocent courage of his opinions with a vengeance. Point out a great idea or a crying need to him, and as soon as he felt sure of it, he would rush off at once, with a quite comical urgency, to apply it. If, however, it proves a certain *greenness*, it is a greenness that sometimes ripens into gold. At any rate it is quite incompatible with any such inherent deceptiveness as the writer of " The Real Shelley" has imputed to him. A touch more of that dissimulative concern for the world's opinion which often passes for prudence, and gives an aspect of virtue to what is merely social astuteness, would have saved him from many false and dishonourable indictments, such as those which wrung a cry from him in a memorable letter to his wife :—" My greatest content would be utterly to desert all human society· I would retire with you and our child to a solitary island in the sea, would build a boat, and shut upon my retreat the flood-gates of the world."

Revelations of the motives and interests of Shelley's life naturally abound in the Letters, and after having read them in conjunction with the poems, it seems to me impossible that any-one should turn away with anything but a profound belief in their writer's inherent nobility and truth of inspiration. But if this is to be so for the unbeliever, how are they to be envied who bring to the book their first enthusiasm unaltered. A more delightful literary experience can scarcely be conceived, I think, than that of this book, while the music of Shelley's song is still fresh in the ears, filling one with quick desire to know more of " the king of beauty and fancy," as Trelawney charmingly

called him. Impatiently foregoing the order of the book, and
turning first to the Letters to get the spirit and atmosphere of
Shelley's surroundings at one time and another, we could not
fail to be fascinated by the glimpses afforded of the year of
marvels which saw the birth of the *Prometheus Unbound* and
other great poems, showing how ideally environed the poet's
days then were. We can choose almost at random from the
letters of that time ; here is a passage from one, written from
Rome towards the end of March, when the *Prometheus Unbound*
was in process of composition :—

"I walk forth in the purple and golden light of an Italian
evening, and return by star or moonlight, through this scene.
The elms are just budding, and the warm spring winds bring
unknown odours, all sweet from the country. I see the radiant
Orion through the mighty columns of the temple of Concord,
and the mellow fading light softens down the modern buildings
of the capitol, the only ones that interfere with the sublime
desolation of the scene. On the steps of the capitol itself stand
two colossal statues of Castor and Pollux, each with his horse,
finely executed, though far inferior to those of Monte Cavallo,
the cast of one of which you know we saw together in London.
This walk is close to our lodging, and this is my evening walk."

While we are at Rome with Shelley in the spirit, one other
passage we must take, describing the burying-place which
received all that remained of him after the death's ordeal of fire
and water some three years later, and which by that time, too,
held the body of Keats. He begins in the same paragraph by
speaking of Rome as "a city, as it were, of the dead, or rather
of those who cannot die, and who survive the puny generations
which inhabit and pass over the spot which they have made
sacred to eternity;" and then, after describing the fields and the
"grassy lanes and copses winding among the ruins," and the
gardens of the palaces, and the "great green hill, lonely and
bare, which overhangs the Tiber," he writes :—

"The English burying-place is a green slope near the walls,
under the pyramidal tomb of Cestius, and is, I think, the most
beautiful and solemn cemetery I ever beheld. To see the sun

shining on its bright grass, fresh, when we first visited it, with
the autumnal dews, and hear the whispering of the wind among
the leaves of the trees which have overgrown the tomb of
Cestius, and the soil which is stirring in the sun-warm earth,
and to mark the tombs, mostly of women and young people
who were buried there, one might, if one were to die, desire the
sleep they seem to sleep."

With this passage may well be placed those two well-known
verses of the *Adonais*, describing the same scene :—

> " Go thou to Rome,—at once the paradise,
>   The grave, the city, and the wilderness ;
> And where its wrecks like shattered mountains rise,
>   And flowering weeds, and fragrant copses dress
>   The bones of desolation's nakedness,
> Pass, till the Spirit of the spot shall lead
>   Thy footsteps to a slope of green access,
> Where, like an infant's smile, over the dead
> A light of laughing flowers along the grass is spread.
>
> And grey walls moulder round, on which dull time
>   Feeds, like slow fire upon a hoary brand ;
> And one keen pyramid with wedge sublime,
>   Pavilioning the dust of him who planned
>   This refuge for his memory, doth stand
> Like flame transformed to marble ; and beneath
>   A field is spread, on which a newer band
> Have pitched in heaven's smile their camp of death,
> Welcoming him we lose with scarce extinguished breath."

One is tempted to go on endlessly, quoting and discussing
the beauty and fascination of the Letters, embodying so
much as they do of all things true and lovely. Of the
changing interests of travel they are in especial full, and
these in a land whose interests are so irresistible, and
with a little band of travellers whose wayside adventures
and excitements are so touched by the thought of the
noble creations in poetry that they helped to form.
Without troubling ourselves much about possible reproaches

of "word-painting," satisfied that the art of writing is
the handmaiden of all the other arts, who while she
retains the naïveté and modesty that are peculiarly her
own cannot get far astray, we shall not fail to follow with
delight those excursions immortally associated now with Venice
and Florence and Rome and Naples, the plains of Lombardy,
the Euganean Hills, and many another region of the "Paradise
of Exiles." In all the list of poets' friends and lovers, there
never was, surely, correspondent so favoured as Peacock, to
receive as he did, often in the enhancing contrasted dullness of
the Indian House, these letters from Italy. What a glimpse is
this to be received by post in a London office, malodorous with
coal-smoke and foolscap!—Shelley is describing a journey
through the Apennines, towards Salerno, when, after a day of
rain, storm, and tempest, amid the mountains, they catch sight
of the sea, illumined by the sudden burst of sunset between
the orange and lemon groves of a lovely village:—"A burst of
the declining sunlight illumined it," he writes. "The road led
along the brink of the precipice towards Salerno. Nothing
could be more glorious than the scene. The immense
mountains covered with the rare and divine vegetation of this
climate, with many-folding vales, and deep, dark recesses,
which the fancy scarcely could penetrate, descended from their
many summits precipitously to the sea. Before us was Salerno,
built into a declining plain, between the mountains and the sea.
Beyond, the other shore of sky-cleaving mountains, then dim
with the mist of tempest. Underneath, from the base of the
precipice where the road conducted, rocky promontories jutted
into the sea, covered with olive and ilex woods, or with the
ruined battlements of some Norman or Saracen fortress. We
slept at Salerno, and the next morning before daybreak proceeded to Posidonia. The night had been tempestuous, and
our way lay by the sea-sand. It was utterly dark, except when
the long line of wave burst, with a sound like thunder, beneath
the starless sky, and cast up a kind of mist of cold white
lustre. When morning came, we found ourselves travelling in
a wide desert plain, perpetually interrupted by wild irregular

glens, and bounded on all sides by the Apennines and the sea."

If the sketches of human life and character in the Letters are, as one might expect, knowing Shelley's comparative lack of closer sympathy with average human personality, and the greater abundance in a land like Italy of Nature's interest, less frequent than his sketches of Nature, they are nevertheless full of charm. Glimpses of Byron and of the others who helped to form the Shelley circle at different times abound; and with such variety of character as Byron, Leigh Hunt, the Gisbornes, the Williams's, Emilia Viviani, and others, afford, it would be strange, indeed, if we were not interested, apart from the vivid reflection of Shelley's irradiating consciousness. We think of that unusual little society, stationed on the lonely shores of the Mediterranean and the Adriatic, where the voices of Nature are apparent at all times, with curious imagination now of those days of memorable association,—days often as trivially or greatly troubled, however, as many others which in memory are only bright. Still more interesting are the occasional little descriptions of Shelley himself at his poet's work, so characteristic, many of them, of the maker of "Prometheus" and the "Witch of Atlas." Here is one such account, written to Peacock from Livorno:— " I have a study here in a tower, something like Scythrop's, where I am just beginning to recover the faculties of reading and writing. . . . From my tower I see the sea, with its islands, Gorgona, Capraja, Elba, and Corsica, on one side, and the Apennines on the other." The letter from which this is quoted is dated July 6th, 1819, and by turning to the one following, we get an exact account of the hours of every day at that time—a time, be it recalled, when Shelley's genius was on every side splendidly active, advancing yet again into the social and political field, as well as daringly further into that of poetry. And so throughout we find the Letters a most delightful and luminous commentary upon the poetry ; we see in them the poems in the making, lit up by a hundred glimpses of the unique life out of which the poems grew, and we turn from them

b

with a larger apprehension altogether of their writer. On the purely literary side, we shall only be able to appraise Shelley with complete critical appraisal, with a view to his practice in verse and prose, when his writings of both kinds have been paralleled and compared, as was suggested by the Rev. Stopford Brooke, in his eloquent address at the inaugural meeting of the Shelley Society.

Sooner or later, in reading the Letters, some significant reference or other to poetic aims is sure to recall the wish to know more fully what Shelley's theory of poetry really was, and in this we have the singular good fortune to be in possession of exact evidence in the essay on "The Defence of Poetry," which presents us with so imposing a statement of the poetic ideal. After searching through all Shelley's utterances about life and thought, and their expression in forms of poetry, on coming to their epitome in this essay, we soon find that their real basis is of the simplest, one that it needs no careful knowledge of metaphysics to comprehend, being indeed nothing more or less than LOVE itself. Upon this simple basis, however, he built a philosophical superstructure, that, as time went on, promised, had he only lived, to form a very elaborate and noble temple of thought. Whether it would have ever reached completion is another matter ; the main scheme of it was fairly clear to him, but he recognised, if somewhat tardily, the insufficiency of the materials and the powers at our command, and his poet's instinct would probably have warned him in time from binding himself to any final statement of matters infinite, whose expression must always be a progressive one. As for poetry, which Shelley regarded as the natural voice of our deepest insight into the ideas with which philosophy concerns itself, his treatment in the "Defence" is wonderfully lucid and perspicuous, especially for one hovering on the dangerous edge of metaphysics as he does. His whole standpoint is admirably expressed in the following passage from the essay by Robert Browning, already quoted from, which forms an incomparable prelude to the *Essays and Letters*. Taking Shelley as a type of the subjective poet, the passage dilates :—" He, gifted

like the objective poet with the fuller perception of nature and
man, is impelled to embody the thing he perceives, not so much
with reference to the many below as to the one above him,
the supreme Intelligence which apprehends all things in their
absolute truth—an ultimate view ever aspired to, if but partially
attained, by the poet's own soul. Not what man sees, but what
God sees—the *Ideas* of Plato, seeds of creation lying burningly
on the Divine Hand—it is towards these that he struggles.
Not with the combination of humanity in action, but with the
primal elements of humanity, he has to do ; and he digs where
he stands,—preferring to seek them in his own soul as the
nearest reflex of that absolute Mind, according to the intuitions of which he desires to perceive and speak." The
exact terms of this exposition Shelley himself might have
questioned, but it states his position nevertheless very perfectly.
Poetry was to him anything but a plaything, even the divine
plaything that it was to Heine, according to a famous con-
fession of that sublime cynic in the vein of which Byron, the
opposite pole in this to Shelley, is our most famous exponent ;
and it was certainly anything but an indifferent alternative to
other unconventional social exercises, or fashionable or un-
fashionable pastimes. To Shelley it was the voice of a
religion, an instrument which responded to the eternal verities,
making harmony for the dull ear of man out of all apparent
discords. "A poem," he cries, "is the very image of life
expressed in its eternal truth," and his "Defence of Poetry" is
throughout imbued with a spirit of passionate belief in the poet's
transcendent functions. Using the differentiation, enforced by
Ruskin, of the terms *æsthetic* and *theoretic*, Shelley was not at
all content to consider things æsthetically only, and according to
sensuous impress and gratification ; he was determinedly theoretic all through. When things of beauty seized his imagination
it was consciously as images of the everlasting principle of
beauty and the perfect harmony which lie behind, though of
course he was too true a poet to vaguely abandon the poet's
safeguards of the concrete. Examples of this theoretic relating
of his subject-matter abound even in his poetry, and this essay

is completely interpenetrated with its spirit. Nor need it matter
greatly that Shelley never reached any dogmatic position as
to the ultimate of these relations ; it is enough that he ideally
recognised this ultimate, even if he did not do so categorically.
In this profound religious way he keeps returning again and
again to exclaim upon the high origin and destiny of his
subject :—" Poetry is indeed something divine," he insists, " it is
at once the centre and circumference of knowledge ; it is that
which comprehends all science, and that to which all science
must be referred. It is at the same time the root and the
blossom of all other systems of thought ; it is that from which
all spring, and that which adorns all ; and that which, if
blighted, denies the fruit and the seed, and withholds from the
barren world the nourishment and the succession of the scions
of the tree of life. It is the perfect and consummate surface and
bloom of all things ; it is as the odour and the colour of the rose
to the texture of the elements which compose it, as the form and
splendour of unfaded beauty to the secrets of anatomy and
corruption." We have but to continue with citations from
the immediately succeeding paragraphs to for ever convert,
surely, all who disbelieve in the high function of poetry. We
gain from them, too, an incidental account of the mysterious
coming of inspiration, which naturally relates itself to the processes of imagination in Shelley's own mind.   " We are aware,"
he says, " of evanescent visitations of thought and feeling sometimes associated with place or person, sometimes regarding our
own mind alone, and always arising unforeseen and departing
unbidden, but elevating and delightful beyond all expression ;
so that even in the desire and the regret they leave, there cannot
but be pleasure, participating as it does in the nature of its
object. It is, as it were, the interpenetration of a diviner nature
through our own ; but its footsteps are like those of a wind over
the seas which the coming calm erases, and whose traces
remain only as on the wrinkled sand which paves it." The
first part of this passage suggests what has always seemed to
me one of the most characteristic episodes in Shelley's life, as
related by Mrs. Shelley—his solitary excursion to Monte San

Pellegrino in the August of 1820, returning to reproduce the
atmosphere and ideal essence of the days of this pilgrimage in
" The Witch of Atlas,"—characteristic outcome! exquisite
mouse of fancy brought forth by what mountain of Shelleyan
imagination !

Proceeding through the rest of the Essays in the light of the
Defence of Poetry, it is not needed to examine them here in
exact detail ; their connection with the different sides of
Shelley's genius and literary development are readily seen.
The *Discourse* on Athenian life and manners, in especial relation
to the subject of Love, which unfortunately breaks off at the
point of entering upon the most interesting part of its subject, is
yet very significant in its bearing upon Shelley's Hellenic
sympathies. How much we have lost by his having left it a
fragment we can only guess ruefully when we remember the
impassioned utterance in praise of love by Agathon and his
comrades, with the judicial deliverance by Socrates that follows,
in Plato's *Symposium*, to which Shelley's *Discourse* was intended
to form an introduction. Shelley's beautiful translation of the
Symposium it is intended to issue in a volume of Plato in the
present series, and it has therefore been omitted here, albeit
somewhat unwillingly, to make way for more of his original
writings. The immense stimulus that Plato gave to Shelley we
are reminded of again and again in the Essays and Letters, and
it must be kept in mind constantly in estimating either prose or
verse. Shelley's devotion to Plato was unwavering from the
day when he first began to read the Dialogues. Hogg, in
describing the poet's Oxford days, tells some exquisite anecdotes
of his enthusiastic Platonism, notably one, most comic, of an
attempt, when crossing a bridge one day, to elicit from a baby,
lifted from the arms of its startled mother, direct evidence about
a state of pre-existence. To the end Plato continued to
exercise Shelley as greatly, if to less eccentric result.
Corroborated by Berkeley and other idealists, Plato taught him
how to reconcile beauty and goodness, the æsthetic and the
moral sides of life, and so in great part formed the basis for the
Shelleyan religion. This is therefore, in many ways, the most

considerable influence in all Shelley's history, accounting for much that would else be very perplexing.

The remaining essays have each their own significance, throwing new light in one way and another, which is simply and clearly indicated as a rule by their titles. In some respects it is no doubt best to study them in the order of their production by Shelley. We come to understand then the evolution of the more perfected Shelley of the later years, and are able to trace the steps of his literary advance. Want of space again has prevented the inclusion of most of the earlier polemical writings, which, however, are not likely to be his latest memorial, and enough is included in the *Appendix* to enable judgment of their general worth. Some excerpts, of special interest in this present political crisis, are given from the Irish Address of 1812, so touched with curious associations of the excitable boyish liberator who went over with such charming faith to conquer a nation by love and its transcendental heroics. *The Declaration of Rights*, which shows a remarkable advance upon the two Irish pamphlets, from the beneficial restraints of the condensation necessary for such a manifesto, is given in full. The famous *Letter to Lord Ellenborough* is also given complete, and in this, which admirably displays all the qualities and faults of Shelley's early prose, we first recognise the capable mastery of expression which its author afterwards attained. *The Necessity of Atheism*, *The Refutation of Deism*, and the Vegetarian pamphlet, slightly interesting in themselves, are embodied in the notes to *Queen Mab*, which can be referred to in almost any edition of the poems, and they are therefore omitted here. The other early political papers are of too occasional a nature to be of much general interest. With the early fragment of romance entitled *The Assassins* we reach another side of Shelley altogether, and it is peculiarly interesting, Mr. H. Buxton Forman has told us, as showing behind its melodramatic crudity in certain portions a marked advance in human sympathy upon the merely intellectual enthusiasms that underlie the previous juvenilia. In it we detect, too, the achievement, afterwards confirmed in the *Coliseum* fragment, of that imaginative atmosphere without which romance utterly fails—that atmosphere of which Hawthorne so knew the secret. And turning at this point to consider the whole excellence of Shelley's prose style, there is something, it seems to me, in its impalpable, individual charm, which, with a hundred differences, is more like Hawthorne than anyone else. Seeing how in his prose Shelley almost entirely dispensed with the glittering equipment of metaphor and parti-coloured, teeming fancy that he wore in his verse exploits, it is wonderful that in his very plainest prose this exquisite individual flavour is almost as distinct as in *The Sensitive Plant* or *Prometheus Unbound*. While always touched with this facile, limpid, Shelleyan native quality, the prose at its best is of true classic excellence,—easily capable, lucid, reasoned, vigorous, unaffected ; and at its worst fails chiefly from indefiniteness and consequent diffuseness of expression ; never, except perhaps here and there in the very early writings, from graver lack of taste or rightness of utterance. For examples of its varied excellence, in the expression of quite different subjects, besides many such passages as have already been given from the Letters and the *Defence of Poetry*, the best of the notes upon the Sculpture of the age of Pericles, and the *Essay on Christianity* can be turned to. About the two last-mentioned writings, one might wish to say a further word with reference to Shelley's ideas upon fine-art and religion, but in the case of religion enough has perhaps already been said, and in the other, if it is remembered that Shelley lived at a day when art-primers and magazines did not abound to supply everybody with ready-made admirations and ecstasies, it will be seen that there is nothing very damning in the fact that he admired the melodrama of Salvator Rosa's, and somewhat depreciated the noble tragedy of Michael Angêlo's art.

The arrangement of the Essays in this volume is in the main that adopted by Mrs. Shelley in her first edition of the *Essays and Letters from Abroad*, while of course there is much that has been added since that time, of which the latest is the review of Hogg's *Alexy Haimatoff*. This review, which was discovered by Professor Dowden two or three years ago in an old magazine—*The Critical Review*—is given here in preference to Shelley's other better known reviews, as, for instance, those on *Frankenstein* and Godwin's *Mandeville.* There are certain other omissions which the scope of a volume such as this has made unavoidable, both in the Essays and the Letters, but, even as it is, this collection of the prose is by far the completest that has yet been brought, like the poems, within multitudinous reach, and there is enough and to spare to give a perfect idea of this side of Shelley's genius. Taken with the other side, of his verse, we have the high record of a noble life, noble even in its imperfections, which ended, let us remember, almost before it was mature, and which we must believe in, if not on the internal evidence that this record contains, at any rate on the testimony of so many and such opposites natures, from Byron to Henri Beyle, who, having known him, have borne witness to the beauty and nobility of his character. In this way the best of these prose-writings may be trusted to continue into time, not, I imagine, as has been said with authority, outlasting their author's verse, but, the prose with the verse, continuing as the incomparable representation of one of those difficultly ideal natures which, while the years go on, will always draw men impelled by the same ideal desires and defeated by the same errors.

ERNEST RHYS.

_____

[NOTE.—The thanks of the editor of this volume are here heartily given to all who have helped to make this edition of Shelley's Prose so far perfect, whether by permission to use copyright matter, as has been so freely granted by Sir Percy F. Shelley, Bart., or by literary aid and suggestion, received in various ways, from, first and foremost, the Shelley Society generally, and then from many of its members individually, including Mr. H. Buxton Forman, Dr. Furnivall, Dr. Garnett, Mr. William Bell Scott, and Mr. Thomas J. Wise. Of these Mr. Wise must be further specially mentioned for the unselfish assistance rendered by him in procuring scarce Shelleyana for the preparation of copy.]

MIXED ESSAYS AND FRAGMENTS.

A DEFENCE OF POETRY.

PART I.

ACCORDING to one mode of regarding those two classes of mental action, which are called reason and imagination, the former may be considered as mind contemplating the relations borne by one thought to another, however produced , and the latter, as mind acting upon those thoughts so as to colour them with its own light, and composing from them, as from elements, other thoughts, each containing within itself the principle of its own integrity. The one is the τὸ ποιειν, or the principle of synthesis, and has for its objects those forms which are common to universal nature and existence itself; the other is the τὸ λογιζειν, or principle of analysis, and its action regards the relations of things simply as relations; considering thoughts, not in their integral unity, but as the algebraical representations which conduct to certain general results. Reason is the enumeration of qualities already

82

known ; imagination is the perception of the value of those quantities, both separately and as a whole. Reason respects the differences, and imagination the similitudes of things. Reason is to imagination as the instrument to the agent, as the body to the spirit, as the shadow to the substance.

Poetry, in a general sense, may be defined to be "the expression of the imagination :" and poetry is connate with the origin of man. Man is an instrument over which a series of external and internal impressions are driven, like the alternations of an ever-changing wind over an Æolian lyre, which move it by their motion to ever-changing melody. But there is a principle within the human being, and perhaps within all sentient beings, which acts otherwise than in the lyre, and produces not melody alone, but harmony, by an internal adjustment of the sounds or motions thus excited to the impressions which excite them. It is as if the lyre could accommodate its chords to the motions of that which strikes them, in a determined proportion of sound ; even as the musician can accommodate his voice to the sound of the lyre. A child at play by itself will express its delight by its voice and motions ; and every inflexion of tone and every gesture will bear exact relation to a corresponding antitype in the pleasurable impressions which awakened it ; it will be the reflected image of that impression ; and as the lyre trembles and sounds after the wind has died away, so the child seeks, by prolonging in its voice and motions the duration of the effect, to prolong also a consciousness of the cause. In relation to the objects which delight a child, these expressions are, what poetry is to higher objects. The savage (for the savage is to ages what the child is to years) expresses the emotions produced in him by surrounding objects in a similar

manner; and language and gesture, together with plastic or
pictorial imitation, become the image of the combined effect
of those objects, and of his apprehension of them.   Man in
society, with all his passions and his pleasures, next
becomes the object of the passions and pleasures of man;
an additional class of emotions produces an augmented
treasure of expressions; and language, gesture, and the
imitative arts, become at once the representation and the
medium, the pencil and the picture, the chisel and the
statue, the chord and the harmony.   The social sympathies,
or those laws from which, as from its elements, society
results, begin to develop themselves from the moment that
two human beings co-exist; the future is contained within
the present, as the plant within the seed; and equality,
diversity, unity, contrast, mutual dependence, become the
principles alone capable of affording the motives according
to which the will of a social being is determined to action,
inasmuch as he is social; and constitute pleasure in sensation, virtue in sentiment, beauty in art, truth in reasoning,
and love in the intercourse of kind.   Hence men, even in
the infancy of society, observe a certain order in their
words and actions, distinct from that of the objects and the
impressions represented by them, all expression being subject to the laws of that from which it proceeds.   But let us
dismiss those more general considerations which might
involve an inquiry into the principles of society itself, and
restrict our view to the manner in which the imagination is
expressed upon its forms.

In the youth of the world, men dance and sing and
imitate natural objects, observing in these actions, as in all
others, a certain rhythm or order.   And, although all men
observe a similar, they observe not the same order, in the
motions of the dance, in the melody of the song, in the

combinations of language, in the series of their imitations
of natural objects. For there is a certain order or rhythm
belonging to each of these classes of mimetic representation,
from which the hearer and the spectator receive an intenser
and purer pleasure than from any other : the sense of an
approximation to this order has been called taste by
modern writers. Every man in the infancy of art, observes
an order which approximates more or less closely to that
from which this highest delight results : but the diversity
is not sufficiently marked, as that its gradations should be
sensible, except in those instances where the predominance
of this faculty of approximation to the beautiful (for so we
may be permitted to name the relation between this highest
pleasure and its cause) is very great. Those in whom it
exists in excess are poets, in the most universal sense of
the word ; and the pleasure resulting from the manner in
which they express the influence of society or nature upon
their own minds, communicates itself to others, and gathers
a sort of reduplication from that community. Their
language is vitally metaphorical ; that is, it marks the
before unapprehended relations of things and perpetuates
their apprehension, until the words which represent them,
become, through time, signs for portions or classes of
thoughts instead of pictures of integral thoughts ; and then
if no new poets should arise to create afresh the associations which have been thus disorganised, language will be
dead to all the nobler purposes of human intercourse.
These similitudes or relations are finely said by Lord
Bacon to be " the same footsteps of nature impressed upon
the various subjects of the world " *—and he considers the
faculty which perceives them as the storehouse of axioms
common to all knowledge. In the infancy of society every

* De Augment. Scient., cap. 1, lib. iii.

author is necessarily a poet, because language itself is poetry ; and to be a poet is to apprehend the true and the beautiful, in a word, the good which exists in the relation, subsisting, first between existence and perception, and secondly between perception and expression. Every original language near to its source is in itself the chaos of a cyclic poem : the copiousness of lexicography and the distinctions of grammar are the works of a later age, and are merely the catalogue and the form of the creations of poetry.

But poets, or those who imagine and express this indestructible order, are not only the authors of language and of music, of the dance, and architecture, and statuary, and painting : they are the institutors of laws, and the founders of civil society, and the inventors of the arts of life, and the teachers, who draw into a certain propinquity with the beautiful and the true, that partial apprehension of the agencies of the invisible world which is called religion. Hence all original religions are allegorical, or susceptible of allegory, and, like Janus, have a double face of false and true. Poets, according to the circumstances of the age and nation in which they appeared, were called, in the earlier epochs of the world, legislators, or prophets : a poet essentially comprises and unites both these characters. For he not only beholds intensely the present as it is, and discovers those laws according to which present things ought to be ordered, but he beholds the future in the present, and his thoughts are the germs of the flower and the fruit of latest time. Not that I assert poets to be prophets in the gross sense of the word, or that they can foretell the form as surely as they foreknow the spirit of events : such is the pretence of superstition, which would make poetry an attribute of prophecy, rather than prophecy an attribute of poetry. A poet participates in the eternal, the infinite, and the one; as far as relates to his conceptions, time and place and number are not. The grammatical forms which express the moods of time, and the difference of persons, and the distinction of place, are convertible with respect to the highest poetry without injuring it as poetry ; and the choruses of Æschylus, and the book of Job, and Dante's Paradise, would afford, more than any other writings, examples of this fact, if the limits of this essay did not forbid citation. The creations of sculpture, painting, and music are illustrations still more decisive.

Language, colour, form, and religious and civil habits of action, are all the instruments and materials of poetry ; they may be called poetry by that figure of speech which considers the effect as a synonyme of the cause. But poetry in a more restricted sense expresses those arrangements of language, and especially metrical language, which are created by that imperial faculty, whose throne is curtained within the invisible nature of man. And this springs from the nature itself of language, which is a more direct representation of the actions and passions of our internal being, and is susceptible of more various and delicate combinations, than colour, form, or motion, and is more plastic and obedient to the control of that faculty of which it is the creation. For language is arbitrarily produced by the imagination, and has relation to thoughts alone ; but all other materials, instruments, and conditions of art have relations among each other, which limit and interpose between conception and expression. The former is as a mirror which reflects, the latter as a cloud which enfeebles, the light of which both are mediums of communication. Hence the fame of sculptors, painters, and musicians, although the intrinsic powers of the great masters of these arts may yield in no degree to that of those who have employed language as the hieroglyphic of their thoughts, has never equalled that of poets in the restricted sense of the term; as two performers of equal skill will produce unequal effects from a guitar and a harp. The fame of legislators and founders of religions, so long as their institutions last, alone seems to exceed that of poets in the restricted sense; but it can scarcely be a question, whether, if we deduct the celebrity which their flattery of the gross opinions of the vulgar usually conciliates, together with that which belonged to them in their higher character of poets, any excess will remain.

We have thus circumscribed the word poetry within the limits of that art which is the most familiar and the most perfect expression of the faculty itself. It is necessary, however, to make the circle still narrower, and to determine the distinction between measured and unmeasured language; for the popular division into prose and verse is inadmissible in accurate philosophy.

Sounds as well as thoughts have relation both between each other and towards that which they represent, and a perception of the order of those relations has always been found connected with a perception of the order of the relations of thoughts. Hence the language of poets has ever affected a certain uniform and harmonious recurrence of sound, without which it were not poetry, and which is scarcely less indispensable to the communication of its influence, than the words themselves, without reference to that peculiar order. Hence the vanity of translation; it were as wise to cast a violet into a crucible that you might discover the formal principle of its colour and odour, as seek to transfuse from one language into another the creations of a poet. The plant must spring again from its seed, or it will bear no flower—and this is the burthen of the curse of Babel.

An observation of the regular mode of the recurrence of harmony in the language of poetical minds, together with its relation to music, produced metre, or a certain system of traditional forms of harmony and language. Yet it is by no means essential that a poet should accommodate his language to this traditional form, so that the harmony, which is its spirit, be observed. The practice is indeed convenient and popular, and to be preferred, especially in such composition as includes much action: but every great poet must inevitably innovate upon the example of his predecessors in the exact structure of his peculiar versification. The distinction between poets and prose writers is a vulgar error. The distinction between philosophers and poets has been anticipated. Plato was essentially a poet— the truth and splendour of his imagery, and the melody of his language, are the most intense that it is possible to conceive. He rejected the measure of the epic, dramatic, and lyrical forms, because he sought to kindle a harmony in thoughts divested of shape and action, and he forebore to invent any regular plan of rhythm which would include, under determinate forms, the varied pauses of his style. Cicero sought to imitate the cadence of his periods, but with little success. Lord Bacon was a poet.* His language has a sweet and majestic rhythm, which satisfies the sense, no less than the almost superhuman wisdom of his philosophy satisfies the intellect; it is a strain which distends, and then bursts the circumference of the reader's mind, and pours itself forth together with it into the universal element with which it has perpetual sympathy.

* See the Filum Labyrinthi, and the Essay on Death particularly.

All the authors of revolutions in opinion are not only necessarily poets as they are inventors, nor even as their words unveil the permanent analogy of things by images which participate in the life of truth; but as their periods are harmonious and rhythmical, and contain in themselves the elements of verse; being the echo of the eternal music. Nor are those supreme poets, who have employed traditional forms of rhythm on account of the form and action of their subjects, less capable of perceiving and teaching the truth of things, than those who have omitted that form.   Shakespeare, Dante, and Milton (to confine ourselves to modern writers) are philosophers of the very loftiest power.

A poem is the very image of life expressed in its eternal truth.   There is this difference between a story and a poem, that a story is a catalogue of detached facts, which have no other connection than time, place, circumstance, cause and effect; the other is the creation of actions according to the unchangeable forms of human nature, as existing in the mind of the Creator, which is itself the image of all other minds.   The one is partial, and applies only to a definite period of time, and a certain combination of events which can never again recur; the other is universal, and contains within itself the germ of a relation to whatever motives or actions have place in the possible varieties of human nature. Time, which destroys the beauty and the use of the story of particular facts, stripped of the poetry which should invest them, augments that of poetry, and for ever develops new and wonderful applications of the eternal truth which it contains.   Hence epitomes have been called the moths of just history; they eat out the poetry of it.   A story of particular facts is as a mirror which obscures and distorts that which should be beautiful: poetry is a mirror which makes beautiful that which is distorted.

The parts of a composition may be poetical, without the composition as a whole being a poem. A single sentence may be considered as a whole, though it may be found in the midst of a series of unassimilated portions; a single word even may be a spark of inextinguishable thought. And thus all the great historians, Herodotus, Plutarch, Livy, were poets; and although the plan of these writers, especially that of Livy, restrained them from developing this faculty in its highest degree, they made copious and ample amends for their subjection, by filling all the interstices of their subjects with living images.

Having determined what is poetry, and who are poets, let us proceed to estimate its effects upon society.

Poetry is ever accompanied with pleasure : all spirits on which it falls open themselves to receive the wisdom which is mingled with its delight. In the infancy of the world, neither poets themselves nor their auditors are fully aware of the excellence of poetry : for it acts in a divine and un-apprehended manner, beyond and above consciousness; and it is reserved for future generations to contemplate and measure the mighty cause and effect in all the strength and splendour of their union. Even in modern times, no living poet ever arrived at the fulness of his fame; the jury which sits in judgment upon a poet, belonging as he does to all time, must be composed of his peers: it must be impanneled by Time from the selectest of the wise of many generations. A poet is a nightingale, who sits in darkness and sings to cheer its own solitude with sweet sounds; his auditors are as men entranced by the melody of an unseen musician, who feel that they are moved and softened, yet know not whence or why. The poems of Homer and his contempo-raries were the delight of infant Greece; they were the elements of that social system which is the column upon which all succeeding civilisation has reposed. Homer embodied the ideal perfection of his age in human character; nor can we doubt that those who read his verses were awakened to an ambition of becoming like to Achilles, Hector, and Ulysses: the truth and beauty of friendship, patriotism, and persevering devotion to an object, were unveiled to the depths in these immortal creations: the sentiments of the auditors must have been refined and enlarged by a sympathy with such great and lovely impersonations, until from admiring they imitated, and from imitation they identified themselves with the objects of their admiration. Nor let it be objected, that these characters are remote from moral perfection, and that they can by no means be considered as edifying patterns for general imitation. Every epoch, under names more or less specious, has deified its peculiar errors; Revenge is the naked idol of the worship of a semi-barbarous age; and Self-deceit is the veiled image of unknown evil, before which luxury and satiety lie prostrate. But a poet considers the vices of his contemporaries as the temporary dress in which his creations must be arrayed, and which cover without concealing the eternal proportions of their beauty. An epic or dramatic personage is understood to wear them around his soul, as he may the ancient armour or the modern uniform around his body; whilst it is easy to conceive a dress more graceful than either. The beauty of the internal nature cannot be so far concealed by its accidental vesture, but that the spirit of its form shall communicate itself to the very disguise, and indicate the shape it hides from the manner in which it is worn. A majestic form and graceful motions will express themselves through the most barbarous and tasteless costume. Few poets of the highest class have chosen to exhibit the beauty of their conceptions in its naked truth and splendour; and it is doubtful whether the alloy of costume, habit, etc., be not necessary to temper this planetary music for mortal ears.

The whole objection, however, of the immorality of poetry rests upon a misconception of the manner in which poetry acts to produce the moral improvement of man. Ethical science arranges the elements which poetry has created, and propounds schemes and proposes examples of civil and domestic life: nor is it for want of admirable doctrines that men hate, and despise, and censure, and deceive, and subjugate one another. But poetry acts in another and diviner manner. It awakens and enlarges the mind itself by rendering it the receptacle of a thousand unapprehended combinations of thought. Poetry lifts the veil from the hidden beauty of the world, and makes familiar objects be as if they were not familiar; it reproduces all that it represents, and the impersonations clothed in its Elysian light stand thenceforward in the minds of those who have once contemplated them, as memorials of that gentle and exalted content which extends itself over all thoughts and actions with which it coexists. The great secret of morals is love; or a going out of our nature, and an identification of ourselves with the beautiful which exists in thought, action, or person, not our own. A man, to be greatly good, must imagine intensely and comprehensively; he must put himself in the place of another and of many others; the pains and pleasures of his species must become his own. The great instrument of moral good is the imagination; and poetry administers to the effect by acting upon the cause. Poetry enlarges the circumference of the imagination by replenishing it with thoughts of ever new delight, which have the power of attracting and assimilating to their own nature all other thoughts, and which form

new intervals and interstices whose void for ever craves
fresh food. Poetry strengthens the faculty which is the
organ of the moral nature of man, in the same manner as
exercise strengthens a limb. A poet therefore would do
ill to embody his own conceptions of right and wrong,
which are usually those of his place and time, in his
poetical creations, which participate in neither. By this
assumption of the inferior office of interpreting the effect,
in which perhaps after all he might acquit himself but
imperfectly, he would resign a glory in a participation
in the cause. There was little danger that Homer, or any
of the eternal poets, should have so far misunderstood
themselves as to have abdicated this throne of their widest
dominion. Those in whom the poetical faculty, though
great, is less intense, as Euripides, Lucan, Tasso, Spenser,
have frequently affected a moral aim, and the effect of
their poetry is diminished in exact proportion to the
degree in which they compel us to advert to this
purpose.

Homer and the cyc.ic poets were followed at a certain
interval by the dramatic and lyrical poets of Athens, who
flourished contemporaneously with all that is most perfect
in the kindred expressions of the poetical faculty ; architecture, painting, music, the dance, sculpture, philosophy,
and we may add, the forms of civil life. For although the
scheme of Athenian society was deformed by many
imperfections which the poetry existing in chivalry and
Christianity has erased from the habits and institutions of
modern Europe ; yet never at any other period has so much
energy, beauty, and virtue been developed ; never was
blind strength and stubborn form so disciplined and
rendered subject to the will of man, or that will less
repugnant to the dictates of the beautiful and the true, as

during the century which preceded the death of Socrates.
Of no other epoch in the history of our species have we
records and fragments stamped so visibly with the image of
the divinity in man.   But it is poetry alone, in form, in
action, or in language, which has rendered this epoch memorable above all others, and the storehouse of examples to
everlasting time.   For written poetry existed at that
epoch simultaneously with the other arts, and it is an idle
inquiry to demand which gave and which received the
light, which all, as from a common focus, have scattered
over the darkest periods of succeeding time.   We know no
more of cause and effect than a constant conjunction of
events : poetry is ever found to co-exist with whatever
other arts contribute to the happiness and perfection of
man.   I appeal to what has already been established to
distinguish between the cause and the effect.

It was at the period here adverted to, that the drama
had its birth ; and however a succeeding writer may have
equalled or surpassed those few great specimens of the
Athenian drama which have been preserved to us, it is
indisputable that the art itself never was understood or
practised according to the true philosophy of it, as at
Athens.   For the Athenians employed language, action,
music, painting, the dance, and religious institutions, to
produce a common effect in the representation of the highest
idealisms of passion and of power; each division in the art
was made perfect in its kind by artists of the most consummate skill, and was disciplined into a beautiful proportion
and unity one towards the other.   On the modern stage a
few only of the elements capable of expressing the image of
the poet's conception are employed at once.   We have
tragedy without music and dancing; and music and
dancing without the highest impersonations of which they

are the fit accompaniment, and both without religion and solemnity. Religious institution has indeed been usually banished from the stage. Our system of divesting the actor's face of a mask, on which the many expressions appropriated to his dramatic character might be moulded into one permanent and unchanging expression, is favourable only to a partial and inharmonious effect; it is fit for nothing but a monologue, where all the attention may be directed to some great master of ideal mimicry. The modern practice of blending comedy with tragedy, though liable to great abuse in point of practice, is undoubtedly an extension of the dramatic circle; but the comedy should be as in King Lear, universal, ideal, and sublime. It is perhaps the intervention of this principle which determines the balance in favour of King Lear against the Œdipus Tyrannus or the Agamemnon, or, if you will, the trilogies with which they are connected; unless the intense power of the choral poetry, especially that of the latter, should be considered as restoring the equilibrium. King Lear, if it can sustain this comparison, may be judged to be the most perfect specimen of the dramatic art existing in the world; in spite of the narrow conditions to which the poet was subjected by the ignorance of the philosophy of the drama which has prevailed in modern Europe. Calderon, in his religious Autos, has attempted to fulfil some of the high conditions of dramatic representation neglected by Shakespeare; such as the establishing a relation between the drama and religion, and the accommodating them to music and dancing; but he omits the observation of conditions still more important, and more is lost than gained by the substitution of the rigidly-defined and ever-repeated idealisms of a distorted superstition for the living impersonations of the truth of human passion.

But I digress.—The connection of scenic exhibitions with the improvement or corruption of the manners of men, has been universally recognised; in other words, the presence or absence of poetry in its most perfect and universal form has been found to be connected with good and evil in conduct or habit. The corruption which has been imputed to the drama as an effect, begins, when the poetry employed in its constitution ends: I appeal to the history of manners whether the periods of the growth of the one and the decline of the other have not corresponded with an exactness equal to any example of moral cause and effect.

The drama at Athens, or wheresoever else it may have approached to its perfection, ever co-existed with the moral and intellectual greatness of the age. The tragedies of the Athenian poets are as mirrors in which the spectator beholds himself, under a thin disguise of circumstance, stript of all but that ideal perfection and energy which every one feels to be the internal type of all that he loves, admires, and would become. The imagination is enlarged by a sympathy with pains and passions so mighty, that they distend in their conception the capacity of that by which they are conceived; the good affections are strengthened by pity, indignation, terror and sorrow; and an exalted calm is prolonged from the satiety of this high exercise of them into the tumult of familiar life: even crime is disarmed of half its horror and all its contagion by being represented as the fatal consequence of the unfathomable agencies of nature; error is thus divested of its wilfulness; men can no longer cherish it as the creation of their choice. In a drama of the highest order there is little food for censure or hatred; it teaches rather self-knowledge and self-respect. Neither the eye nor the mind can see itself, unless reflected upon that which it resembles. The drama, so long as it continues to express poetry, is as a prismatic and many-sided mirror, which collects the brightest rays of human nature and divides and reproduces them from the simplicity of these elementary forms, and touches them with majesty and beauty, and multiplies all that it reflects, and endows it with the power of propagating its like wherever it may fall.

But in periods of the decay of social life, the drama sympathises with that decay. Tragedy becomes a cold imitation of the form of the great masterpieces of antiquity, divested of all harmonious accompaniment of the kindred arts ; and often the very form misunderstood, or a weak attempt to teach certain doctrines, which the writer considers as moral truths ; and which are usually no more than specious flatteries of some gross vice or weakness, with which the author, in common with his auditors, are infected. Hence what has been called the classical and domestic drama. Addison's " Cato " is a specimen of the one ; and would it were not superfluous to cite examples of the other ! To such purposes poetry cannot be made subservient. Poetry is a sword of lightning, ever unsheathed, which consumes the scabbard that would contain it. And thus we observe that all dramatic writings of this nature are unimaginative in a singular degree ; they affect sentiment and passion, which, divested of imagination, are other names for caprice and appetite. The period in our own history of the grossest degradation of the drama is the reign of Charles II., when all forms in which poetry had been accustomed to be expressed became hymns to the triumph of kingly power over liberty and virtue. Milton stood alone illuminating an age unworthy of him. At such periods the calculating principle pervades all the forms of dramatic exhibition, and poetry ceases to be expressed upon them Comedy loses its ideal universality : wit suceeds to humour ; we laugh from self-complacency and triumph, instead of pleasure ; malignity, sarcasm, and contempt succeed to sympathetic merriment ; we hardly laugh, but we smile. Obscenity, which is ever blasphemy against the divine beauty in life, becomes, from the very veil which it assumes, more active if less disgusting : it is a monster for which the corruption of society for ever brings forth new food, which it devours in secret.

The drama being that form under which a greater number of modes of expression of poetry are susceptible of being combined than any other, the connexion of poetry and social good is more observable in the drama than in whatever other form.   And it is indisputable that the highest perfection of human society has ever corresponded with the highest dramatic excellence ; and that the corruption or the extinction of the drama in a nation where it has once flourished, is a mark of a corruption of manners, and an extinction of the energies which sustain the soul of social life.   But, as Machiavelli says of political institutions, that life may be preserved and renewed, if men should arise capable of bringing back the drama to its principles.   And this is true with respect to poetry in its most extended sense : all language, institution and form, require not only to be produced but to be sustained : the office and character of a poet participates in the divine nature as regards providence, no less than as regards creation.

Civil war, the spoils of Asia, and the fatal predominance first of the Macedonian, and then of the Roman arms, were so many symbols of the extinction or suspension of the creative faculty in Greece.   The bucolic writers, who found patronage under the lettered tyrants of Sicily and Egypt, were the latest representatives of its most glorious reign. Their poetry is intensely melodious ; like the odour of the tuberose, it overcomes and sickens the spirit with excess of sweetness ; whilst the poetry of the preceding age was as a meadow-gale of June, which mingles the fragrance of all the flowers of the field, and adds a quickening and harmonising spirit of its own which endows the sense with a power of sustaining its extreme delight. The bucolic and erotic delicacy in written poetry is correlative with that softness in statuary, music, and the kindred arts, and even in manners and institutions, which distinguished the epoch to which I now refer. Nor is it the poetical faculty itself, or any misapplication of it, to which this want of harmony is to be imputed. An equal sensibility to the influence of the senses and the affections is to be found in the writings of Homer and Sophocles: the former, especially, has clothed sensual and pathetic images with irresistible attractions. Their superiority over these succeeding writers consists in the presence of those thoughts which belong to the inner faculties of our nature, not in the absence of those which are connected with the external : their incomparable perfection consists in a harmony of the union of all. It is not what the erotic poets have, but what they have not, in which their imperfection consists. It is not inasmuch as they were poets, but inasmuch as they were not poets, that they can be considered with any plausibility as connected with the corruption of their age. Had that corruption availed so as to extinguish in them the sensibility to pleasure, passion, and natural scenery, which is imputed to them as an imperfection, the last triumph of evil would have been achieved. For the end of social corruption is to destroy all sensibility to pleasure ; and, therefore, it is corruption. It begins at the imagination and the intellect

as at the core, and distributes itself thence as a paralysing
venom, through the affections into the very appetites, until
all become a torpid mass in which hardly sense survives.
At the approach of such a period, poetry ever addresses
itself to those faculties which are the last to be destroyed,
and its voice is heard, like the footsteps of Astræa, departing from the world.   Poetry ever communicates all the
pleasure which men are capable of receiving: it is ever
still the light of life ; the source of whatever of beautiful
or generous or true can have place in an evil time.   It will
readily be confessed that those among the luxurious citizens
of Syracuse and Alexandria, who were delighted with the
poems of Theocritus, were less cold, cruel, and sensual than
the remnant of their tribe.   But corruption must utterly
have destroyed the fabric of human society before poetry
can ever cease.   The sacred links of that chain have never
been entirely disjoined, which descending through the
minds of many men is attached to those great minds,
whence as from a magnet the invisible effluence is sent
forth, which at once connects, animates, and sustains the
life of all.   It is the faculty which contains within itself
the seeds at once of its own and of social renovation.   And
let us not circumscribe the effects of the bucolic and
erotic poetry within the limits of the sensibility of those to
whom it was addressed.   They may have perceived the
beauty of those immortal compositions, simply as fragments
and isolated portions : those who are more finely organised,
or, born in a happier age, may recognise them as episodes
to that great poem, which all poets, like the co-operating
thoughts of one great mind, have built up since the
beginning of the world.

The same revolutions within a narrower sphere had place
in ancient Rome ; but the actions and forms of its social

life never seem to have been perfectly saturated with the
poetical element. The Romans appear to have considered
the Greeks as the selectest treasuries of the selectest forms
of manners and of nature, and to have abstained from
creating in measured language, sculpture, music, or architecture, anything which might bear a particular relation
to their own condition, whilst it should bear a general one
to the universal constitution of the world. But we judge
from partial evidence, and we judge perhaps partially.
Ennius, Varro, Pacuvius, and Accius, all great poets, have
been lost. Lucretius is in the highest, and Virgil in a very
high sense, a creator. The chosen delicacy of expressions
of the latter, are as a mist of light which conceal from us
the intense and exceeding truth of his conceptions of
nature. Livy is instinct with poetry. Yet Horace,
Catullus, Ovid, and generally the other great writers of the
Virgilian age, saw man and nature in the mirror of Greece.
The institutions also, and the religion of Rome, were less
poetical that those of Greece, as the shadow is less vivid
than the substance. Hence poetry in Rome seemed to
follow, rather than accompany, the perfection of political
and domestic society. The true poetry of Rome lived in
its institutions; for whatever of beautiful, true, and
majestic, they contained, could have sprung only from the
faculty which creates the order in which they consist. The
life of Camillus, the death of Regulus; the expectation of
the senators, in their godlike state, of the victorious
Gauls; the refusal of the republic to make peace with
Hannibal, after the battle of Cannæ, were not the
consequences of a refined calculation of the probable
personal advantage to result from such a rhythm and order
in the shows of life, to those who were at once the poets
and the actors of these immortal dramas. The imagination

beholding the beauty of this order, created it out of itself
according to its own idea ; the consequence was empire, and
the reward ever-living fame.   These things are not the less
poetry, *quia carent vate sacro.*   They are the episodes of
that cyclic poem written by Time upon the memories
of men.   The Past, like an inspired rhapsodist, fills
the theatre of everlasting generations with their
harmony.

At length the ancient system of religion and manners
had fulfilled the circle of its revolutions.   And the world
would have fallen into utter anarchy and darkness, but
that there were found poets among the authors of the
Christian and chivalric systems of manners and religion,
who created forms of opinion and action never before
conceived ; which, copied into the imaginations of men,
became as generals to the bewildered armies of their
thoughts.   It is foreign to the present purpose to touch
upon the evil produced by these systems : except that we
protest, on the ground of the principles already established, that no portion of it can be attributed to the poetry
they contain.

It is probable that the poetry of Moses, Job, David,
Solomon, and Isaiah had produced a great effect upon the
mind of Jesus and his disciples.   The scattered fragments
preserved to us by the biographers of this extraordinary
person, are all instinct with the most vivid poetry.   But
his doctrines seem to have been quickly distorted.   At
a certain period after the prevalence of a system of opinions
founded upon those promulgated by him, the three forms
into which Plato had distributed the faculties of mind
underwent a sort of apotheosis, and became the object of
the worship of the civilised world.   Here it is to be
confessed that " Light seems to thicken," and

" The crow makes wing to the rooky wood,
Good things of day begin to droop and drowse,
And night's black agents to their preys do rouse."

But mark how beautiful an order has sprung from the dust
and blood of this fierce chaos ! how the world, as from a
resurrection, balancing itself on the golden wings of knowledge and of hope, has reassumed its yet unwearied flight
into the heaven of time. Listen to the music, unheard by
outward ears, which is as a ceaseless and invisible
wind, nourishing its everlasting course with strength and
swiftness.

The poetry in the doctrines of Jesus Christ, and the
mythology and institutions of the Celtic conquerors of the
Roman empire, outlived the darkness and the convulsions
connected with their growth and victory, and blended
themselves in a new fabric of manners and opinion. It is
an error to impute the ignorance of the dark ages to the
Christian doctrines or the predominance of the Celtic
nations. Whatever of evil their agencies may have contained sprang from the extinction of the poetical principle,
connected with the progress of despotism and superstition.
Men, from causes too intricate to be here discussed, had
become insensible and selfish : their own will had become
feeble, and yet they were its slaves, and thence the slaves
of the will of others : lust, fear, avarice, cruelty, and fraud,
characterised a race amongst whom no one was to be found
capable of *creating* in form, language, or institution. The
moral anomalies of such a state of society are not justly to
be charged upon any class of events immediately connected
with them, and those events are most entitled to our approbation which could dissolve it most expeditiously. It is
unfortunate for those who cannot distinguish words from

thoughts, that many of these anomalies have been incorporated into our popular religion.

It was not until the eleventh century that the effects of the poetry of the Christian and chivalric systems began to manifest themselves. The principle of equality had been discovered and applied by Plato in his Republic, as the theoretical rule of the mode in which the materials of pleasure and of power produced by the common skill and labour of human beings ought to be distributed among them. The limitations of this rule were asserted by him to be determined only by the sensibility of each, or the utility to result to all. Plato, following the doctrines of Timæus and Pythagoras, taught also a moral and intellectual system of doctrine, comprehending at once the past, the present, and the future condition of man. Jesus Christ divulged the sacred and eternal truths contained in these views to mankind, and Christianity, in its abstract purity, became the exoteric expression of the esoteric doctrines of the poetry and wisdom of antiquity. The incorporation of the Celtic nations with the exhausted population of the south, impressed upon it the figure of the poetry existing in their mythology and institutions. The result was a sum of the action and reaction of all the causes included in it ; for it may be assumed as a maxim that no nation or religion can supersede any other without incorporating into itself a portion of that which it supersedes. The abolition of personal and domestic slavery, and the emancipation of women from a great part of the degrading restraints of antiquity, were among the consequences of these events.

The abolition of personal slavery is the basis of the highest political hope that it can enter into the mind of man to conceive. The freedom of women produced the poetry of sexual love. Love became a religion, the idols of whose worship were ever present. It was as if the statues of Apollo and the Muses had been endowed with life and motion, and had walked forth among their worshippers; so that earth became peopled by the inhabitants of a diviner world. The familiar appearance and proceedings of life became wonderful and heavenly, and a paradise was created as out of the wrecks of Eden. And as this creation itself is poetry, so its creators were poets; and language was the instrument of their art: "Galeotto fù il libro, e chi lo scrisse." The Provençal Trouveurs, or inventors, preceded Petrarch, whose verses are as spells, which unseal the inmost enchanted fountains of the delight which is in the grief of love. It is impossible to feel them without becoming a portion of that beauty which we contemplate : it were superfluous to explain how the gentleness and the elevation of mind connected with these sacred emotions can render men more amiable, more generous and wise, and lift them out of the dull vapours of the little world of self. Dante understood the secret things of love even more than Petrarch. His *Vita Nuova* is an inexhaustible fountain of purity of sentiment and language : it is the idealised history of that period, and those intervals of his life which were dedicated to love. His apotheosis of Beatrice in Paradise, and the gradations of his own love and her loveliness, by which as by steps he feigns himself to have ascended to the throne of the Supreme Cause, is the most glorious imagination of modern poetry. The acutest critics have justly reversed the judgment of the vulgar, and the order of the great acts of the "Divine Drama," in the measure of the admiration which they accord to the Hell, Purgatory, and Paradise. The latter is a perpetual hymn of everlasting love. Love, which found a worthy poet in

Plato alone of all the ancients, has been celebrated by a chorus of the greatest writers of the renovated world ; and the music has penetrated the caverns of society, and its echoes still drown the dissonance of arms and superstition. At successive intervals, Ariosto, Tasso, Shakspeare, Spenser, Calderon, Rousseau, and the great writers of our own age, have celebrated the dominion of love, planting as it were trophies in the human mind of that sublimest victory over sensuality and force. The true relation borne to each other by the sexes into which human kind is distributed, has become less misunderstood ; and if the error which confounded diversity with inequality of the powers of the two sexes has been partially recognised in the opinions and institutions of modern Europe, we owe this great benefit to the worship of which chivalry was the law, and poets the prophets.

The poetry of Dante may be considered as the bridge thrown over the stream of time, which unites the modern and ancient world. The distorted notions of invisible things which Dante and his rival Milton have idealised, are merely the mask and the mantle in which these great poets walk through eternity enveloped and disguised. It is a difficult question to determine how far they were conscious of the distinction which must have subsisted in their minds between their own creeds and that of the people. Dante at least appears to wish to mark the full extent of it by placing Riphæus, whom Virgil calls *justissimus unus*, in Paradise, and observing a most heretical caprice in his distribution of rewards and punishments. And Milton's poem contains within itself a philosophical refutation of that system, of which, by a strange and natural antithesis, it has been a chief popular support. Nothing can exceed the energy and magnificence of the character of Satan as

expressed in "Paradise Lost." It is a mistake to suppose
that he could ever have been intended for the popular personification of evil. Implacable hate, patient cunning, and
a sleepless refinement of device to inflict the extremest
anguish on an enemy, these things are evil; and, although
venial in a slave, are not to be forgiven in a tyrant;
although redeemed by much that ennobles his defeat in one
subdued, are marked by all that dishonours his conquest in
the victor. Milton's Devil as a moral being is as far
superior to his God, as one who perseveres in some purpose
which he has conceived to be excellent in spite of adversity
and torture, is to one who in the cold security of undoubted
triumph inflicts the most horrible revenge upon his enemy,
not from any mistaken notion of inducing him to repent of
a perseverance in enmity, but with the alleged design of
exasperating him to deserve new torments. Milton has so
far violated the popular creed (if this shall be judged to be
a violation) as to have alleged no superiority of moral virtue
to his God over his Devil. And this bold neglect of a
direct moral purpose is the most decisive proof of the
supremacy of Milton's genius. He mingled as it were the
elements of human nature as colours upon a single pallet,
and arranged them in the composition of his great picture
according to the laws of epic truth; that is, according
to the laws of that principle by which a series of actions
of the external universe and of intelligent and ethical
beings is calculated to excite the sympathy of succeeding
generations of mankind. The Divina Commedia and
Paradise Lost have conferred upon modern mythology a
systematic form; and when change and time shall have
added one more superstition to the mass of those which
have arisen and decayed upon the earth, commentators
will be learnedly employed in elucidating the religion of

ancestral Europe, only not utterly forgotten because it will have been stamped with the eternity of genius.

Homer was the first and Dante the second epic poet: that is, the second poet, the series of whose creations bore a defined and intelligible relation to the knowledge and sentiment and religion of the age in which he lived, and of the ages which followed it, developing itself in correspondence with their development. For Lucretius had limed the wings of his swift spirit in the dregs of the sensible world; and Virgil, with a modesty that ill became his genius, had affected the fame of an imitator, even whilst he created anew all that he copied; and none among the flock of mock-birds, though their notes were sweet, Apollonius Rhodius, Quintus Calaber, Nonnus, Lucan, Statius, or Claudian, have sought even to fulfil a single condition of epic truth. Milton was the third epic poet. For if the title of epic in its highest sense be refused to the Æneid, still less can it be conceded to the Orlando Furioso, the Gerusalemme Liberata, the Lusiad, or the Fairy Queen.

Dante and Milton were both deeply penetrated with the ancient religion of the civilised world; and its spirit exists in their poetry probably in the same proportion as its forms survived in the unreformed worship of modern Europe. The one preceded and the other followed the Reformation at almost equal intervals. Dante was the first religious reformer, and Luther surpassed him rather in the rudeness and acrimony, than in the boldness of his censures of papal usurpation. Dante was the first awakener of entranced Europe; he created a language, in itself music and persuasion, out of a chaos of inharmonious barbarisms. He was the congregator of those great spirits who presided over the resurrection of learning; the Lucifer of that starry flock which in the thirteenth century shone forth from republican

Italy, as from a heaven, into the darkness of the benighted world. His very words are instinct with spirit; each is as a spark, a burning atom of inextinguishable thought; and many yet lie covered in the ashes of their birth, and pregnant with the lightning which has yet found no conductor. All high poetry is infinite; it is as the first acorn, which contained all oaks potentially. Veil after veil may be undrawn, and the inmost naked beauty of the meaning never exposed. A great poem is a fountain for ever overflowing with the waters of wisdom and delight; and after one person and one age has exhausted all its divine effluence which their peculiar relations enable them to share, another and yet another succeeds, and new relations are ever developed, the source of an unforeseen and an unconceived delight.

The age immediately succeeding to that of Dante, Petrarch, and Boccaccio, was characterised by a revival of painting, sculpture, and architecture. Chaucer caught the sacred inspiration, and the superstructure of English literature is based upon the materials of Italian invention.

But let us not be betrayed from a defence into a critical history of poetry and its influence on society. Be it enough to have pointed out the effects of poets, in the large and true sense of the word, upon their own and all succeeding times.

But poets have been challenged to resign the civic crown to reasoners and mechanists, on another plea. It is admitted that the exercise of the imagination is most delightful, but it is alleged that that of reason is more useful. Let us examine as the grounds of this distinction what is here meant by utility. Pleasure or good, in a general sense, is that which the consciousness of a sensitive and intelligent being seeks, and in which, when found, it acquiesces.   There are two kinds of pleasure, one durable, universal, and permanent; the other transitory and particular.   Utility may either express the means of producing the former or the latter.   In the former sense, whatever strengthens and purifies the affections, enlarges the imagination, and adds spirit to sense, is useful.   But a narrower meaning may be assigned to the word utility, confining it to express that which banishes the importunity of the wants of our animal nature, the surrounding men with security of life, the dispersing the grosser delusions of superstition, and the conciliating such a degree of mutual forbearance among men as may consist with the motives of personal advantage.

Undoubtedly the promoters of utility, in this limited sense, have their appointed office in society.   They follow the footsteps of poets, and copy the sketches of their creations into the book of common life.   They make space, and give time.   Their exertions are of the highest value, so long as they confine their administration of the concerns of the inferior powers of our nature within the limits due to the superior ones.   But whilst the sceptic destroys gross superstitions, let him spare to deface, as some of the French writers have defaced, the eternal truths charactered upon the imaginations of men.   Whilst the mechanist abridges, and the political economist combines labour, let them beware that their speculations, for want of correspondence with those first principles which belong to the imagination, do not tend, as they have in modern England, to exasperate at once the extremes of luxury and want.   They have exemplified the saying, "To him that hath, more shall be given; and from him that hath not, the little that he hath shall be taken away."   The rich have become richer, and the poor have become poorer; and the vessel of the state is driven between the Scylla and Charybdis of anarchy and despotism. Such are the effects which must ever flow from an unmitigated exercise of the calculating faculty.

It is difficult to define pleasure in its highest sense; the definition involving a number of apparent paradoxes. For, from an inexplicable defect of harmony in the constitution of human nature, the pain of the inferior is frequently connected with the pleasures of the superior portions of our being. Sorrow, terror, anguish, despair itself, are often the chosen expressions of an approximation to the highest good. Our sympathy in tragic fiction depends on this principle; tragedy delights by affording a shadow of the pleasure which exists in pain. This is the source also of the melancholy which is inseparable from the sweetest melody. The pleasure that is in sorrow is sweeter than the pleasure of pleasure itself. And hence the saying, " It is better to go to the house of mourning, than to the house of mirth." Not that this highest species of pleasure is necessarily linked with pain. The delight of love and friendship, the ecstacy of the admiration of nature, the joy of the perception and still more of the creation of poetry, is often wholly unalloyed.

The production and assurance of pleasure in this highest sense is true utility. Those who produce and preserve this pleasure are poets or poetical philosophers.

The exertions of Locke, Hume, Gibbon, Voltaire, Rousseau,* and their disciples, in favour of oppressed and deluded humanity, are entitled to the gratitude of mankind. Yet it is easy to calculate the degree of moral and intellectual improvement which the world would have exhibited, had they never lived. A little more nonsense

---

* Although Rousseau has been thus classed, he was essentially a poet. The others, even Voltaire, were mere reasoners.

would have been talked for a century or two ; and perhaps a few more men, women, and children burnt as heretics. We might not at this moment have been congratulating each other on the abolition of the Inquisition in Spain. But it exceeds all imagination to conceive what would have been the moral condition of the world if neither Dante, Petrarch, Boccaccio, Chaucer, Shakspeare, Calderon, Lord Bacon, nor Milton, had ever existed ; if Raphael and Michael Angelo had never been born; if the Hebrew poetry had never been translated ; if a revival of the study of Greek literature had never taken place; if no monuments of ancient sculpture had been handed down to us; and if the poetry of the religion of the ancient world had been extinguished together with its belief. The human mind could never, except by the intervention of these excitements, have been awakened to the invention of the grosser sciences, and that application of analytical reasoning to the aberrations of society, which it is now attempted to exalt over the direct expression of the inventive and creative faculty itself.

We have more moral, political, and historical wisdom than we know how to reduce into practice ; we have more scientific and economical knowledge than can be accommodated to the just distribution of the produce which it multiplies. The poetry in these systems of thought is concealed by the accumulation of facts and calculating processes. There is no want of knowledge respecting what is wisest and best in morals, government, and political economy, or at least, what is wiser and better than what men now practise and endure. But we let "*I dare not* wait upon *I would,* like the poor cat in the adage." We want the creative faculty to imagine that which we know ; we want the generous impulse to act that which we imagine ; we

want the poetry of life : our calculations have outrun conception ; we have eaten more than we can digest. The
cultivation of those sciences which have enlarged the limits
of the empire of man over the external world, has, for want
of the poetical faculty, proportionally circumscribed those
of the internal world ; and man, having enslaved the
elements, remains himself a slave. To what but a cultivation of the mechanical arts in a degree disproportioned to
the presence of the creative faculty, which is the basis of all
knowledge, is to be attributed the abuse of all invention for
abridging and combining labour, to the exasperation of the
inequality of mankind? From what other cause has it
arisen that the discoveries which should have lightened,
have added a weight to the curse imposed on Adam?
Poetry, and the principle of Self, of which money is the
visible incarnation, are the God and Mammon of the world.

The functions of the poetical faculty are two-fold; by one
it creates new materials of knowledge, and power, and
pleasure ; by the other it engenders in the mind a desire to
reproduce and arrange them according to a certain rhythm
and order which may be called the beautiful and the good.
The cultivation of poetry is never more to be desired than
at periods when, from an excess of the selfish and calculating principle, the accumulation of the materials of external
life exceed the quantity of the power of assimilating them
to the internal laws of human nature. The body has then
become too unwieldy for that which animates it.

Poetry is indeed something divine. It is at once the
centre and circumference of knowledge ; it is that which
comprehends all science, and that to which all science must
be referred. It is at the same time the root and blossom
of all other systems of thought; it is that from which all
spring, and that which adorns all ; and that which, if

blighted, denies the fruit and the seed, and withholds from the barren world the nourishment and the succession of the scions of the tree of life. It is the perfect and consummate surface and bloom of all things; it is as the odour and the colour of the rose to the texture of the elements which compose it, as the form and splendour of unfaded beauty to the secrets of anatomy and corruption. What were virtue, love, patriotism, friendship—what were the scenery of this beautiful universe which we inhabit; what were our consolations on this side of the grave—and what were our aspirations beyond it, if poetry did not ascend to bring light and fire from those eternal regions where the owl-winged faculty of calculation dare not ever soar? Poetry is not like reasoning, a power to be exerted according to the determination of the will. A man cannot say, " I will compose poetry." The greatest poet even cannot say it; for the mind in creation is as a fading coal, which some invisible influence, like an inconstant wind, awakens to transitory brightness; this power arises from within, like the colour of a flower which fades and changes as it is developed, and the conscious portions of our natures are unprophetic either of its approach or its departure. Could this influence be durable in its original purity and force, it is impossible to predict the greatness of the results; but when composition begins, inspiration is already on the decline, and the most glorious poetry that has ever been communicated to the world is probably a feeble shadow of the original conceptions of the poet. I appeal to the greatest poets of the present day, whether it is not an error to assert that the finest passages of poetry are produced by labour and study. The toil and the delay recommended by critics can be justly interpreted to mean no more than a careful observation of the inspired moments, and an artificial connexion of the spaces between their suggestions by the intertexture of conventional expressions ; a necessity only imposed by the limitedness of the poetical faculty itself : for Milton conceived the "Paradise Lost" as a whole before he executed it in portions. We have his own authority also for the muse having "dictated" to him the "unpremeditated song." And let this be an answer to those who would allege the fifty-six various readings of the first line of the "Orlando Furioso." Compositions so produced are to poetry what mosaic is to painting. This instinct and intuition of the poetical faculty is still more observable in the plastic and pictorial arts ; a great statue or picture grows under the power of the artist as a child in the mother's womb ; and the very mind which directs the hands in formation is incapable of accounting to itself for the origin, the gradations, or the media of the process.

Poetry is the record of the best and happiest moments of the happiest and best minds. We are aware of evanescent visitations of thought and feeling sometimes associated with place or person, sometimes regarding our own mind alone, and always arising unforeseen and departing unbidden, but elevating and delightful beyond all expression : so that even in the desire and the regret they leave, there cannot but be pleasure, participating as it does in the nature of its object. It is as it were the interpenetration of a diviner nature through our own ; but its footsteps are like those of a wind over the sea, which the coming calm erases, and whose traces remain only as on the wrinkled sands which paves it. These and corresponding conditions of being are experienced principally by those of the most delicate sensibility and the most enlarged imagination ; and the state of mind produced by them is at war with every base desire. The enthusiasm of virtue, love, patriotism, and friendship

is essentially linked with such emotions; and whilst they
last, self appears as what it is, an atom to a universe.
Poets are not only subject to these experiences as spirits
of the most refined organisation, but they can colour all
that they combine with the evanescent hues of this ethereal
world; a word, a trait in the representation of a scene or a
passion will touch the enchanted chord, and reanimate, in
those who have ever experienced these emotions, the sleeping, the cold, the buried image of the past. Poetry thus
makes immortal all that is best and most beautiful in the
world; it arrests the vanishing apparitions which haunt
the interlunations of life, and veiling them, or in language
or in form, sends them forth among mankind, bearing sweet
news of kindred joy to those with whom their sisters abide
—abide, because there is no portal of expression from the
caverns of the spirit which they inhabit into the universe
of things. Poetry redeems from decay the visitations of
the divinity in man.

Poetry turns all things to loveliness; it exalts the
beauty of that which is most beautiful, and it adds beauty
to that which is most deformed; it marries exultation and
horror, grief and pleasure, eternity and change; it subdues
to union under its light yoke all irreconcilable things. It
transmutes all that it touches, and every form moving
within the radiance of its presence is changed by wondrous
sympathy to an incarnation of the spirit which it breathes:
its secret alchemy turns to potable gold the poisonous waters
which flow from death through life; it strips the veil of
familiarity from the world, and lays bare the naked and
sleeping beauty, which is the spirit of its forms.

All things exist as they are perceived: at least in
relation to the percipient. "The mind is its own place,
and of itself can make a heaven of hell, a hell of heaven."

But poetry defeats the curse which binds us to be subjected to the accident of surrounding impressions. And whether it spreads its own figured curtain, or withdraws life's dark veil from before the scene of things, it equally creates for us a being within our being. It makes us the inhabitants of a world to which the familiar world is a chaos. It reproduces the common universe of which we are portions and percipients, and it purges from our inward sight the film of familiarity which obscures from us the wonder of our being. It compels us to feel that which we perceive, and to imagine that which we know. It creates anew the universe, after it has been annihilated in our minds by the recurrence of impressions blunted by reiteration. It justifies the bold and true words of Tasso—*Non merita nome di creatore, se non Iddio ed il Poeta.*

A poet, as he is the author to others of the highest wisdom, pleasure, virtue, and glory, so he ought personally to be the happiest, the best, the wisest, and the most illustrious of men. As to his glory, let time be challenged to declare whether the fame of any other institutor of human life be comparable to that of a poet. That he is the wisest, the happiest, and the best, inasmuch as he is a poet, is equally incontrovertible : the greatest poets have been men of the most spotless virtue, of the most consummate prudence, and, if we would look into the interior of their lives, the most fortunate of men : and the exceptions, as they regard those who possessed the poetic faculty in a high yet inferior degree, will be found on consideration to confine rather than destroy the rule. Let us for a moment stoop to the arbitration of popular breath, and usurping and uniting in our own persons the incompatible characters of accuser, witness, judge, and executioner, let us decide without trial, testimony, or form, that certain motives

of those who are "there sitting where we dare not soar,"
are reprehensible.   Let us assume that Homer was a
drunkard, that Virgil was a flatterer, that Horace was a
coward, that Tasso was a madman, that Lord Bacon was a
peculator, that Raphael was a libertine, that Spenser was a
poet laureate.   It is inconsistent with this division of our
subject to cite living poets, but posterity has done ample
justice to the great names now referred to.   Their errors
have been weighed and found to have been dust in the
balance ; if their sins "were as scarlet, they are now white
as snow;" they have been washed in the blood of the
mediator and redeemer, Time.   Observe in what a ludicrous
chaos the imputations of real or fictitious crime have been
confused in the contemporary calumnies against poetry and
poets; consider how little is, as it appears—or appears, as it is;
look to your own motives, and judge not, lest ye be judged.

Poetry, as has been said, differs in this respect from
logic, that it is not subject to the control of the active
powers of the mind, and that its birth and recurrence have
no necessary connection with the consciousness or will.   It
is presumptuous to determine that these are the necessary
conditions of all mental causation, when mental effects are
experienced unsusceptible of being referred to them.   The
frequent recurrence of the poetical power, it is obvious to
suppose, may produce in the mind a habit of order and
harmony correlative with its own nature and with its effects
upon other minds.   But in the intervals of inspiration, and
they may be frequent without being durable, a poet becomes
a man, and is abandoned to the sudden reflux of the
influences under which others habitually live.   But as he is
more delicately organised than other men, and sensible to
pain and pleasure, both his own and that of others, in a
degree unknown to them, he will avoid the one and pursue

the other with an ardour proportioned to this difference. And he renders himself obnoxious to calumny, when he neglects to observe the circumstances under which these objects of universal pursuit and flight have disguised themselves in one another's garments.

But there is nothing necessarily evil in this error, and thus cruelty, envy, revenge, avarice, and the passions purely evil, have never formed any portion of the popular imputations on the lives of poets.

I have thought it most favourable to the cause of truth to set down these remarks according to the order in which they were suggested to my mind, by a consideration of the subject itself, instead of observing the formality of a polemical reply ; but if the view which they contain be just, they will be found to involve a refutation of the arguers against poetry, so far at least as regards the first division of the subject. I can readily conjecture what should have moved the gall of some learned and intelligent writers who quarrel with certain versifiers ; I confess myself, like them, unwilling to be stunned by the Theseids of the hoarse Codri of the day. Bavius and Mævius undoubtedly are, as they ever were, insufferable persons. But it belongs to a philosophical critic to distinguish rather than confound.

The first part of these remarks has related to poetry in its elements and principles ; and it has been shown, as well as the narrow limits assigned them would permit, that what is called poetry, in a restricted sense, has a common source with all other forms of order and of beauty, according to which the materials of human life are susceptible of being arranged, and which is poetry in an universal sense.

The second part will have for its object an application of these principles to the present state of the cultivation of poetry, and a defence of the attempt to idealise the modern forms of manners and opinions, and compel them into a subordination to the imaginative and creative faculty. For the literature of England, an energetic development of which has ever preceded or accompanied a great and free development of the national will, has arisen as it were from a new birth. In spite of the low-thoughted envy which would undervalue contemporary merit, our own will be a memorable age in intellectual achievements, and we live among such philosophers and poets as surpass beyond comparison any who have appeared since the last national struggle for civil and religious liberty. The most unfailing herald, companion, and follower of the awakening of a great people to work a beneficial change in opinion or institution, is poetry. At such periods there is an accumulation of the power of communicating and receiving intense and impassioned conceptions respecting man and nature. The persons in whom this power resides, may often, as far as regards many portions of their nature, have little apparent correspondence with that spirit of good of which they are the ministers. But even whilst they deny and abjure, they are yet compelled to serve, the power which is seated on the throne of their own soul. It is impossible to read the compositions of the most celebrated writers of the present day without being startled with the electric life which burns within their words. They measure the circumference and sound the depths of human nature with a comprehensive and all-penetrating spirit, and they are themselves perhaps the most sincerely astonished at its manifestations; for it is less their spirit than the spirit of the age. Poets are the hierophants of an unapprehended inspiration; the mirrors of the gigantic shadows which futurity casts upon the present; the words which express what they understand not; the trumpets which sing to battle, and feel not what they inspire ; the influence which is moved not, but moves.   Poets are the unacknowledged legislators of the world.

A DISCOURSE

ON THE MANNERS OF THE ANCIENTS, RELATIVE TO THE SUBJECT OF LOVE.

A FRAGMENT.*

THE period which intervened between the birth of Pericles and the death of Aristotle, is undoubtedly, whether considered in itself or with reference to the effects which it has produced upon the subsequent destinies of civilised man, the most memorable in the history of the world.   What was the combination of moral and political circumstances which produced so unparelleled a progress during that period in literature and the arts ;—why that progress, so rapid and so sustained, so soon received a check, and became retrograde,—are problems left to the wonder and conjecture of posterity.   The wrecks and fragments of those subtle and profound minds, like the ruins of a fine statue, obscurely suggest to us the grandeur and perfection of the whole.   Their very language—a type of the understandings of which it was the creation and the image—in variety, in simplicity, in flexibility, and in copiousness, excels every other language of the western world.   Their sculptures are such as we, in our presumption, assume to be the models of ideal truth and beauty,

---

* This Essay was intended to be a commentary on the Symposium, or Banquet of Plato, but it breaks off at the moment when the main subject is about to be discussed.

and to which no artist of modern times can produce forms in any degree comparable. Their paintings, according to Pliny and Pausanias, were full of delicacy and harmony; and some even were powerfully pathetic, so as to awaken, like tender music or tragic poetry, the most overwhelming emotions. We are accustomed to conceive the painters of the sixteenth century, as those who have brought their art to the highest perfection, probably because none of the ancient paintings have been preserved. For all the inventive arts maintain, as it were, a sympathetic connexion between each other, being no more than various expressions of one internal power, modified by different circumstances, either of an individual, or of society; and the paintings of that period would probably bear the same relation as is confessedly borne by the sculptures to all succeeding ones. Of their music we know little; but the effects which it is said to have produced, whether they be attributed to the skill of the composer, or the sensibility of his audience, are far more powerful than any which we experience from the music of our own times; and if, indeed, the melody of their compositions were more tender and delicate, and inspiring, than the melodies of some modern European nations, their superiority in this art must have been something wonderful, and wholly beyond conception.

Their poetry seems to maintain a very high, though not so disproportionate a rank, in the comparison. Perhaps Shakspeare, from the variety and comprehension of his genius, is to be considered, on the whole, as the greatest individual mind, of which we have specimens remaining. Perhaps Dante created imaginations of greater loveliness and energy than any that are to be found in the ancient literature of Greece. Perhaps nothing has been discovered in the fragments of the Greek lyric poets equivalent to the sublime and chivalric sensibility of Petrarch.—But, as a poet, Homer must be acknowledged to excel Shakspeare in the truth, the harmony, the sustained grandeur, the satisfying completeness of his images, their exact fitness to the illustration, and to that to which they belong. Nor could Dante, deficient in conduct, plan, nature, variety, and temperance, have been brought into comparison with these men, but for those fortunate isles, laden with golden fruit, which alone could tempt any one to embark in the misty ocean of his dark and extravagant fiction.

But, omitting the comparison of individual minds, which can afford no general inference, how superior was the spirit and system of their poetry to that of any other period. So that, had any other genius equal in other respects to the greatest that ever enlightened the world, arisen in that age, he would have been superior to all, from this circumstance alone—that his conceptions would have assumed a more harmonious and perfect form. For it is worthy of observation, that whatever the poets of that age produced is as harmonious and perfect as possible. If a drama, for instance, were the composition of a person of inferior talent, it was still homogeneous and free from inequalities ; it was a whole, consistent with itself. The compositions of great minds bore throughout the sustained stamp of their greatness. In the poetry of succeeding ages the expectations are often exalted on Icarean wings, and fall, too much disappointed to give a memory and a name to the oblivious pool in which they fell.

In physical knowledge Aristotle and Theophrastus had already—no doubt assisted by the labours of those of their predecessors whom they criticise—made advances worthy of the maturity of science. The astonishing invention of geometry, that series of discoveries which have enabled man to command the elements and foresee future events, before the subjects of his ignorant wonder, and which have opened as it were the doors of the mysteries of nature, had already been brought to great perfection. Metaphysics, the science of man's intimate nature, and logic, or the grammar and elementary principles of that science, received from the latter philosophers of the Periclean age a firm basis. All our more exact philosophy is built upon the labours of these great men, and many of the words which we employ in metaphysical distinctions were invented by them to give accuracy and system to their reasonings. The science of morals, or the voluntary conduct of men in relation to themselves or others, dates from this epoch. How inexpressibly bolder and more pure were the doctrines of those great men, in comparison with the timid maxims which prevail in the writings of the most esteemed modern moralists. They were such as Phocion, and Epaminondas, and Timoleon, who formed themselves on their influence, were to the wretched heroes of our own age.

Their political and religious institutions are more difficult to bring into comparison with those of other times. A summary idea may be formed of the worth of any political and religious system, by observing the comparative degree of happiness and of intellect produced under its influence. And whilst many institutions and opinions, which in ancient Greece were obstacles to the improvement of the human race, have been abolished among modern nations, how many pernicious superstitions and new contrivances of misrule, and unheard-of complications of public mischief, have not been invented among them by the ever-watchful spirit of avarice and tyranny.

The modern nations of the civilised world owe the

progress which they have made—as well in those physical sciences in which they have already excelled their masters, as in the moral and intellectual inquiries, in which, with all the advantage of the experience of the latter, it can scarcely be said that they have yet equalled them,—to what is called the revival of learning; that is, the study of the writers of the age which preceded and immediately followed the government of Pericles, or of subsequent writers, who were, so to speak, the rivers flowing from those immortal fountains. And though there seems to be a principle in the modern world, which, should circumstances analogous to those which modelled the intellectual resources of the age to which we refer, into so harmonious a proportion, again arise, would arrest and perpetuate them, and consign their results to a more equal, extensive, and lasting improvement of the condition of man—though justice and the true meaning of human society are, if not more accurately, more generally understood; though perhaps men know more, and therefore are more, as a mass, yet this principle has never been called into action, and requires indeed a universal and almost appalling change in the system of existing things. The study of modern history is the study of kings, financiers, statesmen, and priests. The history of ancient Greece is the study of legislators, philosophers, and poets; it is the history of men, compared with the history of titles. What the Greeks were, was a reality, not a promise. And what we are and hope to be, is derived, as it were, from the influence and inspiration of these glorious generations.

Whatever tends to afford a further illustration of the manners and opinions of those to whom we owe so much, and who were, perhaps, on the whole, the most perfect specimens of humanity of whom we have authentic record,

were infinitely valuable. Let us see their errors, their
weaknesses, their daily actions, their familiar conversation,
and catch the tone of their society. When we discover
how far the most admirable community ever framed, was
removed from that perfection to which human society is
impelled by some active power within each bosom, to aspire,
how great ought to be our hopes, how resolute our struggles.
For the Greeks of the Periclean age were widely different
from us. It is to be lamented that no modern writer has
hitherto dared to show them precisely as they were.
Barthélemi cannot be denied the praise of industry and
system; but he never forgets that he is a Christian and a
Frenchman. Wieland, in his delightful novels, makes
indeed a very tolerable Pagan, but cherishes too many
political prejudices, and refrains from diminishing the
interest of his romances by painting sentiments in which
no European of modern times can possibly sympathise.
There is no book which shows the Greeks precisely as they
were; they seem all written for children, with the caution
that no practice or sentiment, highly inconsistent with our
present manners, should be mentioned, lest those manners
should receive outrage and violation. But there are many
to whom the Greek language is inaccessible, who ought not
to be excluded by this prudery from possessing an exact
and comprehensive conception of the history of man; for
there is no knowledge concerning what man has been and
may be, from partaking of which a person can depart,
without becoming in some degree more philosophical,
tolerant, and just.

One of the chief distinctions between the manners of
ancient Greece and modern Europe consisted in the regulations and the sentiments respecting sexual intercourse.
Whether this difference arises from some imperfect

influence of the doctrines of Jesus Christ, who alleges the
absolute and unconditional equality of all human beings, or
from the institutions of chivalry, or from a certain funda-
mental difference of physical nature existing in the Celts,
or from a combination of all or any of these causes, acting
on each other, is a question worthy of voluminous investigation. The fact is, that the modern Europeans have in this
circumstance, and in the abolition of slavery, made an
improvement the most decisive in the regulation of human
society ; and all the virtue and the wisdom of the
Periclean age arose under other institutions, in spite of the
diminution which personal slavery and the inferiority of
women, recognised by law and opinion, must have produced
in the delicacy, the strength, the comprehensiveness, and
the accuracy of their conceptions, in moral, political, and
metaphysical science, and perhaps in every other art and
science.

The women, thus degraded, became such as it was
expected they would become. They possessed, except with
extraordinary exceptions, the habits and the qualities of
slaves. They were probably not extremely beautiful ; at
least there was no such disproportion in the attractions of
the external form between the female and male sex among
the Greeks, as exists among the modern Europeans. They
were certainly devoid of that moral and intellectual loveliness with which the acquisition of knowledge and the
cultivation of sentiment animates, as with another life of
overpowering grace, the lineaments and the gestures of
every form which they inhabit. Their eyes could not have
been deep and intricate from the workings of the mind,
and could have entangled no heart in soul-enwoven
labyrinths.

Let it not be imagined that because the Greeks were

deprived of its legitimate object, they were incapable of sentimental love, and that this passion is the mere child of chivalry and the literature of modern times. This object, or its archetype, forever exists in the mind, which selects among those who resemble it, that which most resembles it; and instinctively fills up the interstices of the imperfect image, in the same manner as the imagination moulds and completes the shapes in clouds, or in the fire, into the resemblances of whatever form, animal, building, etc., happens to be present to it. Man is in his wildest state a social being: a certain degree of civilisation and refinement ever produces the want of sympathies still more intimate and complete; and the gratification of the senses is no longer all that is sought in sexual connection. It soon becomes a very small part of that profound and complicated sentiment, which we call love, which is rather the universal thirst for a communion not merely of the senses, but of our whole nature, intellectual, imaginative, and sensitive; and which, when individualised, becomes an imperious necessity, only to be satisfied by the complete or partial, actual or supposed, fulfilment of its claims. This want grows more powerful in proportion to the development which our nature receives from civilisation; for man never ceases to be a social being. The sexual impulse, which is only one, and often a small party of those claims, serves, from its obvious and external nature, as a kind of type or expression of the rest, a common basis, an acknowledged and visible link. Still it is a claim which even derives a strength not its own from the accessory circumstances which surround it, and one which our nature thirsts to satisfy. To estimate this, observe the degree of intensity and durability of the love of the male towards the female in animals and savages; and acknowledge all the duration and intensity observable in the love of civilised beings beyond that of savages to be produced from other causes. In the susceptibility of the external senses there is probably no important difference.

Among the ancient Greeks the male sex, one half of the human race, received the highest cultivation and refinement ; whilst the other, so far as intellect is concerned, were educated as slaves, and were raised but few degrees in all that related to moral or intellectual excellence above the condition of savages. The gradations in the society of man present us with a slow improvement in this respect. The Roman women held a higher consideration in society, and were esteemed almost as the equal partners with their husbands in the regulation of domestic economy and the education of their children. The practices and customs of modern Europe are essentially different from and incomparably less pernicious than either, however remote from what an enlightened mind cannot fail to desire as the future destiny of human beings.

ON THE SYMPOSIUM,

OR, PREFACE TO THE BANQUET OF PLATO.

A FRAGMENT.

THE dialogue entitled " The Banquet," was selected by the translator as the most beautiful and perfect among all the works of Plato.* He despairs of having communicated to the English language any portion of the surpassing graces

* The Republic, though replete with considerable errors of speculation, is, indeed, the greatest repository of important truths of all the works of Plato. This, perhaps, is because it is the longest. He first, and perhaps last, maintained that a state ought to be governed, not

of the composition, or having done more than present an
imperfect shadow of the language and the sentiment of this
astonishing production.

Plato is eminently the greatest among the Greek philosophers, and from, or, rather, perhaps through him, his
master Socrates, have proceeded those emanations of moral
and metaphysical knowledge, on which a long series and an
incalculable variety of popular superstitions have sheltered
their absurdities from the slow contempt of mankind.
Plato exhibits the rare union of close and subtle logic, with
the Pythian enthusiasm of poetry, melted by the splendour
and harmony of his periods into one irresistible stream of
musical impressions, which hurry the persuasions onward, as
in a breathless career. His language is that of an immortal
spirit, rather than a man. Lord Bacon is, perhaps, the only
writer, who, in these particulars, can be compared with him:
his imitator, Cicero, sinks in the comparison into an ape
mocking the gestures of a man. His views into the nature
of mind and existence are often obscure, only because they
are profound ; and though his theories respecting the
government of the world, and the elementary laws of
moral action, are not always correct, yet there is scarcely
any of his treatises which do not, however stained by
puerile sophisms, contain the most remarkable intuitions
into all that can be the subject of the human mind. His
excellence consists especially in intuition, and it is this
faculty which raises him far above Aristotle, whose genius,
though vivid and various, is obscure in comparison with
that of Plato.

by the wealthiest, or the most ambitious, or the most cunning, but by
the wisest; the method of selecting such rulers, and the laws by which
such a selection is made, must correspond with and arise out of the
moral freedom and refinement of the people.

The dialogue entitled " The Banquet," is called
or a Discussion upon Love, and is supposed to have taken
place at the house of Agathon, at one of a series of
festivals given by that poet, on the occasion of his gaining
the prize of tragedy at the Dionysiaca. The account of the
debate of this occasion is supposed to have been given by
Apollodorus, a pupil of Socrates, many years after it had
taken place, to a companion who was curious to hear it.
This Apollodorus appears, both from the style in which he
is represented in this piece, as well as from a passage in the
Phædon, to have been a person of an impassioned and
enthusiastic disposition; to borrow an image from the
Italian Painters, he seems to have been the St. John of
the Socratic group. The drama (for so the lively distinction of character and the various and well-wrought
circumstances of the story almost entitle it to be called)
begins by Socrates persuading Aristodemus to sup at
Agathon's, uninvited. The whole of this introduction
affords the most lively conception of refined Athenian
manners.

[UNFINISHED.]

ON LOVE.

WHAT is love? Ask him who lives, what is life? ask him
who adores, what is God?

I know not the internal constitution of other men, nor
even thine, whom I now address. I see that in some
external attributes they resemble me, but when, misled
by that appearance, I have thought to appeal to something
in common, and unburthen my inmost soul to them, I have

found my language misunderstood, like one in a distant and savage land. The more opportunities they have afforded me for experience, the wider has appeared the interval between us, and to a greater distance have the points of sympathy been withdrawn. With a spirit ill fitted to sustain such proof, trembling and feeble through its tenderness, I have everywhere sought sympathy, and have found only repulse and disappointment.

Thou demandest what is love? It is that powerful attraction towards all that we conceive, or fear, or hope beyond ourselves, when we find within our own thoughts the chasm of an insufficient void, and seek to awaken in all things that are, a community with what we experience within ourselves. If we reason, we would be understood; if we imagine, we would that the airy children of our brain were born anew within another's; if we feel, we would that another's nerves should vibrate to our own, that the beams of their eyes should kindle at once and mix and melt into our own, that lips of motionless ice should not reply to lips quivering and burning with the heart's best blood. This is Love. This is the bond and the sanction which connects not only man with man, but with everything which exists. We are born into the world, and there is something within us which, from the instant that we live, more and more thirsts after its likeness. It is probably in correspondence with this law that the infant drains milk from the bosom of its mother; this propensity develops itself with the development of our nature. We dimly see within our intellectual nature a miniature as it were of our entire self, yet deprived of all that we condemn or despise, the ideal prototype of everything excellent or lovely that we are capable of conceiving as belonging to the nature of man. Not only the portrait of our external being, but an assemblage of the minutest particles of which our nature is composed ; * a mirror whose surface reflects only the forms of purity and brightness ; a soul within our soul that describes a circle around its proper paradise, which pain, and sorrow, and evil dare not overleap. To this we eagerly refer all sensations, thirsting that they should resemble or correspond with it. The discovery of its antitype ; the meeting with an understanding capable of clearly estimating our own ; an imagination which should enter into and seize upon the subtle and delicate peculiarities which we have delighted to cherish and unfold in secret ; with a frame whose nerves, like the chords of two exquisite lyres, strung to the accompaniment of one delightful voice, vibrate with the vibrations of our own ; and of a combination of all these in such proportion as the type within demands ; this is the invisible and unattainable point to which Love tends : and to attain which, it urges forth the powers of man to arrest the faintest shadow of that, without the possession of which there is no rest nor respite to the heart over which it rules. Hence in solitude, or in that deserted state when we are surrounded by human beings, and yet they sympathise not with us, we love the flowers, the grass, and the waters, and the sky. In the motion of the very leaves of spring, in the blue air, there is then found a secret correspondence with our heart. There is eloquence in the tongueless wind, and a melody in the flowing brooks and the rustling of the reeds beside them, which by their inconceivable relation to something within the soul, awaken the spirits to a dance of breathless rapture, and bring tears of mysterious tenderness to the eyes, like the enthusiasm of patriotic success, or the voice of one beloved singing to you

* These words are ineffectual and metaphorical. Most words are so—No help !

alone. Sterne says that, if he were in a desert, he would
love some cypress. So soon as this want or power is dead,
man becomes the living sepulchre of himself, and what yet
survives is the mere husk of what once he was.

THE COLISEUM.

A FRAGMENT.

AT the hour of noon, on the feast of the Passover, an old
man, accompanied by a girl, apparently his daughter,
entered the Coliseum at Rome. They immediately passed
through the Arena, and seeking a solitary chasm among the
arches of the southern part of the ruin, selected a fallen
column for their seat, and clasping each other's hands, sate
as in silent contemplation of the scene. But the eyes of
the girl were fixed upon her father's lips, and his countenance, sublime and sweet, but motionless as some Praxitelean
image of the greatest of poets, filled the silent air with
smiles, not reflected from external forms.

It was the great feast of the Resurrection, and the whole
native population of Rome, together with all the foreigners
who flock from all parts of the earth to contemplate its
celebration, were assembled round the Vatican. The most
awful religion of the world went forth surrounded by
emblazonry of mortal greatness, and mankind had assembled
to wonder at and worship the creations of their own power.
No straggler was to be met with in the streets and grassy
lanes which led to the Coliseum. The father and daughter
had sought this spot immediately on their arrival.

A figure, only visible at Rome in night or solitude, and
then only to be seen amid the desolated temples of the

Forum, or gliding among the weed-grown galleries of the Coliseum, crossed their path. His form, which, though emaciated, displayed the elementary outlines of exquisite grace, was enveloped in an ancient chlamys, which half concealed his face; his snow-white feet were fitted with ivory sandals, delicately sculptured in the likeness of two female figures, whose wings met upon the heel, and whose eager and half-divided lips seemed quivering to meet. It was a face, once seen, never to be forgotten. The mouth and the moulding of the chin resembled the eager and impassioned tenderness of the statues of Antinous; but instead of the effeminate sullenness of the eye, and the narrow smoothness of the forehead, shone an expression of profound and piercing thought; the brow was clear and open, and his eyes deep, like two wells of crystalline water which reflect the all-beholding heavens. Over all was spread a timid expression of womanish tenderness and hesitation, which contrasted, yet intermingled strangely, with the abstracted and fearless character that predominated in his form and gestures.

He avoided, in an extraordinary degree, all communication with the Italians, whose language he seemed scarcely to understand, but was occasionally seen to converse with some accomplished foreigner, whose gestures and appearance might attract him amid his solemn haunts. He spoke Latin, and especially Greek, with fluency, and with a peculiar but sweet accent; he had apparently acquired a knowledge of the northern languages of Europe. There was no circumstance connected with him that gave the least intimation of his country, his origin, or his occupation. His dress was strange, but splendid and solemn. He was forever alone. The literati of Rome thought him a curiosity, but there was something in his manner unintelligible but impressive, which awed their obtrusions into distance and silence.   The countrymen, whose path he rarely crossed, returning by starlight from their market at Campo Vaccino, called him, with that strange mixture of religious and historical ideas so common in Italy, *Il Diavolo di Bruto.*

Such was the figure which interrupted the contemplations, if they were so engaged, of the strangers, by addressing them in the clear, and exact, but unidiomatic phrases of their native language :—" Strangers, you are two ; behold the third in this great city, to whom alone the spectacle of these mighty ruins is more delightful than the mockeries of a superstition which destroyed them."

" I see nothing," said the old man.

" What do you here, then ? "

' I listen to the sweet singing of the birds, and the sound of my daughter's breathing composes me like the soft murmur of water—and I feel the sunwarm wind—and this is pleasant to me."

" Wretched old man, know you not that these are the ruins of the Coliseum ? "

" Alas ! stranger," said the girl, in a voice like mournful music, " speak not so—he is blind."

The stranger's eyes were suddenly filled with tears, and the lines of his countenance became relaxed.   " Blind ? " he exclaimed, in a tone of suffering, which was more than an apology ; and seated himself apart on a flight of shattered and mossy stairs which wound up among the labyrinths of the ruin.

" My sweet Helen," said the old man, " you did not tell me that this was the Coliseum ? "

" How should I tell you, dearest father, what I knew not ?   I was on the point of inquiring the way to that building, when we entered this circle of ruins, and, until the stranger accosted us, I remained silent, subdued by the greatness of what I see."

" It is your custom, sweetest child, to describe to me the objects that give you delight. You array them in the soft radiance of your words, and whilst you speak I only feel the infirmity which holds me in such dear dependence, as a blessing. Why have you been silent now ? "

" I know not—first the wonder and pleasure of the sight, then the words of the stranger, and then thinking on what he had said, and how he had looked—and now, beloved father, your own words."

" Well, tell me now, what do you see ? "

" I see a great circle of arches built upon arches, and shattered stones lie around, that once made a part of the solid wall. In the crevices, and on the vaulted roofs, grow a multitude of shrubs, the wild olive and the myrtle—and intricate brambles, and entangled weeds and plants I never saw before. The stones are immensely massive, and they jut out one from the other. There are terrible rifts in the wall, and broad windows through which you see the blue heaven. There seems to be more than a thousand arches, some ruined, some entire, and they are all immensely high and wide. Some are shattered, and stand forth in great heaps, and the underwood is tufted on their crumbling summits. Around us lie enormous columns, shattered and shapeless—and fragments of capitals and cornice, fretted with delicate sculptures."

" It is open to the blue sky ? " said the old man.

" Yes. We see the liquid death of heaven above through the rifts and the windows ; and the flowers, and the weeds, and the grass and creeping moss are nourished by its unforbidden rain. The blue sky is above—the wide, bright, blue sky—it flows through the great rents on high, and through the bare boughs of the marble-rooted fig-tree, and through the leaves and flowers of the weeds, even to the dark arcades beneath. I see—I feel its clear and piercing beams fill the universe, and impregnate the joy-inspiring wind with life and light, and casting the veil of its splendour over all things—even me. Yes, and through the highest rift the noonday waning moon is hanging, as it were, out of the solid sky, and this shows that the atmosphere has all the clearness which it rejoices me that you feel."

" What else see you ? "

" Nothing."

" Nothing ? "

" Only the bright-green mossy ground, speckled by tufts of dewy clover-grass that run into the interstices of the shattered arches, and round the isolated pinnacles of the ruin."

" Like the lawny dells of soft short grass which wind among the pine forests and precipices in the Alps of Savoy ? "

" Indeed, father, your eye has a vision more serene than mine."

" And the great wrecked arches, the shattered masses of precipitous ruin, overgrown with the younglings of the forest, and more like chasms rent by an earthquake among the mountains, than like the vestige of what was human workmanship—what are they ? "

" Things awe-inspiring and wonderful."

" Are they not caverns such as the untamed elephant might choose, amid the Indian wilderness, wherein to hide her cubs ? such as, were the sea to overflow the earth, the mightiest monsters of the deep would change into their spacious chambers ? "

"Father, your words image forth what I would have expressed, but alas! could not."

"I hear the rustling of leaves, and the sound of waters,—but it does not rain,—like the fast drops of a fountain among woods."

"It falls from among the heaps of ruin over our heads—it is, I suppose, the water collected in the rifts by the showers."

"A nursling of man's art, abandoned by his care, and transformed by the enchantment of Nature into a likeness of her own creations, and destined to partake their immortality! Changed into a mountain cloven with woody dells, which overhang its labyrinthine glades, and shattered into toppling precipices. Even the clouds, intercepted by its craggy summit, feed its eternal fountains with their rain. By the column on which I sit, I should judge that it had once been crowned by a temple or a theatre, and that on sacred days the multitude wound up its craggy path to spectacle or the sacrifice——It was such itself! * Helen, what sound of wings is that?"

"It is the wild pigeons returning to their young. Do you not hear the murmur of those that are brooding in their nests."

"Ay, it is the language of their happiness. They are as

* Nor does a recollection of the use to which it may have been destined interfere with these emotions. Time has thrown its purple shadow athwart this scene, and no more is visible than the broad and everlasting character of human strength and genius, that pledge of all that is to be admirable and lovely in ages yet to come. Solemn temples, where the senate of the world assembled, palaces, triumphal arches, and cloud-surrounded columns, loaded with the sculptured annals of conquest and domination—what actions and deliberations have they been destined to enclose and commemorate? Superstitious rites, which in their mildest form, outrage reason, and obscure the moral sense of mankind; schemes for wide-extended murder, and devastation,

happy as we are, child, but in a different manner. They know not the sensations which this ruin excites within us. Yet it is pleasure to them to inhabit it; and the succession of its forms as they pass, is connected with associations in their minds, sacred to them, as these to us. The internal nature of each being is surrounded by a circle, not to be surmounted by his fellows; and it is this repulsion which constitutes the misfortune of the condition of life. But there is a circle which comprehends, as well as one which mutually excludes, all things which feel. And, with respect to man, his public and his private happiness consists in diminishing the circumference which includes those resembling himself, until they become one with him, and he with them. It is because we enter into the meditations, designs, and destinies of something beyond ourselves, that the contemplation of the ruins of human power excites an elevating sense of awfulness and beauty. It is therefore that the ocean, the glacier, the cataract, the tempest, the volcano, have each a spirit which animates the extremities of our frame with tingling joy. It is therefore that the singing of birds, and the motion of leaves, the sensation of the odorous earth beneath, and the freshness of the living wind around, is sweet. And this is Love. This is the religion of eternity, whose votaries have been exiled

and misrule, and servitude; and, lastly, these schemes brought to their tremendous consummations, and a human being returning in the midst of festival and solemn joy, with thousands and thousands of his enslaved and desolated species chained behind his chariot, exhibiting, as titles to renown, the labour of ages, and the admired creations of genius, overthrown by the brutal force, which was placed as a sword within his hand, and,—contemplation fearful and abhorred!— he himself, a being capable of the gentlest and best emotions, inspired with the persuasion that he has done a virtuous deed! We do not forget these things. . . .

from among the multitude of mankind. O Power!" cried
the old man, lifting his sightless eyes towards the undazzling
sun, " thou which interpenetratest all things ; and without
which this glorious world were a blind and formless chaos,
Love, Author of Good, God, King, Father! Friend of these
thy worshippers! Two solitary hearts invoke thee, may
they be divided never! If the contentions of mankind
have been their misery ; if to give and seek that happiness
which thou art, has been their choice and destiny ; if in the
contemplation of these majestic records of the power of
their kind, they see the shadow and the prophecy of that
which thou mayst have decreed that he should become ; if
the justice, the liberty, the loveliness, the truth, which are
thy footsteps, have been sought by them, divide them not!
It is thine to unite, to eternise ; to make outlive the limits
of the grave those who have left among the living,
memorials of thee. When this frame shall be senseless
dust, may the hopes, and the desires, and the delights
which animate it now, never be extinguished in my child ;
even as, if she were borne into the tomb, my memory
would be the written monument of all her nameless
excellencies!"

The old man's countenance and gestures, radiant with
the inspiration of his words, sunk, as he ceased, into more
than its accustomed calmness, for he heard his daughter's
sobs, and remembered that he had spoken of death.—" My
father, how can I outlive you?" said Helen.

" Do not let us talk of death," said the old man, suddenly
changing his tone. "Heraclitus, indeed, died at my age,
and if I had so sour a disposition, there might be some
danger. But Democritus reached a hundred-and-twenty,
by the mere dint of a joyous and unconquerable mind. He
only died at last, because he had no gentle and beloved

ministering spirit, like my Helen, for whom it would have been his delight to live. You remember his gay old sister requested him to put off starving himself to death until she had returned from the festival of Ceres; alleging, that it would spoil her holiday if he refused to comply, as it was not permitted to appear in the procession immediately after the death of a relation; and how good-temperedly the sage acceded to her request."

The old man could not see his daughter's grateful smile, but he felt the pressure of her hand by which it was expressed.—"In truth," he continued, "that mystery, death, is a change which neither for ourselves nor for others is the just object of hope or fear. We know not if it be good or evil, we only know, it is. The old, the young, may alike die; no time, no place, no age, no foresight, exempts us from death, and the chance of death. We have no knowledge, if death be a state of sensation, of any precaution that can make those sensations fortunate, if the existing series of events shall not produce that effect. Think not of death, or think of it as something common to us all. It has happened," said he, with a deep and suffering voice, "that men have buried their children."

" Alas! then, dearest father, how I pity you. Let us speak no more."

They arose to depart from the Coliseum, but the figure which had first accosted them interposed itself :—" Lady," he said, " if grief be an expiation of error, I have grieved deeply for the words which I spoke to your companion. The men who anciently inhabited this spot, and those from whom they learned their wisdom, respected infirmity and age. If I have rashly violated that venerable form, at once majestic and defenceless, may I be forgiven?"

" It gives me pain to see how much your mistake afflicts

you," she said; "if you can forget, doubt not that we forgive."

"You thought me one of those who are blind in spirit," said the old man, "and who deserve, if any human being can deserve, contempt and blame. Assuredly, contemplating this monument as I do, though in the mirror of my daughter's mind, I am filled with astonishment and delight; the spirit of departed generations seems to animate my limbs, and circulate through all the fibres of my frame. Stranger, if I have expressed what you have ever felt, let us know each other more."

"The sound of your voice, and the harmony of your thoughts, are delightful to me," said the youth, "and it is a pleasure to see any form which expresses so much beauty and goodness as your daughter's; if you reward me for my rudeness, by allowing me to know you, my error is already expiated, and you remember my ill words no more. I live a solitary life, and it is rare that I encounter any stranger with whom it is pleasant to talk; besides, their meditations, even though they be learned, do not always agree with mine; and, though I can pardon this difference, they cannot. Nor have I ever explained the cause of the dress I wear, and the difference which I perceive between my language and manners, and those with whom I have intercourse. Not but that it is painful to me to live without communion with intelligent and affectionate beings. You are such, I feel."

ON THE PUNISHMENT OF DEATH.

A FRAGMENT.

THE first law which it becomes a Reformer to propose and support, at the approach of a period of great political change, is the abolition of the punishment of death.

It is sufficiently clear that revenge, retaliation, atonement, expiation, are rules and motives, so far from deserving a place in any enlightened system of political life, that they are the chief sources of a prodigious class of miseries in the domestic circles of society. It is clear that however the spirit of legislation may appear to frame institutions upon more philosophical maxims, it has hitherto, in those cases which are termed criminal, done little more than palliate the spirit, by gratifying a portion of it; and afforded a compromise between that which is best;—the inflicting of no evil upon a sensitive being, without a decisively beneficial result in which he should at least participate: and that which is worst; that he should be put to torture for the amusement of those whom he may have injured, or may seem to have injured.

Omitting these remoter considerations, let us inquire what *Death* is; that punishment which is applied as a measure of transgressions of indefinite shades of distinction, so soon as they shall have passed that degree and colour of enormity, with which it is supposed no inferior infliction is commensurate.

And first, whether death is good or evil, a punishment or a reward, or whether it be wholly indifferent, no man can take upon himself to assert. That that within us which thinks and feels, continues to think and feel after the dissolution of the body, has been the almost universal opinion of mankind, and the accurate philosophy of what I may be permitted to term the modern Academy, by showing the prodigious depth and extent of our ignorance respecting the causes and nature of sensation, renders probable the affirmative of a proposition, the negative of which it is so difficult to conceive, and the popular arguments against which, derived from what is called the atomic system, are proved to be applicable only to the relation which one object bears to another, as apprehended by the mind, and not to existence itself, or the nature of that essence which is the medium and receptacle of objects

The popular system of religion suggests the idea that the mind, after death, will be painfully or pleasurably affected according to its determinations during life. However ridiculous and pernicious we must admit the vulgar accessories of this creed to be, there is a certain analogy, not wholly absurd, between the consequences resulting to an individual during life from the virtuous or vicious, prudent or imprudent, conduct of his external actions, to those consequences which are conjectured to ensue from the discipline and order of his internal thoughts, as affecting his condition in a future state. They omit, indeed, to calculate upon the accidents of disease, and temperament, and organisation, and circumstance, together with the multitude of independent agencies which affect the opinions, the conduct, and the happiness of individuals, and produce determinations of the will, and modify the judgment, so as to produce effects the most opposite in natures considerably similar. These are those operations in the order of the whole of nature, tending, we are prone to believe, to some definite mighty end, to which the agencies of our peculiar nature are subordinate ; nor is there any reason to suppose, that in a future state they

86

should become suddenly exempt from that subordination. The philosopher is unable to determine whether our existence in a previous state has affected our present condition, and abstains from deciding whether our present condition will affect us in that which may be future. That, if we continue to exist, the manner of our existence will be such as no inference nor conjectures, afforded by a consideration of our earthly experience, can elucidate, is sufficiently obvious. The opinion that the vital principle within us, in whatever mode it may continue to exist, must lose that consciousness of definite and individual being which now characterises it, and become a unit in the vast sum of action and of thought which disposes and animates the universe, and is called God, seems to belong to that class of opinion which has been designated as indifferent.

To compel a person to know all that can be known by the dead, concerning that which the living fear, hope, or forget; to plunge him into the pleasure or pain which there awaits him; to punish or reward him in a manner and in a degree incalculable and incomprehensible by us; to disrobe him at once from all that intertexture of good and evil with which Nature seems to have clothed every form of individual existence, is to inflict on him the doom of death.

A certain degree of pain and terror usually accompany the infliction of death. This degree is infinitely varied by the infinite variety in the temperament and opinions of the sufferers. As a measure of punishment, strictly so considered, and as an exhibition, which, by its known effects on the sensibility of the sufferer, is intended to intimidate the spectators from incurring a similar liability, it is singularly inadequate.

Firstly,—Persons of energetic character, in whom, as in

men who suffer for political crimes, there is a large mixture
of enterprise, and fortitude, and disinterestedness, and the
elements, though misguided and disarranged, by which the
strength and happiness of a nation might have been
cemented, die in such a manner, as to make death appear
not evil, but good. The death of what is called a traitor,
that is, a person who, from whatever motive, would abolish
the government of the day, is as often a triumphant exhibition of suffering virtue, as the warning of a culprit. The
multitude, instead of departing with a panic-stricken
approbation of the laws which exhibited such a spectacle,
are inspired with pity, admiration and sympathy ; and the
most generous among them feel an emulation to be the
authors of such flattering emotions, as they experience
stirring in their bosoms. Impressed by what they see and
feel, they make no distinction between the motives which
incited the criminals to the actions for which they suffer,
or the heroic courage with which they turned into good
that which their judges awarded to them as evil, or the
purpose itself of those actions, though that purpose may
happen to be eminently pernicious. The laws in this case
lose that sympathy, which it ought to be their chief object
to secure, and in a participation of which consists their
chief strength in maintaining those sanctions by which the
parts of the social union are bound together, so as to
product, as nearly as possible, the ends for which it is
instituted.

Secondly,—Persons of energetic character, in communities not modelled with philosophical skill to turn all the
energies which they contain to the purposes of common
good, are prone also to fall into the temptation of under-
taking, and are peculiarly fitted for despising the perils
attendant upon consummating, the most enormous crimes.

Murder, rapes, extensive schemes of plunder, are the actions
of persons belonging to this class ; and death is the penalty
of conviction. But the coarseness of organisation, peculiar
to men capable of committing acts wholly selfish, is usually
found to be associated with a proportionate insensibility to
fear or pain. Their sufferings communicate to those of the
spectators, who may be liable to the commission of similar
crimes, a sense of the lightness of that event, when closely
examined, which, at a distance, as uneducated persons are
accustomed to do, probably they regarded with horror.
But a great majority of the spectators are so bound up in
the interests and the habits of social union that no temptation would be sufficiently strong to induce them to a
commission of the enormities to which this penalty is
assigned.   The more powerful, and the richer among
them—and a numerous class of little tradesmen are richer
and more powerful than those who are employed by them,
and the employer, in general, bears this relation to the
employed—regard their own wrongs as, in some degree,
avenged, and their own rights secured by this punishment,
inflicted as the penalty of whatever crime. In cases of
murder or mutilation, this feeling is almost universal. In
those, therefore, whom this exhibition does not awaken to
the sympathy which extenuates crime and discredits the
law which restrains it, it produces feelings more directly at
war with the genuine purposes of political society.   It
excites those emotions which it is the chief object of civilisation to extinguish for ever, and in the extinction of which
alone there can be any hope of better institutions than
those under which men now misgovern one another. Men
feel that their revenge is gratified, and that their security
is established by the extinction and the sufferings of beings,
in most respects resembling themselves ; and their daily

occupations constraining them to a precise form in all their thoughts, they come to connect inseparably the idea of their own advantage with that of the death and torture of others. It is manifest that the object of sane polity is directly the reverse; and that laws founded upon reason should accustom the gross vulgar to associate their ideas of security and of interest with the reformation, and the strict restraint, for that purpose alone, of those who might invade it.

The passion of revenge is originally nothing more than an habitual perception of the ideas of the sufferings of the person who inflicts an injury, as connected, as they are in a savage state, or in such portions of society as are yet undisciplined to civilisation, with security that that injury will not be repeated in future. This feeling, engrafted upon superstition and confirmed by habit, at last loses sight of the only object for which it may be supposed to have been implanted, and becomes a passion and a duty to be pursued and fulfilled, even to the destruction of those ends to which it originally tended. The other passions, both good and evil, Avarice, Remorse, Love, Patriotism, present a similar appearance; and to this principle of the mind over-shooting the mark at which it aims, we owe all that is eminently base or excellent in human nature; in providing for the nutriment or the extinction of which, consists the true art of the legislator.*

Nothing is more clear than that the infliction of punishment in general, in a degree which the reformation and the

* The savage and the illiterate are but faintly aware of the distinction between the future and the past : they make actions belonging to periods so distinct, the subjects of similar feelings ; they live only in the present, or in the past, as it is present. It is in this that the philosopher excels one of the many ; it is this which distinguishes the doctrine of philosophic necessity from fatalism ; and that determination of the will, bv which it is the active source of future events, from

restraint of those who transgress the laws does not render indispensable, and none more than death, confirms all the inhuman and unsocial impulses of men. It is almost a proverbial remark, that those nations in which the penal code has been particularly mild, have been distinguished from all others by the rarity of crime. But the example is to be admitted to be equivocal. A more decisive argument is afforded by a consideration of the universal connection of ferocity of manners, and a contempt of social ties, with the contempt of human life. Governments which derive their institutions from the existence of circumstances of barbarism and violence, with some rare exceptions, perhaps, are bloody in proportion as they are despotic, and form the manners of their subjects to a sympathy with their own spirit.

The spectators who feel no abhorrence at a public execution, but rather a self-applauding superiority, and a sense of gratified indignation, are surely excited to the most inauspicious emotions. The first reflection of such a one is the sense of his own internal and actual worth, as preferable to that of the victim, whom circumstances have led to destruction. The meanest wretch is impressed with a sense of his own comparative merit. He is one of those on whom the tower of Siloam fell not—he is such a one as Jesus Christ found not in all Samaria, who, in his own soul, throws the first stone at the woman taken in adultery. The

that liberty or indifference, to which the abstract liability of irremediable actions is attached, according to the notions of the vulgar.

This is the source of the erroneous excesses of Remorse and Revenge; the one extending itself over the future, and the other over the past; provinces in which their suggestions can only be the sources of evil. The purpose of a resolution to act more wisely and virtuously in future, and the sense of a necessity of caution in repressing an enemy, are the sources from which the enormous superstitions implied in the words cited have arisen.

popular religion of the country takes its designation from that illustrious person whose beautiful sentiment I have quoted. Any one who has stript from the doctrines of this person the veil of familiarity, will perceive how adverse their spirit is to feelings of this nature.

ON LIFE.

LIFE and the world, or whatever we call that which we are and feel, is an astonishing thing. The mist of familiarity obscures from us the wonder of our being. We are struck with admiration at some of its transient modifications, but it is itself the great miracle. What are changes of empires, the wreck of dynasties, with the opinions which supported them; what is the birth and the extinction of religious and of political systems to life? What are the revolutions of the globe which we inhabit, and the operations of the elements of which it is composed, compared with life? What is the universe of stars, and suns, of which this inhabited earth is one, and their motions, and their destiny, compared with life? Life, the great miracle, we admire not, because it is so miraculous. It is well that we are thus shielded by the familiarity of what is at once so certain and so unfathomable, from an astonishment which would otherwise absorb and overawe the functions of that which is its object.

If any artist, I do not say had executed, but had merely conceived in his mind the system of the sun, and the stars, and planets, they not existing, and had painted to us in words, or upon canvas, the spectacle now afforded by the nightly cope of heaven, and illustrated it by the wisdom of astronomy, great would be our admiration. Or had he imagined the scenery of this earth, the mountains, the seas, and the rivers ; the grass, and the flowers, and the variety of the forms and masses of the leaves of the woods, and the colours which attend the setting and the rising sun, and the hues of the atmosphere, turbid or serene, these things not before existing, truly we should have been astonished, and it would not have been a vain boast to have said of such a man, "Non merita nome di creatore, se non Iddio ed il Poeta." But now these things are looked on with little wonder, and to be conscious of them with intense delight is esteemed to be the distinguishing mark of a refined and extraordinary person. The multitude of men care not for them. It is thus with Life—that which includes all.

What is life? Thoughts and feelings arise, with or without our will, and we employ words to express them. We are born, and our birth is unremembered, and our infancy remembered but in fragments ; we live on, and in living we lose the apprehension of life. How vain is it to think that words can penetrate the mystery of our being ! Rightly used they may make evident our ignorance to ourselves, and this is much. For what are we? Whence do we come? and whither do we go? Is birth the commencement, is death the conclusion of our being? What is birth and death?

The most refined abstractions of logic conduct to a view of life, which, though startling to the apprehension, is, in fact, that which the habitual sense of its repeated combinations has extinguished in us. It strips, as it were, the painted curtain from this scene of things. I confess that I am one of those who am unable to refuse my assent to the conclusions of those philosophers who assert that nothing exists but as it is perceived.

It is a decision against which all our persuasions struggle, and we must be long convicted before we can be convinced that the solid universe of external things is "such stuff as dreams are made of." The shocking absurdities of the popular philosophy of mind and matter, its fatal consequences in morals, and their violent dogmatism concerning the source of all things, had early conducted me to materialism. This materialism is a seducing system to young and superficial minds. It allows its disciples to talk, and dispenses them from thinking. But I was discontented with such a view of things as it afforded; man is a being of high aspirations, "looking both before and after," whose "thoughts wander through eternity," disclaiming alliance with transience and decay; incapable of imagining to himself annihilation; existing but in the future and the past; being, not what he is, but what he has been and shall be. Whatever may be his true and final destination, there is a spirit within him at enmity with nothingness and dissolution. This is the character of all life and being. Each is at once the centre and the circumference; the point to which all things are referred, and the line in which all things are contained. Such contemplations as these, materialism and the popular philosophy of mind and matter alike forbid; they are only consistent with the intellectual system.

It is absurd to enter into a long recapitulation of arguments sufficiently familiar to those inquiring minds, whom alone a writer on abstruse subjects can be conceived to address. Perhaps the most clear and vigorous statement of the intellectual system is to be found in Sir William Drummond's Academical Questions. After such an exposition, it would be idle to translate into other words what could only lose its energy and fitness by the change.

Examined point by point, and word by word, the most discriminating intellects have been able to discern no train of thoughts in the process of reasoning, which does not conduct inevitably to the conclusion which has been stated.

What follows from the admission? It establishes no new truth, it gives us no additional insight into our hidden nature, neither its action nor itself. Philosophy, impatient as it may be to build, has much work yet remaining, as pioneer for the overgrowth of ages. It makes one step towards this object; it destroys error, and the roots of error. It leaves, what it is too often the duty of the reformer in political and ethical questions to leave, a vacancy. It reduces the mind to that freedom in which it would have acted, but for the misuse of words and signs, the instruments of its own creation. By signs, I would be understood in a wide sense, including what is properly meant by that term, and what I peculiarly mean. In this latter sense, almost all familiar objects are signs, standing, not for themselves, but for others in their capacity of suggesting one thought which shall lead to a train of thoughts. Our whole life is thus an education of error.

Let us recollect our sensations as children. What a distinct and intense apprehension had we of the world and of ourselves! Many of the circumstances of social life were then important to us which are now no longer so. But that is not the point of comparison on which I mean to insist. We less habitually distinguished all that we saw and felt, from our ourselves. They seemed as it were to constitute one mass. There are some persons who, in this respect, are always children. Those who are subject to the state called reverie, feel as if their nature were dissolved into the surrounding universe, or as if the surrounding universe were absorbed into their being.

They are conscious of no distinction. And these are states which precede, or accompany, or follow an unusually intense and vivid apprehension of life. As men grow up this power commonly decays, and they become mechanical and habitual agents. Thus feelings and then reasonings are the combined result of a multitude of entangled thoughts, and of a series of what are called impressions, planted by reiteration.

The view of life presented by the most refined deductions of the intellectual philosophy, is that of unity. Nothing exists but as it is perceived. The difference is merely nominal between those two classes of thought, which are vulgarly distinguished by the names of ideas and of external objects. Pursuing the same thread of reasoning, the existence of distinct individual minds, similar to that which is employed in now questioning its own nature, is likewise found to be a delusion. The words *I, you, they,* are not signs of any actual difference subsisting between the assemblage of thoughts thus indicated, but are merely marks employed to denote the different modifications of the one mind.

Let it not be supposed that this doctrine conducts to the monstrous presumption that I, the person who now write and think, am that one mind. I am but a portion of it. The words *I,* and *you,* and *they* are grammatical devices invented simply for arrangement, and totally devoid of the intense and exclusive sense usually attached to them. It is difficult to find terms adequate to express so subtle a conception as that to which the Intellectual Philosophy has conducted us. We are on that verge where words abandon us, and what wonder if we grow dizzy to look down the dark abyss of how little we know.

The relations of *things* remain unchanged, by whatever

system. By the word *things* is to be understood any
object of thought, that is any thought upon which any
other thought is employed, with an apprehension of
distinction.   The relations of these remain unchanged ;
and such is the material of our knowledge.

What is the cause of life ? that is, how was it produced,
or what agencies distinct from life have acted or act upon
life ?   All recorded generations of mankind have wearily
busied themselves in inventing answers to this question ;
and the result has been,—Religion. Yet, that the basis of
all things cannot be, as the popular philosophy alleges,
mind, is sufficiently evident.   Mind, as far as we have any
experience of its properties, and beyond that experience
how vain is argument ! cannot create, it can only perceive.
It is said also to be the cause.   But cause is only a word
expressing a certain state of the human mind with regard
to the manner in which two thoughts are apprehended to
be related to each other.   If any one desires to
know how unsatisfactorily the popular philosophy employs
itself upon this great question, they need only impartially
reflect upon the manner in which thoughts develop themselves in their minds.   It is infinitely improbable that the
cause of mind, that is, of existence, is similar to mind.

ON A FUTURE STATE.

IT has been the persuasion of an immense majority of
human beings in all ages and nations that we continue to
live after death,—that apparent termination of all the
functions of sensitive and intellectual existence.   Nor has
mankind been contented with supposing that species of

existence which some philosophers have asserted; namely, the resolution of the component parts of the mechanism of a living being into its elements, and the impossibility of the minutest particle of these sustaining the smallest diminution. They have clung to the idea that sensibility and thought, which they have distinguished from the objects of it, under the several names of spirit and matter, is, in its own nature, less susceptible of division and decay, and that, when the body is resolved into its elements, the principle which animated it will remain perpetual and unchanged. Some philosophers—and those to whom we are indebted for the most stupendous discoveries in physical science, suppose, on the other hand, that intelligence is the mere result of certain combinations among the particles of its objects; and those among them who believe that we live after death, recur to the interposition of a supernatural power, which shall overcome the tendency inherent in all material combinations to dissipate and be absorbed into other forms.

Let us trace the reasonings which in one and the other have conducted to these two opinions, and endeavour to discover what we ought to think on a question of such momentous interest. Let us analyse the ideas and feelings which constitute the contending beliefs, and watchfully establish a discrimination between words and thoughts. Let us bring the question to the test of experience and fact; and ask ourselves, considering our nature in its entire extent, what light we derive from a sustained and comprehensive view of its component parts, which may enable us to assert, with certainty, that we do or do not live after death.

The examination of this subject requires that it should be stript of all those accessory topics which adhere to it in the

common opinion of men.   The existence of a God, and a
future state of rewards and punishments, are totally foreign
to the subject.   If it be proved that the world is ruled by a
Divine Power, no inference necessarily can be drawn from
that circumstance in favour of a future state.   It has been
asserted, indeed, that as goodness and justice are to be
numbered among the attributes of the Deity, he will
undoubtedly compensate the virtuous who suffer during life,
and that he will make every sensitive being, who does not
deserve punishment, happy for ever.   But this view of the
subject, which it would be tedious as well as superfluous to
develop and expose, satisfies no person, and cuts the knot
which we now seek to untie.   Moreover, should it be proved,
on the other hand, that the mysterious principle which
regulates the proceedings of the universe, is neither
intelligent nor sensitive, yet it is not an inconsistency to
suppose at the same time, that the animating power
survives the body which it has animated, by laws as
independent of any supernatural agent as those through
which it first became united with it.   Nor, if a future state
be clearly proved, does it follow that it will be a state of
punishment or reward.

By the word death, we express that condition in which
natures resembling ourselves apparently cease to be that
which they were.   We no longer hear them speak, nor see
them move.   If they have sensations and apprehensions, we
no longer participate in them.   We know no more than
that those external organs, and all that fine texture of material frame, without which we have no experience that life
or thought can subsist, are dissolved and scattered abroad.
The body is placed under the earth, and after a certain
period there remains no vestige even of its form.   This is
that contemplation of inexhaustible melancholy, whose

shadow eclipses the brightness of the world. The common
observer is struck with dejection at the spectacle. He
contends in vain against the persuasion of the grave, that
the dead indeed cease to be. The corpse at his feet is
prophetic of his own destiny. Those who have preceded
him, and whose voice was delightful to his ear; whose
touch met his like sweet and subtle fire; whose aspect
spread a visionary light upon his path—these he cannot
meet again. The organs of sense are destroyed, and the
intellectual operations dependent on them have perished
with their sources. How can a corpse see or feel? its eyes
are eaten out, and its heart is black and without motion.
What intercourse can two heaps of putrid clay and crumbling bones hold together? When you can discover where
the fresh colours of the faded flower abide, or the music of
the broken lyre, seek life among the dead. Such are the
anxious and fearful contemplations of the common observer,
though the popular religion often prevents him from
confessing them even to himself.

The natural philosopher, in addition to the sensations
common to all men inspired by the event of death, believes
that he sees with more certainty that it is attended with
the annihilation of sentiment and thought. He observes
the mental powers increase and fade with those of the body,
and even accommodate themselves to the most transitory
changes of our physical nature. Sleep suspends many of
the faculties of the vital and intellectual principle; drunkenness and disease will either temporarily or permanently
derange them. Madness or idiotcy may utterly extinguish
the most excellent and delicate of those powers. In old age
the mind gradually withers; and as it grew and was
strengthened with the body, so does it together with the
body sink into decrepitude. Assuredly these are convincing

evidences that so soon as the organs of the body are subjected to the laws of inanimate matter, sensation, and
perception, and apprehension, are at an end.   It is probable
that what we call thought is not an actual being, but no
more than the relation between certain parts of that
infinitely varied mass, of which the rest of the universe is
composed, and which ceases to exist as soon as those parts
change their position with regard to each other.   Thus
colour, and sound, and taste, and odour exist only relatively.   But let thought be considered as some peculiar substance, which permeates, and is the cause of, the animation
of living beings.   Why should that substance be assumed
to be something essentially distinct from all others, and
exempt from subjection to those laws from which no other
substance is exempt?   It differs, indeed, from all other substances, as electricity, and light, and magnetism, and the
constituent parts of air and earth, severally differ from all
others.   Each of these is subject to change and to decay
and to conversion into other forms.   Yet the difference
between light and earth is scarcely greater than that which
exists between life, or thought, and fire.   The difference
between the two former was never alleged as an argument
for the eternal permanence of either, in that form under
which they first might offer themselves to our notice.   Why
should the difference between the two latter substances be
an argument for the prolongation of the existence of one and
not the other, when the existence of both has arrived at
their apparent termination?   To say that fire exists without manifesting any of the properties of fire, such as light,
heat, etc., or that the principle of life exists without
consciousness, or memory, or desire, or motive, is to resign,
by an awkward distortion of language, the affirmative of
the dispute.   To say that the principle of life *may* exist in

distribution among various forms, is to assert what cannot be proved to be either true or false, but which, were it true, annihilates all hope of existence after death, in any sense in which that event can belong to the hopes and fears of men. Suppose, however, that the intellectual and vital principle differs in the most marked and essential manner from all other known substances; that they have all some resemblance between themselves which it in no degree participates. In what manner can this concession be made an argument for its imperishability? All that we see or know perishes and is changed. Life and thought differ indeed from anything else. But that it survives that period, beyond which we have no experience of its existence, such distinction and dissimilarity affords no shadow of proof, and nothing but our own desires could have led us to conjecture or imagine.

Have we existed before birth? It is difficult to conceive the possibility of this. There is, in the generative principle of each animal and plant, a power which converts the substances by which it is surrounded into a substance homogeneous with itself. That is, the relations between certain elementary particles of matter undergo a change, and submit to new combinations. For when we use the words *principle, power, cause,* etc., we mean to express no real being, but only to class under those terms a certain series of co-existing phenomena; but let it be supposed that this principle is a certain substance which escapes the observation of the chemist and anatomist. It certainly *may be;* though it is sufficiently unphilosophical to allege the possibility of an opinion as a proof of its truth. Does it see, hear, feel, before its combination with those organs on which sensation depends? Does it reason, imagine, apprehend, without those ideas which sensation alone can

87

communicate? If we have not existed before birth; if, at
the period when the parts of our nature on which thought
and life depend, seem to be woven together, they are woven
together; if there are no reasons to suppose that we have
existed before that period at which our existence apparently
commences, then there are no grounds for supposition
that we shall continue to exist after our existence has apparently ceased. So far as thought and life is concerned,
the same will take place with regard to us, individually
considered, after death, as had place befo re our birth.

It is said that it is possible that we should continue to
exist in some mode totally inconceivable to us at present.
This is a most unreasonable presumption. It casts on the
adherents of annihilation the burthen of proving the
negative of a question, the affirmative of which is not
supported by a single argument, and which, by its very
nature, lies beyond the experience of the human understanding. It is sufficiently easy, indeed, to form any
proposition, concerning which we are ignorant, just not
so absurd as not to be contradictory in itself, and defy
refutation. The possibility of whatever enters into the
wildest imagination to conceive is thus triumphantly
vindicated. But it is enough that such assertions should
be either contradictory to the known laws of nature, or
exceed the limits of our experience, that their fallacy or
irrelevancy to our consideration should be demonstrated.
They persuade, indeed, only those who desire to be
persuaded.

This desire to be for ever as we are; the reluctance to a
violent and unexperienced change, which is common to all
the animated and inanimate combinations of the universe,
is, indeed, the secret persuasion which has given birth to
the opinions of a future state.

ESSAY ON CHRISTIANITY.

THE Being who has influenced in the most memorable manner the opinions and the fortunes of the human species, is Jesus Christ. At this day, his name is connected with the devotional feelings of two hundred millions of the race of man. The institutions of the most civilized portion of the globe derive their authority from the sanction of his doctrines; he is the hero, the God, of our popular religion. His extraordinary genius, the wide and rapid effect of his unexampled doctrines, his invincible gentleness and benignity, the devoted love borne to him by his adherents, suggested a persuasion to them that he was something divine. The supernatural events which the historians of this wonderful man subsequently asserted to have been connected with every gradation of his career, established the opinion.

His death is said to have been accompanied by an accumulation of tremendous prodigies. Utter darkness fell upon the earth, blotting the noonday sun; dead bodies, arising from their graves, walked through the public streets, and an earthquake shook the astonished city, rending the rocks of the surrounding mountains. The philosopher may attribute the application of these events to the death of a reformer, or the events themselves to a visitation of that universal Pan who——

.   .   .   .

The thoughts which the word "God" suggests to the human mind are susceptible of as many variations as human minds themselves. The Stoic, the Platonist, and the Epicurean, the Polytheist, the Dualist, and the Trinitarian, differ infinitely in their conceptions of its meaning. They agree only in considering it the most awful and most venerable of names, as a common term devised to express all of mystery, or majesty, or power, which the invisible world contains.   And not only has every sect distinct conceptions of the application of this name, but scarcely two individuals of the same sect, who exercise in any degree the freedom of their judgment, or yield themselves with any candour of feeling to the influences of the visible world, find perfect coincidence of opinion to exist between them.   It is [interesting] to inquire in what acceptation Jesus Christ employed this term.

We may conceive his mind to have been predisposed on this subject to adopt the opinions of his countrymen.   Every human being is indebted for a multitude of his sentiments to the religion of his early years.   Jesus Christ probably [studied] the historians of his country with the ardour of a spirit seeking after truth.   They were undoubtedly the companions of his childish years, the food and nutriment and materials of his youthful meditations.   The sublime dramatic poem entitled *Job* had familiarized his imagination with the boldest imagery afforded by the human mind and the material world.   *Ecclesiastes* had diffused a seriousness and solemnity over the frame of his spirit, glowing with youthful hope, and [had] made audible to his listening heart

> "The still, sad music of humanity,
>   Not harsh or grating, but of ample power
>   To chasten and subdue."

He had contemplated this name as having been profanely perverted to the sanctioning of the most enormous and abominable crimes.   We can distinctly trace, in the tissue of his doctrines, the persuasion that God is some universal Being, differing from man and the mind of man.   According

to Jesus Christ, God is neither the Jupiter, who sends
rain upon the earth; nor the Venus, through whom all
living things are produced; nor the Vulcan, who presides
over the terrestrial element of fire; nor the Vesta, that
preserves the light which is enshrined in the sun and moon
and stars. He is neither the Proteus nor the Pan of the
material world. But the word God, according to the
acceptation of Jesus Christ, unites all the attributes which
these denominations contain, and is the [interpoint] and
overruling Spirit of all the energy and wisdom included
within the circle of existing things. It is important to
observe that the author of the Christian system had a
conception widely differing from the gross imaginations of
the vulgar relatively to the ruling Power of the universe.
He everywhere represents this Power as something
mysteriously and illimitably pervading the frame of
things. Nor do his doctrines practically assume any
proposition which they theoretically deny. They do not
represent God as a limitless and inconceivable mystery;
affirming, at the same time, his existence as a Being subject
to passion and capable——

. . . .

" Blessed are the pure in heart, for they shall see God."
Blessed are those who have preserved internal sanctity of
soul; who are conscious of no secret deceit; who are the
same in act as they are in desire; who conceal no thought,
no tendencies of thought, from their own conscience; who
are faithful and sincere witnesses, before the tribunal
of their own judgments, of all that passes within their
mind. Such as these shall see God. What! after death,
shall their awakened eyes behold the King of Heaven?
Shall they stand in awe before the golden throne on which
He sits, and gaze upon the venerable countenance of the

paternal Monarch ?   Is this the reward of the virtuous and
the pure ?   These are the idle dreams of the visionary, or
the pernicious representations of impostors, who have
fabricated from the very materials of wisdom a cloak
for their own dwarfish or imbecile conceptions.

Jesus Christ has said no more than the most excellent
philosophers have felt and expressed—that virtue is its
own reward.   It is true that such an expression as he has
used was prompted by the energy of genius, and was
the overflowing enthusiasm of a poet; but it is not
the less literally true [because] clearly repugnant to the
mistaken conceptions of the multitude.   God, it has been
asserted, was contemplated by Jesus Christ as every poet
and every philosopher must have contemplated that
mysterious principle.   He considered that venerable word
to express the overruling Spirit of the collective energy of
the moral and material world.   He affirms, therefore, no
more than that a simple, sincere mind is the indispensable
requisite of true science and true happiness.   He affirms
that a being of pure and gentle habits will not fail, in
every thought, in every object of every thought, to be
aware of benignant visitings from the invisible energies by
which he is surrounded.

Whosoever is free from the contamination of luxury and
licence, may go forth to the fields and to the woods,
inhaling joyous renovation from the breath of Spring, or
catching from the odours and sounds of Autumn some
diviner mood of sweetest sadness, which improves the
softened heart.   Whosoever is no deceiver or destroyer of
his fellow-men—no liar, no flatterer, no murderer—may
walk among his species, deriving, from the communion
with all which they contain of beautiful or of majestic,
some intercourse with the Universal God.   Whosoever has

maintained with his own heart the strictest correspondence
of confidence, who dares to examine and to estimate every
imagination which suggests itself to his mind—whosoever
is that which he designs to become, and only aspires to that
which the divinity of his own nature shall consider and
approve—he has already seen God.

We live and move and think; but we are not the
creators of our own origin and existence. We are not the
arbiters of every motion of our own complicated nature;
we are not the masters of our own imaginations and moods
of mental being. There is a Power by which we are
surrounded, like the atmosphere in which some motionless
lyre is suspended, which visits with its breath our silent
chords at will.

Our most imperial and stupendous qualities—those on
which the majesty and the power of humanity is erected—
are, relatively to the inferior portion of its mechanism,
active and imperial; but they are the passive slaves of
some higher and more omnipotent Power. This Power is
God; and those who have seen God have, in the period of
their purer and more perfect nature, been harmonized by
their own will to so exquisite [a] consentaneity of power as
to give forth divinest melody, when the breath of universal
being sweeps over their frame. That those who are pure
in heart shall see God, and that virtue is its own reward,
may be considered as equivalent assertions. The former
of these propositions is a metaphorical repetition of the
latter. The advocates of literal interpretation have been
the most efficacious enemies of those doctrines whose
nature they profess to venerate. Thucydides, in particular,
affords a number of instances calculated——

.   .   .   .   .

Tacitus says, that the Jews held God to be something

eternal and supreme, neither subject to change nor to decay; therefore, they permit no statues in their cities or their temples. The universal Being can only be described or defined by negatives which deny his subjection to the laws of all inferior existences. Where indefiniteness ends idolatry and anthropomorphism begin. God is, as Lucan has expressed,

> " Quocunque vides, quodcunque moveris,
> Et cœlum et virtus."

The doctrine of what some fanatics have termed "a peculiar Providence"—that is, of some power beyond and superior to that which ordinarily guides the operations of the Universe, interfering to punish the vicious and reward the virtuous—is explicitly denied by Jesus Christ. The absurd and execrable doctrine of vengeance, in *all its shapes*, seems to have been contemplated by this great moralist with the profoundest disapprobation; nor would he permit the most venerable of names to be perverted into a sanction for the meanest and most contemptible propensities incident to the nature of man. "Love your enemies' bless those who curse you, that ye may be the sons of your Heavenly Father, who makes the sun to shine on the good and on the evil, and the rain to fall on the just and unjust." How monstrous a calumny have not impostors dared to advance against the mild and gentle author of this just sentiment, and against the whole tenor of his doctrines and his life, overflowing with benevolence and forbearance and compassion! They have represented him asserting that the Omnipotent God—that merciful and benignant Power who scatters equally upon the beautiful earth all the elements of security and happiness—whose influences are distributed to all whose natures admit of a participation in them—who sends to the weak and vicious creatures of his will all the benefits which they are capable of sharing—that this God has devised a scheme whereby the body shall live after its apparent dissolution, and be rendered capable of indefinite torture. He is said to have compared the agonies which the vicious shall then endure to the excruciations of a living body bound among the flames, and being consumed sinew by sinew, and bone by bone.

And this is to be done, not because it is supposed (and the supposition would be sufficiently detestable) that the moral nature of the sufferer would be improved by his tortures—it is done because it *is just* to be done. My neighbour, or my servant, or my child, has done me an injury, and it is just that he should suffer an injury in return. Such is the doctrine which Jesus Christ summoned his whole resources of persuasions to oppose. "Love your enemy, bless those who curse you:" such, he says, is the practice of God, and such must ye imitate if ye would be the children of God.

Jesus Christ would hardly have cited, as an example of all that is gentle and beneficent and compassionate, a Being who shall deliberately scheme to inflict on a large portion of the human race tortures indescribably intense and indefinitely protracted: who shall inflict them, too, without any mistake as to the true nature of pain —without any view to future good—merely because it is just.

This, and no other, is justice :—to consider, under all the circumstances and consequences of a particular case, how the greatest quantity and purest quality of happiness will ensue from any action ; [this] is to be just, and there is no other justice. The distinction between justice and mercy was first imagined in the courts of tyranny. Man-

kind receive every relaxation of their tyranny as a
circumstance of grace or favour.

Such was the clemency of Julius Cæsar, who, having
achieved by a series of treachery and bloodshed the ruin of
the liberties of his country, receives the fame of mercy
because, possessing the power to slay the noblest men of
Rome, he restrained his sanguinary soul, arrogating to
himself as a merit an abstinence from actions which if he
had committed, he would only have added one other
atrocity to his deeds. His assassins understood justice
better. They saw the most virtuous and civilised community of mankind under the most insolent dominion
of one wicked man; and they murdered him. They
destroyed the usurper of the liberties of their countrymen,
not because they hated him, not because they would
revenge the wrongs which they had sustained (Brutus, it is
said, was his most familiar friend ; most of the conspirators
were habituated to domestic intercourse with the man whom
they destroyed) : it was in affection, inextinguishable love
for all that is venerable and dear to the human heart, in the
names of Country, Liberty, and Virtue ; it was in a serious
and solemn and reluctant mood, that these holy patriots
murdered their father and their friend. They would have
spared his violent death, if he could have deposited the
rights which he had assumed. His own selfish and narrow
nature necessitated the sacrifices they made. They
required that he should change all those habits which
debauchery and bloodshed had twined around the fibres of
his inmost frame of thought ; that he should participate
with them and with his country those privileges which,
having corrupted by assuming to himself, he would no
longer value. They would have sacrificed their lives if
they could have made him worthy of the sacrifice. Such

are the feelings which Jesus Christ asserts to belong to the ruling Power of the world. He desireth not the death of a sinner : he makes the sun to shine upon the just and unjust.

The nature of a narrow and malevolent spirit is so essentially incompatible with happiness as to render it inaccessible to the influences of the benignant God. All that his own perverse propensities will permit him to receive, that God abundantly pours forth upon him. If there is the slightest overbalance of happiness, which can be allotted to the most atrocious offender, consistently with the nature of things, that is rigidly made his portion by the ever-watchful Power of God. In every case, the human mind enjoys the utmost pleasure which it is capable of enjoying. God is represented by Jesus Christ as the Power from which, and through which, the streams of all that is excellent and delightful flow ; the Power which models, as they pass, all the elements of this mixed universe to the purest and most perfect shape which it belongs to their nature to assume. Jesus Christ attributes to this Power the faculty of Will. How far such a doctrine, in its ordinary sense, may be philosophically true, or how far Jesus Christ intentionally availed himself of a metaphor easily understood, is foreign to the subject to consider. This much is certain, that Jesus Christ represents God as the fountain of all goodness, the eternal enemy of pain and evil, the uniform and unchanging motive of the salutary operations of the material world. The supposition that this cause is excited to action by some principle analogous to the human will, adds weight to the persuasion that it is foreign to its beneficent nature to inflict the slightest pain. According to Jesus Christ, and according to the indisputable facts of the case, some evil spirit has dominion in this imperfect world. But there

will come a time when the human mind shall be visited
exclusively by the influences of the benignant Power. Men
shall die, and their bodies shall rot under the ground ;
all the organs through which their knowledge and their
feelings have flowed, or in which they have originated,
shall assume other forms, and become ministrant to purposes the most foreign from their former tendencies.
There is a time when we shall neither be heard or be seen
by the multitude of beings like ourselves by whom we
have been so long surrounded. They shall go to graves ;
where then ?

It appears that we moulder to a heap of senseless dust ;
to a few worms, that arise and perish, like ourselves.
Jesus Christ asserts that these appearances are fallacious,
and that a gloomy and cold imagination alone suggests the
conception that thought can cease to be. Another and a
more extensive state of being, rather than the complete
extinction of being, will follow from that mysterious change
which we call Death. There shall be no misery, no pain,
no fear. The empire of evil spirits extends not beyond the
boundaries of the grave. The unobscured irradiations
from the fountain-fire of all goodness shall reveal all that
is mysterious and unintelligible, until the mutual communications of knowledge and of happiness throughout all
thinking natures constitute a harmony of good that ever
varies and never ends.

This is Heaven, when pain and evil cease, and when the
Benignant Principle, untrammelled and uncontrolled, visits
in the fulness of its power the universal frame of things.
Human life, with all its unreal ills and transitory hopes, is
as a dream, which departs before the dawn, leaving no
trace of its evanescent hues. All that it contains of pure
or of divine visits the passive mind in some serenest mood.

Most holy are the feelings through which our fellow-beings are rendered dear and [venerable] to the heart. The remembrance of their sweetness, and the completion of the hopes which they [excite], constitute, when we awaken from the sleep of life, the fulfilment of the prophecies of its most majestic and beautiful visions.

We die, says Jesus Christ; and, when we awaken from the languor of disease, the glories and the happiness of Paradise are around us. All evil and pain have ceased for ever. Our happiness also corresponds with, and is adapted to, the nature of what is most excellent in our being. We see God, and we see that he is good. How delightful a picture, even if it be not true! How magnificent is the conception which this bold theory suggests to the contemplation, even if it be no more than the imagination of some sublimest and most holy poet, who, impressed with the loveliness and majesty of his own nature, is impatient and discontented with the narrow limits which this imperfect life and the dark grave have assigned for ever as his melancholy portion. It is not to be believed that Hell, or punishment, was the conception of this daring mind. It is not to be believed that the most prominent group of this picture, which is framed so heart-moving and lovely—the accomplishment of all human hope, the extinction of all morbid fear and anguish—would consist of millions of sensitive beings enduring, in every variety of torture which Omniscient vengeance could invent, immortal agony.

Jesus Christ opposed with earnest eloquence the panic fears and hateful superstitions which have enslaved mankind for ages. Nations had risen against nations, employing the subtlest devices of mechanism and mind to waste, and excruciate, and overthrow. The great community of mankind had been subdivided into ten thousand each organized for the ruin of the other. Wheel within wheel, the vast machine was instinct with the restless spirit of desolation. Pain had been inflicted ; therefore, pain should be inflicted in return. Retaliation of injuries is the only remedy which can be applied to violence, because it teaches the injurer the true nature of his own conduct, and operates as a warning against its repetition. Nor must the same measure of calamity be returned as was received. If a man borrows a certain sum from me, he is bound to repay that sum. Shall no more be required of the enemy who destroys my reputation, or ravages my fields ? It is just that he should suffer ten times the loss which he has inflicted, that the legitimate consequences of his deed may never be obliterated from his remembrance, and that others may clearly discern and feel the danger of invading the peace of human society. Such reasonings, and the impetuous feelings arising from them, have armed nation against nation, family against family, man against man.

An Athenian soldier, in the Ionian army which had assembled for the purpose of vindicating the liberty of the Asiatic Greeks, accidentally set fire to Sardis. The city, being composed of combustible materials, was burned to the ground. The Persians believed that this circumstance of aggression made it their duty to retaliate on Athens. They assembled successive expeditions on the most extensive scale. Every nation of the East was united to ruin the Grecian States. Athens was burned to the ground, the whole territory laid waste, and every living thing which it contained [destroyed]. After suffering and inflicting incalculable mischiefs, they desisted from their purpose only when they became impotent to effect it. The desire of revenge for the aggression of Persia outlived, among the

Greeks, that love of liberty which had been their most glorious distinction among the nations of mankind; and Alexander became the instrument of its completion. The mischiefs attendant on this consummation of fruitless ruin are too manifold and too tremendous to be related. If all the thought which had been expended on the construction of engines of agony and death—the modes of aggression and defence, the raising of armies, and the acquirement of those arts of tyranny and falsehood without which mixed multitudes could neither be led nor governed—had been employed to promote the true welfare and extend the real empire of man, how different would have been the present situation of human society! how different the state of knowledge in physical and moral science, upon which the power and happiness of mankind essentially depend! What nation has the example of the desolation of Attica by Mardonius and Xerxes, or the extinction of the Persian empire by Alexander of Macedon, restrained from outrage? Was not the pretext of this latter system of spoliation derived immediately from the former? Had revenge in this instance any other effect than to increase, instead of diminishing, the mass of malice and evil already existing in the world?

The emptiness and folly of retaliation are apparent from every example which can be brought forward. Not only Jesus Christ, but the most eminent professors of every sect of philosophy, have reasoned against this futile superstition. Legislation is, in one point of view, to be considered as an attempt to provide against the excesses of this deplorable mistake. It professes to assign the penalty of all private injuries, and denies to individuals the right of vindicating their proper cause. This end is certainly not attained without some accommodation to the propensities which it

desires to destroy.   Still, it recognises no principle but the
production of the greatest eventual good with the least
immediate injury ; and regards the torture, or the death, of
any human being as unjust, of whatever mischief he may
have been the author, so that the result shall not more than
compensate for the immediate pain.

Mankind, transmitting from generation to generation
the legacy of accumulated vengeances, and pursuing with
the feelings of duty the misery of their fellow-beings, have
not failed to attribute to the Universal Cause a character
analogous with their own.   The image of this invisible,
mysterious Being is more or less excellent and perfect—
resembles more or less its original—in proportion to the
perfection of the mind on which it is impressed.   Thus,
that nation which has arrived at the highest step in the
scale of moral progression will believe most purely in that
God, the knowledge of whose real attributes is considered
as the firmest basis of the true religion.   The reason of the
belief of each individual, also, will be so far regulated by
his conceptions of what is good.   Thus, the conceptions
which any nation or individual entertains of the God of its
popular worship may be inferred from their own actions
and opinions, which are the subjects of their approbation
among their fellow-men.   Jesus Christ instructed his disciples to be perfect, as their Father in Heaven is perfect,
declaring at the same time his belief that human perfection
requires the refraining from revenge and retribution in any
of its various shapes.

The perfection of the human and the divine character is
thus asserted to be the same.   Man, by resembling God,
fulfils most accurately the tendencies of his nature : and
God comprehends within himself all that constitutes human
perfection.   Thus, God is a model through which the

excellence of man is to be estimated, whilst the *abstract* perfection of the human character is the type of the *actual* perfection of the divine. It is not to be believed that a person of such comprehensive views as Jesus Christ could have fallen into so manifest a contradiction as to assert that men would be tortured after death by that Being whose character is held up as a model to human kind, because he is incapable of malevolence and revenge. All the arguments which have been brought forward to justify retribution fail, when retribution is destined neither to operate as an example to other agents, nor to the offender himself. How feeble such reasoning is to be considered, has been already shown ; but it is the character of an evil Dæmon to consign the beings whom he has endowed with sensation to unprofitable anguish. The peculiar circum- stances attendant on the conception of God casting sinners to burn in Hell for ever, combine to render that conception the most perfect specimen of the greatest imaginable crime. Jesus Christ represented God as the principle of all good, the source of all happiness, the wise and benevolent Creator and Preserver of all living things. But the interpreters of his doctrines have confounded the good and the evil principle. They observe the emanations of their universal natures to be inextricably entangled in the world, and, trembling before the power of the cause of all things, addressed to it such flattery as is acceptable to the ministers of human tyranny, attributing love and wisdom to those energies which they felt to be exerted indifferently for the purposes of benefit and calamity.

Jesus Christ expressly asserts that distinction between the good and evil principle which it has been the practice of all theologians to confound. How far his doctrines, or their interpretation, may be true, it would scarcely have been worth while to inquire, if the one did not afford an example and an incentive to the attainment of true virtue, whilst the other holds out a sanction and apology for every species of mean and cruel vice.

It cannot be precisely ascertained in what degree Jesus Christ accommodated his doctrines to the opinions of his auditors ; or in what degree he really said all that he is related to have said. He has left no written record of himself, and we are compelled to judge from the imperfect and obscure information which his biographers (persons certainly of very undisciplined and undiscriminating minds) have transmitted to posterity. These writers (our only guides) impute sentiments to Jesus Christ which flatly contradict each other. They represent him as narrow, superstitious, and exquisitely vindictive and malicious. They insert, in the midst of a strain of impassioned eloquence or sagest exhortations, a sentiment only remarkable for its naked and drivelling folly. But it is not difficult to distinguish the inventions by which these historians have filled up the interstices of tradition, or corrupted the simplicity of truth, from the real character of their rude amazement. They have left sufficiently clear indications of the genuine character of Jesus Christ to rescue it for ever from the imputations cast upon it by their ignorance and fanaticism. We discover that he is the enemy of oppression and of falsehood ; that he is the advocate of equal justice ; that he is neither disposed to sanction bloodshed nor deceit ; under whatsoever pretences their practice may be vindicated. We discover that he was a man of weak and majestic demeanour, calm in danger ; of natural and simple thought and habits ; beloved to adoration by his adherents ; unmoved, solemn, and severe.

It is utterly incredible that this man said, that if you hate your enemy, you would find it to your account to return him good for evil, since, by such a temporary oblivion of vengeance, you would heap coals of fire on his head. Where such contradictions occur, a favourable construction is warranted by the general innocence of manners and comprehensiveness of views which he is represented to possess. The rule of criticism to be adopted in judging of the life, actions, and words of a man who has acted any conspicuous part in the revolutions of the world, should not be narrow. We ought to form a general image of his character and of his doctrines, and refer to -this whole the distinct portions of actions and speech by which they are diversified. It is not here asserted that no contradictions are to be admitted to have taken place in the system of Jesus Christ, between doctrines promulgated in different states of feeling or information, or even such as are implied in the enunciation of a scheme of thought, various and obscure through its immensity and depth. It is not asserted that no degree of human indignation ever hurried him, beyond the limits which his calmer mood had placed, to disapprobation against vice and folly Those deviations from the history of his life are alone to be vindicated, which represent his own essential character in contradiction with itself.

Every human mind has what Bacon calls its "*idola specûs*"—peculiar images which reside in the inner cave of thought. These constitute the essential and distinctive character of every human being; to which every action and every word have intimate relation; and by which, in depicting a character, the genuineness and meaning of these words and actions are to be determined. Every fanatic or enemy of virtue is not at liberty to misrepresent

the greatest geniuses and most heroic defenders of all that
is valuable in this mortal world. History, to gain any
credit, must contain some truth, and that truth shall thus
be made a sufficient indication of prejudice and deceit.

With respect to the miracles which these biographers
have related, I have already declined to enter into any
discussion on their nature or their existence. The supposition of their falsehood or their truth would modify in
no degree the hues of the picture which is attempted to be
delineated.   To judge truly of the moral and philosophical
character of Socrates, it is not necessary to determine the
question of the familiar Spirit which [it] is supposed that
he believed to attend on him. The power of the human
mind, relatively to intercourse with or dominion over the
invisible world, is doubtless an interesting theme of discussion ; but the connection of the instance of Jesus Christ
with the established religion of the country in which I
write, renders it dangerous to subject oneself to the imputation of introducing new Gods or abolishing old ones; nor
is the duty of mutual forbearance sufficiently understood to
render it certain that the metaphysician and the moralist,
even though he carefully sacrifice a cock to Esculapius,
may not receive something analogous to the bowl of hemlock for the reward of his labours. Much, however, of
what his [Christ's] biographers have asserted is not to be
rejected merely because inferences inconsistent with the
general spirit of his system are to be adduced from its
admission.   Jesus Christ did what every other reformer
who has produced any considerable effect upon the world has
done. He accommodated his doctrines to the prepesses-
sions of those whom he addressed. He used a language
for this view sufficiently familiar to our comprehensions.
He said—However new or strange my doctrines may

appear to you, they are in fact only the restoration and re-establishment of those original institutions and ancient customs of your own law and religion. The constitutions of your faith and policy, although perfect in their origin, have become corrupt and altered, and have fallen into decay. I profess to restore them to their pristine authority and splendour. "Think not that I am come to destroy the Law and the Prophets. I am come not to destroy, but to fulfil. Till heaven and earth pass away, one jot or one tittle shall in nowise pass away from the Law, till all be fulfilled." Thus, like a skilful orator (see Cicero, *De Oratore*), he secures the prejudices of his auditors, and induces them, by his professions of sympathy with their feelings, to enter with a willing mind into the exposition of his own. The art of persuasion differs from that of reasoning ; and it is of no small moment, to the success even of a true cause, that the judges who are to determine on its merits should be free from those national and religious predilections which render the multitude both deaf and blind.

Let not this practice be considered as an unworthy artifice. It were best for the cause of reason that mankind should acknowledge no authority but its own ; but it is useful, to a certain extent, that they should not consider those institutions which they have been habituated to reverence as opposing an obstacle to its admission. All reformers have been compelled to practice this misrepresentation of their own true feelings and opinions. It is deeply to be lamented that a word should ever issue from human lips which contains the minutest alloy of dissimulation, or simulation, or hyprocrisy, or exaggeration, or anything but the precise and rigid image which is present to the mind, and which ought to dictate the expression.

But the practice of utter sincerity towards other men would avail to no good end, if they were incapable of practising it towards their own minds. In fact, truth cannot be communicated until it is perceived. The interests, therefore, of truth require that an orator should, as far as possible, produce in his hearers that state of mind on which alone his exhortations could fairly be contemplated and examined.

Having produced this favourable disposition of mind, Jesus Christ proceeds to qualify, and finally to abrogate, the system of the Jewish law. He descants upon its insufficiency as a code of moral conduct, which it professed to be, and absolutely selects the law of retaliation as an instance of the absurdity and immorality of its institutions. The conclusion of the speech is in a strain of the most daring and most impassionate speculation. He seems emboldened by the success of his exculpation to the multitude, to declare in public the utmost singularity of his faith. He tramples upon all received opinions, on all the cherished luxuries and superstitions of mankind. He bids them cast aside the claims of custom and blind faith by which they have been encompassed from the very cradle of their being, and receive the imitator and minister of the Universal God.

EQUALITY OF MANKIND.

" The spirit of the Lord is upon me, because he hath chosen me to preach the gospel to the poor : He hath sent me to heal the broken-hearted, to preach deliverance to the captives and recovery of sight to the blind, and to set at liberty them that are bruised." (Luke, ch. iv., ver. 18.) This is an enunciation of all that Plato and Diogenes have speculated upon the equality of mankind. They saw that the great majority of the human species were reduced to the situation of squalid ignorance and moral imbecility, for the purpose of purveying for the luxury of a few, and contributing to the satisfaction of their thirst for power. Too mean-spirited and too feeble in resolve to attempt the conquest of their own evil passions and of the difficulties of the material world, men sought dominion over their fellow-men, as an easy method to gain that apparent majesty and power which the instinct of their nature requires. Plato wrote the scheme of a republic, in which law should watch over the equal distribution of the external instruments of unequal power—honours, property etc. Diogenes devised a nobler and a more worthier system of opposition to the system of the slave and tyrant. He said: "It is in the power of each individual to level the inequality which is the topic of the complaint of mankind. Let him be aware of his own worth, and the station which he occupies in the scale of moral beings. Diamonds and gold, palaces and sceptres, derive their value from the opinion of mankind. The only sumptuary law which can be imposed on the use and fabrication of these instruments of mischief and deceit, these symbols of successful injustice, is the law of opinion. Every man possesses the power, in this respect, to legislate for himself. Let him be well aware of his own worth and moral dignity. Let him yield in meek reverence to any wiser or worthier than he, so long as he accords no veneration to the splendour of his apparel, the luxury of his food, the multitude of his flatterers and slaves. It is because, mankind, ye value and seek the empty pageantry of wealth and social power, that ye are enslaved to its possessions. Decrease your physical wants; learn to live, so far as nourishment and shelter are concerned, like the beast of the forest and the birds of the air; ye will need not to complain, that other individuals of your species are surrounded by the diseases of luxury and the vices of subserviency and oppression." With all those who are truly wise, there will be an entire community, not only of thoughts and feelings, but also of external possessions. Insomuch, therefore, as ye live [wisely], ye may enjoy the community of whatsoever benefits arise from the inventions of civilized life. They are of value only for purposes of mental power ; they are of value only as they are capable of being shared and applied to the common advantage of philosophy ; and if there be no love among men, whatever institutions they may frame must be subservient to the same purpose—to the continuance of inequality. If there be no love among men, it is best that he who sees through the hollowness of their professions should fly from their society, and suffice to his own soul. In wisdom, he will thus lose nothing ; in power, he will gain everything. In proportion to the love existing among men, so will be the community of property and power. Among true and real friends, all is common ; and, were ignorance and envy and superstition banished from the world, all mankind would be friends. The only perfect and genuine republic is that which comprehends every living being. Those distinctions which have been artificially set up, of nations, societies, families, and religions, are only general names, expressing the abhorrence and contempt with which men blindly consider their fellow-men. I love my country ; I love the city in which I was born, my parents, my wife, and the children of my care ; and to this city, this woman, and this nation it is incumbent on me to do all the benefit in my power. To what do these distinctions point, but to an evident denial of the duty which humanity imposes on you, of doing every possible good to every individual, under whatéver denomination he may be comprehended, to whom you have the power of doing it? You ought to love all mankind; nay, every individual of mankind. You ought not to love the individuals of your domestic circle less, but to love those who exist beyond it more. Once make the feelings of confidence and of affection universal, and the distinctions of property and power will vanish; nor are they to be abolished without substituting something equivalent in mischief to them, until all mankind shall acknowledge an entire community of rights.

But, as the shades of night are dispelled by the faintest glimmerings of dawn, so shall the minutest progress of the benevolent feelings disperse, in some degree, the gloom of tyranny, and [curb the] ministers of mutual suspicion and abhorrence. Your physical wants are few, whilst those of your mind and heart cannot be numbered or described, from their multitude and complication. To secure the gratification of the former, you have made yourselves the bond-slaves of each other.

They have cultivated these meaner wants to so great an excess as to judge nothing so valuable or desirable [as] what relates to their gratification. Hence has arisen a system of passions which loses sight of the end they were originally awakened to attain. Fame, power, and gold, are loved for their own sakes—are worshipped with a blind, habitual idolatry. The pageantry of empire, and the fame of irresistible might, are contemplated by the possessor with unmeaning complacency, without a retrospect to the properties which first made him consider them of value. It is from the cultivation of the most contemptible properties of human nature that discord and torpor and indifference, by which the moral universe is disordered, essentially depend. So long as these are the ties by which human society is connected, let it not be admitted that théy are fragile.

Before man can be free, and equal, and truly wise, he must cast aside the chains of habit and superstition; he must strip sensuality of its pomp, and selfishness of its excuses, and contemplate actions and objects as they really are. He will discover the wisdom of universal love; he will feel the meanness and the injustice of sacrificing the reason and the liberty of his fellow-men to the indulgence of his physical appetites, and becoming a party to their degradation by the consummation of his own.

Such, with those differences only incidental to the age and state of society in which they were promulgated, appear to have been the doctrines of Jesus Christ. It is not too much to assert that they have been the doctrines of every just and compassionate mind that ever speculated on the social nature of man. The dogma of the equality of mankind has been advocated, with various success, in different ages of the world. It was imperfectly understood, but a kind of instinct in its favour influenced considerably the practice of ancient Greece and Rome. Attempts to establish usages founded on this dogma have been made in modern Europe, in several instances, since the revival of literature and the arts. Rousseau has vindicated this opinion with all the eloquence of sincere and earnest faith; and is, perhaps, the philosopher among the moderns who, in the structure of his feelings and understanding, resembles most nearly the mysterious sage of Judea. It is impossible to read those passionate words in which Jesus Christ upbraids the pusillanimity and sensuality of mankind, without being strongly reminded of the more connected and systematic enthusiasm of Rousseau. "No man,"

says Jesus Christ, " can serve two masters. Take, therefore, no thought for to-morrow, for the morrow shall
take thought for the things of itself. Sufficient unto the
day is the evil [thereof." If we would profit by the
wisdom of a sublime and poetical mind, we must beware of
the vulgar error of interpreting literally every expression it
employs. Nothing can well be more remote from truth
than the literal and strict construction of such expressions
as Jesus Christ delivers, or than [to imagine that] it were
best for man that he should abandon all his acquirements
in physical and intellectual science, and depend on the
spontaneous productions of nature for his subsistence.
Nothing is more obviously false than that the remedy for
the inequality among men consists in their return to the
condition of savages and beasts. Philosophy will never be
understood if we approach the study of its mysteries with
so narrow and illiberal conceptions of its universality.
Rousseau certainly did not mean to persuade the immense
population of his country to abandon all the arts of life,
destroy their habitations and their temples, and become the
inhabitants of the woods. He addressed the most
enlightened of his compatriots, and endeavoured to
persuade them to set the example of a pure and simple life,
by placing in the strongest point of view his conceptions of
the calamitous and diseased aspect which, overgrown as it
is with the vices of sensuality and selfishness, is exhibited
by civilized society. Nor can it be believed that Jesus
Christ endeavoured to prevail on the inhabitants of
Jerusalem neither to till their fields, nor to frame a shelter
against the sky, nor to provide food for the morrow. He
simply exposes, with the passionate rhetoric of enthusiastic
love towards all human beings, the miseries and mischiefs
of that system which makes all things subservient to the

subsistence of the material frame of man. He warns them
that no man can serve two masters—God and Mammon;
that it is impossible at once to be high-minded and just and
wise, and to comply with the accustomed forms of human
society, seek power, wealth, or empire, either from the
idolatry of habit, or as the direct instruments of sensual
gratification. He instructs them that clothing and food
and shelter are not, as they suppose, the true end of human
life, but only certain means, to be valued in proportion to
their subserviency to that end. These means it is right of
every human being to possess, and that in the same degree.
In this respect, the fowls of the air and the lilies of
the field are examples for the imitation of mankind. They
are clothed and fed by the Universal God. Permit, therefore, the Spirit of this benignant Principle to visit your
intellectual frame, or, in other words, become just and pure.
When you understand the degree of attention which the
requisitions of your physical nature demand, you will
perceive how little labour suffices for their satisfaction.
Your heavenly Father knoweth you have need of these
things. The universal Harmony, or Reason, which makes
your passive frame of thought its dwelling, in proportion to
the purity and majesty of its nature will instruct you, if ye
are willing to attain that exalted condition, in what
manner to possess all the objects necessary for
your material subsistence. All men are [impelled] to
become thus pure and happy. All men are called to
participate in the community of Nature's gifts. The man
who has fewest bodily wants approaches nearest to the
Divine Nature. Satisfy these wants at the cheapest rate,
and expend the remaining energies of your nature in the
attainment of virtue and knowledge. The mighty frame
of the wonderful and lovely world is the food of your

contemplation, and living beings who resemble your own nature, and are bound to you by similarity of sensations, are destined to be the nutriment of your affection; united, they are the consummation of the widest hopes your mind can contain. Ye can expend thus no labour on mechanism consecrated to luxury and pride. How abundant will not be your progress in all that truly ennobles and extends human nature! By rendering yourselves thus worthy, ye will be as free in your imaginations as the swift and many-coloured fowls of the air, and as beautiful in pure simplicity as the lilies of the field. In proportion as mankind becomes wise—yes, in exact proportion to that wisdom—should be the extinction of the unequal system under which they now subsist. Government is, in fact, the mere badge of their depravity. They are so little aware of the inestimable benefits of mutual love as to indulge, without thought, and almost without motive, in the worst excesses of selfishness and malice. Hence, without graduating human society into a scale of empire and subjection, its very existence has become impossible. It is necessary that universal benevolence should supersede the regulations of precedent and prescription, before these regulations can safely be abolished. Meanwhile, their very subsistence depends on the system of injustice and violence which they have been devised to palliate. They suppose men endowed with the power of deliberating and determining for their equals; whilst these men, as frail and as ignorant as the multitude whom they rule, possess, as a practical consequence of this power, the right which they of necessity exercise to prevent (together with their own) the physical and moral and intellectual nature of all mankind.

It is the object of wisdom to equalize the distinctions on which this power depends, by exhibiting in their proper worthlessness the objects, a contention concerning which renders its existence a necessary evil. The evil, in fact, is virtually abolished wherever *justice* is practised; and it is abolished in precise proportion to the prevalence of true virtue.

The whole frame of human things is infected by an insidious poison. Hence it is that man is blind in his understanding, corrupt in his moral sense, and diseased in his physical functions. The wisest and most sublime of the ancient poets saw this truth, and embodied their conception of its value in retrospect to the earliest ages of mankind. They represented equality as the reign of Saturn, and taught that mankind had gradually degenerated from the virtue which enabled them to enjoy or maintain this happy state. Their doctrine was philosophically false. Later and more correct observations have instructed us that uncivilized man is the most pernicious and miserable of beings, and that the violence and injustice, which are the genuine indications of real inequality, obtain in the society of these beings without palliation. Their imaginations of a happier state of human society were referred, in truth, to the Saturnian period; they ministered, indeed, to thoughts of despondency and sorrow. But they were the children of airy hope—the prophets and parents of man's futurity. Man was once as a wild beast; he has become a moralist, a metaphysician, a poet, and an astronomer. Lucretius or Virgil might have referred the comparison to themselves; and, as a proof of the progress of the nature of man, challenged a comparison with the cannibals of Scythia.* The experience of the ages which have intervened between the present period and that in which Jesus Christ taught, tends to prove his doctrine, and to illustrate theirs. There

* Jesus Christ foresaw what the poets retrospectively imagined.

is more equality because there is more justice, and there is more justice because there is more universal knowledge.

To the accomplishment of such mighty hopes were the views of Jesus Christ extended; such did he believe to be the tendency of his doctrines—the abolition of artificial distinctions among mankind, so far as the love which it becomes all human beings to bear towards each other, and the knowledge of truth from which that love will never fail to be produced, avail to their destruction. A young man came to Jesus Christ, struck by the miraculous dignity and simplicity of his character, and attracted by the words of power which he uttered. He demanded to be considered as one of the followers of his creed. "Sell all that thou hast," replied the philosopher; "give it to the poor, and follow me." But the young man had large possessions, and he went away sorrowing.

The system of equality was attempted, after Jesus Christ's death, to be carried into effect by his followers. "They that believed had all things in common; they sold their possessions and goods, and parted them to all men, as every man had need; and they continued daily with one accord in the temple, and breaking bread from house to house, did eat their meat with gladness and singleness of heart." (Acts, ch. ii.)

The practical application of the doctrines of strict justice to a state of society established in its contempt, was such as might have been expected. After the transitory glow of enthusiasm had faded from the minds of men, precedent and habit resumed their empire; they broke like a universal deluge on one shrinking and solitary island. Men to whom birth had allotted ample possession, looked with complacency on sumptuous apartments and luxurious food, and those ceremonials of delusive majesty which surround

the throne of power and the court of wealth.   Men from
whom these things were withheld by their condition, began
again to gaze with stupid envy on pernicious splendour ;
and, by desiring the false greatness of another's state, to
sacrifice the intrinsic dignity of their own.   The demagogues of the infant republic of the Christian sect, attaining,
through eloquence or artifice, to influence amongst its
members, first violated (under the pretence of watching
over their integrity) the institutions established for the
common and equal benefit of all.   These demagogues
artfully silenced the voice of the moral sense among
them by engaging them to attend, not so much to the
cultivation of a virtuous and happy life in this mortal
scene, as to the attainment of a fortunate condition after
death ; not so much to the consideration of those means
by which the state of man is adorned and improved, as an
inquiry into the secrets of the connexion between God and
the world—things which, they well knew, were not to be
explained, or even to be conceived.   The system of equality
which they established necessarily fell to the ground,
because it is a system that must result from, rather than
precede, the moral improvement of human kind.   It was a
circumstance of no moment that the first adherents of the
system of Jesus Christ cast their property into a common
stock.   The same degree of real community of property
could have subsisted without this formality, which served
only to extend a temptation of dishonesty to the treasurers
of so considerable a patrimony.   Every man, in proportion
to his virtue, considers himself, with respect to the great
community of mankind, as the steward and guardian of
their interests in the property which he chances to possess.
Every man, in proportion to his wisdom, sees the manner
in which it is his duty to employ the resources which the

consent of mankind has intrusted to his discretion. Such is the [annihilation] of the unjust inequality of powers and conditions existing in the world; and so gradually and inevitably is the progress of equality accommodated to the progress of wisdom and of virtue among mankind.

Meanwhile, some benefit has not failed to flow from the imperfect attempts which have been made to erect a system of equal rights to property and power upon the basis of arbitrary institutions. They have undoubtedly, in every case, from the instability of their formation, failed. Still, they constitute a record of those epochs at which a true sense of justice suggested itself to the understandings of men, so that they consented to forego all the cherished delights of luxury, all the habitual gratifications arising out of the possession or the expectation of power, all the superstitions with which the accumulated authority of ages had made them dear and venerable. They are so many trophies erected in the enemy's land, to mark the limits of the victorious progress of truth and justice.

[THE REST IS WANTING.]

SPECULATIONS ON METAPHYSICS.

I.—THE MIND.

I. IT is an axiom in mental philosophy, that we can think of nothing which we have not perceived. When I say that we can think of nothing, I mean, we can imagine nothing, we can reason of nothing. The most astonishing combinations of poetry, the subtlest deductions of logic and mathematics, are no other than combinations which the intellect

89

makes of sensations according to its own laws. A catalogue of all the thoughts of the mind, and of all their possible modifications, is a cyclopedic history of the universe.

But, it will be objected, the inhabitants of the various planets of this and other solar systems; and the existence of a Power bearing the same relation to all that we perceive and are, as what we call a cause does to what we call effect, were never subjects of sensation, and yet the laws of mind almost universally suggest, according to the various disposition of each, a conjecture, a persuasion, or a conviction of their existence. The reply is simple; these thoughts are also to be included in the catalogue of existence; they are modes in which thoughts are combined; the objection only adds force to the conclusion, that beyond the limits of perception and thought nothing can exist.

Thoughts, or ideas, or notions, call them what you will, differ from each other, not in kind, but in force. It has commonly been supposed that those distinct thoughts which affect a number of persons, at regular intervals, during the passage of a multitude of other thoughts, which are called *real*, or *external objects*, are totally different in kind from those which affect only a few persons, and which recur at irregular intervals, and are usually more obscure and indistinct, such as hallucinations, dreams, and the ideas of madness. No essential distinction between any one of these ideas, or any class of them, is founded on a correct observation of the nature of things, but merely on a consideration of what thoughts are most invariably subservient to the security and happiness of life; and if nothing more were expressed by the distinction, the philosopher might safely accommodate his language to that of the vulgar. But they pretend to assert an essential difference, which has no foundation in truth, and which suggests a narrow and false conception of universal nature, the parent of the most fatal errors in speculation. A specific difference between every thought of the mind, is, indeed, a necessary consequence of that law by which it perceives diversity and number; but a generic and essential difference is wholly arbitrary. The principle of the agreement and similarity of all thoughts, is, that they are all thoughts; the principle of their disagreement consists in the variety and irregularity of the occasions on which they arise in the mind. That in which they agree, to that in which they differ, is as everything to nothing. Important distinctions, of various degrees of force, indeed, are to be established between them, if they were, as they may be, subjects of ethical and œconomical discussion; but that is a question altogether distinct.

By considering all knowledge as bounded by perception, whose operations may be indefinitely combined, we arrive at a conception of Nature inexpressibly more magnificent, simple and true, than accords with the ordinary systems of complicated and partial consideration. Nor does a contemplation of the universe, in this comprehensive and synthetical view, exclude the subtlest analysis of its modifications and parts.

———

A scale might be formed, graduated according to the degrees of a combined ratio of intensity, duration, connection, periods of recurrence, and utility, which would be the standard, according to which all ideas might be measured, and an uninterrupted chain of nicely shadowed distinctions would be observed, from the faintest impression on the senses, to the most distinct combination of those impressions; from the simplest of those combinations, to that mass of knowledge which, including our own nature, constitutes what we call the universe.

We are intuitively conscious of our own existence, and of that connection in the train of our successive ideas, which we term our identity. We are conscious also of the existence of other minds; but not intuitively. Our evidence, with respect to the existence of other minds, is founded upon a very complicated relation of ideas, which it is foreign to the purpose of this treatise to anatomise. The basis of this relation is, undoubtedly, a periodical recurrence of masses of ideas, which our voluntary determinations have, in one peculiar direction, no power to circumscribe or to arrest, and against the recurrence of which they can only imperfectly provide. The irresistible laws of thought constrain us to believe that the precise limits of our actual ideas are not the actual limits of possible ideas; the law, according to which these deductions are drawn, is called analogy; and this is the foundation of all our inferences, from one idea to another, inasmuch as they resemble each other.

———

We see trees, houses, fields, living beings in our own shape, and in shapes more or less analogous to our own. These are perpetually changing the mode of their existence relatively to us. To express the varieties of these modes, we say, *we move, they move;* and as this motion is continual, though not uniform, we express our conception of the diversities of its course by—*it has been, it is, it shall be.* These diversities are events or objects, and are essential, considered relatively to human identity, for the existence of the human mind. For if the inequalities, produced by what has been termed the operations of the external universe, were levelled by the perception of our being, uniting, and filling up their interstices, motion and mensuration, and time, and space; the elements of the human mind being thus abstracted, sensation and imagination cease. Mind cannot be considered pure.

II.—WHAT METAPHYSICS ARE. ERRORS IN THE USUAL METHODS OF CONSIDERING THEM.

WE do not attend sufficiently to what passes within ourselves. We combine words, combined a thousand times before. In our minds we assume entire opinions; and in the expression of those opinions, entire phrases, when we would philosophise. Our whole style of expression and sentiment is infected with the tritest plagiarisms. Our words are dead, our thoughts are cold and borrowed.

Let us contemplate facts; let us, in the great study of ourselves, resolutely compel the mind to a rigid consideration of itself. We are not content with conjecture, and inductions, and syllogisms, in sciences regarding external objects. As in these, let us also, in considering the phenomena of mind, severely collect those facts which cannot be disputed. Metaphysics will thus possess this conspicuous advantage over every other science, that each student, by attentively referring to his own mind, may ascertain the authorities upon which any assertions regarding it are supported. There can thus be no deception, we ourselves being the depositories of the evidence of the subject which we consider.

Metaphysics may be defined as an inquiry concerning those things belonging to, or connected with, the internal nature of man.

It is said that mind produces motion; and it might as well have been said, that motion produces mind.

III.—DIFFICULTY OF ANALYZING THE HUMAN MIND.

IF it were possible that a person should give a faithful history of his being, from the earliest epochs of his recollection, a picture would be presented such as the world has never contemplated before. A mirror would be held up to all men in which they might behold their own recollections, and, in dim perspective, their shadowy hopes and fears,— all that they dare not, or that daring and desiring, they could not expose to the open eyes of day. But thought can with difficulty visit the intricate and winding chambers which it inhabits. It is like a river whose rapid and perpetual stream flows outward;—like one in dread who speeds through the recesses of some haunted pile, and dares not look behind. The caverns of the mind are obscure, and shadowy; or pervaded with a lustre, beautifully bright indeed, but shining not beyond their portals. If it were possible to be where we have been, vitally and indeed—if, at the moment of our presence there, we could define the results of our experience—if the passage from sensation to reflection—from a state of passive perception to voluntary contemplation, were not so dizzying and so tumultuous, this attempt would be less difficult.

IV.—HOW THE ANALYSIS SHOULD BE CARRIED ON.

MOST of the errors of philosophers have arisen from considering the human being in a point of view too detailed and circumscribed. He is not a moral and an intellectual, —but also, and pre-eminently, an imaginative being. His own mind is his law; his own mind is all things to him. If we would arrive at any knowledge which should be serviceable from the practical conclusions to which it leads, we ought to consider the mind of man and the universe as the great whole on which to exercise our speculations. Here, above all, verbal disputes ought to be laid aside, though this has long been their chosen field of battle. It imports little to inquire whether thought be distinct from the objects of thought. The use of the words *external* and *internal*, as applied to the establishment of this distinction, has been the symbol and the source of much dispute. This is merely an affair of words, and as the dispute deserves, to say, that when speaking of the objects of thought, we indeed only describe one of the forms of thought—or that, speaking of thought, we only apprehend one of the operations of the universal system of beings.

V.—CATALOGUE OF THE PHENOMENA OF DREAMS, AS
CONNECTING SLEEPING AND WAKING.

1. LET us reflect on our infancy, and give as faithfully as possible a relation of the events of sleep.

And first I am bound to present a faithful picture of my own peculiar nature relatively to sleep. I do not doubt that were every individual to imitate me, it would be found that among many circumstances peculiar to their individual nature, a sufficiently general resemblance would be found to prove the connection existing between those peculiarities and the most universal phenomena. I shall employ caution, indeed, as to the facts which I state, that they contain nothing false or exaggerated. But they contain no more than certain elucidations of my own nature; concerning the degree in which it resembles, or differs from, that of others, I am by no means accurately aware. It is sufficient, however, to caution the reader against drawing general inferences from particular instances.

I omit the general instances of delusion in fever or delirium, as well as mere dreams considered in themselves. A delineation of this subject, however inexhaustible and interesting, is to be passed over.

What is the connection of sleeping and of waking?

———

2. I distinctly remember dreaming three several times, between intervals of two or more years, the same precise dream. It was not so much what is ordinarily called a dream ; the single image, unconnected with all other images, of a youth who was educated at the same school with myself, presented itself in sleep. Even now, after the lapse of many years, I can never hear the name of this youth, without the three places where I dreamed of him presenting themselves distinctly to my mind.

———

3. In dreams, images acquire associations peculiar to dreaming ; so that the idea of a particular house, when it recurs a second time in dreams, will have relation with the idea of the same house, in the first time, of a nature entirely different from that which the house excites, when seen or thought of in relation to waking ideas.

———

4. I have beheld scenes, with the intimate and unaccountable connection of which with the obscure parts of my own nature, I have been irresistibly impressed. I have beheld a scene which has produced no unusual effect on my thoughts. After the lapse of many years I have dreamed of this scene. It has hung on my memory, it has haunted my thoughts, at intervals, with the pertinacity of an object connected with human affections. I have visited this scene again. Neither the dream could be dissociated from the landscape, nor the landscape from the dream, nor

feelings, such as neither singly could have awakened, from both. But the most remarkable event of this nature, which ever occurred to me, happened five years ago at Oxford. I was walking with a friend, in the neighbourhood of that city, engaged in earnest and interesting conversation. We suddenly turned the corner of a lane, and the view, which its high banks and hedges had concealed, presented itself. The view consisted of a windmill, standing in one among many plashy meadows, enclosed with stone walls; the irregular and broken ground, between the wall and the road on which we stood; a long low hill behind the windmill, and a grey covering of uniform cloud spread over the evening sky. It was that season when the last leaf had just fallen from the scant and stunted ash. The scene surely was a common scene; the season and the hour little calculated to kindle lawless thought; it was a tame uninteresting assemblage of objects, such as would drive the imagination for refuge in serious and sober talk, to the evening fireside, and the dessert of winter fruits and wine. The effect which it produced on me was not such as could have been expected. I suddenly remembered to have seen that exact scene in some dream of long *————

* *Here I was obliged to leave off, overcome by thrilling horror.* This remark closes this fragment, which was written in 1815. I remember well his coming to me from writing it, pale and agitated, to seek refuge in conversation from the fearful emotions it excited. No man, as these fragments prove, had such keen sensations as Shelley. His nervous temperament was wound up by the delicacy of his health to an intense degree of sensibility, and while his active mind pondered for ever upon, and drew conclusions from his sensations, his reveries increased their vivacity, till they mingled with, and made one with thought, and both became absorbing and tumultuous, even to physical pain.—*M. S.*

SPECULATIONS ON MORALS.

I.— PLAN OF A TREATISE ON MORALS.

THAT great science which regards nature and the
operations of the human mind, is popularly divided into
morals and metaphysics. The latter relates to a just
classification, and the assignment of distinct names to its
ideas ; the former regards simply the determination of that
arrangement of them which produces the greatest and most
solid happiness. It is admitted that a virtuous or moral
action, is that action which, when considered in all its accessories and consequences, is fitted to produce the highest
pleasure to the greatest number of sensitive beings. The
laws according to which all pleasure, since it cannot be
equally felt by all sensitive beings, ought to be distributed
by a voluntary agent, are reserved for a separate chapter.

The design of this little treatise is restricted to the
development of the elementary principles of morals. As far
as regards that purpose, metaphysical science will be
treated merely so far as a source of negative truth ; whilst
morality will be considered as a science, respecting which
we can arrive at positive conclusions.

The misguided imaginations of men have rendered the
ascertaining of what *is not true*, the principal direct service
which metaphysical science can bestow upon moral science.
Moral science itself is the doctrine of the voluntary actions
of man, as a sentient and social being. These actions
depend on the thoughts in his mind. But there is a mass
of popular opinion, from which the most enlightened persons
are seldom wholly free, into the truth or falsehood of which
it is incumbent on us to inquire, before we can arrive at
any firm conclusions as to the conduct which we ought to

pursue in the regulation of our own minds, or towards our fellow-beings; or before we can ascertain the elementary laws, according to which these thoughts, from which these actions flow, are originally combined.

The object of the forms according to which human society is administered, is the happiness of the individuals composing the communities which they regard, and these forms are perfect or imperfect in proportion to the degree in which they promote this end.

This object is not merely the quantity of happiness enjoyed by individuals as sensitive beings, but the mode in which it should be distributed among them as social beings. It is not enough, if such a coincidence can be conceived as possible, that one person or class of persons should enjoy the highest happiness, whilst another is suffering a disproportionate degree of misery. It is necessary that the happiness produced by the common efforts, and preserved by the common care, should be distributed according to the just claims of each individual; if not, although the quantity produced should be the same, the end of society would remain unfulfilled. The object is in a compound proportion to the quantity of happiness produced, and the correspondence of the mode in which it is distributed, to the elementary feelings of man as a social being.

The disposition in an individual to promote this object is called virtue; and the two constituent parts of virtue, benevolence and justice, are correlative with these two great portions of the only true object of all voluntary actions of a human being. Benevolence is the desire to be the author of good, and justice the apprehension of the manner in which good ought to be done.

Justice and benevolence result from the elementary laws of the human mind.

CHAPTER I.

ON THE NATURE OF VIRTUE.

SECT. 1. General View of the Nature and Objects of Virtue.—2. The
Origin and Basis of Virtue, as founded on the Elementary
Principles of Mind.—3. The Laws which flow from the nature of
Mind regulating the application of those principles to human
actions.—4. Virtue, a possible attribute of man.

WE exist in the midst of a multitude of beings like ourselves, upon whose happiness most of our actions exert some
obvious and decisive influence.

The regulation of this influence is the object of moral
science.

We know that we are susceptible of receiving painful or
pleasurable impressions of greater or less intensity and
duration. That is called good which produces pleasure;
that is called evil which produces pain. These are general
names applicable to every class of causes, from which an
overbalance of pain or pleasure may result. But when a
human being is the active instrument of generating or
diffusing happiness, the principle through which it is
most effectually instrumental to that purpose, is called
virtue. And benevolence, or the desire to be the author of
good, united with justice, or an apprehension of the manner
in which that good is to be done, constitutes virtue.

But, wherefore should a man be benevolent and just?
The immediate emotions of his nature, especially in its
most inartificial state, prompt him to inflict pain, and to
arrogate dominion. He desires to heap superfluities to his
own store, although others perish with famine. He is pro-
pelled to guard against the smallest invasion of his own
liberty, though he reduces others to a condition of the most

pitiless servitude. He is revengeful, proud and selfish. Wherefore should he curb these propensities?

It is inquired, for what reason a human being should engage in procuring the happiness, or refrain from producing the pain of another? When a reason is required to prove the necessity of adopting any system of conduct, what is it that the objector demands? He requires proof of that system of conduct being such as will most effectually promote the happiness of mankind. To demonstrate this, is to render a moral reason. Such is the object of Virtue.

A common sophism, which, like many others, depends on the abuse of a metaphorical expression to a literal purpose, has produced much of the confusion which has involved the theory of morals. It is said that no person is bound to be just or kind, if, on his neglect, he should fail to incur some penalty. Duty is obligation. There can be no obligation without an obliger. Virtue is a law, to which it is the will of the lawgiver that we should conform; which will we should in no manner be bound to obey, unless some dreadful punishment were attached to disobedience. This is the philosophy of slavery and superstition.

In fact, no person can be *bound* or *obliged*, without some power preceding to bind and oblige. If I observe a man bound hand and foot, I know that some one bound him. But if I observe him returning self-satisfied from the performance of some action, by which he has been the willing author of extensive benefit, I do not infer that the anticipation of hellish agonies, or the hope of heavenly reward, has constrained him to such an act.*

.   .   .   .

* A leaf of manuscript is wanting here, manifestly treating of self-love and disinterestedness.—*M. S.*

It remains to be stated in what manner the sensations which constitute the basis of virtue originate in the human mind; what are the laws which it receives there; how far the principles of mind allow it to be an attribute of a human being; and, lastly, what is the probability of persuading mankind to adopt it as a universal and systematic motive of conduct.

BENEVOLENCE.

THERE is a class of emotions which we instinctively avoid. A human being, such as is man considered in his origin, a child a month old, has a very imperfect consciousness of the existence of other natures resembling itself. All the energies of its being are directed to the extinction of the pains with which it is perpetually assailed. At length it discovers that it is surrounded by natures susceptible of sensations similar to its own. It is very late before children attain to this knowledge. If a child observes, without emotion, its nurse or its mother suffering acute pain, it is attributable rather to ignorance than insensibility. So soon as the accents and gestures, significant of pain, are referred to the feelings which they express, they awaken in the mind of the beholder a desire that they should cease. Pain is thus apprehended to be evil for its own sake, without any other necessary reference to the mind by which its existence is perceived, than such as is indispensable to its perception. The tendencies of our original sensations, indeed, all have for their object the preservation of our individual being. But these are passive and unconscious. In proportion as the mind acquires an active power, the empire of these tendencies becomes limited. Thus an infant, a savage, and a solitary

beast, is selfish, because its mind is incapable of receiving
an accurate intimation of the nature of pain as existing in
beings resembling itself. The inhabitant of a highly
civilised community will more acutely sympathise with the
sufferings and enjoyments of others, than the inhabitant of
a society of a less degree of civilisation. He who shall
have cultivated his intellectual powers by familiarity with
the highest specimens of poetry and philosophy, will usually
sympathise more than one engaged in the less refined
functions of manual labour. Every one has experience of
the fact, that to sympathise with the sufferings of another,
is to enjoy a transitory oblivion of his own.

The mind thus acquires, by exercise, a habit, as it were,
of perceiving and abhorring evil, however remote from the
immediate sphere of sensations with which that individual
mind is conversant. Imagination or mind employed in
prophetically imaging forth its objects, is that faculty of
human nature on which every gradation of its progress,
nay, every, the minutest, change, depends. Pain or
pleasure, if subtly analysed, will be found to consist
entirely in prospect. The only distinction between the
selfish man and the virtuous man is, that the imagination of
the former is confined within a narrow limit, whilst that of
the latter embraces a comprehensive circumstance. In this
sense, wisdom and virtue may be said to be inseparable,
and criteria of each other. Selfishness is the offspring of
ignorance and mistake; it is the portion of unreflecting
infancy, and savage solitude, or of those whom toil or evil
occupations have blunted or rendered torpid; disinterested
benevolence is the product of a cultivated imagination,
and has an intimate connexion with all the arts which add
ornament, or dignity, or power, or stability to the social
state of man. Virtue is thus entirely a refinement of

civilised life : a creation of the human mind ; or, rather, a combination which it has made, according to elementary rules contained within itself, of the feelings suggested by the relations established between man and man.

All the theories which have refined and exalted humanity, or those which have been devised as alleviations of its mistakes and evils, have been based upon the elementary emotions of disinterestedness, which we feel to constitute the majesty of our nature. Patriotism, as it existed in the ancient republics, was never, as has been supposed, a calculation of personal advantages. When Mutius Scævola thrust his hand into the burning coals, and Regulus returned to Carthage, and Epicharis sustained the rack silently, in the torments of which she knew that she would speedily perish, rather than betray the conspirators to the tyrant ;* these illustrious persons certainly made a small estimate of their private interest. If it be said that they sought posthumous fame ; instances are not wanting in history which prove that men have even defied infamy for the sake of good. But there is a great error in the world with respect to the selfishness of fame. It is certainly possible that a person should seek distinction as a medium of personal gratification. But the love of fame is frequently no more than a desire that the feelings of others should confirm, illustrate, and sympathise with, our own. In this respect it is allied with all that draws us out of ourselves. It is the "last infirmity of noble minds." Chivalry was likewise founded on the theory of self-sacrifice. Love possesses so extraordinary a power over the human heart, only because disinterestedness is united with the natural propensities. These propensities themselves are comparatively impotent in cases where the imagination

* Tacitus.

of pleasure to be given, as well as to be received, does not enter into the account. Let it not be objected that patriotism, and chivalry, and sentimental love, have been the fountains of enormous mischief. They are cited only to establish the proposition that, according to the elementary principles of mind, man is capable of desiring and pursuing good for its own sake.

JUSTICE.

THE benevolent propensities are thus inherent in the human mind. We are impelled to seek the happiness of others. We experience a satisfaction in being the authors of that happiness. Everything that lives is open to impressions of pleasure and pain. We are led by our benevolent propensities to regard every human being indifferently with whom we come in contact. They have preference only with respect to those who offer themselves most obviously to our notice. Human beings are indiscriminating and blind ; they will avoid inflicting pain, though that pain should be attended with eventual benefit ; they will seek to confer pleasure without calculating the mischief that may result. They benefit one at the expense of many.

There is a sentiment in the human mind that regulates benevolence in its application as a principle of action. This is the sense of justice. Justice, as well as benevolence, is an elementary law of human nature. It is through this principle that men are impelled to distribute any means of pleasure which benevolence may suggest the communication of to others, in equal portions among an equal number of applicants. If ten men are shipwrecked on a desert island, they distribute whatever subsistence may remain to them,

90

into equal portions among themselves. If six of them conspire to deprive the remaining four of their share, their conduct is termed unjust.

The existence of pain has been shown to be a circumstance which the human mind regards with dissatisfaction, and of which it desires the cessation. It is equally according to its nature to desire that the advantages to be enjoyed by a limited number of persons should be enjoyed equally by all. This proposition is supported by the evidence of indisputable facts. Tell some ungarbled tale of a number of persons being made the victims of the enjoyments of one, and he who would appeal in favour of any system which might produce such an evil to the primary emotions of our nature, would have nothing to reply. Let two persons, equally strangers, make application for some benefit in the possession of a third to bestow, and to which he feels that they have an equal claim. They are both sensitive beings ; pleasure and pain affect them alike.

⋅　　⋅　　⋅　　⋅　　⋅　　⋅　　⋅

CHAPTER II.

It is foreign to the general scope of this little Treatise to encumber a simple argument by controverting any of the trite objections of habit or fanaticism. But there are two ; the first, the basis of all political mistake, and the second, the prolific cause and effect of religious error, which it seems useful to refute.

First, it is inquired, "Wherefore should a man be benevolent and just?" The answer has been given in the preceding chapter.

If a man persists to inquire why he ought to promote the happiness of mankind, he demands a mathematical or metaphysical reason for a moral action. The absurdity of this scepticism is more apparent, but not less real than the exacting a moral reason for a mathematical or metaphysical fact. If any person should refuse to admit that all the radii of a circle are of equal length, or that human actions are necessarily determined by motives, until it could be proved that these radii and these actions uniformly tended to the production of the greatest general good, who would not wonder at the unreasonable and capricious association of his ideas?

The writer of a philosophical treatise may, I imagine, at this advanced era of human intellect, be held excused from entering into a controversy with those reasoners, if such there are, who would claim an exemption from its decrees in favour of anyone among those diversified systems of obscure opinion respecting morals, which, under the name of religions, have in various ages and countries prevailed among mankind. Besides that if, as these reasoners have pretended, eternal torture or happiness will ensue as the consequence of certain actions, we should be no nearer the possession of a standard to determine what actions were right and wrong, even if this pretended revelation, which is by no means the case, had furnished us with a complete catalogue of them. The character of actions as virtuous or vicious would by no means be determined alone by the personal advantage or disadvantage of each moral agent individually considered. Indeed, an action is often virtuous in proportion to the greatness of the personal calamity which the author willingly draws upon himself by daring to perform it. It is because an action produces an overbalance of pleasure or pain to the greatest number of sentient beings, and not merely because its consequences are beneficial or injurious to the author of that action, that it is good or evil. Nay, this latter consideration has a tendency to pollute the purity of virtue, inasmuch as it consists in the motive rather than in the consequences of an action. A person who should labour for the happiness of mankind lest he should be tormented eternally in Hell, would, with reference to that motive, possess as little claim to the epithet of virtuous, as he who should torture, imprison, and burn them alive, a more usual and natural consequence of such principles, for the sake of the enjoyments of Heaven.

My neighbour, presuming on his strength, may direct me to perform or to refrain from a particular action; indicating a certain arbitrary penalty in the event of disobedience within his power to inflict. My action, if modified by his menaces, can in no degree participate in virtue. He has afforded me no criterion as to what is right or wrong. A king, or an assembly of men, may publish a proclamation affixing any penalty to any particular action, but that is not immoral because such penalty is affixed. Nothing is more evident than that the epithet of virtue is inapplicable to the refraining from that action on account of the evil arbitrarily attached to it. If the action is in itself beneficial, virtue would rather consist in not refraining from it, but in firmly defying the personal consequences attached to its performance.

Some usurper of supernatural energy might subdue the whole globe to his power; he might possess new and unheard-of resources for enduing his punishments with the most terrible attributes of pain. The torments of his victims might be intense in their degree, and protracted to an infinite duration. Still the "will of the lawgiver" would afford no surer criterion as to what actions were right or wrong. It would only increase the possible virtue of those who refuse to become the instruments of his tyranny.

II.—MORAL SCIENCE CONSISTS IN CONSIDERING THE DIFFER-
ENCE, NOT THE RESEMBLANCE, OF PERSONS.

THE internal influence, derived from the constitution of
the mind from which they flow, produces that peculiar
modification of actions, which makes them intrinsically
good or evil.

To attain an apprehension of the importance of this distinction, let us visit, in imagination, the proceedings of some
metropolis. Consider the multitude of human beings who
inhabit it, and survey, in thought, the actions of the several
classes into which they are divided. Their obvious actions
are apparently uniform: the stability of human society
seems to be maintained sufficiently by the uniformity of the
conduct of its members, both with regard to themselves,
and with regard to others. The labourer arises at a certain
hour, and applies himself to the task enjoined him. The
functionaries of government and law are regularly employed
in their offices and courts. The trader holds a train of
conduct from which he never deviates. The ministers of
religion employ an accustomed language, and maintain a
decent and equable regard. The army is drawn forth, the
motions of every soldier are such as they were expected to
be ; the general commands, and his words are echoed from
troop to troop. The domestic actions of men are, for the
most part, undistinguishable one from the other, at a
superficial glance. The actions which are classed under the
general appellation of marriage, education, friendship, etc.,
are perpetually going on, and to a superficial glance, are
similar one to the other.

But, if we would see the truth of things, they must be
stripped of this fallacious appearance of uniformity. In
truth, no one action has, when considered in its whole

extent, any essential resemblance with any other. Each individual, who composes the vast multitude which we have been contemplating, has a peculiar frame of mind, which, whilst the features of the great mass of his actions remain uniform, impresses the minuter lineaments with its peculiar hues. Thus, whilst his life, as a whole, is like the lives of other men, in detail, it is most unlike ; and the more subdivided the actions become ; that is, the more they enter into that class which have a vital influence on the happiness of others and his own, so much the more are they distinct from those of other men.

> ——"Those little, nameless, unremembered acts
> Of kindness and of love,"

as well as those deadly outrages which are inflicted by a look, a word—or less—the very refraining from some faint and most evanescent expression of countenance ; these flow from a profounder source than the series of our habitual conduct, which, it has been already said, derives its origin from without. These are the actions, and such as these, which make human life what it is, and are the fountains of all the good and evil with which its entire surface is so widely and impartially overspread ; and though they are called minute, they are called so in compliance with the blindness of those who cannot estimate their importance. It is in the due appreciating the general effects of their peculiarities, and in cultivating the habit of acquiring decisive knowledge respecting the tendencies arising out of them in particular cases, that the most important part of moral science consists. The deepest abyss of these vast and multitudinous caverns, it is necessary that we should visit.

This is the difference between social and individual man. Not that this distinction is to be considered definite, or characteristic of one human being as compared with another, it denotes rather two classes of agency, common in a degree to every human being. None is exempt, indeed, from that species of influence which affects, as it were, the surface of his being, and gives the specific outline to his conduct. Almost all that is ostensible submits to that legislature created by the general representation of the past feelings of mankind—imperfect as it is from a variety of causes, as it exists in the government, the religion, and domestic habits. Those who do not nominally, yet actually, submit to the same power. The external features of their conduct, indeed, can no more escape it, than the clouds can escape from the stream of the wind; and his opinion, which he often hopes he has dispassionately secured from all contagion of pre-judice and vulgarity, would be found, on examination, to be the inevitable excrescence of the very usages from which he vehemently dissents. Internally all is conducted other-wise; the efficiency, the essence, the vitality of actions, derives its colour from what is no ways contributed to from any external source. Like the plant, which while it derives the accident of its size and shape from the soil in which it springs, and is cankered, or distorted, or inflated, yet retains those qualities which essentially divide it from all others; so that hemlock continues to be poison, and the violet does not cease to emit its odour in whatever soil it may grow.

We consider our own nature too superficially. We look on all that in ourselves with which we can discover a resem-blance in others; and consider those resemblances as the materials of moral knowledge. It is in the differences that it actually consists.

THE AGE OF PERICLES:

WITH CRITICAL NOTICES OF THE SCULPTURE IN THE FLORENCE GALLERY.

THE period which intervened between the birth of Pericles and the death of Aristotle, is undoubtedly, whether considered in itself, or with reference to the effects which it produced upon the subsequent destinies of civilized man, the most memorable in the history of the world. What was the combination of moral and political circumstances which produced so unparalleled a progress during that period in literature and the arts ;—why that progress, so rapid and so sustained, so soon received a check, and became retrograde,—are problems left to the wonder and conjecture of posterity. The wrecks and fragments of those subtle and profound minds, like the ruins of a fine statue, obscurely suggest to us the grandeur and perfection of the whole. Their very language,—a type of the understanding, of which it was the creation and the image,—in variety, in simplicity, in flexibility, and in copiousness, excels every other language of the western world. Their sculptures are such as, in our perception, assume to be the models of ideal truth and beauty, and to which, no artist of modern times can produce forms in any degree comparable. Their paintings, according to Pausanias, were full of delicacy and harmony ; and some were powerfully pathetic, so as to awaken, like tender music or tragic poetry, the most overwhelming emotions. We are accustomed to consider the painters of the sixteenth century as those who have brought this art to the highest perfection, probably because none of the ancient pictures have been preserved.

All the inventive arts maintain, as it were, a sympathetic connexion between each other, being no more than various expressions of one internal power, modified by different circumstances, either of an individual, or of society.

The paintings of that period would probably bear the same relation as is confessedly borne by the sculptures to all successive ones. Of their music we know little; but the effects which it is said to have produced, whether they be attributed to the skill of the composer, or the sensibility of his audience, were far more powerful than any which we experience from the music of our times; and if, indeed, the melody of their compositions were more tender, and delicate, and inspiring, than the melodies of some modern European nations, their progress in this art must have been something wonderful, and wholly beyond conception. Their poetry seems to maintain a high, though not so disproportionate a rank, in comparison. Perhaps Shakespeare, from the variety and comprehension of his genius, is to be considered as the greatest individual mind, of which we have specimens remaining;—perhaps Dante created imaginations of greater loveliness and beauty than any that are to be found in the ancient literature of Greece;—perhaps nothing has been discovered in the fragments of the Greek lyric poets equivalent to the sublime and chivalrous sensibility of Petrarch:—but, as a poet, Homer must be acknowledged to excel Shakespeare in the truth and harmony, the sustained grandeur, and satisfying completeness of his images, their exact fitness to the illustration, and to that which they belong. Nor could Dante, deficient in conduct, plan, nature, variety, and temperance, have been brought into comparison, but for the fortunate isles, laden with golden fruit, which alone could tempt any one to embark in the misty ocean of his dark and extravagant fiction.

ON THE NIOBE.

OF all the remains to us of Greek antiquity, this figure is perhaps the most consummate personification of loveliness, with regard to its countenance, as that of the Venus of the Tribune is with regard to its entire form of woman. It is colossal; the size adds to its value; because it allows to the spectator the choice of a greater number of points of view, and affords him a more analytical one, in which to catch a greater number of the infinite modes of expression, of which any form approaching ideal beauty is necessarily composed. It is the figure of a mother in the act of sheltering, from some divine and inevitable peril, the last, we may imagine, of her surviving children.

The little creature, terrified, as we may conceive, at the strange destruction of all its kindred, has fled to its mother, and is hiding its head in the folds of her robe, and casting back one arm, as in a passionate appeal for defence, where it never before could have been sought in vain. She is clothed in a thin tunic of delicate woof; and her hair is fastened on her head into a knot, probably by that mother whose care will never fasten it again. Niobe is enveloped in profuse drapery, a portion of which the left hand has gathered up, and is in the act of extending it over the child in the instinct of shielding her from what reason knows to be inevitable. The right (as the restorer has properly imagined,) is drawing up her daughter to her: and with that instinctive gesture, and by its gentle pressure, is encouraging the child to believe that it can give security. The countenance of Niobe is the consummation of feminine majesty and loveliness, beyond which the imagination scarcely doubts that it can conceive anything.

That masterpiece of the poetic harmony of marble

expresses other feelings. There is embodied a sense of the inevitable and rapid destiny which is consummating around her, as if it were already over. It seems as if despair and beauty had combined, and produced nothing but the sublimity of grief. As the motions of the form expressed the instinctive sense of the possibility of protecting the child, and the accustomed and affectionate assurance that she would find an asylum within her arms, so reason and imagination speak in the countenance the certainty that no mortal defence is of avail. There is no terror in the countenance, only grief—deep, remediless grief. There is no anger :—of what avail is indignation against what is known to be omnipotent? There is no selfish shrinking from personal pain—there is no panic at supernatural agency—there is no adverting to herself as herself : the calamity is mightier than to leave scope for such emotions.

Everything is swallowed up in sorrow : she is all tears : her countenance, in assured expectation of the arrow piercing its last victim in her embrace, is fixed on her omnipotent enemy. The pathetic beauty of the expression of her tender, and inexhaustible, and unquenchable despair, is beyond the effect of sculpture. As soon as the arrow shall pierce her last tie upon earth, the fable that she was turned into stone, or dissolved into a fountain of tears, will be but a feeble emblem of the sadness of hopelessness, in which the few and evil years of her remaining life, we feel, must flow away.

It is difficult to speak of the beauty of the countenance, or to make intelligible in words, from what such astonishing loveliness results.

The head, resting somewhat backward upon the full and flowing contour of the neck, is as in the act of watching an event momently to arrive. The hair is delicately divided on the forehead, and a gentle beauty gleams from the broad and clear forehead, over which its strings are drawn. The face is of an oval fulness, and the features conceived with the daring of a sense of power. In this respect it resembles the careless majesty which Nature stamps upon the rare masterpieces of her creation, harmonizing them as it were from the harmony of the spirit within. Yet all this not only consists with, but is the cause of the subtlest delicacy of clear and tender beauty—the expression at once of innocence and sublimity of soul—of purity and strength— of all that which touches the most removed and divine of the chords that make music in our thoughts—of that which shakes with astonishment even the most superficial.

THE MINERVA.

THE head is of the highest beauty. It has a close helmet, from which the hair, delicately parted on the forehead, half escapes. The attitude gives entire effect to the perfect form of the neck, and to that full and beautiful moulding of the lower part of the face and mouth, which is in living beings the seat of the expression of a simplicity and integrity of nature. Her face, upraised to heaven, is animated with a profound, sweet, and impassioned melancholy, with an earnest, and fervid, and disinterested pleading against some vast and inevitable wrong. It is the joy and poetry of sorrow making grief beautiful, and giving it that nameless feeling which, from the imperfection of language, we call pain, but which is not all pain, though a feeling which makes not only its possessor, but the spectator of it, prefer it to what is called pleasure, in which all is not pleasure. It is difficult to think that this head, though of the highest ideal beauty, is the head of Minerva, although the attributes and attitude of the lower part of the statue certainly suggest that idea. The Greeks rarely, in their representations of the characters of their gods,—unless we call the poetic enthusiasm of Apollo a mortal passion,—expressed the disturbance of human feeling; and here is deep and impassioned grief animating a divine countenance. It is, indeed, divine. Wisdom (which Minerva may be supposed to emblem,) is pleading earnestly with Power,—and invested with the expression of that grief, because it must ever plead so vainly. The drapery of the statue, the gentle beauty of the feet, and the grace of the attitude, are what may be seen in many other statues belonging to that astonishing era which produced it : such a countenance is seen in few.

This statue happens to be placed on a pedestal, the subject of whose reliefs is in a spirit wholly the reverse. It was probably an altar to Bacchus—possibly a funeral urn. Under the festoons of fruits and flowers that grace the pedestal, the corners of which are ornamented with the skulls of goats, are sculptured some figures of Mænads under the inspiration of the god. Nothing can be conceived more wild and terrible than their gestures, touching, as they do, the verge of distortion, into which their fine limbs and lovely forms are thrown. There is nothing, however, that exceeds the possibility of nature, though it borders on its utmost line.

The tremendous spirit of superstition, aided by drunkenness, producing something beyond insanity, seems to have caught them in its whirlwinds, and to bear them over the earth, as the rapid volutions of a tempest have the ever-changing trunk of a waterspout, or as the torrent of a mountain river whirls the autumnal leaves resistlessly along in its full eddies. The hair, loose and floating, seems caught in the tempest of their own tumultuous motion;

their heads are thrown back, leaning with a strange delirium upon their necks, and looking up to heaven, whilst they totter and stumble even in the energy of their tempestuous dance.

One represents Agave with the head of Pentheus in one hand, and in the other a great knife ; a second has a spear with its pine cone, which was the Thyrsus ; and another dances with mad voluptuousness; the fourth is beating a kind of tambourine.

This was indeed a monstrous superstition, even in Greece, where it was alone capable of combining ideal beauty and poetical and abstract enthusiasm with the wild errors from which it sprung. In Rome it had a more familiar, wicked, and dry appearance ; it was not suited to the severe and exact apprehensions of the Romans, and their strict morals were violated by it, and sustained a deep injury, little analogous to its effects upon the Greeks, who turned all things—superstition, prejudice, murder, madness—to beauty.

ON THE VENUS CALLED ANADYOMINE.

She has just issued from the bath, and yet is animated with the enjoyment of it.

She seems all soft and mild enjoyment, and the curved lines of her fine limbs flow into each other with a never-ending sinuosity of sweetness. Her face expresses a breathless, yet passive and innocent voluptuousness, free from affectation. Her lips, without the sublimity of lofty and impetuous passion, the grandeur of enthusiastic imagination of the Apollo of the Capitol, or the union of both, like the Apollo Belvidere, have the tenderness of arch, yet pure and affectionate desire, and the mode in which the ends of the mouth are drawn in, yet lifted or half-opened, with the smile that for ever circles round them, and the tremulous curve into which they are wrought by inextinguishable desire, and the tongue lying against the lower lip, as in the listlessness of passive joy, express love, still love.

Her eyes seem heavy and swimming with pleasure, and her small forehead fades on both sides into that sweet swelling and thin declension of the bone over the eye, in the mode which expresses simple and tender feelings.

The neck is full, and panting as with the aspiration of delight, and flows with gentle curves into her perfect form.

Her form is indeed perfect. She is half-sitting and half-rising from a shell, and the fulness of her limbs, and their complete roundness and perfection, do not diminish the vital energy with which they seem to be animated. The position of the arms, which are lovely beyond imagination, is natural, unaffected, and easy. This, perhaps, is the finest personification of Venus, the deity of superficial desire, in all antique statuary. Her pointed and pear-like person, ever virgin, and her attitude modesty itself.

A BAS-RELIEF.

Probably the sides of a Sarcophagus.

THE lady is lying on a couch, supported by a young woman, and looking extremely exhausted ; her dishevelled hair is floating about her shoulder, and she is half-covered with drapery that falls on the couch.

Her tunic is exactly like a chemise, only the sleeves are longer, coming half way down the upper part of the arm. An old wrinkled woman, with a cloak over her head, and an enormously sagacious look, has a most *professional* appearance, and is taking hold of her arm gently with one hand, and with the other is supporting it. I think she is feeling her pulse. At the side of the couch sits a woman as in grief, holding her head in her hands. At the bottom of the bed is another matron tearing her hair, and in the act of screaming out most violently, which she seems, however, by the rest of her gestures, to do with the utmost deliberation, as having come to the resolution, that it was a correct thing to do so. Behind her is a gossip of the most ludicrous ugliness, crying, I suppose, or praying, for her arms are crossed upon her neck. There is also a fifth setting up a wail. To the left of the couch a nurse is sitting on the ground dandling the child in her arms, and wholly occupied in so doing. The infant is swaddled. Behind her is a female who appears to be in the act of rushing in with dishevelled hair and violent gesture, and in one hand brandishing a whip or a thunder-bolt. This is probably some emblematic person, the messenger of death, or a fury, whose personification would be a key to the whole. What they are all wailing at, I know not ; whether the lady is dying, or the father has directed the child to be exposed : but if the mother be not dead, such a tumult would kill a woman in the straw in these days.

The other compartment, in the second scene of the drama, tells the story of the presentation of the child to its father. An old man has it in his arms, and with professional and mysterious officiousness is holding it out to the father. The father, a middle-aged and very respectable-looking man, perhaps not long married, is looking with the admiration of a bachelor on his first child, and perhaps thinking, that he was once such a strange little creature himself. His hands are clasped, and he is gathering up between his arms the folds of his cloak, an emblem of his gathering up all his faculties to understand the tale the gossip is bringing.

An old man is standing beside him, probably his father, with some curiosity, and much tenderness in his looks. Around are collected a host of his relations, of whom the youngest, a handsome girl, seems the least concerned. It is altogether an admirable piece, quite in the spirit of the comedies of Terence.*

MICHAEL ANGELO'S BACCHUS.

THE countenance of this figure is a most revolting mistake of the spirit and meaning of Bacchus. It looks drunken, brutal, narrow-minded, and has an expression of dissoluteness the most revolting. The lower part of the figure is stiff, and the manner in which the shoulders are united to the breast, and the neck to the head, abundantly inharmonious. It is altogether without unity, as was the idea of the deity of Bacchus in the conception of a Catholic. On the other hand, considered only as a piece of workmanship, it has many merits. The arms are executed in a style of the most perfect and manly beauty. The body is conceived with great energy, and the manner in which the lines mingle into each other, of the highest boldness and truth. It wants unity as a work of art—as a representation of Bacchus it wants everything.

A JUNO.

A STATUE of great merit. The countenance expresses a stern and unquestioned severity of dominion, with a certain sadness. The lips are beautiful—susceptible of expressing scorn—but not without sweetness. With fine lips a person

* This bas-relief is not antique. It is of the Cinquecento.

9¹

is never wholly bad, and they never belong to the expression
of emotions wholly selfish—lips being the seat of imagination. The drapery is finely conceived, and the manner in
which the act of throwing back one leg is expressed, in the
diverging folds of the drapery of the left breast fading in
bold yet graduated lines into a skirt, as it descends from
the left shoulder, is admirably imagined.

AN APOLLO,

with serpents twining round a wreath of laurel on which
the quiver is suspended. It probably was, when complete,
magnificently beautiful. The restorer of the head and
arms, following the indication of the muscles of the right
side, has lifted the arm, as in triumph, at the success of an
arrow, imagining to imitate the Lycian Apollo in that, so
finely described by Apollonius Rhodius, when the dazzling
radiance of his beautiful limbs shone over the dark Euxine.
The action, energy, and godlike animation of these limbs
speak a spirit which seems as if it could not be consumed.

ON THE REVIVAL OF LITERATURE.

In the fifteenth century of the Christian era, a new and
extraordinary event roused Europe from her lethargic
state, and paved the way to her present greatness. The
writings of Dante in the thirteenth, and of Petrarch in the
fourteenth, were the bright luminaries which had afforded
glimmerings of literary knowledge to the almost benighted
traveller toiling up the hill of Fame. But on the taking of
Constantinople, a new and sudden light appeared : the
dark clouds of ignorance rolled into distance, and Europe

was inundated by learned monks, and still more by the quantity of learned manuscripts which they brought with them from the scene of devastation. The Turks settled themselves in Constantinople, where they adopted nothing but the vicious habits of the Greeks: they neglected even the small remains of its ancient learning, which, filtered and degenerated as it was by the absurd mixture of Pagan and Christian philosophy, proved, on its retirement to Europe, the spark which spread gradually and successfully the light of knowledge over the world.

Italy, France, and England—for Germany still remained many centuries less civilised than the surrounding countries —swarmed with monks and cloisters. Superstition, of whatever kind, whether earthly or divine, has hitherto been the weight which clogged man to earth, and prevented his genius from soaring aloft amid its native skies. The enterprises, and the effects of the human mind, are something more than stupendous: the works of nature are material and tangible: we have a half insight into their kind, and in many instances we predict their effects with certainty. But mind seems to govern the world without visible or substantial means. Its birth is unknown; its action and influence unperceived; and its being seems eternal. To the mind both humane and philosophical, there cannot exist a greater subject of grief than the reflection of how much superstition has retarded the progress of intellect, and consequently the happiness of man.

The monks in their cloisters were engaged in trifling and ridiculous disputes: they contented themselves with teaching the dogmas of their religion, and rushed impatiently forth to the colleges and halls, where they disputed with an acrimony and meanness little befitting the resemblance of their pretended holiness. But the situation of a monk is a situation the most unnatural that bigotry, proud in the invention of cruelty, could conceive; and their vices may be pardoned as resulting from the wills and devices of a few proud and selfish bishops, who enslaved the world that they might live at ease.

The disputes of the schools were mostly scholastical; it was the discussion of words, and had no relation to morality. Morality,—the great means and end of man,— was contained, as they affirmed, in the extent of a few hundred pages of a certain book, which others have since contended were but scraps of martyrs' last dying words, collected together and imposed on the world. In the refinements of the scholastic philosophy, the world seemed in danger of losing the little real wisdom that still remained as her portion; and the only valuable part of their disputes was such as tended to develop the system of the Peripatetic Philosophers. Plato, the wisest, the profoundest, and Epicurus, the most humane and gentle among the ancients, were entirely neglected by them. Plato interfered with their peculiar mode of thinking concerning heavenly matters; and Epicurus, maintaining the rights of man to pleasure and happiness, would have afforded a seducing contrast to their dark and miserable code of morals. It has been asserted, that these holy men solaced their lighter moments in a contraband worship of Epicurus and profaned the philosophy which maintained the rights of all by a selfish indulgence of the rights of a few. Thus it is: the laws of nature are invariable, and man sets them aside that he may have the pleasure of travelling through a labyrinth in search of them again.

Pleasure, in an open and innocent garb, by some strange process of reasoning, is called vice; yet man (so closely is he linked to the chains of necessity—so irresistibly is he impelled to fulfil the end of his being,) must seek her at whatever price : he becomes a hypocrite, and braves damnation with all its pains.

Grecian literature,—the finest the world has ever produced,—was at length restored : its form and mode we obtained from the manuscripts which the ravages of time, of the Goths, and of the still more savage Turks, had spared. The burning of the library at Alexandria was an evil of importance. This library is said to have contained volumes of the choicest Greek authors.

REVIEW OF HOGG'S *MEMOIRS OF PRINCE ALEXY HAIMATOFF.*

[*Memoirs of Prince Alexy Haimatoff*. Translated from the original Latin MSS. under the immediate inspection of the Prince. By JOHN BROWN, Esq. Pp. 236. 12mo. Hookham, 1814.]

Is the suffrage of mankind the legitimate criterion of intellectual energy ? Are complaints of the aspirants to literary fame to be considered as the honourable disappointment of neglected genius, or the sickly impatience of a dreamer miserably self deceived ? the most illustrious ornaments of the annals of the human race, have been stigmatised by the contempt and abhorrence of entire communities of man ; but this injustice arose out of some temporary superstition, some partial interest, some national doctrine : a glorious redemption awaited their remembrance. There is indeed, nothing so remarkable in the contempt of the ignorant for the enlightened : the vulgar pride of folly, delights to triumph upon mind. This is an intelligible process : the infancy [infamy ?] or ingloriousness that can be thus explained, detracts nothing from the beauty of virtue or the sublimity of genius. But what does utter obscurity express ? if the public do not advert even in censure to a performance, has that performance already received its condemnation ?

The result of this controversy is important to the ingenuous critic. His labours are indeed, miserably worthless, if their objects may invariably be attained before their application. He should know the limits of his prerogative. He should not be ignorant, whether it is his duty to promulgate the decisions of others, or to cultivate his taste and judgment that he may be enabled to render a ' reason for his own.

Circumstances the least connected with intellectual nature have contributed, for a certain period, to retain in obscurity, the most memorable specimens of human genius. The author re[f]rains perhaps from introducing his production to the world with all the pomp of empirical bibliopolism. A sudden tide in the affairs of men may make the neglect or contradiction of some insignificant doctrine, a badge of obscurity and discredit : those even who are exempt fiom the action of these absurd predilections, are necessarily in an indirect manner affected by their influence. It is perhaps the product of an imagination daring and undisciplined : the majority of readers ignorant and disdaining toleration refuse to pardon a neglect of common rules; their canons of criticism are carelessly infringed, it is less religious than a charity sermon, less methodical and cold than a French tragedy, where all the unities are preserved : no excellencies, where prudish cant and dull regularity are absent, can preserve it from the contempt and abhorrence of the multitude. It is evidently not difficult to imagine an instance in which the most elevated genius shall be recompensed with neglect. Mediocrity alone seems unvaryingly to escape rebuke and obloquy, it accom[m]odates its attempts to the spirit of the age, which has produced it, and adopts with mimic effrontery the cant of the day and hour for which alone it lives.

We think that " the Memoirs of Prince Alexy Haima-toff" deserves to be regarded as an example of the fact, by the frequency of which criticism is vindicated from the imputation of futility and impertinence. We do not hesitate to consider this fiction, as the product of a bold and original mind. We hardly remember even [ever ?] to have seen surpassed the subtle delicacy of imagination, by which the manifest distinctions of character, and form are seized and pictured in colours, that almost make nature more beautiful than herself. The vulgar observe no resemblances or discrepancies, but such as are gross and glaring. The science of mind to which history, poetry, biography serve as the materials, consists in the discernment of shades and distinctions where the unenlightened discover nothing but a shapeless and unmeaning mass. The faculty for this discernment distinguishes genius from dulness. There are passages in the production before us, which afford instances of just and rapid intuition belonging only to intelligences that possess this faculty in no ordinary degree. As a composition the book is far from faultless. Its abruptness and angularities do not appear to have received the slightest polish or correction. The author has written with fervour but has disdained to revise at leisure. These errors are the errors of youth and genius and the fervid impatience of sensibilities impetuously disburthening their fulness. The author is proudly negligent of connecting the incidents of his tale. It appears more like the recorded day dream of a poet, not unvisited by the sublimest and most lovely visions, than the tissue of a romance skilfully interwoven for the purpose of maintaining the interest of the reader, and conducting his sympathies by dramatic gradations to the denouement. It is, what it professes to be, a memoir, not a novel. Yet its claims to the former appellation are established, only by the impatience and inexperience of the author, who, possessing in an eminent degree, the higher qualifications of a novelist, we had almost said a poet, has neglected the number by which that success would probably have been secured, which, in this instance, merit[s] of a far nobler stamp, have unfortunately failed to acquire. Prince Alexy is by no means an unnatural, although no common character. We think we can discern his counterpart in Alfieri's* delineation of himself. The same propensities, the same ardent devotion to his purposes, the same chivalric and unproductive attachment to unbounded liberty, characterizes both. We are inclined to doubt whether the author has not attributed to his hero, the doctrines of universal philanthropy in a spirit of profound and almost unsearchable irony : at least he appears biassed by no peculiar principles, and it were perhaps an insoluble inquiry whether any, and if any, what moral truth he designed to illustrate by his tale. Bruhle, the tutor of Alexy, is a character delineated with consummate skill ; the power of intelligence and virtue over external deficiencies is forcibly exemplified. The calmness, patience and magnanimity of this singular man, are truly rare and admirable : his disinterestedness, his equanimity, his irresistible gentleness form a finished and delightful portrait. But we cannot regard his commendation to his pupil to indulge in

* *Alfien's* in the original.

promiscuous concubinage without horror and detestation.
The author appears to deem the loveless intercourse of brutal
appetite, a venial offence against delicacy and virtue ! he
asserts that a transient connection with a cultivated female
may contribute to form the heart without essentially
vitiating the sensibilities. It is our duty to protest
against so pernicious and disgusting an opinion. No man
can rise pure from the poisonous embraces of a prostitute,
or sinless from the desolated hopes of a confiding heart.
Whatever may be the claims of chastity, whatever the
advantages of simple and pure affections, these ties, these
benefits are of equal obligation to either sex.* Domestic
relations depend for their integrity upon a complete reci-
procity of duties.   But the author himself has in the
adventure of the sultana, Debesh-Sheptuti afforded a most
impressive and tremendous allegory of the cold blooded and
malignant selfishness of sensuality.

We are incapacitated by the unconnected and vague
narrative from forming an analysis of the incidents, they
would consist indeed, simply of a catalogue of events, and
which, divested of the aërial tinge of genius might appear
trivial and common. We shall content ourselves, therefore with selecting some passages calculated to exemplify
the peculiar powers of the author. The following description of the simple and interesting Rosalie is in the highest
style of delineation : " Her hair was unusually black, she
truly had raven locks, the same glossiness, the same varying
shade, the same mixture of purple and sable for which the
plumage of the raven is remarkable, were found in the long
elastic tresses depending from her head and covering her
shoulders. Her complexion was dark and clear ; the
colours which composed the brown that dyed her smooth

* *Six* in the original.

skin, were so well mixed, that not one blot, not one varied
tinge injured its brightness, and when the blush of animation or of modesty flushed her cheek, the tint was so rare,
that could a painter have dipped his pencil in it, that
single shade would have rendered him immortal.   The
bone above her eye was sharp, and beautifully curved ;
much as I have admired the wonderful properties of curves,
I am convinced that their most stupendous properties
collected, would fall far short of that magic line.   The eye
brow was pencilled with extreme nicety ; in the centre it
consisted of the deepest shade of black, at the edges it was
hardly perceptible, and no man could have been hardy
enough to have attempted to define the precise spot at
which it ceased : in short the velvet drapery of the eye-
brow was only to be rivalled by the purple of the long
black eyelashes that terminated the ample curtain.
Rosalie's eyes were large and full ; they appeared at a
distance uniformly dark, but upon close inspection the
innumerable strokes of various hues of infinite fineness and
endless variety drawn in concentric circles behind the
pellucid chrystal, filled the mind with wonder and admiration, and could only be the work of infinite power directed
by infinite wisdom."

Alexy's union with Aür-Ahebeh the Circassian slave is
marked by circumstances of deep pathos, and the sweetest
tenderness of sentiment.   The description of his misery
and madness at her death, deserves to be remarked as
affording evidence of an imagination vast, profound and
full of energy.

"Alexy, who gained the friendship, perhaps the love of the native
Rosalie : the handsome Haimatoff, the philosophic Haimatoff, the
haughty Haimatoff, Haimatoff the gay, the witty, the accomplished,
the bold hunter, the friend of liberty, the chivalric lover of all that is

feminine, the hero, the enthusiast ; see him now, that is he, mark him ! he appears in the shades of evening, he stalk[s] as a spectre, he has just risen from the damps of the charnel house ; see, the dews still hang on his forehead. He will vanish at cock-crowing, he never heard the song of the lark, nor the busy hum of men ; the sun's rays never warmed him, the pale moonbeam alone shews his unearthly figure, which is fanned by the wing of the owl, which scarce obstructs the slow flight of the droning beetle,* or of the drowsy bat. Mark him ! he stops, his lean arms are crossed on his bosom ; he is bowed to the earth, his sunken eye gazes from its deep cavity on vacuity, as the toad skulking in the corner of a sepulchre, peeps with malignity through the circum[am]bient gloom. His cheek is hollow ; the glowing tints of his complexion, which once resembled the autumnal sunbeam on the autumnal beech, are gone, the cadaverous yellow, the livid hue have usurped their place, the sable honours of his head have perished, they once waved in the wind like the jetty pinions of the raven, the skull is only covered by the shrivelled skin, which the rook views wistfully, and calls to her young ones. His gaunt bones start from his wrinkled garments, his voice is deep, hollow, sepulchral[;] it is the voice which wakes the dead, he has long held converse with the departed. He attempts to walk he knows not whither, his legs totter under him, he falls, the boys hoot him, the dogs bark at him, he hears them not, he sees them not.—Rest there, Alexy, it beseemeth thee, thy bed is the grave, thy bride is the worm, yet once thou stoodest erect, thy cheek was flushed with joyful ardour, thy eye blazing told what thy head conceived, what thy heart felt, thy limbs were vigour and activity, thy bosom expanded with pride, ambition, and desire, every nerve thrilled to feel, every muscle swelled to execute.

"Haimatoff, the blight has tainted thee, thou ample roomy web of life, whereon were traced the gaudy characters, the gay embroidery of pleasure, how has the moth battened on thee ; Haimatoff, how has the devouring flame scorched the plains, once yellow with the harvest ! the simoon, the parching breath of the desert, has swept over the laughing plains, the carpet of verdure rolled away at its approach, and has bared amid desolation. Thou stricken deer, thy leather coat, thy dappled hide hangs loose upon thee, it was a deadly arrow, how has it wasted thee, thou scathed oak, how has the red lightning drank thy sap :

* *beatle* in the original.

Haimatoff, Haimatoff, eat thy soul with vexation. Let the immeasureable ocean roll between thee and pride: you must not dwell together." P. 129.

The episode of Viola is affecting, natural, and beautiful. We do not ever remember to have seen the unforgiving fastidiousness of family honor more awfully illustrated. After the death of her lover, Viola still expects that he will esteem, still cherishes the delusion that he is not lost to her for ever.

"She used frequently to go to the window to look for him, or walk in the Park to meet him, but without the least impatience, at his delay. She learnt a new tune, or a new song to amuse him, she stood behind the door to startle him as he entered, or disguised herself to surprise him."

The character of Mary, deserves, we think, to be considered as the only complete failure in the book. Every other female whom the author has attempted to describe is designated by an individuality peculiarly marked and true. They constitute finished portraits of whatever is eminently simple, graceful, gentle, or disgustingly atrocious and vile. Mary alone is the miserable parasite of fashion, the tame slave of drivelling and drunken folly, the cold hearted coquette, the lying and meretricious prude. The means employed to gain this worthless prize corresponds exactly with its worthlessness. Sir Fulke * Hildebrand is a strenuous tory, Alexy, on his arrival in England professes himself inclined to the principles of the whig party, finding that the Baronet had sworn that his daughter should never marry a whig, he sacrifices his principles and with inconceiveable effrontry thus palliates his apostacy and falsehood.

* *Eulke* in the original.

" The prejudices of the Baronet, were strong in proportion as they were irrational. I resolved rather to humour than to thwart them. I contrived to be invited to dine in company with him ; I always proposed the health of the minister, I introduced politics and defended the tory party in long speeches, I attended clubs and public dinners of that interest. I do not know whether this conduct was justifiable ; it may certainly be excused when the circumstances of my case are duly considered. I would tear myself in pieces, if I suspected that I could be guilty of the slightest falsehood or prevarication ; (see Lord Chesterfield's letters for the courtier-like distinction between simulation and dissimulation,) but there was nothing of that sort here. I was of no party, consequently, I could not be accused of deserting anyone. I did not defend the injustice of any body of men, I did not detract from the merits of any virtuous character. I praised what was laudable in the tory party, and blamed what was reprehensible in the whigs : I was silent with regard to whatever was culpable in the former or praiseworthy in the latter. The stratagem was innocent, which injured no one, and which promoted the happiness of two individuals, especially of the most amiable woman the world ever knew."

An instance of more deplorable perversity of the human understanding we do not recollect ever to have witnessed. It almost persuades us to believe that scepticism or indifference concerning certain sacred truths may occasionally produce a subtlety of sophism, by which the conscience of the criminal may be bribed to overlook his crime.

Towards the conclusion of this strange and powerful performance it must be confessed that *aliquando bonus dormitat Homerus.* The adventure of the Eleutheri, although the sketch of a profounder project, is introduced and concluded with unintelligible abruptness. Bruhle dies, purposely as it should seem that his pupil may renounce the romantic sublimity of his nature, and that his inauspicious union and prostituted character, might be exempt from the censure of violated friendship. Numerous indications of profound and vigorous thought are scattered over even the most negligently compacted portions of the narrative. It is an unweeded garden where nightshade is interwoven with sweet jessamine, and the most delicate spices of the east, peep over struggling stalks of rank and poisonous hemlock.

In the delineation of the more evanescent feelings and uncommon instances of strong and delicate passion we conceive the author to have exhibited new and unparalleled powers. He has noticed some peculiarities of female character, with a delicacy and truth singularly exquisite. We think that the interesting subject of sexual relations requires for its successful development the application of a mind thus organised and endowed. Yet even here how great the deficiencies; this mind must be pure from the fashionable superstitions of gallantry, must be exempt from the sordid feelings which with blind idolatry worship * the image and blaspheme the deity, reverence the type, and degrade the realty of which it is an emblem.

We do not hesitate to assert that the author of this volume is a man of ability. His great though indisciplinable energies and fervid rapidity of conception embody † scenes and situations, and ‡ passions affording inexhaustible food for wonder and delight. The interest is deep and irresistible. A moral enchanter seems to have conjured up the shapes of all that is beautiful and strange to suspend the faculties in fascination and astonishment.

* *Worships* in the original.
† *Embodies* in the original.
‡ "And *of* passions" in the original.

THE ASSASSINS.

A FRAGMENT OF A ROMANCE.

———◆———

CHAPTER I.

JERUSALEM, goaded on to resistance by the incessant usurpations and insolence of Rome, leagued together its discordant factions to rebel against the common enemy and tyrant. Inferior to their foe in all but the unconquerable hope of liberty, they surrounded their city with fortifications of uncommon strength, and placed in array before the temple a band rendered desperate by patriotism and religion. Even the women preferred to die, rather than survive the ruin of their country. When the Roman army approached the walls of the sacred city, its preparations, its discipline, and its numbers, evinced the conviction of its leader, that he had no common barbarians to subdue. At the approach of the Roman army, the strangers withdrew from the city.

Among the multitudes which from every nation of the East had assembled at Jerusalem, was a little congregation of Christians. They were remarkable neither for their numbers nor their importance. They contained among them neither philosophers nor poets. Acknowledging no laws but those of God, they modelled their conduct towards their fellow-men by the conclusions of their individual judgment on the practical application of these laws. And it was apparent from the simplicity and severity of their manners, that this contempt for human institutions had

produced among them a character superior in singleness
and sincere self-apprehension to the slavery of pagan
customs and the gross delusions of antiquated superstition.
Many of their opinions considerably resembled those of the
sect afterwards known by the name of Gnostics. They
esteemed the human understanding to be the paramount
rule of human conduct; they maintained that the obscurest
religious truth required for its complete elucidation no
more than the strenuous application of the energies of
mind. It appeared impossible to them that any doctrine
could be subversive of social happiness which is not capable
of being confuted by arguments derived from the nature of
existing things. With the devoutest submission to the law
of Christ, they united an intrepid spirit of inquiry as to the
correctest mode of acting in particular instances of conduct
that occur among men. Assuming the doctrines of the
Messiah concerning benevolence and justice for the regulation of their actions, they could not be persuaded to
acknowledge that there was apparent in the divine code
any prescribed rule whereby, for its own sake, one action
rather than another, as fulfilling the will of their great
Master, should be preferred.

The contempt with which the magistracy and priesthood
regarded this obscure community of speculators, had
hitherto protected them from persecution. But they had
arrived at that precise degree of eminence and prosperity
which is peculiarly obnoxious to the hostility of the rich
and powerful. The moment of their departure from
Jerusalem was the crisis of their future destiny. Had they
continued to seek a precarious refuge in a city of the
Roman empire, this persecution would not have delayed to
impress a new character on their opinions and their
conduct; narrow views, and the illiberality of sectarian

patriotism, would not have failed speedily to obliterate the magnificence and beauty of their wild and wonderful condition.

Attached from principle to peace, despising and hating the pleasures and the customs of the degenerate mass of mankind, this unostentatious community of good and happy men fled to the solitudes of Lebanon. To Arabians and enthusiasts the solemnity and grandeur of these desolate recesses possessed peculiar attractions. It well accorded with the justice of their conceptions on the relative duties of man towards his fellow in society, that they should labour in unconstrained equality to dispossess the wolf and the tiger of their empire, and establish on its ruins the dominion of intelligence and virtue. No longer would the worshippers of the God of Nature be indebted to a hundred hands for the accommodation of their simple wants. No longer would the poison of a diseased civilisation embrue their very nutriment with pestilence. They would no longer owe their very existence to the vices, the fears, and the follies of mankind. Love, friendship, and philanthropy, would now be the characteristic disposers of their industry. It is for his mistress or his friend that the labourer consecrates his toil ; others are mindful, but he is forgetful, of himself. "God feeds the hungry ravens, and clothes the lilies of the fields, and yet Solomon in all his glory is not like to one of these."

Rome was now the shadow of her former self. The light of her grandeur and loveliness had passed away. The latest and the noblest of her poets and historians had foretold in agony her approaching slavery and degradation. The ruins of the human mind, more awful and portentous than the desolation of the most solemn temples, threw a shade of gloom upon her golden palaces which the brutal vulgar could not see, but which the mighty felt with inward trepidation and despair. The ruins of Jerusalem lay defenceless and uninhabited upon the burning sands; none visited, but in the depth of solemn awe, this accursed and solitary spot. Tradition says that there was seen to linger among the scorched and shattered fragments of the temple, one being, whom he that saw dared not to call man, with clasped hands, immoveable eyes, and a visage horribly serene. Not on the will of the capricious multitude, nor the constant fluctuations of the many and the weak, depends the change of empires and religions. These are the mere insensible elements from which a subtler intelligence moulds its enduring statuary. They that direct the changes of this mortal scene breathe the decrees of their dominion from a throne of darkness and of tempest. The power of man is great.

After many days of wandering, the Assassins pitched their tents in the vallay of Bethzatanai. For ages had this fertile valley lain concealed from the adventurous search of man, among mountains of everlasting snow. The men of elder days had inhabited this spot. Piles of monumental marble and fragments of columns that in their integrity almost seemed the work of some intelligence more sportive and fantastic than the gross conceptions of mortality, lay in heaps beside the lake, and were visible beneath its transparent waves. The flowering orange-tree, the balsam, and innumerable odoriferous shrubs, grew wild in the desolated portals. The fountain tanks had overflowed; and, amid the luxuriant vegetation of their margin, the yellow snake held its unmolested dwelling. Hither came the tiger and the bear to contend for those once domestic animals who had forgotten the secure servitude of their ancestors. No sound, when the famished beast of prey

had retreated in despair from the awful desolation of this
place, at whose completion he had assisted, but the shrill
cry of the stork, and the flapping of his heavy wings from
the capital of the solitary column, and the scream of the
hungry vulture baffled of its only victim. The lore of
ancient wisdom was sculptured in mystic characters on the
rocks. The human spirit and the human hand had been
busy here to accomplish its profoundest miracles. It was a
temple dedicated to the God of knowledge and of truth.
The palaces of the Caliphs and the Cæsars might easily
surpass these ruins in magnitude and sumptuousness : but
they were the design of tyrants and the work of slaves.
Piercing genius and consummate prudence had planned and
executed Bethzatanai. There was deep and important
meaning in every lineament of its fantastic sculpture.
The unintelligible legend, once so beautiful and perfect, so
full of poetry and history, spoke, even in destruction,
volumes of mysterious import, and obscure significance.

But in the season of its utmost prosperity and magnificence, art might not aspire to vie with nature in the
valley of Bethzatanai. All that was wonderful and lovely
was collected in this deep seclusion. The fluctuating elements seemed to have been rendered everlastingly permanent in forms of wonder and delight. The mountains of
Lebanon had been divided to their base to form this happy
valley ; on every side their icy summits darted their white
pinnacles into the clear blue sky, imaging, in their grotesque
outline, minarets, and ruined domes, and columns worn
with time. Far below, the silver clouds rolled their bright
volumes in many beautiful shapes, and fed the eternal
springs that, spanning the dark chasms like a thousand
radiant rainbows, leaped into the quiet vale, then lingering
in many a dark glade among the groves of cypress and of

palm, lost themselves in the lake. The immensity of these precipitous mountains, with their starry pyramids of snow, excluded the sun, which overtopped not, even in its meridian, their overhanging rocks. But a more heavenly and serener light was reflected from their icy mirrors, which, piercing through the many-tinted clouds, produced lights and colours of inexhaustible variety. The herbage was perpetually verdant, and clothed the darkest recesses of the caverns and the woods.

Nature, undisturbed, had become an enchantress in these solitudes : she had collected here all that was wonderful and divine from the armoury of her omnipotence. The very winds breathed health and renovation, and the joyousness of youthful courage. Fountains of crystalline water played perpetually among the aromatic flowers, and mingled a freshness with their odour. The pine boughs became instruments of exquisite contrivance, among which every varying breeze waked music of new and more delightful melody. Meteoric shapes, more effulgent than the moonlight, hung on the wandering clouds, and mixed in discordant dance around the spiral fountains. Blue vapours assumed strange lineaments under the rocks and among the ruins, lingering like ghosts with slow and solemn step. Through a dark chasm to the east, in the long perspective of a portal glittering with the unnumbered riches of the subterranean world, shone the broad moon, pouring in one yellow and unbroken stream her horizontal beams. Nearer the icy region, autumn and spring held an alternate reign. The sere leaves fell and choked the sluggish brooks ; the chilling fogs hung diamonds on every spray ; and in the dark cold evening the howling winds made melancholy music in the trees. Far above, shone the bright throne of winter, clear, cold, and dazzling. Sometimes there was seen the snow-flakes to fall before the sinking orb of the beamless sun, like a shower of fiery sulphur. The cataracts, arrested in their course, seemed, with their transparent columns, to support the dark-browed rocks. Sometimes the icy whirlwind scooped the powdery snow aloft, to mingle with the hissing meteors, and scatter spangles through the rare and rayless atmosphere.

Such strange scenes of chaotic confusion and harrowing sublimity, surrounding and shutting in the vale, added to the delights of its secure and voluptuous tranquillity. No spectator could have refused to believe that some spirit of great intelligence and power had hallowed these wild and beautiful solitudes to a deep and solemn mystery.

The immediate effect of such a scene, suddenly presented to the contemplation of mortal eyes, is seldom the subject of authentic record. The coldest slave of custom cannot fail to recollect some few moments in which the breath of spring or the crowding clouds of sunset, with the pale moon shining through their fleecy skirts, or the song of some lonely bird perched on the only tree of an unfrequented heath, has awakened the touch of nature. And they were Arabians who entered the valley of Bethzatanai; men who idolized nature and the God of nature; to whom love and lofty thoughts, and the apprehensions of an uncorrupted spirit, were sustenance and life. Thus securely excluded from an abhorred world, all thought of its judgment was cancelled by the rapidity of their fervid imaginations. They ceased to acknowledge, or deigned not to advert to, the distinctions with which the majority of base and vulgar minds control the longings and struggles of the soul towards its place of rest. A new and sacred fire was kindled in their hearts and sparkled in their eyes. Every ges-ture, every feature, the minutest action, was modelled to beneficence and beauty by the holy inspiration that had descended on their searching spirits. The epidemic transport communicated itself through every heart with the rapidity of a blast from heaven. They were already disembodied spirits ; they were already the inhabitants of paradise. To live, to breathe, to move, was itself a sensation of immeasurable transport. Every new contemplation of the condition of his nature brought to the happy enthusiast an added measure of delight, and impelled to every organ, where mind is united with external things, a keener and more exquisite perception of all that they contain of lovely and divine. To love, to be beloved, suddenly became an insatiable famine of his nature, which the wide circle of the universe, comprehending beings of such inexhaustible variety and stupendous magnitude of excellence, appeared too narrow and confined to satiate.

Alas, that these visitings of the spirit of life should fluctuate and pass away ! That the moments when the human mind is commensurate with all that it can conceive of excellent and powerful, should not endure with its existence and survive its most momentous change ! But the beauty of a vernal sunset, with its overhanging curtains of empurpled cloud, is rapidly dissolved, to return at some unexpected period, and spread an alleviating melancholy over the dark vigils of despair.

It is true the enthusiasm of overwhelming transport which had inspired every breast among the Assassins is no more. The necessity of daily occupation and the ordinariness of that human life, the burthen of which it is the destiny of every human being to bear, had smothered, not extinguished, that divine and eternal fire. Not the less indelible and permanent were the impressions communicated to all; not the more unalterably were the features of their social character modelled and determined by its influence.

CHAPTER II.

ROME had fallen. Her senate-house had become a polluted den of thieves and liars; her solemn temples, the arena of theological disputants, who made fire and sword the missionaries of their inconceivable beliefs. The city of the monster Constantine, symbolizing, in the consequences of its foundation, the wickedness and weakness of his successors, feebly imaged with declining power the substantial eminence of the Roman name. Pilgrims of a new and mightier faith crowded to visit the lonely ruins of Jerusalem, and weep and pray before the sepulchre of the Eternal God. The earth was filled with discord, tumult, and ruin. The spirit of disinterested virtue had armed one-half of the civilised world against the other. Monstrous and detestable creeds poisoned and blighted the domestic charities. There was no appeal to natural love, or ancient faith, from pride, superstition, and revenge.

Four centuries had passed thus, terribly characterised by the most calamitous revolutions. The Assassins, meanwhile, undisturbed by the surrounding tumult, possessed and cultivated their fertile valley. The gradual operation of their peculiar condition had matured and perfected the singularity and excellence of their character. That cause, which had ceased to act as an immediate and overpowering excitement, became the unperceived law of their lives, and sustenance of their natures. Their religious tenets had also undergone a change, corresponding with the exalted condition of their moral being. The gratitude which they owed to the benignant Spirit by which their limited intelligences

had not only been created but redeemed, was less frequently adverted to, became less the topic of comment
or contemplation ; not, therefore, did it cease to be their
presiding guardian, the guide of their inmost thoughts, the
tribunal of appeal for the minutest particulars of their conduct. They learned to identify this mysterious benefactor
with the delight that is bred among the solitary rocks, and
has its dwelling alike in the changing colours of the clouds
and the inmost recesses of the caverns. Their future also
no longer existed, but in the blissful tranquillity of the
present. Time was measured and created by the vices and
the miseries of men, between whom and the happy nation
of the Assassins, there was no analogy nor comparison.
Already had their eternal peace commenced. The darkness
had passed away from the open gates of death.

The practical results produced by their faith and condition
upon their external conduct were singular and memorable.
Excluded from the great and various community of mankind,
these solitudes became to them a sacred hermitage, in which
all formed, as it were, one being, divided against itself by
no contending will or factious passions. Every impulse
conspired to one end, and tended to a single object. Each
devoted his powers to the happiness of the other. Their
republic was the scene of the perpetual contentions of
benevolence ; not the heartless and assumed kindness of
commercial man, but the genuine virtue that has a legible
superscription in every feature of the countenance, and
every motion of the frame. The perverseness and calamities
of those who dwelt beyond the mountains that encircled
their undisturbed possessions, were unknown and
unimagined. Little embarrassed by the complexities of
civilised society, they knew not to conceive any happiness
that can be satiated without participation, or that thirsts

not to reproduce and perpetually generate itself. The path of virtue and felicity was plain and unimpeded. They clearly acknowledged, in every case, that conduct to be entitled to preference which would obviously produce the greatest pleasure. They could not conceive an instance in which it would be their duty to hesitate, in causing, at whatever expense, the greatest and most unmixed delight.

Hence arose a peculiarity which only failed to germinate in uncommon and momentous consequences, because the Assassins had retired from the intercourse of mankind, over whom other motives and principles of conduct than justice and benevolence prevail. It would be a difficult matter for men of such a sincere and simple faith, to estimate the final results of their intentions, among the corrupt and slavish multitude. They would be perplexed also in their choice of the means, whereby their intentions might be fulfilled. To produce immediate pain or disorder for the sake of future benefit, is consonant, indeed, with the purest religion and philosophy, but never fails to excite invincible repugnance in the feelings of the many. Against their predilections and distastes an Assassin, accidentally the inhabitant of a civil-ised community, would wage unremitting hostility from principle. He would find himself compelled to adopt means which they would abhor, for the sake of an object which they could not conceive that he should propose to himself. Secure and self-enshrined in the magnificence and pre-eminence of his conceptions, spotless as the light of heaven, he would be the victim among men of calumny and persecution. Incapable of distinguishing his motives, they would rank him among the vilest and most atrocious criminals. Great, beyond all comparison with them, they would despise him in the presumption of their ignorance. Because his spirit burned with an unquenchable passion for their welfare, they would lead him, like his illustrious master, amidst scoffs, and mockery, and insult, to the remuneration of an ignominious death.

Who hesitates to destroy a venomous serpent that has crept near his sleeping friend, except the man who selfishly dreads lest the malignant reptile should turn his fury on himself? And if the poisoner has assumed a human shape, if the bane be distinguished only from the viper's venom by the excess and extent of its devastation, will the saviour and avenger here retract and pause entrenched behind the superstition of the indefeasible divinity of man? Is the human form, then, the mere badge of a prerogative for unlicensed wickedness and mischief? Can the power derived from the weakness of the oppressed, or the ignorance of the deceived, confer the right in security to tyrannise and defraud?

The subject of regular governments, and the disciple of established superstition, dares not to ask this question. For the sake of the eventual benefit, he endures what he esteems a transitory evil, and the moral degradation of man disquiets not his patience. But the religion of an Assassin imposes other virtues than endurance, when his fellow-men groan under tyranny, or have become so bestial and abject that they cannot feel their chains. An Assassin believes that man is eminently man, and only then enjoys the prerogatives of his privileged condition, when his affections and his judgment pay tribute to the God of Nature. The perverse, and vile, and vicious—what were they? Shapes of some unholy vision, moulded by the spirit of Evil, which the sword of the merciful destroyer should sweep from this beautiful world. Dreamy nothings; phantasms of misery and mischief, that hold their death-like state on glittering thrones, and in the loathsome dens of poverty.

No Assassin would submissively temporise with vice, and in cold charity become a pander to falsehood and desolation. His path through the wilderness of civilised society would be marked with the blood of the oppressor and the ruiner. The wretch, whom nations tremblingly adore, would expiate in his throttling grasp a thousand licensed and venerable crimes.

How many holy liars and parasites, in solemn guise, would his saviour arm drag from their luxurious couches, and plunge in the cold charnel, that the green and many-legged monsters of the slimy grave might eat off at their leisure the lineaments of rooted malignity and detested cunning. The respectable man—the smooth, smiling, polished villain, whom all the city honours; whose very trade is lies and murder; who buys his daily bread with the blood and tears of men, would feed the ravens with his limbs. The Assassin would cater nobly for the eyeless worms of earth, and the carrion fowls of heaven.

Yet here, religion and human love had imbued the manners of those solitary people with inexpressible gentleness and benignity. Courage and active virtue, and the indignation against vice, which becomes a hurrying and irresistible passion, slept like the imprisoned earthquake, or the lightning shafts that hang in the golden clouds of evening. They were innocent, but they were capable of more than innocence; for the great principles of their faith were perpetually acknowledged and adverted to; nor had they forgotten, in this uninterrupted quiet, the author of their felicity.

Four centuries had thus worn away without producing an event. Men had died, and natural tears had been shed upon their graves, in sorrow that improves the heart. Those who had been united by love had gone to death

together, leaving to their friends the bequest of a most
sacred grief, and of a sadness that is allied to pleasure.
Babes that hung upon their mothers' breasts had become
men ; men had died ; and many a wild luxuriant weed
that overtopped the habitations of the vale, had twined its
roots around their disregarded bones. Their tranquil state
was like a summer sea, whose gentle undulations disturb
not the reflected stars, and break not the long still line of
the rainbow hues of sunrise.

CHAPTER III.

WHERE all is thus calm, the slightest circumstance is
recorded and remembered. Before the sixth century had
expired one incident occurred, remarkable and strange. A
young man, named Albedir, wandering in the woods, was
startled by the screaming of a bird of prey, and, looking up,
saw blood fall, drop by drop, from among the intertwined
boughs of a cedar. Having climbed thetree, he beheld a
terrible and dismaying spectacle. A naked human body
was impaled on the broken branch. It was maimed and
mangled horribly ; every limb bent and bruised into frightful distortion, and exhibiting a breathing image of the
most sickening mockery of life. A monstrous snake had
scented its prey from among the mountains—and above
hovered a hungry vulture. From amidst this mass of desolated humanity, two eyes, black and inexpressibly brilliant,
shone with an unearthly lustre. Beneath the blood-stained
eyebrows their steady rays manifested the serenity of an
immortal power, the collected energy of a deathless mind,
spell-secured from dissolution. A bitter smile of mingled
abhorrence and scorn distorted his wounded lip—he appeared

calmly to observe and measure all around—self-possession had not deserted the shattered mass of life.

The youth approached the bough on which the breathing corpse was hung. As he approached, the serpent reluctantly unwreathed his glittering coils, and crept towards his dark and loathsome cave. The vulture, impatient of his meal, fled to the mountain, that re-echoed with his hoarse screams. The cedar branches creaked with their agitating weight, faintly, as the dismal wind arose. All else was deadly silent.

At length a voice issued from the mangled man. It rattled in hoarse murmurs from his throat and lungs—his words were the conclusion of some strange mysterious soliloquy. They were broken, and without apparent connection, completing wide intervals of inexpressible conceptions.

" The great tyrant is baffled, even in success. Joy ! joy ! to his tortured foe ! Triumph to the worm whom he tramples under his feet ! Ha ! His suicidal hand might dare as well abolish the mighty frame of things ! Delight and exultation sit before the closed gates of death !—I fear not to dwell beneath their black and ghastly shadow. Here thy power may not avail ! Thou createst—'tis mine to ruin and destroy.—I was thy slave—I am thy equal, and thy foe.—Thousands tremble before thy throne, who, at my voice, shall dare to pluck the golden crown from thine unholy head ! " He ceased. The silence of noon swallowed up his words. Albedir clung tighter to the tree—he dared not for dismay remove his eyes. He remained mute in the perturbation of deep and creeping horror.

" Albedir ! " said the same voice, " Albedir ! in the name of God, approach. He that suffered me to fall, watches thee ;—the gentle and merciful spirits of sweet human love, delight not in agony and horror. For pity's sake approach, in the name of thy good God, approach, Albedir !" The tones were mild and clear as the responses of Æolian music. They floated to Albedir's ear like the warm breath of June that lingers in the lawny groves, subduing all to softness. Tears of tender affection started into his eyes. It was as the voice of a beloved friend. The partner of his childhood, the brother of his soul, seemed to call for aid, and pathetically to remonstrate with delay. He resisted not the magic impulse, but advanced towards the spot, and tenderly attempted to remove the wounded man. He cautiously descended the tree with his wretched burthen, and deposited it on the ground.

A period of strange silence intervened. Awe and cold horror were slowly succeeding to the softer sensations of tumultuous pity, when again he heard the silver modulations of the same enchanting voice. "Weep not for me, Albedir! What wretch so utterly lost, but might inhale peace and renovation from this paradise! I am wounded, and in pain ; but having found a refuge in this seclusion, and a friend in you, I am worthier of envy than compassion. Bear me to your cottage secretly : I would not disturb your gentle partner by my appearance. She must love me more dearly than a brother. I must be the playmate of your children ; already I regard them with a father's love. My arrival must not be regarded as a thing of mystery and wonder. What, indeed, but that men are prone to error and exaggeration, is less inexplicable, than that a stranger, wandering on Lebanon, fell from the rocks into the vale? Albedir," he continued, and his deepening voice assumed awful solemnity, " in return for the affection with which I cherish thee and thine, thou owest this submission."

Albedir implicity submitted ; not even a thought had

power to refuse its deference. He reassumed his burthen, and proceeded towards the cottage. He watched until Khaled should be absent, and conveyed the stranger into an apartment appropriated for the reception of those who occasionally visited their habitation. He desired that the door should be securely fastened, and that he might not be visited until the morning of the following day.

Albedir waited with impatience for the return of Khaled. The unaccustomed weight of even so transitory a secret, hung on his ingenuous and unpractised nature, like a blighting, clinging curse. The stranger's accents had lulled him to a trance of wild and delightful imagination. Hopes, so visionary and aerial, that they had assumed no denomination, had spread themselves over his intellectual frame, and, phantoms as they were, had modelled his being to their shape. Still his mind was not exempt from the visitings of disquietude and perturbation. It was a troubled stream of thought, over whose fluctuating waves unsearchable fate seemed to preside, guiding its unforeseen alterations with an inexorable hand. Albedir paced earnestly the garden of his cottage, revolving every circumstance attendant on the incident of the day. He re-imaged with intense thought the minutest recollections of the scene. In vain—he was the slave of suggestions not to be controlled. Astonishment, horror, and awe—tumultuous sympathy, and a mysterious elevation of soul, hurried away all activity of judgment, and overwhelmed, with stunning force, every attempt at deliberation or inquiry.

His reveries were interrupted at length by the return of Khaled. She entered the cottage, that scene of undisturbed repose, in the confidence that change might as soon overwhelm the eternal world, as disturb this inviolable sanctuary. She started to behold Albedir. Without preface or remark, he recounted with eager haste the occurrences of the day. Khaled's tranquil spirit could hardly keep pace with the breathless rapidity of his narration. She was bewildered with staggering wonder even to hear his confused tones, and behold his agitated countenance.

CHAPTER IV.

ON the following morning Albedir arose at sunrise, and visited the stranger. He found him already risen, and employed in adorning the lattice of his chamber with flowers from the garden. There was something in his attitude and occupation singularly expressive of his entire familiarity with the scene. Albedir's habitation seemed to have been his accustomed home. He addressed his host in a tone of gay and affectionate welcome, such as never fails to communicate by sympathy the feelings from which it flows.

"My friend," said he, "the balm of the dew of our vale is sweet; or is this garden the favoured spot where the winds conspire to scatter the best odours they can find? Come, lend me your arm awhile, I feel very weak." He motioned to walk forth, but, as if unable to proceed, rested on the seat beside the door. For a few moments they were silent, if the interchange of cheerful and happy looks is to be called silence. At last he observed a spade that rested against the wall. "You have only one spade, brother," said he; "you have only one, I suppose, of any of the instruments of tillage. Your garden ground, too, occupies a certain space which it will be necessary to enlarge. This must be quickly remedied. I cannot earn my supper of to-night, nor of to-morrow; but henceforward, I do not mean to eat the bread of idleness. I know that you would

willingly perform the additional labour which my nourishment would require ; I know, also, that you would feel a
degree of pleasure in the fatigue arising from this employment, but I shall contest with you such pleasures as these,
and such pleasures as these alone." His eyes were somewhat
wan, and the tone of his voice languid as he spoke.

As they were thus engaged, Khaled came towards them.
The stranger beckoned to her to sit beside him, and taking
her hands within his own, looked attentively on her mild
countenance. Khaled inquired if he had been refreshed
by sleep. He replied by a laugh of careless and
inoffensive glee ; and placing one of her hands within
Albedir's, said, "If this be sleep, here in this odorous
vale, where these sweet smiles encompass us, and the
voices of those who love are heard—if these be the visions
of sleep, sister, those who lie down in misery shall arise
lighter than the butterflies. I came from amid the tumult
of a world, how different from this ! I am unexpectedly
among you, in the midst of a scene such as my imagination never dared to promise. I must remain here—I
must not depart." Khaled, recovering from the admiration
and astonishment caused by the stranger's words and
manner, assured him of the happiness which she should
feel in such an addition to her society. Albedir, too, who
had been more deeply impressed than Khaled by the event
of his arrival, earnestly re-assured him of the ardour of the
affection with which he had inspired them. The stranger
smiled gently to hear the unaccustomed fervour of
sincerity which animated their address, and was rising
to retire, when Khaled said, "You have not yet seen our
children, Maimuna and Abdallah. They are by the water-
side, playing with their favourite snake. We have only to
cross yonder little wood, and wind down a path cut in the

rock that overhangs the lake, and we shall find them beside a recess which the shore makes there, and which a chasm, as it were, among the rocks and woods, encloses. Do you think you could walk there ? "—"To see your children, Khaled ? I think I could, with the assistance of Albedir's arm, and yours."—So they went through the wood of ancient cypress, intermingled with the brightness of many-tinted blooms, which gleamed like stars through its romantic glens. They crossed the green meadow, and entered among the broken chasms, beautiful as they were in their investiture of odoriferous shrubs. They came at last, after pursuing a path which wound through the intricacies of a little wilderness, to the borders of the lake. They stood on the rock which overhung it, from which there was a prospect of all the miracles of nature and of art which encircled and adorned its shores. The stranger gazed upon it with a countenance unchanged by any emotion, but, as it were, thoughtfully and contemplatingly. As he gazed, Khaled ardently pressed his hand, and said, in a low yet eager voice, "Look, look, lo there ! "   He turned towards her, but her eyes were not on him. She looked below—her lips were parted by the feelings which possessed her soul—her breath came and went regularly but inaudibly. She leaned over the precipice, and her dark hair hanging beside her face, gave relief to its fine lineaments, animated by such love as exceeds utterance. The stranger followed her eyes, and saw that her children were in the glen below ; then raising his eyes, exchanged with her affectionate looks of congratulation and delight. The boy was apparently eight years, the girl about two years younger. The beauty of their form and countenance was something so divine and strange, as overwhelmed the senses of the beholder like a delightful dream, with insupportable

ravishment. They were arrayed in a loose robe of
linen, through which the exquisite proportions of their form
appeared. Unconscious that they were observed, they did
not relinquish the occupation in which they were engaged.
They had constructed a little boat of the bark of trees, and
had given it sails of interwoven feathers, and launched it
on the water. They sate beside a white flat stone, on
which a small snake lay coiled, and when their work was
finished, they arose and called to the snake in melodious
tones, so that it understood their language. For it unwreathed its shining circles and crept to the boat, into
which no sooner had it entered, than the girl loosened the
band which held it to the shore, and it sailed away. Then
they ran round and round the little creek, clapping their
hands, and melodiously pouring out wild sounds, which the
snake seemed to answer by the restless glancing of his
neck. At last a breath of wind came from the shore, and
the boat changed its course, and was about to leave the
creek, which the snake perceived and leaped into the water,
and came to the little children's feet. The girl sang to it,
and it leaped into her bosom, and she crossed her fair hands
over it, as if to cherish it there. Then the boy answered
with a song, and it glided from beneath her hands and
crept towards him. While they were thus employed,
Maimuna looked up, and seeing her parents on the cliff,
ran to meet them up the steep path that wound around it;
and Abdallah, leaving his snake, followed joyfully.

LETTERS.

I.—To Thomas Hookham, Old Bond Street.

Lymouth, Barnstaple, Aug. 18*th,* 1812.

DEAR SIR,
            Your parcel arrived last night, for which I am much obliged. Before I advert to any other topic, I will explain the contents of mine in which this is enclosed. In the first place, I send you fifty copies of the Letter [to Lord Ellenborough]. I send you a copy of a work which I have procured from America, and which I am exceedingly anxious should be published. It developes, as you will perceive by the most superficial reading, the actual state of republicanized Ireland, and appears to me, above all things, calculated to remove the prejudices which have too long been cherished of that oppressed country. I enclose also two pamphlets which I printed and distributed whilst in Ireland some months ago (no bookseller daring to publish them). They were on that account attended with only partial success, and I request your opinion as to the probable result of publishing them with the annexed suggestions in one pamphlet, with an explanatory preface, in *London.* They would find their way to Dublin.

You confer on me an obligation, and involve a high compliment, by your advice. I shall, if possible, prepare a volume of essays, moral and *religious*, by November ; but, all my MSS. now being in Dublin, and from peculiar circumstances not immediately obtainable, I do not know whether I can. I enclose also, by way of specimen, all that I have written of a little poem begun since my arrival in England. I conceive I have matter enough for six more cantos. You will perceive that I have not attempted to temper my constitutional enthusiasm in that poem. Indeed, a poem is safe : the iron-souled Attorney-General would scarcely dare to attack [it]. The Past, the Present, and the Future, are the grand and comprehensive topics of this poem. I have not yet half exhausted the second of them.*

I shall take the liberty of retaining the two poems which you have sent me (Mr. Peacock's), and only regret that my powers are so circumscribed as to prevent me from becoming extensively useful to your friend. The poems abound with a genius, an information, the power and extent of which I admire, in proportion as I lament the object of their application. Mr. Peacock conceives that commerce is prosperity ; that the glory of the British flag is the happiness of the British people ; that George III., so far from having been a warrior and a tyrant, has been a patriot. To me it appears otherwise ; and I have rigidly accustomed myself not to be seduced by the loveliest eloquence or the sweetest strains to regard with intellectual toleration that which ought not to be tolerated by those who love liberty, truth, and virtue. I mean not to say that Mr. Peacock does not love them ; but I mean to say that he regards those means [as] instrumental to their progress, which I regard [as] instrumental to their destruction. (See *Genius of the Thames*, pp. 24, 26, 28, 76, 98.) At the same time, I am free to say that the poem appears to be far beyond mediocrity in genius and versification, and the conclusion of *Palmyra* the finest piece of poetry I ever read. I have not had time to read the *Philosophy of Melancholy*, and of course am only half acquainted with that genius and those powers whose application I should consider myself rash and impertinent in criticising, did I not conceive that frankness and justice demand it.

I should esteem it as a favour if you would present the enclosed letter to the Chevalier Lawrence. I have read his *Empire of the Nairs;* nay, have it. Perfectly and decidedly do I subscribe to the truth of the principles which it is designed to establish.

I hope you will excuse, nay, and doubt not but you will, the frankness I have used. Characters of our liberality are so

* The poem here alluded to is *Queen Mab.*—L. S.

wondrous rare, that the sooner they know each other, and the fuller and more complete that knowledge is, the better.

Dear Sir, permit me to remain.

Yours, very truly,

PERCY B. SHELLEY.

I am about translating an old French work, professedly by M. Mirabaud—not the famous one—*La Système de la Nature.* Do you know anything of it ?

———

II.—TO THOMAS HOOKHAM.

Tanyralt, Dec. 17th, 1812.

MY DEAR SIR,

You will receive the *Biblical Extracts* * in a day or two by the twopenny post. I confide them to the care of a person going to London. Would not Daniel J. Eaton publish them ? Could the question be asked him in any manner ?

I am also preparing a volume of minor poems, respecting whose publication I shall request your judgment, both as publisher and friend. A very obvious question would be— Will they sell or not ? Subjoined is a list of books which I wish you to send me very soon. I am determined to apply myself to a study that is hateful and disgusting to my very soul, but which is, above all studies, necessary for him who would be listened to as a mender of antiquated abuses. I mean that record of crimes and miseries, History. You see that the metaphysical works to which my heart hankers are not numerous in this list. One thing will you take care of for me ? that those standard and respectable works on history, etc., be of the cheapest possible editions. With respect to metaphysical works, I am less scrupulous.

Spinoza you may or may not be able to obtain. Kant is translated into Latin by some Englishman. I would prefer that the Greek classics should have Latin or English versions printed opposite. If not to be obtained thus, they must be sent otherwise.

Mrs. Shelley is attacking Latin with considerable resolution, and can already read many odes in Horace. She unites with her sister and myself in best wishes to yourself and brother.

Your very sincere friend,

P. B. SHELLEY.

———

* This work has never been published.—L. S.

III.—To Thomas Hookham.

February, 1813.

My Dear Sir,

I am boiling with indignation at the horrible injustice and tyranny of the sentence pronounced on Hunt and his brother ; and it is on this subject that I write to you. Surely the seal of abjectness and slavery is indelibly stamped upon the character of England.

Although I do not retract in the slightest degree my wish for a subscription for the widows and children of those poor men hung at York, yet this £1,000 which the Hunts are sentenced to pay is an affair of more consequence. Hunt is a brave, a good, and an enlightened man. Surely the public, for whom Hunt has done so much, will repay in part the great debt of obligation which they owe the champion of their liberties and virtues ; or are they dead, cold, stone-hearted, and insensible—brutalized by centuries of unremitting bondage ? However that may be, they surely may be excited into some slight acknowledgment of his merits. Whilst hundreds of thousands are sent to the tyrants of Russia, he pines in a dungeon, far from all that can make life desired.

Well, I am rather poor at present ; but I have £20 which is not immediately wanted. Pray, begin a subscription for the Hunts ; put down my name for that sum, and, when I hear that you have complied with my request, I will send it you.* Now, if there are any difficulties in the way of this scheme of ours, for the love of liberty and virtue, overcome them. Oh ! that I might wallow for one night in the Bank of England !

Queen Mab is finished and transcribed. I am now preparing the notes, which shall be long and philosophical. You will receive it with the other poems. I think that the whole should form one volume ; but of that we can speak hereafter.

As to the French *Encyclopédie*, it is a book which I am desirous—very desirous—of possessing ; and, if you could get me a few months' credit (being at present rather low in cash), I should very much desire to have it.

My dear sir, excuse the earnestness of the first part of my letter. I feel warmly on this subject, and I flatter myself that,

---

* The Hunts, however, refused to accept any subscription, public or private, and paid the fine entirely out of their own pockets.—L. S.

so long as your own independence and liberty remain uncompromised, you are inclined to second my desires.

Your very sincere friend,

P. B. SHELLEY.

P.S.—If no other way can be devised for this subscription, will you take the trouble on yourself of writing an appropriate advertisement for the papers, inserting, by way of stimulant, my subscription?

On second thoughts, I enclose the £20.

IV.—TO THOMAS JEFFERSON HOGG.

Bishopgate, September, 1815.

MY DEAR FRIEND,

Your letter has lain by me for the last week, reproaching me every day. I found it on my return from a water excursion on the Thames, the particulars of which will have been recounted in another letter. The exercise and dissipation of mind attached to such an expedition have produced so favourable an effect on my health, that my habitual dejection and irritability have almost deserted me, and I can devote six hours in the day to study without difficulty. I have been engaged lately in the commencement of several literary plans, which, if my present temper of mind endures, I shall probably complete in the winter. I have consequently deserted Cicero, or proceed but slowly with his philosophic dialogues. I have read the Oration for the poet Archias, and am only disappointed with its brevity.

I have been induced by one of the subjects which I am now pursuing to consult Bayle. I think he betrays great obliquity of understanding and coarseness of feeling. I have also read the four finest books of Lucan's *Pharsalia*—a poem, as it appears to me, of wonderful genius and transcending *Virgil*. Mary has finished the fifth book of the *Æneid*, and her progress in Latin is such as to satisfy my best expectations.

The east wind—the wind of autumn—is abroad, and even now the leaves of the forest are shattered at every gust. When may we expect you? September is almost passed, and October, the month of your promised return, is at hand, when we shall be happy to welcome you again to our fireside.

No events, as you know, disturb our tranquillity. Adieu.

Ever affectionately yours,

PERCY B. SHELLEY.

V.—To Thomas Love Peacock.

Hotel de Sécheron, Geneva, May 15, 1816.

After a journey of ten days, we arrived at Geneva. The journey, like that of life, was variegated with intermingled rain and sunshine, though these many showers were to me, as you know, April showers, quickly passing away, and foretelling the calm brightness of summer.

The journey was in some respects exceedingly delightful, but the prudential considerations arising out of the necessity of preventing delay, and the continual attention to pecuniary disbursements, detract terribly from the pleasure of all travelling schemes.

.   .   .   .

You live by the shores of a tranquil stream, among low and woody hills. You live in a free country, where you may act without restraint, and possess that which you possess in security ; and so long as the name of country and the selfish conceptions it includes shall subsist, England, I am persuaded, is the most free and the most refined.

Perhaps you have chosen wisely, but if I return and follow your example, it will be no subject of regret to me that I have seen other things. Surely there is much of bad and much of good, there is much to disgust and much to elevate, which he cannot have felt or known who has never passed the limits of his native land.

So long as man is such as he now is, the experience of which I speak will never teach him to despise the country of his birth—far otherwise, like Wordsworth, he will never know what love subsists between that and him until absence shall have made its beauty more heartfelt ; our poets and philosophers, our mountains and our lakes, the rural lanes and fields which are so especially our own, are ties which, until I become utterly senseless, can never be broken asunder.

These, and the memory of them, if I never should return, these and the affections of the mind, with which, having been once united, [they] are inseparable, will make the name of England dear to me for ever, even if I should permanently return to it no more.

But I suppose you did not pay the postage of this, expecting nothing but sentimental gossip, and I fear it will be long before

I play the tourist properly, I will, however, tell you that to come to Geneva we crossed the Jura branch of the Alps.

The mere difficulties of horses, high bills, postilions, and cheating, lying *aubergistes*, you can easily conceive ; fill up that part of the picture according to your own experience, and it cannot fail to resemble.

The mountains of Jura exhibit scenery of wonderful sublimity. Pine forests of impenetrable thickness, and untrodden, nay, inaccessible expanse, spreading on every side. Sometimes descending, they follow the route into the valleys, clothing the precipitous rocks, and struggling with knotted roots between the most barren clefts. Sometimes the road winds high into the regions of frost, and there these forests become scattered, and loaded with snow.

The trees in these regions are incredibly large, and stand in scattered clumps over the white wilderness. Never was scene more utterly desolate than that which we passed on the evening of our last day's journey.

The natural silence of that uninhabited desert contrasted strangely with the voices of the people who conducted us, for it was necessary in this part of the mountain to take a number of persons, who should assist the horses to force the chaise through the snow, and prevent it from falling down the precipice.

We are now at Geneva, where, or in the neighbourhood, we shall remain probably until the autumn. I may return in a fortnight or three weeks, to attend to the last exertions which L—— is to make for the settlement of my affairs ; of course I shall then see you ; in the meantime it will interest me to hear all that you have to tell of yourself.

P. B. SHELLEY.

VI.—To T. L. PEACOCK.

MEILLERIE, CLARENS, CHILLON, VEVAI, LAUSANNE.

Montalegre, near Coligni, Geneva, July 12th, [1816.]

IT is nearly a fortnight since I have returned from Vevai. This journey has been on every account delightful, but most especially, because then I first knew the divine beauty of Rousseau's imagination, as it exhibits itself in Julie. It is inconceivable what an enchantment the scene itself lends to those delineations, from which its own most touching charm arises. But I will give you an abstract of our voyage, which lasted eight days, and if you have a map of Switzerland, you can follow me.

We left Montalegre at half-past two on the 23rd of June. The lake was calm, and after three hours of rowing we arrived at Hermance, a beautiful little village, containing a ruined tower, built, the villagers say, by Julius Cæsar. There were three other towers similar to it, which the Genevese destroyed for their own fortifications in 1560. We got into the tower by a kind of window. The walls are immensely solid, and the stone of which it is built so hard, that it yet retained the mark of chisels. The boatman said, that this tower was once three times higher than it is now. There are two staircases in the thickness of the walls, one of which is entirely demolished, and the other half ruined, and only accessible by a ladder. The town itself, now an inconsiderable village inhabited by a few fishermen, was built by a queen of Burgundy, and reduced to its present state by the inhabitants of Berne, who burnt and ravaged everything they could find.

Leaving Hermance, we arrived at sunset at the village of Herni. After looking at our lodgings, which were gloomy and dirty, we walked out by the side of the lake. It was beautiful to see the vast expanse of these purple and misty waters broken by the craggy islets near to its slant and "beached margin." There were many fish sporting in the lake, and multitudes were collected close to the rocks to catch the flies which inhabited them.

On returning to the village, we sat on a wall beside the lake, looking at some children who were playing at a game like nine-pins. The children here appeared in an extraordinary way deformed and diseased. Most of them were crooked, and with enlarged throats; but one little boy had such exquisite grace in his mien and motions, as I never before saw equalled in a child. His countenance was beautiful for the expression with which it overflowed. There was a mixture of pride and gentleness in his eyes and lips, the indications of sensibility, which his education will probably pervert to misery or seduce to crime; but there was more of gentleness than of pride, and it seemed that the pride was tamed from its original wildness by the habitual exercise of milder feelings. My companion gave him a piece of money, which he took without speaking, with a sweet smile of easy thankfulness, and then with an embarrassed air turned to his play. All this might scarcely be; but the imagination surely could not forbear to breathe into the most inanimate forms, some likeness of its own visions, on such a serene and glowing evening, in this remote and romantic village, beside the calm lake that bore us hither.

On returning to our inn, we found that the servant had arranged our rooms, and deprived them of the greater portion of their former disconsolate appearance. They reminded my companion of Greece : it was five years, he said, since he had slept in such beds. The influence of the recollections excited by this circumstance on our conversation gradually faded, and I retired to rest with no unpleasant sensations, thinking of our journey to-morrow, and of the pleasure of recounting the little adventures of it when we return.

The next morning we passed Yvoire, a scattered village with an ancient castle, whose houses are interspersed with trees, and which stands at a little distance from Nerni, on the promontory which bounds a deep bay, some miles in extent. So soon as we arrived at this promontory, the lake began to assume an aspect of wilder magnificence. The mountains of Savoy, whose summits were bright with snow, descended in broken slopes to the lake : on high, the rocks were dark with pine forests, which become deeper and more immense, until the ice and snow mingle with the points of naked rock that pierce the blue air ; but below, groves of walnut, chestnut, and oak, with openings of lawny fields, attested the milder climate.

As soon as we had passed the opposite promontory, we saw the river Drance, which descends from between a chasm in the mountains, and makes a plain near the lake, intersected by its divided streams. Thousands of *besolets*, beautiful water-birds, like sea-gulls, but smaller, with purple on their backs, take their station on the shallows where its waters mingle with the lake. As we approached Evian, the mountains descended more precipitously to the lake, and masses of intermingled wood and rock overhung its shining spire.

We arrived at this town about seven o'clock, after a day which involved more rapid changes of atmosphere than I ever recollect to have observed before. The morning was cold and wet ; then an easterly wind, and the clouds hard and high ; then thunder showers, and wind shifting to every quarter ; then a warm blast from the south, and summer clouds hanging over the peaks, with bright blue sky between. About half an hour after we had arrived at Evian, a few flashes of lightning came from a dark cloud, directly over head, and continued after the cloud had dispersed. "Diespiter per pura tonantes egit equos : " a phenomenon which certainly had no influence on me, corresponding with that which it produced on Horace.

The appearance of the inhabitants of Evian is more wretched, diseased, and poor, than I ever recollect to have seen. The contrast indeed between the subjects of the King of Sardinia and the citizens of the independent republics of Switzerland, affords a powerful illustration of the blighting mischiefs of despotism, within the space of a few miles. They have mineral waters here, *eaux savonneuses*, they call them. In the evening we had some difficulty about our passports, but so soon as the syndic heard my companion's rank and name, he apologised for the circumstance. The inn was good. During our voyage, on the distant height of a hill, covered with pine-forests, we saw a ruined castle, which reminded me of those on the Rhine.

We left Evian on the following morning, with a wind of such violence as to permit but one sail to be carried. The waves also were exceedingly high, and our boat so heavily laden, that there appeared to be some danger. We arrived, however, safe at Meillerie, after passing with great speed mighty forests which overhung the lake, and lawns of exquisite verdure, and mountains with bare and icy points, which rose immediately from the summit of the rocks, whose bases were echoing to the waves.

We here heard that the Empress Maria Louisa had slept at Meillerie—before the present inn was built, and when the accommodations were those of the most wretched village—in remembrance of St. Preux. How beautiful it is to find that the common sentiments of human nature can attach themselves to those who are the most removed from its duties and its enjoyments, when Genius pleads for their admission at the gate of Power. To own them was becoming in the Empress, and confirms the affectionate praise contained in the regret of a great and enlightened nation. A Bourbon dared not even to have remembered Rousseau. She owed this power to that democracy which her husband's dynasty outraged, and of which it was, however, in some sort, the representative among the nations of the earth. This little incident shows at once how unfit and how impossible it is for the ancient system of opinions, or for any power built upon a conspiracy to revive them, permanently to subsist among mankind. We dined there, and had some honey, the best I have ever tasted, the very essence of the mountain flowers, and as fragrant. Probably the village derives its name from this production. Meillerie is the well-known scene of St. Preux's visionary exile ; but Meillerie is indeed enchanted ground, were Rousseau no magician. Groves of pine, chestnut, and walnut overshadow it; magnificent and unbounded forests to which England affords no parallel. In the midst of these woods are dells of lawny expanse, inconceivably verdant, adorned with a thousand of the rarest flowers, and odorous with thyme.

The lake appeared somewhat calmer as we left Meillerie, sailing close to the banks, whose magnificence augmented with the turn of every promontory. But we congratulated ourselves too soon : the wind gradually increased in violence, until it blew tremendously ; and, as it came from the remotest extremity of the lake, produced waves of a frightful height, and covered the whole surface with a chaos of foam. One of our boatmen, who was a dreadfully stupid fellow, persisted in holding the sail at a time when the boat was on the point of being driven under water by the hurricane. On discovering his error, he let it entirely go, and the boat for a moment refused to obey the helm ; in addition, the rudder was so broken as to render the management of it very difficult ; one wave fell in, and then another. My companion, an excellent swimmer, took off his coat, I did the same, and we sat with our arms crossed, every instant expecting to be swamped. The sail was, however, again held, the boat obeyed the helm, and still in imminent peril from the immensity of the waves, we arrived in a few minutes at a sheltered port, in the village of St. Gingoux.

I felt in this near prospect of death a mixture of sensations, among which terror entered, though but subordinately. My feelings would have been less painful had I been alone ; but I knew that my companion would have attempted to save me, and I was overcome with humiliation, when I thought that his life might have been risked to preserve mine. When we arrived at St. Gingoux, the inhabitants, who stood on the shore, unaccustomed to see a vessel as frail as ours, and fearing to venture at all on such a sea, exchanged looks of wonder and congratulation with our boatmen, who, as well as ourselves, were well pleased to set foot on shore.

St. Gingoux is even more beautiful than Meillerie ; the mountains are higher, and their loftiest points of elevation descend more abruptly to the lake. On high, the aerial summits still cherish great depths of snow in their ravines, and in the paths of their unseen torrents. One of the highest of these is called Roche de St. Julien, beneath whose pinnacles the forests become deeper and more extensive ; the chestnut gives a peculiarity to the scene, which is most beautiful, and will make a picture in my memory, distinct from all other mountain scenes which I have ever before visited.

As we arrived here early, we took a *voiture* to visit the mouth of the Rhone. We went between the mountains and the lake, under groves of mighty chestnut trees, beside perpetual streams, which are nourished by the snows above, and form stalactites on the rocks, over which they fall. We saw an immense chestnut tree, which had been overthrown by the hurricane of the morning. The place where the Rhone joins the lake was marked by a line of tremendous breakers ; the river is as rapid as when it leaves the lake, but is muddy and dark. We went about a league farther on the road to La Valais, and stopped at a castle called La Tour de Bouverie, which seems to be the frontier of Switzerland and Savoy, as we were asked for our passports, on the supposition of our proceeding to Italy.

On one side of the road was the immense Roche de St. Julien, which overhung it ; through the gateway of the castle we saw the snowy mountains of La Valais, clothed in clouds, and, on the other side, was the willowy plain of the Rhone, in a character of striking contrast with the rest of the scene, bounded by the dark mountains that overhang Clarens, Vevai, and the lake that rolls between. In the midst of the plain rises a little isolated hill, on which the white spire of a church peeps from among the tufted chestnut woods. We returned to St. Gingoux before sunset, and I passed the evening in reading *Julie.*

As my companion rises late, I had time before breakfast, on the ensuing morning, to hunt the waterfalls of the river that fall into the lake of St. Gingoux. The stream is, indeed, from the declivity over which it falls, only a succession of waterfalls, which roar over the rocks with a perpetual sound, and suspend their unceasing spray on the leaves and flowers that overhang and adorn its savage banks. The path that conducted along this river sometimes avoided the precipices of its shores, by leading through meadows ; sometimes threaded the base of the perpendicular and caverned rocks. I gathered in these meadows a nosegay of such flowers as I never saw in England, and which I thought more beautiful for that rarity.

On my return, after breakfast, we sailed for Clarens, determining first to see the three mouths of the Rhone, and then the Castle of Chillon ; the day was fine, and the water calm. We passed from the blue waters of the lake over the stream of the Rhone, which is rapid even at a great distance from its confluence with the lake ; the turbid waters mixed with those of the lake, but mixed with them unwillingly. (*See Nouvelle Hèloïse,*

Lettre 17, *Part.* 4). I read Julie all day ; an overflowing, as it now seems, surrounded by the scenes which it has so wonderfully peopled, of sublimest genius, and more than human sensibility. Meillerie, the Castle of Chillon, Clarens, the mountains of La Valais and Savoy, present themselves to the imagination as monuments of things that were once familiar, and of beings that were once dear to it. They were created indeed by one mind, but a mind so powerfully bright as to cast a shade of falsehood on the records that are called reality.

We passed on to the castle of Chillon, and visited its dungeons and towers. These prisons are excavated below the lake ; the principal dungeon is supported by seven columns, whose branching capitals support the roof. Close to the very walls, the lake is eight hundred feet deep ; iron rings are fastened to these columns, and on them were engraven a multitude of names, partly those of visitors, and partly doubtless of the prisoners, of whom now no memory remains, and who thus beguiled a solitude which they have long ceased to feel. One date was as ancient as 1670. At the commencement of the Reformation, and indeed long after that period, this dungeon was the receptacle of those who shook, or who denied the system of idolatry, from the effects of which mankind is even now slowly emerging.

Close to this long and lofty dungeon was a narrow cell, and beyond it one larger and far more lofty and dark, supported upon two unornamented arches. Across one of these arches was a beam, now black and rotten, on which prisoners were hung in secret. I never saw a monument more terrible of that cold and inhuman tyranny, which it had been the delight of man to exercise over man. It was indeed one of those many tremendous fulfilments which render the "pernicies humani generis" of the great Tacitus so solemn and irrefragable a prophecy. The gendarme, who conducted us over this castle, told us that there was an opening to the lake, by means of a secret spring, connected with which the whole dungeon might be filled with water before the prisoners could possibly escape !

We proceeded with a contrary wind to Clarens against a heavy swell. I never felt more strongly than on landing at Clarens, that the spirit of old times had deserted its once cherished habitation. A thousand times, thought I, have Julia and St. Preux walked on this terraced road, looking towards these mountains which I now behold ; nay, treading on the ground where I now tread. From the window of our lodging our landlady pointed out "le bosquet de Julie." At least the inhabitants of this village are impressed with an idea, that the persons of that romance had actual existence. In the evening we walked thither. It is, indeed, Julia's wood. The hay was making under the trees; the trees themselves were aged, but vigorous, and interspersed with younger ones, which are destined to be their successors, and in future years, when we are dead, to afford a shade to future worshippers of nature, who love the memory of that tenderness and peace of which this was the imaginary abode. We walked forward among the vineyards, whose narrow terraces overlook this affecting scene. Why did the cold maxims of the world compel me at this moment to repress the tears of melancholy transport which it would have been so sweet to indulge, immeasurably, even until the darkness of night had swallowed up the objects which excited them.

I forgot to remark, what indeed my companion remarked to me, that our danger from the storm took place precisely in the spot where Julie and her lover were nearly overset, and where St. Preux was tempted to plunge with her into the lake.

On the following day we went to see the castle of Clarens, a square strong house, with very few windows, surrounded by a double terrace that overlooks the valley, or rather the plain of Clarens. The road which conducted to it wound up the steep ascent through woods of walnut and chestnut. We gathered roses on the terrace, in the feeling that they might be the posterity of some planted by Julie's hand. We sent their dead and withered leaves to the absent.

We went again to "the bosquet de Julie," and found that the precise spot was now utterly obliterated, and a heap of stones marked the place where the little chapel had once stood. Whilst we were execrating the author of this brutal folly, our guide informed us that the land belonged to the convent of St. Bernard, and that this outrage had been committed by their orders. I knew before, that if avarice could harden the hearts of men, a system of prescriptive religion has an influence far more inimical to natural sensibility. I know that an isolated man is sometimes restrained by shame from outraging the venerable feelings arising out of the memory of genius, which once made nature even lovelier than itself; but associated man holds it as the very sacrament of his union to forswear all delicacy, all benevolence, all remorse; all that is true, or tender, or sublime.

We sailed from Clarens to Vevai. Vevai is a town more

94

beautiful in its simplicity than any I have ever seen. Its market-place, a spacious square interspersed with trees, looks directly upon the mountains of Savoy and La Valais, the lake, and the valley of the Rhone. It was at Vevai that Rousseau conceived the design of *Julie.*

From Vevai we came to Ouchy, a village near Lausanne. The coasts of the Pays de Vaud, though full of villages and vineyards, present an aspect of tranquillity and peculiar beauty which well compensates for the solitude which I am accustomed to admire. The hills are very high and rocky, crowned and interspersed with woods. Waterfalls echo from the cliffs, and shine afar. In one place we saw the traces of two rocks of immense size, which had fallen from the mountain behind. One of these lodged in a room where a young woman was sleeping, without injuring her. The vineyards were utterly destroyed in its path, and the earth torn up.

The rain detained us two days at Ouchy. We, however, visited Lausanne, and saw Gibbon's house. We were shown the decayed summer-house where he finished his History, and the old acacias on the terrace, from which he saw Mont Blanc, after having written the last sentence. There is something grand and even touching in the regret which he expresses at the completion of his task. It was conceived amid the ruins of the Capitol. The sudden departure of his cherished and accustomed toil must have left him, like the death of a dear friend, sad and solitary.

My companion gathered some acacia leaves to preserve in remembrance of him. I refrained from doing so, fearing to outrage the greater and more sacred name of Rousseau ; the contemplation of whose imperishable creations had left no vacancy in my heart for mortal things. Gibbon had a cold and unimpassioned spirit. I never felt more inclination to rail at the prejudices which cling to such a thing, than now that *Julie* and Clarens, Lausanne and the *Roman Empire*, compelled me to a contrast between Rousseau and Gibbon.

When we returned, in the only interval of sunshine during the day, I walked on the pier which the lake was lashing with its waves. A rainbow spanned the lake, or rather rested one extremity of its arch upon the water, and the other at the foot of the mountains of Savoy. Some white houses, I know not if they were those of Meillerie, shone through the yellow fire.

On Saturday, the 30th of June, we quitted Ouchy, and after two days of pleasant sailing arrived on Sunday evening at Montalegre.

VII.—To T. L. Peacock.

Geneva, July 17th, 1816.

My opinion of turning to one spot of earth and calling it our home, and of the excellencies and usefulness of the sentiments arising out of this attachment, has at length produced in me the resolution of acquiring this possession.

You are the only man who has sufficient regard for me to take an interest in the fulfilment of this design, and whose tastes conform sufficiently to mine to engage me to confide the execution of it to your discretion.

I do not trouble you with apologies for giving you this commission. I require only rural exertion, walks, and circuitous wanderings, some slight negotiations about the letting of a house—the superintendence of a disorderly garden, some palings to be mended, some books to be removed and set up.

I wish you would get all my books and all my furniture from Bishopgate, and all other effects appertaining to me. I have written to . . . to secure all that belongs to me there to you. I have written also to L—— to give up possession of the house on the 3rd of August.

When you have possessed yourself of all my affairs, I wish you to look out for a home for me and Mary and William, and the kitten, who is now *en pension.* I wish you to get an unfurnished house, with as good a garden as may be, near Windsor Forest, and take a lease of it for fourteen or twenty-one years. The house must not be too small. I wish the situation to resemble as nearly as possible that of Bishopgate, and should think that Sunning Hill, or Winkfield Plain, or the neighbourhood of Virginia Water would afford some possibilities.

Houses are now exceedingly cheap and plentiful ; but I entrust the whole of this affair entirely to your own discretion.

. . . .

My present intention is to return to England, and to make that most excellent of nations my perpetual resting place. I think it is extremely probable that we shall return next spring— perhaps before, perhaps after, but certainly we shall return.

On the motives and on the consequences of this journey, I reserve much explanation for some future winter walk or summer expedition. This much alone is certain, that before we return we shall have seen, and felt, and heard, a multiplicity of things which will haunt our talk and make us a little better worth knowing than we were before our departure.

If possible we think of descending the Danube in a boat, of visiting Constantinople and Athens, then Rome and the Tuscan cities, and returning by the south of France, always following great rivers. The Danube, the Po, the Rhone, and the Garonne ; rivers are not like roads, the work of the hands of man ; they imitate mind, which wanders at will over pathless deserts, and flows through nature's loveliest recesses, which are inaccessible to anything besides. They have the viler advantage also of affording a cheaper mode of conveyance.

This eastern scheme is one which has just seized on our imaginations. I fear that the detail of execution will destroy it, as all other wild and beautiful visions ; but at all events you will hear from us wherever we are, and to whatever adventures destiny enforces us.

Tell me in return all English news. What has become of my poem ?* I hope it has already sheltered itself in the bosom of its mother, Oblivion, from whose embraces no one could have been so barbarous as to tear it except me.

Tell me of the political state of England—its literature, of which when I speak Coleridge is in my thoughts ;—yourself, lastly your own employments, your historical labours.

I had written thus far when your letter to Mary dated the 8th arrived. What you say of Bishopgate of course modifies that part of this letter which relates to it. I confess I did not learn the destined ruin without some pain, but it is well for me perhaps that a situation requiring so large an expense should be placed beyond our hopes.

You must shelter my roofless Penates, dedicate some new temple to them, and perform the functions of a priest in my absence. They are innocent deities, and their worship neither sanguinary nor absurd.

Leave Mammon and Jehovah to those who delight in wickedness and slavery—their altars are stained with blood or polluted with gold, the price of blood. But the shrines of the Penates are good wood fires, or window frames intertwined with creeping plants ; their hymns are the purring of kittens, the hissing of kettles ; the long talks over the past and dead, the laugh of children, the warm wind of summer filling the quiet house, and the pelting storm of winter struggling in vain for entrance. In talking of the Penates, will you not liken me to Julius Cæsar dedicating a temple to Liberty ? As I have said in the former part of my letter, I trust entirely to your discretion on the

---

* Presumably *Alastor.*—H. B. F.

subject of a house. Certainly the Forest engages my preference, because of the sylvan nature of the place, and the beasts
with which it is filled. But I am not insensible to the beauties
of the Thames, and any extraordinary eligibility of situation
you mention in your letter would overwhelm our habitual
affection for the neighbourhood of Bishopgate.

Its proximity to the spot you have chosen is an argument
with us in favour of the Thames. Recollect, however, we are
now choosing a fixed, settled, eternal home, and as such its
internal qualities will affect us more constantly than those which
consist in the surrounding scenery, which whatever it may be at
first, will shortly be no more than the colours with which our
own habits shall invest it.

I am glad that circumstances do not permit the choice to be
my own. I shall abide by yours as others abide by the necessity
of their birth.

·   ·   ·   ·   ·   ·   ·

P. B. S.

VIII.—To T. L. Peacock.

ST. MARTIN—SERVOZ—CHAMOUNI—MONTANVERT—
MONT BLANC.

Hôtel de Londres, Chamouni, July 22nd, 1816.

Whilst you, my friend, are engaged in securing a home for
us, we are wandering in search of recollections to embellish it.
I do not err in conceiving that you are interested in details of all
that is majestic or beautiful in nature ; but how shall I describe
to you the scenes by which I am now surrounded ? To exhaust
the epithets which express the astonishment and the admiration—
the very excess of satisfied astonishment, where expectation
scarcely acknowledged any boundary, is this to impress upon
your mind the images which fill mine now, even till it overflow ?
I too have read the raptures of travellers ; I will be warned by
their example ; I will simply detail to you all that I can relate,
or all that, if related, would enable you to conceive, what we
have done or seen since the morning of the 20th, when we left
Geneva.

We commenced our intended journey to Chamouni at half-past
eight in the morning. We passed through the champain

country, which extends from Mont Saléve to the base of the higher Alps. The country is sufficiently fertile, covered with corn-fields and orchards, and intersected by sudden acclivities with flat summits. The day was cloudless and excessively hot, the Alps were perpetually in sight, and as we advanced, the mountains, which form their outskirts, closed in around us. We passed a bridge over a stream, which discharges itself into the Arve. The Arve itself, much swollen by the rains, flows constantly to the right of the road.

As we approached Bonneville through an avenue composed of a beautiful species of drooping poplar, we observed that the corn-fields on each side were covered with inundation. Bonneville is a neat little town, with no conspicuous peculiarity, except the white towers of the prison, an extensive building overlooking the town. At Bonneville the Alps commence, one of which, clothed by forests, rises almost immediately from the opposite bank of the Arve.

From Bonneville to Cluses the road conducts through a spacious and fertile plain, surrounded on all sides by mountains, covered like those of Meillerie with forests of intermingled pine and chestnut. At Cluses the road turns suddenly to the right, following the Arve along the chasm, which it seems to have hollowed for itself among the perpendicular mountains. The scene assumes here a more savage and colossal character : the valley becomes narrow, affording no more space than is sufficient for the river and the road. The pines descend to the banks, imitating, with their irregular spires, the pyramidal crags, which lift themselves far above the regions of forest into the deep azure of the sky, and among the white dazzling clouds. The scene, at the distance of half a mile from Cluses, differs from that of Matlock in little else than in the immensity of its proportions, and in its untameable inaccessible solitude, inhabited only by the goats which we saw browsing on the rocks.

Near Maglans, within a league of each other, we saw two waterfalls. They were no more than mountain rivulets, but the height from which they fell, at least of *twelve* hundred feet, made them assume a character inconsistent with the smallness of their stream. The first fell from the overhanging brow of a black precipice on an enormous rock, precisely resembling some colossal Egyptian statue of a female deity. It struck the head of the visionary image, and gracefully dividing there, fell from it in folds of foam more like to cloud than water, imitating a veil of the most exquisite woof. It then united, concealing the lower part of the statue, and hiding itself in a winding of its channel, burst into a deeper fall, and crossed our route in its path towards the Arve.

The other waterfall was more continuous and larger. The violence with which it fell made it look more like some shape which an exhalation had assumed, than like water, for it streamed beyond the mountain, which appeared dark behind it, as it might have appeared behind an evanescent cloud.

The character of the scenery continued the same until we arrived at St. Martin (called in the maps Sallanches), the mountains perpetually becoming more elevated, exhibiting at every turn of the road more craggy summits, loftier and wider extent of forests, darker and more deep recesses.

The following morning we proceeded from St. Martin, on mules, to Chamouni, accompanied by two guides. We proceeded, as we had done the preceding day, along the valley of the Arve, a valley surrounded on all sides by immense mountains, whose rugged precipices are intermixed on high with dazzling snow. Their bases were still covered with the eternal forests, which perpetually grew darker and more profound as we approached the inner regions of the mountains.

On arriving at a small village at the distance of a league from St. Martin, we dismounted from our mules, and were conducted by our guides to view a cascade. We beheld an immense body of water fall two hundred and fifty feet, dashing from rock to rock, and casting a spray which formed a mist around it, in the midst of which hung a multitude of sunbows, which faded or became unspeakably vivid, as the inconstant sun shone through the clouds. When we approached near to it, the rain of the spray reached us, and our clothes were wetted by the quick-falling but minute particles of water. The cataract fell from above into a deep craggy chasm at our feet, where, changing its character to that of a mountain stream, it pursued its course towards the Arve, roaring over the rocks that impeded its progress.

As we proceeded, our route still lay through the valley, or rather, as it had now become, the vast ravine, which is at once the couch and the creation of the terrible Arve. We ascended, winding between mountains, whose immensity staggers the imagination. We crossed the path of a torrent, which three days since had descended from the thawing snow, and torn the road away.

We dined at Servoz, a little village, where there are lead and copper mines, and where we saw a cabinet of natural curiosities, like those of Keswick and Bethgelert. We saw in this cabinet some chamois' horns, and the horns of an exceedingly rare animal called the bouquetin, which inhabits the deserts of snow to the south of Mont Blanc : it is an animal of the stag kind ; its horns weigh, at least, twenty-seven English pounds. It is inconceivable how so small an animal could support so inordinate a weight. The horns are of a very peculiar con- formation, being broad, massy, and pointed at the ends, and surrounded with a number of rings, which are supposed to afford an indication of its age : there were seventeen rings on the largest of these horns.

From Servoz three leagues remain to Chamouni.—Mont Blanc was before us—the Alps, with their innumerable glaciers on high all around,—closing in the complicated windings of the single vale—forests inexpressibly beautiful, but majestic in their beauty—intermingled beech and pine, and oak, overshadowed our road, or receded, whilst lawns of such verdure as I have never seen before, occupied these openings, and gradually became darker in their recesses. Mont Blanc was before us, but it was covered with cloud ; its base, furrowed with dreadful gaps, was seen above. Pinnacles of snow intolerably bright, part of the chain connected with Mont Blanc, shone through the clouds at intervals on high. I never knew—I never imagined—what mountains were before. The immensity of these aerial summits excited, when they suddenly burst upon the sight, a sentiment of ecstatic wonder, not unallied to mad- ness. And remember this was all one scene, it all pressed home to our regard and our imagination. Though it embraced a vast extent of space, the snowy pyramids which shot into the bright blue sky seemed to overhang our path ; the ravine, clothed with gigantic pines, and black with its depth below, so deep that the very roaring of the untameable Arve, which rolled through it, could not be heard above—all was as much our own, as if we had been the creators of such impressions in the minds of others as now occupied our own. Nature was the poet, whose harmony held our spirits more breathless than that of the divinest.

As we entered the valley of Chamouni, (which in fact, may be considered as a continuation of those which we have followed from Bonneville and Cluses,) clouds hung upon the mountains at the distance perhaps of 6000 feet from the earth, but so as effectually to conceal, not only Mont Blanc, but the other *aiguilles*, as they call them here, attached and subordinate to it. We were travelling along the valley, when suddenly we heard a sound as of the burst of smothered thunder rolling above ; yet there was something in the sound, that told us it could not be thunder. . Our guide hastily pointed out to us a part of the mountain opposite, from whence the sound came. It was an avalanche. We saw the smoke of its path among the rocks, and continued to hear at intervals the bursting of its fall. It fell on the bed of a torrent, which it displaced, and presently we saw its tawny-coloured waters also spread themselves over the ravine, which was their couch.

We did not, as we intended, visit the *Glacier des Bossons* to-day, although it descends within a few minutes' walk of the road, wishing to survey it at least when unfatigued. We saw this glacier, which comes close to the fertile plain, as we passed. Its surface was broken into a thousand unaccountable figures ; conical and pyramidical crystallizations, more than fifty feet in height, rise from its surface, and precipices of ice, of dazzling splendour, overhang the woods and meadows of the vale. This glacier winds upwards from the valley, until it joins the masses of frost from which it was produced above, winding through its own ravine like a bright belt flung over the black region of pines. There is more in all these scenes than mere magnitude of proportion : there is a majesty of outline ; there is an awful grace in the very colours which invest these wonderful shapes— a charm which is peculiar to them, quite distinct even from the reality of their unutterable greatness.

July 24.

Yesterday morning we went to the source of the Arveiron. It is about a league from this village ; the river rolls forth impetuously from an arch of ice, and spreads itself in many streams over a vast space of the valley, ravaged and laid bare by its inundations. The glacier by which its waters are nourished, overhangs this cavern and the plain, and the forests of pine which surround it, with terrible precipices of solid ice. On the other side rises the immense glacier of Montanvert, fifty miles in extent, occupying a chasm among mountains of inconceivable height, and of forms so pointed and abrupt, that they seem to pierce the sky. From this glacier we saw, as we sat on a rock, close to one of the streams of the Arveiron, masses of ice detach themselves from on high, and rush with a loud dull noise into the vale. The violence of their fall turned them into powder, which flowed over the rocks in imitation of water-falls, whose ravines they usurped and filled.

In the evening, I went with Ducrée, my guide, the only

tolerable person I have seen in this country, to visit the glacier of Bossons. This glacier, like that of Montanvert, comes close to the vale, overhanging the green meadows and the dark woods with the dazzling whiteness of its precipices and pinnacles, which are like spires of radiant crystal, covered with a net-work of frosted silver. These glaciers flow perpetually into the valley, ravaging in their slow but irresistible progress the pastures and the forests which surround them, performing a work of desolation in ages, which a river of lava might accomplish in an hour, but far more irretrievably; for where the ice has once descended, the hardiest plant refuses to grow; if even, as in some extraordinary instances, it should recede after its progress has once commenced. The glaciers perpetually move onward, at the rate of a foot each day, with a motion that commences at the spot where, on the boundaries of perpetual congelation, they are produced by the freezing of the waters which arise from the partial melting of the eternal snows. They drag with them, from the regions whence they derive their origin, all the ruins of the mountain, enormous rocks, and immense accumulations of sand and stones. These are driven onwards by the irresistible stream of solid ice; and when they arrive at a declivity of the mountain, sufficiently rapid, roll down, scattering ruin. I saw one of these rocks which had descended in the spring, (winter here is the season of silence and safety,) which measured forty feet in every direction.

The verge of a glacier, like that of Bossons, presents the most vivid image of desolation that it is possible to conceive. No one dares to approach it; for the enormous pinnacles of ice which perpetually fall, are perpetually reproduced. The pines of the forest, which bound it at one extremity, are overthrown and shattered, to a wide extent, at its base. There is something inexpressibly dreadful in the aspect of the few branchless trunks, which, nearest to the ice rifts, still stand in the uprooted soil. The meadows perish, overwhelmed with sand and stones. Within this last year, these glaciers have advanced three hundred feet into the valley. Saussure, the naturalist, says, that they have their periods of increase and decay: the people of the country hold an opinion entirely different; but as I judge, more probable. It is agreed by all, that the snow on the summit of Mont Blanc and the neighbouring mountains perpetually augments, and that ice, in the form of glaciers, subsists without melting in the valley of Chamouni during its transient and variable summer. If the snow which produces this glacier must augment, and the heat of the valley is no obstacle to the

perpetual existence of such masses of ice as have already
descended into it, the consequence is obvious ; the glaciers
must augment and will subsist, at least until they have overflowed
this vale.

I will not pursue Buffon's sublime but gloomy theory—that
this globe which we inhabit will, at some future period, be
changed into a mass of frost by the encroachments of the polar
ice, and of that produced on the most elevated points of the
earth. Do you, who assert the supremacy of Ahriman, imagine
him throned among these desolating snows, among these
palaces of death and frost, so sculptured in this their terrible
magnificence by the adamantine hand of necessity, and that he
casts around him, as the first essays of his final usurpation,
avalanches, torrents, rocks, and thunders, and above all these
deadly glaciers, at once the proof and symbols of his reign ;—
add to this, the degradation of the human species—who, in
these regions, are half deformed or idiotic, and most of whom
are deprived of anything that can excite interest or admiration.
This is part of the subject more mournful and less sublime ;
but such as neither the poet nor the philosopher should disdain
to regard.

This morning we departed, on the promise of a fine day, to
visit the glacier of Montanvert. In that part where it fills a
slanting valley, it is called the Sea of Ice. This valley is 950
toises, or 7600 feet, above the level of the sea. We had not
proceeded far before the rain began to fall, but we persisted
until we had accomplished more than half of our journey, when
we returned, wet through.

Chamouni, July 25th.

We have returned from visiting the glacier of Montanvert, or
as it is called the Sea of Ice, a scene in truth of dizzying
wonder. The path that winds to it along the side of a
mountain, now clothed with pines, now intersected with snowy
hollows, is wide and steep. The cabin of Montanvert is three
leagues from Chamouni, half of which distance is performed on
mules, not so sure-footed but that on the first day the one which
I rode fell in what the guides call a *mauvais pas*, so that I
narrowly escaped being precipitated down the mountain. We
passed over a hollow covered with snow, down which vast
stones are accustomed to roll. One had fallen the preceding
day, a little time after we had returned : our guides desired us
to pass quickly, for it is said that sometimes the least sound

will accelerate their descent.   We arrived at Montanvert, however, safe.

On all sides precipitous mountains, the abodes of unrelenting frost, surround this vale : their sides are banked up with ice and snow, broken, heaped high, and exhibiting terrific chasms. The summits are sharp and naked pinnacles, whose over-hanging steepness will not even permit snow to rest upon them. Lines of dazzling ice occupy here and there their perpendicular rifts, and shine through the driving vapours with inexpressible brilliance : they pierce the clouds like things not belonging to this earth.   The vale itself is filled with a mass of undulating ice, and has an ascent sufficiently gradual even to the remotest abysses of these horrible deserts.   It is only half a league (about two miles) in breadth, and seems much less.   It exhibits an appearance as if frost had suddenly bound up the waves and whirlpools of a mighty torrent.   We walked some distance upon its surface.   The waves are elevated about twelve or fifteen feet from the surface of the mass, which is intersected by long gaps of unfathomable depth, the ice of whose sides is more beautifully azure than the sky.   In these regions everything changes, and is in motion.   This vast mass of ice has one general progress, which ceases neither day nor night ; it breaks and bursts for ever : some undulations sink while others rise ; it is never the same.   The echo of rocks, or of the ice and snow which fall from their overhanging precipices, or roll from their aerial summits, scarcely ceases for one moment.   One would think that Mont Blanc, like the god of the Stoics, was a vast animal, and that the frozen blood for ever circulated through his stony veins.

We dined (M——, C——, and I) on the grass, in the open air, surrounded by this scene.   The air is piercing and clear. We returned down the mountain sometimes encompassed by the driving vapours, sometimes cheered by the sunbeams, and arrived at our inn by seven o'clock.

Montalegre, July 28*th.*

The next morning we returned through the rain to St. Martin. The scenery had lost something of its immensity, thick clouds hanging over the highest mountains ; but visitings of sunlight intervened between the showers, and the blue sky shone between the accumulated clouds of snowy whiteness which brought them ; the dazzling mountains sometimes glittered through a chasm of the clouds above our heads, and all the charm of its grandeur remained. We repassed *Pont Pellisier*, a wooden bridge over the Arve, and the ravine of the Arve. We repassed the pine forests which overhang the defile, the chateau of St. Michael ; a haunted ruin, built on the edge of a precipice, and shadowed over by the eternal forest. We repassed the vale of Servoz, a vale more beautiful, because more luxuriant, than that of Chamouni. Mont Blanc forms one of the sides of this vale also, and the other is inclosed by an irregular amphitheatre of enormous mountains, one of which is in ruins, and fell fifty years ago into the higher part of the valley ; the smoke of its fall was seen in Piedmont, and people went from Turin to investigate whether a volcano had not burst forth among the Alps. It continued falling many days, spreading, with the shock and thunder of its ruin, consternation into the neighbouring vales. In the evening we arrived at St. Martin. The next day we wound through the valley, which I have described before, and arrived in the evening at our home.

We have bought some specimens of minerals and plants, and two or three crystal seals, at Mont Blanc, to preserve the remembrance of having approached it. There is a cabinet of *histoire naturelle* at Chamouni, just as at Keswick, Matlock, and Clifton ; the proprietor of which is the very vilest specimen of that vile species of quack, that, together with the whole army of aubergistes and guides, and indeed the entire mass of the population, subsist on the weakness and credulity of travellers as leeches subsist on the sick. The most interesting of my purchases is a large collection of all the seeds of rare alpine plants, with their names written upon the outside of the papers that contain them. These I mean to colonise in my garden in England, and to permit you to make what choice you please from them. They are companions which the Celandine—the classic Celandine—need not despise ; they are as wild and more daring than he, and will tell him tales of things even as touching and sublime as the gaze of a vernal poet.

Did I tell you that there are troops of wolves among these mountains ? In the winter they descend into the valleys, which the snow occupies six months of the year, and devour everything that they can find out of doors. A wolf is more powerful than the fiercest and strongest dog. There are no bears in these regions. We heard, when we were in Lucerne, that they were occasionally found in the forests which surround that lake.

Adieu, S.

———

IX.—JOURNAL.

Geneva, Sunday, 18*th August,* 1816.

See Apollo's Sexton,* who tells us many mysteries of his trade. We talk of Ghosts. Neither Lord Byron nor M. G. L. seem to believe in them ; and they both agree, in the very face of reason, that none could believe in ghosts without believing in God. I do not think that all the persons who profess to discredit these visitations, really discredit them ; or, if they do in the daylight, are not admonished, by the approach of loneliness and midnight, to think more respectfully of the world of shadows.

Lewis recited a poem, which he had composed at the request of the Princess of Wales. The Princess of Wales, he premised, was not only a believer in ghosts, but in magic and witchcraft, and asserted, that prophecies made in her youth had been accomplished since. The tale was of a lady in Germany.

This lady, Minna, had been exceedingly attached to her husband, and they had made a vow that the one who died first should return after death to visit the other as a ghost. She was sitting one day alone in her chamber, when she heard an unusual sound of footsteps on the stairs. The door opened, and her husband's spectre, gashed with a deep wound across the forehead, and in military habiliments, entered. She appeared startled at the apparition ; and the ghost told her, that when he should visit her in future, she would hear a passing bell toll, and these words distinctly uttered close to her ear, "Minna, I am here." On inquiry, it was found that her husband had fallen in battle on the very day she was visited by the vision. The intercourse between the ghost and the woman continued for some time, until the latter laid aside all terror, and indulged herself in the affection which she had felt for him while living. One evening she went to a ball, and permitted her thoughts to be alienated by the attentions of a Florentine gentleman, more witty, more graceful, and more gentle, as it appeared to her, than any person she had ever seen. As he was conducting her through the dance, a death-bell tolled. Minna, lost in the fascination of the Florentine's attentions, disregarded, or did not hear the sound. A second peal, louder and more deep, startled the whole company, when Minna heard the ghost's accustomed whisper, and raising her eyes, saw in an

* Mr. G. Lewis, so named in *English Bards and Scotch Reviewers.*— M.S.

opposite mirror the reflection of the ghost, standing over her.
She is said to have died of terror.

Lewis told four other stories—all grim.

Thursday, 29th August.—We depart from Geneva, at nine in
the morning. The Swiss are very slow drivers; besides which
we have Jura to mount; we, therefore, go a very few posts
to-day. The scenery is very beautiful, and we see many magnificent views. We pass Les Rousses, which, when we crossed in
the spring, was deep in snow. We sleep at Morrez.

Friday, 30th.—We leave Morrez, and arrive in the evening at
Dôle, after a various day.

Saturday, 31st.—From Dôle we go to Rouvray, where we
sleep. We pass through Dijon; and, after Dijon, take a
different route than that which we followed on the two other
occasions. The scenery has some beauty and singularity in the
line of the mountains which surround the Val de Suzon. Low,
yet precipitous hills, covered with vines or woods, and with
streams, meadows, and poplars, at the bottom.

Sunday, September 1st.—Leave Rouvray, pass Auxerre, where
we dine; a pretty town, and arrive, at two o'clock, at Villeneuve
le Guiard.

Monday, 2nd.—From Villeneuve le Guiard, we arrive at Fontainebleau. The scenery around this palace is wild and even
savage. The soil is full of rocks, apparently granite, which on
every side break through the ground. The hills are low, but
precipitous and rough. The valleys, equally wild, are shaded
by forests. In the midst of this wilderness stands the palace.
Some of the apartments equal in magnificence anything that I
could conceive. The roofs are fretted with gold, and the
canopies of velvet. From Fontainebleau we proceed to Versailles, in the route towards Rouen. We arrive at Versailles at nine.

Tuesday, 3rd.—We saw the palace and gardens of Versailles
and le Grand et Petit Trianon. They surpass Fontainebleau.
The gardens are full of statues, vases, fountains, and colonnades.
In all that essentially belongs to a garden they are extraor-
dinarily deficient. The orangery is a stupid piece of expense.
There was one orange-tree, not apparently so old, sown in 1442.
We saw only the gardens and the theatre at the Petit Trianon.
The gardens are in the English taste, and extremely pretty.
The Grand Trianon was open. It is a summer palace, light,
yet magnificent. We were unable to devote the time it deserved
to the gallery of paintings here. There was a portrait of
Madame de la Vallière, the repentant mistress of Louis XIV.

She was melancholy, but exceedingly beautiful, and was represented as holding a skull, and sitting before a crucifix, pale, and with downcast eyes.

We then went to the great palace. The apartments are unfurnished ; but even with this disadvantage, are more magnificent than those of Fontainebleau. They are lined with marble of various colours, whose pedestals and capitals are gilt, and the ceiling is richly gilt with compartments of painting. The arrangement of these materials has in them, it is true, something effeminate and royal. Could a Grecian architect have commanded all the labour and money which was expended on Versailles, he would have produced a fabric which the whole world has never equalled. We saw the Hall of Hercules, the balcony where the King and the Queen exhibited themselves to the Parisian mob. The people who showed us through the palace, obstinately refused to say anything about the Revolution. We could not even find out in which chamber the rioters of the 10th August found the king. We saw the Salle d'Opéra, where are now preserved the portraits of the kings. There was the race of the house of Orleans, with the exception of Egalité, all extremely handsome. There was Madame de Maintenon, and beside her a beautiful little girl, the daughter of La Vallière. The pictures had been hidden during the Revolution. We saw the library of Louis XVI. The librarian had held some place in the ancient court near Marie-Antoinette. He returned with the Bourbons, and was waiting for some better situation. He showed us a book which he had preserved during the Revolution. It was a book of paintings, representing a tournament at the Court of Louis XIV. ; and it seemed that the present desolation of France, the fury of the injured people, and all the horrors to which they abandoned themselves, stung by their long sufferings, flowed naturally enough from expenditures so immense, as must have been demanded by the magnificence of this tournament. The vacant rooms of this palace imaged well the hollow show of monarchy. After seeing these things we departed towards Havre, and slept at Auxerre.

Wednesday, 4th.—We passed through Rouen, and saw the cathedral, an immense specimen of the most costly and magnificent gothic. The interior of the church disappoints. We saw the burial-place of Richard Cœur de Lion and his brother. The altar of the church is a fine piece of marble. Sleep at Yvetot.

Thursday, 5th.—We arrive at Havre, and wait for the packet —wind contrary.

S.

X.—To Mr. and Mrs. Leigh Hunt.

Great Marlow, 29th June 1817.

MY DEAR FRIENDS,

I performed my promise, and arrived here the night after I set off. Everybody up to this minute has been and continues well. I ought to have written yesterday, for to-day, I know not how, I have so constant a pain in my side, and such a depression of strength and spirits, as to make my holding the pen whilst I write to you an almost intolerable exertion. This, you know, with me is transitory. Do not mention that I am unwell to your nephew; for the advocate of a new system of diet is held bound to be invulnerable by disease, in the same manner as the sectaries of a new system of religion are held to be more moral than other people, or as a reformed parliament must at least be assumed as the remedy of all political evils. No one will change the diet, adopt the religion, or reform the parliament else.

Well, I am very anxious to hear how you get on, and I intreat Marianne to excite Hunt not to delay a minute in writing the necessary letters, and in informing me of the result. Kings are only to be approached through their ministers; who indeed, as Marianne shall know to her cost, if she don't take care, are responsible not only for all their commissions, but, a more dreadful responsibility, for all their *omissions*. And I know not who has a right to the title of king, if not according to the Stoics, he to whom the King of kings had delegated the prerogative of lord of the creation.

Let me know how Henry gets on, and make my best respects to your brother and Mrs. Hunt. Adieu.

Always most affectionately yours,

P. B. S.

XI.—To William Godwin.

Marlow, December 7th, 1817.

MY DEAR GODWIN,—To begin with the subject of most immediate interest: close with Richardson; and when I say this, what relief should I not feel from a thousand distressing emotions, if I could believe that he was in earnest in his offer! I have not heard from Longdill, though I wish earnestly for information.

My health has been materially worse. My feelings at intervals are of a deadly and torpid kind, or awakened to a state of such unnatural and keen excitement, that, only to instance the organ of sight, I find the very blades of grass and the boughs of distant trees present themselves to me with microscopical distinctness. Towards evening, I sink into a state of lethargy and inanimation, and often remain for hours on the sofa, between sleep and waking, a prey to the most painful irritability of thought. Such, with little intermission, is my condition. The hours devoted to study are selected with vigilant caution from among these periods of endurance. It is not for this that I think of travelling to Italy, even if I knew that Italy would relieve me. But I have experienced a decisive pulmonary attack ; and, although at present it has passed away without any very considerable vestige of its existence, yet this symptom sufficiently shows the true nature of my disease to be consumption. It is to my advantage that this malady is in its nature slow, and, if one is sufficiently alive to its advances, is susceptible of cure from a warm climate. In the event of its assuming any decided shape, it would be my *duty* to go to Italy without delay ; and it is only when that measure becomes an indispensable duty that, contrary to both Mary's feelings and to mine, as they regard you, I shall go to Italy. I need not remind you (besides the mere pain endured by the survivors) of the train of evil consequences which my death would cause to ensue. I am thus circumstantial and explicit, because you seem to have misunderstood me. It is not health, but life, that I should seek in Italy ; and that, not for my own sake—I feel that I am capable of trampling on all such weakness—but for the sake of those to whom my life may be a source of happiness, utility, security, and honour, and to some of whom my death might be all that is the reverse.

I ought to say I cannot persevere in the meat diet. What you say of Malthus fills me, as far as my intellect is concerned, with life and strength. I believe that I have a most anxious desire that the time should quickly come that, even so far as you are personally concerned, you should be tranquil and independent. But when I consider the intellectual lustre with which you clothe this world, and how much the last generation of mankind may be benefited by that light flowing forth without the intervention of one shadow, I am elevated above all thoughts which tend to you or myself as an individual, and become, by sympathy, part of those distant and innumerable minds to whom your writings must be present.

I meant to have written to you about *Mandeville* * solely;
but I was so irritable and weak that I could not write, although
I thought I had much to say. I have read *Mandeville*, but I
must read it again soon, for the interest is of that irresistible and
overwhelming kind, that the mind in its influence is like a cloud
borne on by an impetuous wind—like one breathlessly carried
forward, who has no time to pause or observe the causes of his
career. I think the power of *Mandeville* is inferior to nothing
you have done; and, were it not for the character of Falkland,†
no instance in which you have exerted that power of *creation*
which you possess beyond all contemporary writers, might
compare with it. Falkland is still alone; power is, in Falkland,
not, as in *Mandeville*, tumult hurried onward by the tempest,
but tranquillity standing unshaken amid its fiercest rage. But
Caleb Williams never shakes the deepest soul like *Mandeville.*
It must be said of the latter, you rule with a rod of iron. The
picture is never bright; and we wonder whence you drew the
darkness with which its shades are deepened, until the epithet
of tenfold might almost cease to be a metaphor. The *noun
smorfia* touches some cord within us with such a cold and
jarring power, that I started, and for some time could scarce
believe but that I was Mandeville, and that this hideous grin
was stamped upon my own face. In style and strength of
expression, *Mandeville* is wonderfully great, and the energy and
the sweetness of the sentiments scarcely to be equalled.
Clifford's character, as mere beauty, is a divine and soothing
contrast; and I do not think—if, perhaps, I except (and I
know not if I ought to do so) the speech of Agathon in the
Symposium of Plato—that there ever was produced a moral
discourse more characteristic of all that is admirable and
lovely in human nature—more lovely and admirable in itself—
than that of Henrietta to Mandeville, as he is recovering from
madness. Shall I say that, when I discovered that she was
pleading all this time sweetly for her lover, and when at last she
weakly abandoned poor Mandeville, I felt an involuntary
and, perhaps, an unreasonable pang? Adieu!

Always most affectionately yours,

P. S.

---

* Godwin's novel so called.—L. S.
† In the novel of *Caleb Williams.*—L. S.

XII.—To WILLIAM GODWIN.

Marlow, December 11th, 1817.

I have read and considered all that you say about my general powers, and the particular instance of the poem in which I have attempted to develop them. Nothing can be more satisfactory to me than the interest which your admonitions express. But I think you are mistaken in some points with regard to the peculiar nature of my powers, whatever be their amount. I listened with deference and self-suspicion to your censures of *Laon and Cythna;* but the productions of mine which you commend hold a very low place in my own esteem, and this reassured me, in some degree at least. The poem was produced by a series of thoughts which filled my mind with unbounded and sustained enthusiasm. I felt the precariousness of my life, and I resolved in this book to leave some records of myself. Much of what the volume contains was written with the same feeling, as real, though not so prophetic, as the communications of a dying man. I never presumed, indeed, to consider it anything approaching to faultless ; but, when I considered contemporary productions of the same apparent pretensions, I will own that I was filled with confidence. I felt that it was in many respects a genuine picture of my own mind. I felt that the sentiments were true, not assumed : and in this have I long believed—that my power consists in sympathy, and that part of imagination which relates to sentiment and contemplation. I am formed, if for anything not in common with the herd of mankind, to apprehend minute and remote distinctions of feeling, whether relative to external nature or the living beings which surround us, and to communicate the conceptions which result from considering either the moral or the material universe as a whole. . . . Yet, after all, I cannot but be conscious, in much of what I write, of an absence of that tranquillity which is the attribute and accompaniment of power. This feeling alone would make your most kind and wise admonitions, on the subject of the economy of intellectual force, valuable to me. And, if I live, or if I see any trust in coming years, doubt not but that I shall do something, whatever it might be, which a serious and earnest estimate of my powers will suggest to me, and which will be in every respect accommodated to their utmost limits.

XIII.—To Charles Ollier.

Marlow, December 11*th,* 1817.

DEAR SIR,
It is to be regretted that you did not consult your own safety and advantage (if you consider it connected with the non-publication of my book) before your declining the publication, after having accepted it, would have operated to so extensive and serious an injury to my views as now. The instances of abuse and menace which you cite were such as you expected, and were, as I conceived, prepared for. If not, it would have been just to me to have given them their due weight and consideration before. You foresaw, you foreknew, all that these people would say. You do your best to condemn my book before it is given forth, because you publish it, and then withdraw ; so that no other bookseller will publish it, because one has already rejected it. You must be aware of the great injury which you prepare for me. If I had never consulted your advantage, my book would have had a fair hearing. But now it is first published, and then the publisher, as if the author had deceived him as to the contents of the work—and as if the inevitable consequence of its publication would be ignominy and punishment—and as if none should dare to touch it or look at it —retracts, at a period when nothing but the most extraordinary and unforeseen circumstances can justify his retraction.

I beseech you to reconsider the matter, for your sake no less than for my own. Assume the high and secure ground of courage. The people who visit your shop, and the wretched bigot who gave his worthless custom to some other bookseller, are not the public. The public respect talent ; and a large portion of them are already undeceived with regard to the prejudices which my book attacks. You would lose some customers, but you would gain others. Your trade would be diverted into a channel more consistent with your own principles. Not to say that a publisher is in no wise pledged to all the opinions of his publications, or to any ; and that he may enter his protest with each copy sold, either against the truth or the discretion of the principles of the books he sells. But there is a much more important consideration in the case. You are, and have been to a certain extent, the publisher. I don't believe that, if the book was quietly and regularly published, the Government would touch anything of a character so refined, and so remote from the conceptions of the vulgar. They would hesitate before they invaded a member of the higher circles of the republic of letters. But, if they see us tremble, they will make no distinctions ; they will feel their strength. You might bring the arm of the law down upon us by flinching now. Directly these scoundrels see that people are afraid of them, they seize upon them and hold them up to mankind as criminals already convicted by their own fears. You lay yourself prostrate, and they trample on you. How glad they would be to seize on any connection of Hunt's by this most powerful of all their arms—the terrors and self-condemnation of their victim. Read all the *ex officio* cases, and see what reward booksellers and printers have received for their submission.

If, contrary to common sense and justice, you resolve to give me up, you shall receive no detriment from a connection with me in small matters, though you determine to inflict so serious a one on me in great. You shall not be at a farthing's expense. I shall still, so far as my powers extend, do my best to promote your interest. On the contrary supposition, even admitting you derive no benefit from the book itself—and it should be my care that you shall do so—I hold myself ready to make ample indemnity for any loss you may sustain.

There is one compromise you might make, though that would be still injurious to me. Sherwood and Neely wished to be the principal publishers. Call on them, and say that it was through a mistake that you undertook the principal direction of the book, as it was *my wish* that it should be theirs, and that I have written to you to that effect. This, if it would be advantageous to you, would be detrimental to, but not utterly destructive of, my views. To withdraw your name entirely, would be to inflict on me a bitter and undeserved injury.

Let me hear from you by return of post. I hope that you will be influenced to fulfil your engagement with me, and proceed with the publication, as justice to me, and, indeed, a well-under-stood estimate of your own interest and character, demand. I do hope that you will have too much regard to the well-chosen motto of your seal * to permit the murmurs of a few bigots to outweigh the serious and permanent considerations presented in this letter. To their remonstrances you have only to reply, " I did not write the book ; I am not responsible ; here is the author's address—state your objections to him. I do no more than sell it to those who inquire for it ; and, if they are not pleased with their bargain, the author empowers me to receive the book and to return the money." As to the interference of

* " In omnibus libertas."

Government, nothing is more improbable [than] that in any case it would be attempted ; but, if it should, it would be owing entirely to your perseverance in the groundless apprehensions which dictated your communication received this day, and conscious terror would be perverted into an argument of guilt.

I have just received a most kind and encouraging letter from Mr. Moore on the subject of my poem. I have the fairest chance of the public approaching my work with unbiassed and unperverted feeling : the fruit of reputation (and you know for *what purposes* I value it) is within my reach. It is for you, now you have been once named as publisher, and have me in your power, to blast all this, and to hold up my literary character in the eye of mankind as that of a proscribed and rejected outcast. And for no evil that I have ever done you, but in return for a preference which, although you falsely now esteem injurious to you, was solicited by Hunt, and conferred by me, as a source and a proof of nothing but kind intentions.

Dear Sir,
I remain your sincere well-wisher,
PERCY B. SHELLEY.

XIV.—TO LEIGH HUNT.

Lyons, March 22, 1818.

MY DEAR FRIEND,—Why did you not wake me that night before we left England, you and Marianne? I take this as rather an unkind piece of kindness in you ; but which, in consideration of the six hundred miles between us, I forgive.

We have journeyed towards the spring, that has been hastening to meet us from the south ; and though our weather was at first abominable, we have now warm sunny days, and soft winds, and a sky of deep azure, the most serene I ever saw. The heat in this city to-day, is like that of London in the midst of summer. My spirits and health sympathize in the change. Indeed, before I left London, my spirits were as feeble as my health, and I had demands on them which I found it difficult to supply. I have read "Foliage :" with most of the poems I am already familiar. What a delightful poem the "Nymphs" is ! It is truly *poetical*, in the intense and emphatic sense of the word. If six hundred miles were not between us, I should say what pity that *glib* was not omitted, and that the poem is not as faultless as it is beautiful. But, for fear I should *spoil* your next poem, I will not let slip a word upon the subject.

Give my love to Marianne and her sister, and tell Marianne she defrauded me of a kiss by not waking me when she went away, and that, as I have no better mode of conveying it, I must take the best, and ask you to pay the debt. When shall I see you again? Oh, that it might be in Italy! I confess that the thought of how long we may be divided makes me very melancholy. Adieu, my dear friends. Write soon.

Ever most affectionately yours,

P. B. S.

———

XV.—JOURNAL.

March 26, Thursday.

We travel towards the mountains, and begin to enter the valleys of the Alps. The country becomes covered again with verdure and cultivation, and white châteaux and scattered cottages among woods of old oak and walnut trees. The vines are here peculiarly picturesque; they are trellissed upon immense stakes, and the trunks of them are moss-covered and hoary with age. Unlike the French vines, which creep lowly on the ground, they form rows of interlaced bowers, which, when the leaves are green and the red grapes are hanging among those hoary branches, will afford a delightful shadow to those who sit upon the moss underneath. The vines are sometimes planted in the open fields, and sometimes among lofty orchards of apple and pear trees, the twigs of which were just becoming purple with the bursting blossoms.

We dined at Les Echelles, a village at the foot of the mountain of the same name, the boundaries of France and Savoy. Before this we had been stopped at Pont Bonvoisin, where the legal limits of the French and Sardinian territories are placed. We here heard that a Milanese had been sent back all the way to Lyons, because his passport was unauthorised by the Sardinian Consul, a few days before, and that we should be subjected to the same treatment. We, in respect to the character of our nation I suppose, were suffered to pass. Our books, however, were, after a long discussion, sent to Chambery, to be submitted to the censor; a priest, who admits nothing of Rousseau, Voltaire, etc., into the dominions of the King of Sardinia. All such books are burned.

After dinner we ascended Les Echelles, winding along a road cut through perpendicular rocks, of immense elevation, by

Charles Emanuel, Duke of Savoy, in 1582. The rocks, which cannot be less than a thousand feet in perpendicular height, sometimes overhang the road on each side, and almost shut out the sky. The scene is like that described in the Prometheus of Æschylus. Vast rifts and caverns in the granite precipices, wintry mountains with ice and snow above ; the loud sounds of unseen waters within the caverns, and walls of toppling rocks, only to be scaled as he describes, by the winged chariot of the ocean nymphs.

Under the dominion of this tyranny, the inhabitants of the fertile valleys, bounded by these mountains, are in a state of most frightful poverty and disease. At the foot of this ascent, were cut into the rocks in several places, stories of the misery of the inhabitants, to move the compassion of the traveller. One old man, lame and blind, crawled out of a hole in the rock, wet with the perpetual melting of the snows of above, and dripping like a shower-bath.

The country, as we descended to Chambery, continued as beautiful ; though marked with somewhat of a softer character than before : we arrived a little after night-fall.

XVI.—To T. L. Peacock.

Milan, April 1818.

My Dear P.,
    Behold us arrived at the end of our journey—that is, within a few miles of it—because we design to spend the summer on the shore of the lake of Como. Our journey was somewhat painful from the cold—and in no other manner interesting until we passed the Alps : of course I except the Alps themselves ; but no sooner had we arrived at Italy, than the loveliness of the earth and the serenity of the sky made the greatest difference in my sensations. I depend on these things for life ; for in the smoke of cities, and the tumult of human kind, and the chilling fogs and rain of our own country, I can hardly be said to live. With what delight did I hear the woman, who conducted us to see the triumphal arch of Augustus at Susa, speak the clear and complete language of Italy, though half unintelligible to me, after that nasal and abbreviated cacophony of the French ! A ruined arch of magnificent proportions in the Greek taste, standing in a kind of road of green lawn, overgrown with violets and primroses, and in the midst of stupendous mountains, and a *blonde* woman,

of light and graceful manners, something in the style of Fuseli's Eve, were the first things we met in Italy.

This city is very agreeable. We went to the opera last night —which is a most splendid exhibition. The opera itself was not a favourite, and the singers very inferior to our own. But the ballet, or rather a kind of melodrame or pantomimic drama, was the most splendid spectacle I ever saw. We have no Miss Melanie here—in every other respect, Milan is unquestionably superior. The manner in which language is translated into gesture, the complete and full effect of the whole as illustrating the history in question, the unaffected self-possession of each of the actors, even to the children, made this choral drama more impressive than I could have conceived possible. The story is *Othello*, and strange to say, it left no disagreeable impression.

I write, but I am not in the humour to write, and you must expect longer, if not more entertaining, letters soon—that is, in a week or so—when I am a little recovered from my journey. Pray tell us all the news with regard to our own offspring, whom we left at nurse in England ; as well as those of our friends. Mention Cobbett and politics too—and Hunt—to whom Mary is now writing—and particularly your own plans and yourself. You shall hear more of me and my plans soon. My health is improved already—and my spirits something—and I have many literary schemes, and one in particular—which I thirst to be settled that I may begin. I have ordered Ollier to send you some sheets, etc., for revision.

Adieu.—Always faithfully yours,
P. B. S.

———

XVII.—To T. L. PEACOCK.

Milan, April 20, 1818.

MY DEAR P.—I had no conception that the distance between us, measured by time in respect of letters, was so great. I have but just received yours dated the 2nd—and when you will receive mine written from this city somewhat later than the same date, I cannot know. I am sorry to hear that you have been obliged to remain at Marlow ; a certain degree of society being almost a necessity of life, particularly as we are not to see you this summer in Italy. But this, I suppose, must be as it is. I often revisit Marlow in thought. The curse of this life is, that whatever is once known, can never be unknown. You inhabit a spot, which before you inhabit it, is as indifferent to you as any other spot upon earth, and when, persuaded by some necessity, you think to leave it, you leave it not ; it clings to you—and with memories of things, which, in your experience of them, gave no such promise, revenges your desertion. Time flows on, places are changed ; friends who were with us, are no longer with us ; yet what has been seems yet to be, but barren and stripped of life. See, I have sent you a study for Nightmare Abbey.

Since I last wrote to you we have been to Como, looking for a house. This lake exceeds any thing I ever beheld in beauty, with the exception of the arbutus islands of Killarney. It is long and narrow, and has the appearance of a mighty river winding among the mountains and the forests. We sailed from the town of Como to a tract of country called the Tremezina, and saw the various aspects presented by that part of the lake. The mountains between Como and that village, or rather cluster of villages, are covered on high with chestnut forests (the eating chestnuts, on which the inhabitants of the country subsist in time of scarcity), which sometimes descend to the very verge of the lake, overhanging it with their hoary branches. But usually the immediate border of this shore is composed of laurel-trees, and bay, and myrtle, and wild fig-trees, and olives which grow in the crevices of the rocks, and overhang the caverns, and shadow the deep glens, which are filled with the flashing light of the waterfalls. Other flowering shrubs, which I cannot name, grow there also. On high, the towers of village churches are seen white among the dark forests. Beyond, on the opposite shore, which faces the south, the mountains descend less precipitously to the lake, and although they are much higher, and some covered with perpetual snow, there intervenes between them and the lake a range of lower hills, which have glens and rifts opening to the other, such as I should fancy the *abysses* of Ida or Parnassus. Here are plantations of olive, and orange, and lemon trees, which are now so loaded with fruit, that there is more fruit than leaves—and vineyards. This shore of the lake is one continued village, and the Milanese nobility have their villas here. The union of culture and the untameable profusion and loveliness of nature is here so close, that the line where they are divided can hardly be discovered. But the finest scenery is that of the Villa Pliniana ; so called from a fountain which ebbs and flows every three hours, described by the younger Pliny, which is in the court-yard. This house, which was once a magnificent palace, and is now half in ruins, we are endeavouring to procure. It is built upon terraces *raised from* the bottom of the lake, together with its garden, at the foot of a semicircular precipice, overshadowed by profound forests of chestnut. The scene from the colonnade is the most extraordinary, at once, and the most lovely that eye ever beheld. On one side is the mountain, and immediately over you are clusters of cypress-trees of an astonishing height, which seem to pierce the sky. Above you, from among the clouds, as it were, descends a waterfall of immense size, broken by the woody rocks into a thousand channels to the lake. On the other side is seen the blue extent of the lake and the mountains, speckled with sails and spires. The apartments of the Pliniana are immensely large, but ill furnished and antique. The terraces, which overlook the lake, and conduct under the shade of such immense laurel-trees as deserve the epithet of Pythian, are most delightful. We staid at Como two days, and have now returned to Milan, waiting the issue of our negotiation about a house. Como is only six leagues from Milan, and its mountains are seen from the cathedral.

This cathedral is a most astonishing work of art. It is built of white marble, and cut into pinnacles of immense height, and the utmost delicacy of workmanship, and loaded with sculpture. The effect of it, piercing the solid blue with those groups of dazzling spires, relieved by the serene depth of this Italian heaven, or by moonlight when the stars seem gathered among those clustered shapes, is beyond any thing I had imagined architecture capable of producing. The interior, though very sublime, is of a more earthly character, and with its stained glass and massy granite columns overloaded with antique figures, and the silver lamps, that burn for ever under the canopy of black cloth beside the brazen altar and the marble fretwork of the dome, give it the aspect of some gorgeous sepulchre. There is one solitary spot among those aisles, behind the altar, where the light of day is dim and yellow under the storied window, which I have chosen to visit, and read Dante there.

I have devoted this summer, and indeed the next year, to the composition of a tragedy on the subject of Tasso's madness, which I find upon inspection is, if properly treated, admirably dramatic and poetical. But, you will say, I have no dramatic talent; very true, in a certain sense; but I have taken the resolution to see what kind of a tragedy a person without dramatic talent could write. It shall be better morality than Fazio, and better poetry than Bertram, at least. You tell me nothing of Rhododaphne, a book from which, I confess, I expected extraordinary success.

Who lives in my house at Marlow now, or what is to be done with it? I am seriously persuaded that the situation was injurious to my health, or I should be tempted to feel a very absurd interest in who is to be its next possessor. The expense of our journey here has been very considerable—but we are now living at the hotel here, in a kind of Pension, which is very reasonable in respect of price, and when we get into a menage of our own, we have every reason to expect that we shall experience something of the boasted cheapness of Italy. The finest bread, made of a sifted flour, the whitest and the best I ever tasted, is only *one English penny* a pound. All the necessaries of life bear a proportional relation to this. But then the luxuries, tea, etc., are very dear,—and the English, as usual, are cheated in a way that is quite ridiculous, if they have not their wits about them. We do not know a single human being, and the opera, until last night, has been always the same. Lord Byron, we hear, has taken a house for three years, at Venice ; whether we shall see him or not, I do not know. The number of English who pass through this town is very great. They ought to be in their own country in the present crisis. Their conduct is wholly inexcusable. The people here, though inoffensive enough, seem both in body and soul a miserable race. The men are hardly men ; they look like a tribe of stupid and shrivelled slaves, and I do not think that I have seen a gleam of intelligence in the countenance of man since I passed the Alps. The women in enslaved countries are always better than the men ; but they have tight-laced figures, and figures and mien which express (O how unlike the French !) a mixture of the coquette and prude, which reminds me of the worst characteristics of the English.* Everything but humanity is in much greater perfection here than in France. The cleanliness and comfort of the inns is something quite English. The country is beautifully cultivated ; and altogether, if you can, as one ought always to do, find your happiness in yourself, it is a most delightful and commodious place to live in.

Adieu.—Your affectionate friend,

P. B. S.

---

* These impressions of Shelley, with regard to the Italians, formed in ignorance, and with precipitation, became altogether altered after a longer stay in Italy. He quickly discovered the extraordinary intelligence and genius of this wonderful people, amidst the ignorance in

XVIII.—To T. L. Peacock.

Milan, April 30th, 1818.

My Dear P.,—I write, simply to tell you, to direct your next letters, Poste Restante, Pisa. We have engaged a vetturino for that city, and leave Milan to-morrow morning. Our journey will occupy six or seven days.

Pisa is not six miles from the Mediterranean, with which ·it communicates by the river Arno. We shall pass by Piacenza, Parma, Bologna, the Apennines, and Florence, and I will endeavour to tell you something of these celebrated places in my next letter ; but I cannot promise much, for, though my health is much improved, my spirits are unequal, and seem to desert me when I attempt to write.

Pisa, they say, is uninhabitable in the midst of summer—we shall do, therefore, what other people do, retire to Florence, or to the mountains. But I will write to you our plans from Pisa, when I shall understand them better myself.

You may easily conjecture the motives which led us to forego the divine solitude of Como. To me, whose chief pleasure in life is the contemplation of nature, you may imagine how great is this loss.

Let us hear from you *once a fortnight.* Do not forget those who do not forget you.

Adieu.—Ever most sincerely yours,
P. B. Shelley.

XIX.—To T. L. Peacock.

Livorno, June 5, 1818.

My Dear P.,—We have not heard from you since the middle of April—that is, we have received only *one* letter from you since our departure from England. It necessarily follows that some accident has intercepted them. Address, in future, to the care of Mr. Gisborne, Livorno—and I shall receive them, though sometimes somewhat circuitously, yet always securely.

We left Milan on the 1st of May, and travelled across the Apennines to Pisa. This part of the Apennine is far less beauti-

which they are carefully kept by their rulers, and the vices, fostered by a religious system, which these same rulers have used as their most successful engine.—*M. S.*

ful than the Alps ; the mountains are wide and wild, and the whole scenery broad and undetermined—the imagination cannot find a home in it. The Plain of the Milanese, and that of Parma, is exquisitely beautiful—it is like one garden, or rather cultivated wilderness ; because the corn and the meadow-grass grow under high and thick trees, festooned to one another by regular festoons of vines. On the seventh day we arrived at Pisa, where we remained three or four days. A large disagreeable city, almost without inhabitants. We then proceeded to this great trading town, where we have remained a month, and which, in a few days, we leave for the Bagni di Lucca, a kind of watering-place situated in the depth of the Apennines ; the scenery surrounding this village is very fine.

We have made some acquaintance with a very amiable and accomplished lady, Mrs. Gisborne, who is the sole attraction in this most unattractive of cities. We had no idea of spending a month here, but she has made it even agreeable. We shall see something of Italian society at the Bagni di Lucca, where the most fashionable people resort.

When you send my parcel—which, by-the-by, I should request you to direct to Mr. Gisborne—I wish you could contrive to enclose the two last parts of Clarke's Travels, relating to Greece, and belonging to Hookham. You know I subscribe there still—and I have determined to take the Examiner here. You would, therefore, oblige me, by sending it weekly, after having read it yourself, to the same direction, and so clipped, as to make as little weight as possible.

I write as if writing where perhaps my letter may never arrive.

With every good wish from all of us,
Believe me most sincerely yours,
P. B. S.

XX.—To Mr. and Mrs. Gisborne,
(Leghorn).

You cannot know, as some friends in England do, to whom my silence is still more inexcusable, that this silence is no proof of forgetfulness or neglect.

I have, in truth, nothing to say, but that I shall be happy to see you again, and renew our delightful walks, until the desire or the duty of seeing new things hurries us away. We have spent a month here in our accustomed solitude, with the exception of one night at the Casino ; and the choice society of all ages, which I took care to pack up in a large trunk before we left England, have revisited us here. I am employed just now, having little better to do, in translating into my faint and inefficient periods, the divine eloquence of Plato's Symposium ; only as an exercise, or, perhaps, to give Mary some idea of the manners and feelings of the Athenians—so different on many subjects from that of any other community that ever existed.

We have almost finished Ariosto—who is entertaining and graceful, and *sometimes* a poet. Forgive me, worshippers of a more equal and tolerant divinity in poetry, if Ariosto pleases me less than you. Where is the gentle seriousness, the delicate sensibility, the calm and sustained energy, without which true greatness cannot be? He is so cruel, too, in his descriptions ; his most prized virtues are vices almost without disguise. He constantly vindicates and embellishes revenge in its grossest form ; the most deadly superstition that ever infested the world. How different from the tender and solemn enthusiasm of Petrarch—or even the delicate moral sensibility of Tasso, though somewhat obscured by an assumed and artificial style.

We read a good deal here—and we read little in Livorno. We have ridden, Mary and I, once only, to a place called Prato Fiorito, on the top of the mountains : the road, winding through forests, and over torrents, and on the verge of green ravines, affords scenery magnificently fine. I cannot describe it to you, but bid you, though vainly, come and see. I take great delight in watching the changes of the atmosphere here, and the growth of the thunder showers with which the noon is often over-shadowed, and which break and fade away towards evening into flocks of delicate clouds. Our fire-flies are fading away fast ; but there is the planet Jupiter, who rises majestically over the rift in the forest-covered mountains to the south, and the pale summer lightning which is spread out every night, at intervals, over the sky. No doubt Providence has contrived these things, that, when the fire-flies go out, the low-flying owl may see her way home.

Remember me kindly to the Machinista.

With the sentiment of impatience until we see you again in the autumn,

I am, yours most sincerely,

P. B. SHELLEY.

Bagni di Lucca, July 10*th,* 1818.

XXI.—To William Godwin.

Bagni di Lucca, July 25th, 1818.

MY DEAR GODWIN,—We have, as yet, seen nothing of Italy which marks it to us as the habitation of departed greatness. The serene sky, the magnificent scenery, the delightful productions of the climate, are known to us, indeed, as the same with those which the ancients enjoyed. But Rome and Naples —even Florence, are yet to see ; and if we were to write you at present a history of our impressions, it would give you no idea that we lived in Italy.

I am exceedingly delighted with the plan you propose of a book, illustrating the character of our calumniated republicans. It is precisely the subject for Mary ; and I imagine that, but for the fear of being excited to refer to books not within her reach, she would attempt to begin it here, and order the works you notice. I am unfortunately little skilled in English history, and the interest which it excites in me is so feeble, that I find it a duty to attain merely to that general knowledge of it which is indispensable.

Mary has just finished Ariosto with me, and, indeed, has attained a very competent knowledge of Italian. She is now reading Livy. I have been constantly occupied in literature, but have written little—except some translations from Plato, in which I exercised myself, in the despair of producing anything original. The Symposium of Plato seems to me one of the most valuable pieces of all antiquity ; whether we consider the intrinsic merit of the composition, or the light which it throws on the inmost state of manners and opinions among the ancient Greeks. I have occupied myself in translating this, and it has excited me to attempt an Essay upon the cause of some differences in sentiment between the Ancients and Moderns, with respect to the subject of the dialogue.

Two things give us pleasure in your last letters. The resumption of [*your answer to*] Malthus, and the favourable turn of the general election. If Ministers do not find some means, totally inconceivable to me, of plunging the nation in war, do you imagine that they can subsist ? Peace is all that a country, in the present state of England, seems to require, to afford it tranquillity and leisure for attempting some remedy ; not to the universal evils of all constituted society, but to the peculiar system of misrule under which those evils have been exasperated now. I wish that I had health or spirits that would enable me to enter into public affairs, or that I could find words to express all that I feel and know.

The modern Italians seem a miserable people, without sensibility, or imagination, or understanding. Their outside is polished, and an intercourse with them seems to proceed with much facility, though it ends in nothing, and produces nothing. The women are particularly empty, and though possessed of the same kind of superficial grace, are devoid of every cultivation and refinement. They have a ball at the Casino here every Sunday, which we attend—but neither Mary nor C—— dance. I do not know whether they refrain from philosophy or protestantism.

I hear that poor Mary's book is attacked most violently in the Quarterly Review. We have heard some praise of it, and among others, an article of Walter Scott's in Blackwood's Magazine.

If you should have anything to send us—and, I assure you, anything relating to England is interesting to us—commit it to the care of Ollier the bookseller, or P—— ; they send me a parcel every quarter.

My health is, I think, better, and, I imagine, continues to improve, but I still have busy thoughts and dispiriting cares, which I would shake off—and it is now summer.——A thousand good wishes to yourself and your undertakings.

Ever most affectionately yours,
P. B. S.

XXII.—To T. L. Peacock.

Bagni di Lucca, July 25th, 1818.

My Dear Peacock,—I received on the same day your letters marked 5 and 6, the one directed to Pisa and the other to Livorno, and I can assure you that they are most welcome visitors.

Our life here is as unvaried by any external events as if we were at Marlow, where a sail up the river or a journey to London makes an epoch. Since I last wrote to you, I have ridden over to Lucca, once with C., and once alone ; and we have been over to the Casino, where I cannot say there is anything remarkable, the women being far removed from anything which the most liberal annotator would interpret into beauty or grace, and apparently possessing no intellectual excellences to compensate the deficiency. I assure you it is well that it is so, for the dances, especially the waltz, are so exquisitely beautiful that it would be a little dangerous to the newly unfrozen senses and imaginations of us migrators from the neighbourhood of the pole. As it is—except in the dark—there can be no peril. The atmosphere here, unlike that of the rest of Italy, is diversified with clouds, which grow in the middle of the day, and sometimes bring thunder and lightning, and hail about the size of a pigeon's egg, and decrease towards the evening, leaving only those finely woven webs of vapour which we see in English skies, and flocks of fleecy and slowly moving clouds, which all vanish before sunset ; and the nights are for ever serene, and we see a star in the east at sunset—I think it is Jupiter—almost as fine as Venus was last summer ; but it wants a certain silver and aerial radiance, and soft yet piercing splendour, which belongs, I suppose, to the latter planet by virtue of its at once divine and female nature. I have forgotten to ask the ladies if Jupiter produces on them the same effect. I take great delight in watching the changes of the atmosphere. In the evening, Mary and I often take a ride, for horses are cheap in this country. In the middle of the day, I bathe in a pool or fountain, formed in the middle of the forests by a torrent. It is surrounded on all sides by precipitous rocks, and the waterfall of the stream which forms it falls into it on one side with perpetual dashing. Close to it, on the top of the rocks, are alders, and above the great chestnut trees, whose long and pointed leaves pierce the deep blue sky in strong relief. The water of this pool, which, to venture an unrythmical paraphrase, is "sixteen feet long and ten feet wide," is as transparent as the air, so that the stones and sand at the bottom seem, as it were, trembling in the light of noonday. It is exceedingly cold also. My custom is to undress, and sit on the rocks, reading Herodotus, until the perspiration has subsided, and then to leap from the edge of the rock into this fountain—a practice in the hot weather excessively refreshing. This torrent is composed, as it were, of a succession of pools and waterfalls, up which I sometimes amuse myself by climbing when I bathe, and receiving the spray over all my body, whilst I clamber up the moist crags with difficulty.

I have lately found myself totally incapable of original composition. I employed my mornings, therefore, in translating the *Symposium*, which I accomplished in ten days. Mary is now transcribing it, and I am writing a prefatory essay. I have been reading scarcely anything but Greek, and a little Italian poetry with Mary. We have finished *Ariosto* together —a thing I could not have done again alone.

Frankenstein seems to have been well received ; for although the unfriendly criticism of the *Quarterly* is an evil for it, yet it proves that it is read in some considerable degree, and it would be difficult for them with any appearance of fairness, to deny it merit altogether. Their notice of me, and their exposure of their true motives for not noticing my book, shows how well understood an hostility must subsist between me and them.

The news of the result of the elections, especially that of the metropolis, is highly inspiriting. I received a letter, of two day's later date, with yours, which announced the unfortunate termination of that of Westmoreland. I wish you had sent me some of the overflowing villainy of those apostates. What a pitiful wretch that Wordsworth ! That such a man should be such a poet ! I can compare him with no one but Simonides, that flatterer of the Sicilian tyrants, and at the same time the most natural and tender of lyric poets.

What pleasure would it have given me if the wings of imagination could have divided the space which divides us, and I could have been of your party. I have seen nothing so beautiful as Virginia Water in its kind. And my thoughts for ever cling to Windsor Forest, and the copses of Marlow, like the clouds which hang upon the woods of the mountains, low trailing, and though they pass away, leave their best dew when they themselves have faded. You tell me that you have finished *Nightmare Abbey.* I hope that you have given the enemy no quarter. Remember, it is a sacred war. We have found an excellent quotation in Ben Jonson's *Every Man in his Humour.* I will transcribe it, as I do not think you have these plays at Marlow.

"MATTHEW. O, it's only your fine humour, sir. Your true melancholy breeds your fine wit, sir. I am melancholy myself divers times, sir ; and then do I no more but take pen and paper presently, and overflow you half a score or a dozen of sonnets at a sitting.

"ED. KNOWELL. Sure, he utters them by the gross.

"STEPHEN. Truly, sir ; and I love such things out of measure.

"ED. KNOWELL. I' faith, better than in measure, I'll undertake.

"MATTHEW. Why, I pray you, sir, make use of my study; it's at your service.

"STEPHEN. I thank you, sir; I shall be bold, I warrant you. *Have you a stool there to be melancholy upon?*"—*Every Man in his Humour*, Act 3, scene i.

The last expression would not make a bad motto.*

————

XXIII.—TO T. L. PEACOCK.

Bagni de Lucca, Aug. 16th, 1818.

MY DEAR PEACOCK,

No new event has been added to my life since I wrote last: at least none which might not have taken place as well on the banks of the Thames as on those of the Serchio. I project soon a short excursion, of a week or so, to some of the neighbouring cities; and on the tenth of September we leave this place for Florence, when I shall at least be able to tell you of some things which you cannot see from your windows.

I have finished, by taking advantage of a few days of inspiration— which the *Cameonæ* have been lately very backward in conceding—the little poem I began sending to the press in London. Ollier will send you the proofs. Its structure is slight and airy; its subject ideal. The metre corresponds with the spirit of the poem, and varies with the flow of the feeling. I have translated, and Mary has transcribed the *Symposium*, as well as my poem; and I am proceeding to employ myself on a discourse, upon the subject of which the *Symposium* treats, considering the subject with reference to the difference of sentiments respecting it, existing between the Greeks and modern nations; a subject to be handled with that delicate caution which either I cannot or I will not practise in other matters, but which here I acknowledge to be necessary. Not that I have any serious thought of publishing either this discourse or the *Symposium*, at least till I return to England, when we may discuss the propriety of it.

Nightmare Abbey finished. Well, what is in it? What is it? You are as secret as if the priest of Ceres had dictated its sacred

* I adopted this passage as a second motto, omitting E. Knowell's interlocutions.—T. L. P.

pages. However, I suppose I shall see in time, when my second parcel arrives. My first is yet absent. By what conveyance did you send it?

Pray, are you yet cured of your Nympholepsy? 'Tis a sweet disease : but one as obstinate and dangerous as any—even when the Nymph is a Poliad. Whether such be the case or not, I hope your nympholeptic tale is not abandoned. The subject, if treated with a due spice of Bacchic fury, and interwoven with the manners and feelings of those divine people, who, in their very errors, are the mirrors, as it were, in which all that is delicate and graceful contemplates itself, is perhaps equal to any. What a wonderful passage there is in *Phædrus*—the beginning, I think, of one of the speeches of Socrates *—in praise of poetic madness, and in definition of what poetry is, and how a man becomes a poet. Every man who lives in this age and desires to write poetry, ought, as a preservative against the false and narrow systems of criticism which every poetical empiric vents, to impress himself with this sentence, if he would be numbered among those to whom may apply this proud, though sublime, expression of Tasso : "*Non c'è in mondo chi merita nome di creatore, che Dio ed il Poeta.*"

The weather has been brilliantly fine ; and now, among these mountains, the autumnal air is becoming less hot, especially in the mornings and evenings. The chestnut woods are now inexpressibly beautiful, for the chestnuts have become large, and add a new richness to the full foliage. We see here Jupiter in the east ; and Venus, I believe, as the evening star, directly after sunset.

More and better in my next. M. and C. desire their kind remembrances.—Most faithfully your friend,

P. B. SHELLEY.

* The passage alluded to is this :—"There are several kinds," says Socrates, "of divine madness. That which proceeds from the Muses taking possession of a tender and unoccupied soul, awakening, and bacchically inspiring it towards songs and other poetry, adorning myriads of ancient deeds, instructs succeeding generations, but he who, without this madness from the Muses, approaches the poetical gates, having persuaded himself that by art alone he may become sufficiently a poet, will find in the end his own imperfection, and see the poetry of his cold prudence vanish into nothingness before the light of that which has sprung from divine insanity."—*Platonis Phædrus*, p. 245 a.—T. L. P.

XXIV.—To Mrs. Shelley,

(BAGNI DI LUCCA).

Florence, Thursday, 11 *o'clock,*
20th August, 1818.

DEAREST MARY,

We have been delayed in this city four hours, for the Austrian minister's passport, but are now on the point of setting out with a vetturino, who engages to take us on the third day to Padua ; that is, we shall only sleep three nights on the road. Yesterday's journey, performed in a one-horse cab-riolet, almost without springs, over a rough road, was excessively fatiguing. —— suffered most from it ; for, as to myself, there are occasions in which fatigue seems a useful medicine, as I have felt no pain in my side—a most delightful respite—since I left you. The country was various and exceedingly beautiful. Sometimes there were those low cultivated lands, with their vine festoons, and large bunches of grapes just becoming purple —at others we passed between high mountains, crowned with some of the most majestic Gothic ruins I ever saw, which frowned from the bare precipices, or were half seen among the olive-copses. As we approached Florence, the country became cultivated to a very high degree, the plain was filled with the most beautiful villas, and, as far as the eye could reach, the mountains were covered with them ; for the plains are bounded on all sides by blue and misty mountains. The vines are here trailed on low trellisses of reeds interwoven into crosses to sup-port them, and the grapes, now almost ripe, are exceedingly abundant. You everywhere meet those teams of beautiful white oxen, which are now labouring the little vine-divided fields with their Virgilian ploughs and carts. Florence itself, that is the Lung' Arno (for I have seen no more), I think is the most beautiful city I have yet seen. It is surrounded with cultivated hills, and from the bridge which crosses the broad channel of the Arno, the view is the most animated and elegant I ever saw. You see three or four bridges, one apparently supported by Corinthian pillars, and the white sails of the boats, relieved by the deep green of the forest, which comes to the water's edge, and the sloping hills covered with bright villas on every side. Domes and steeples rise on all sides, and the cleanliness is remarkably great. On the other side there are the foldings of the Vale of Arno above ; first the hills of olive and vine, then the chestnut woods, and then the blue and misty pine forests, which invest the aerial Apennines, that fade in the distance. I have seldom seen a city so lovely at first sight as Florence.

We shall travel hence within a few hours, with the speed of the post, since the distance is 190 miles, and we are to do it in three days, besides the half day, which is somewhat more than sixty miles a-day. We have now got a comfortable carriage and two mules, and, thanks to Paolo, have made a very decent bargain, comprising everything, to Padua. I should say we had delightful fruit for breakfast—figs, very fine—and peaches, unfortunately gathered before they were ripe, whose smell was like what one fancies of the wakening of Paradise flowers.

Well, my dearest Mary, are you very lonely? Tell me truth, my sweetest, do you ever cry? I shall hear from you once at Venice, and once on my return here. If you love me you will keep up your spirits—and, at all events, tell me truth about it; for, I assure you, I am not of a disposition to be flattered by your sorrow, though I should be by your cheerfulness; and, above all, by seeing such fruits of my absence as were produced when we were at Geneva. What acquaintances have you made? I might have travelled to Padua with a German, who had just come from Rome, and had scarce recovered from a malaria fever, caught in the Pontine Marshes, a week or two since; and I conceded to ——'s entreaties—and to *your* absent suggestions, and omitted the opportunity, although I have no great faith in such species of contagion. It is not very hot— not at all too much so for my sensations; and the only thing that incommodes me are the gnats at night, who roar like so many humming-tops in one's ear—and I do not always find zanzariere. How is Willmouse and little Clara? They must be kissed for me—and you must particularly remember to speak my name to William, and see that he does not quite forget me before I return. Adieu—my dearest girl, I think that we shall soon meet. I shall write again from Venice. Adieu, dear Mary!

I have been reading the *Noble Kinsmen*, in which, with the exception of that lovely scene, to which you added so much grace in reading to me, I have been disappointed. The Jailor's Daughter is a poor imitation, and deformed. The whole story wants moral discrimination and modesty. I do not believe that Shakspeare wrote a word of it.

XXV.—To Mrs. Shelley,

(BAGNI DI LUCCA).

Venice, Sunday Morning.

My Dearest Mary,

We arrived here last night at twelve o'clock, and it is now before breakfast the next morning. I can, of course, tell you nothing of the future ; and though I shall not close this letter till post time, yet I do not know exactly when that is. Yet, if you are very impatient, look along the letter and you will see another date, when I may have something to relate.

I came from Padua hither in a gondola, and the gondoliere, among other things, without any hint on my part, began talking of Lord Byron. He said he was a *giovinotto Inglese*, with a *nome stravagante*, who lived very luxuriously, and spent great sums of money. This man, it seems, was one of Lord B.'s gondolieri. No sooner had we arrived at the inn, than the waiter began talking about him—said, that he frequented Mrs. H.'s *conversazioni* very much.

Our journey from Florence to Padua contained nothing which may not be related another time. At Padua, as I said, we took a gondola—and left it at three o'clock. These gondolas are the most beautiful and convenient boats in the world. They are finely carpeted and furnished with black, and painted black. The couches on which you lean are extraordinarily soft, and are so disposed as to be the most comfortable to those who lean or sit. The windows have at will either Venetian plate-glass flowered, or Venetian blinds, or blinds of black cloth to shut out the light. The weather here is extremely cold—indeed, sometimes very painfully so, and yesterday it began to rain. We passed the laguna in the middle of the night in a most violent storm of wind, rain, and lightning. It was very curious to observe the elements above in a state of such tremendous convulsion, and the surface of the water almost calm ; for these lagunas, though five miles broad, a space enough in a storm to sink a gondola, are so shallow that the boatmen drive the boat along with a pole. The sea-water, furiously agitated by the wind, shone with sparkles like stars. Venice, now hidden and now disclosed by the driving rain, shone dimly with its lights. We were all this while safe and comfortable. Well, adieu, dearest : I shall, as Miss Byron says, resume the pen in the evening.

Sunday Night, 5 *o'clock in the Morning.*

Well, I will try to relate everything in its order.

At three o'clock I called on Lord Byron: he was delighted to see me.

He took me in his gondola across the laguna to a long sandy island, which defends Venice from the Adriatic. When we disembarked, we found his horses waiting for us, and we rode along the sands of the sea, talking. Our conversation consisted in histories of his wounded feelings, and questions as to my affairs, and great professions of friendship and regard for me. He said, that if he had been in England at the time of the Chancery affair, he would have moved heaven and earth to have prevented such a decision. We talked of literary matters, his Fourth Canto, which, he says, is very good, and indeed repeated some stanzas of great energy to me. When we returned to his palace—which

. . . (*The letter is here torn*).

The Hoppners are the most amiable people I ever knew. They are much attached to each other, and have a nice little boy, seven months old. Mr. H. paints beautifully, and this excursion, which he has just put off, was an expedition to the Julian Alps, in this neighbourhood—for the sake of sketching, to procure winter employment. He has only a fortnight's leisure, and he has sacrificed two days of it to strangers whom he never saw before. Mrs. H. has hazel eyes and sweet looks.

(*Paper torn.*)

Well, but the time presses; I am now going to the banker's to send you money for the journey, which I shall address to you at Florence, Post-office. Pray come instantly to Este, where I shall be waiting in the utmost anxiety for your arrival. You can pack up directly you get this letter, and employ the next day on that. The day after, get up at four o'clock, and go post to Lucca, where you will arrive at six. Then take a vetturino for Florence to arrive the same evening. From Florence to Este is three days' vetturino journey—and you could not, I think, do it quicker by the post. Make Paolo take you to good inns, as we found very bad ones; and pray avoid the Tre Mori at Bologna, perche vi sono cose inespressibili nei letti. I do not think you can, but *try* to get from Florence to Bologna in one day. Do not take the post, for it is not much faster and very expensive. I have been obliged to decide on all these things without you : I have done for the best—and, my own beloved Mary, you must soon come and scold me if I have done wrong, and kiss me if I have done right—for, I am sure, I do not know which—and it is only the event that can show. We shall at least be saved the trouble of introduction, and have formed acquaintance with a lady who is so good, so beautiful, so angelically mild, that were she as wise too, she would be quite a——. Her eyes are like a reflection of yours. Her manners are like yours when you know and like a person.

Do you know, dearest, how this letter was written ? By scraps and patches, and interrupted every minute. The gondola is now come to take me to the banker's. Este is a little place, and the house found without difficulty. I shall count four days for this letter : one day for packing, four for coming here—and on the ninth or tenth day we shall meet.

I am too late for the post—but I send an express to overtake it. Enclosed is an order for fifty pounds. If you knew all that I had to do !—

Dearest love, be well, be happy, come to me—confide in your own constant and affectionate P. B. S.

Kiss the blue-eyed darlings for me, and do not let William forget me. Clara cannot recollect me.

XXVI.—To Mrs. Shelley,

(I CAPPUCCINI—ESTE).

Padua, mezzogiorno.

MY BEST MARY,—I found at Mount Selice a favourable opportunity for going to Venice, where I shall try to make some arrangement for you and little Ca. to come for some days, and shall meet you, if I do not write anything in the meantime, at Padua, on Thursday morning. C. says she is obliged to come to see the Medico, whom we missed this morning, and who has appointed as the only hour at which he can be at leisure—half-past eight in the morning. You must, therefore, arrange matters so that you should come to the Stella d'Oro a little before that hour—a thing to be accomplished only by setting out at half-past three in the morning. You will by this means arrive at Venice very early in the day, and avoid the heat, which might be bad for the babe, and take the time, when she would at least sleep great part of the time. C. will return with the return carriage, and I shall meet you, or send to you at Padua.

Meanwhile remember Charles the First—and do you be prepared to bring at least *some* of Myrra translated ; bring the book also with you, and the sheets of " Prometheus Unbound," which you will find numbered from one to twenty-six on the table of the pavilion. My poor little Clara, how is she to-day ? Indeed I am somewhat uneasy about her, and though I feel secure that there is no danger, it would be very comfortable to have some reasonable person's opinion about her. The Medico at Padua is certainly a man in great practice, but I confess he does not satisfy me.

Am I not like a wild swan to be gone so suddenly ? But, in fact, to set off alone to Venice required an exertion. I felt myself capable of making it, and I knew that you desired it. What will not be—if so it is destined—the lonely journey through that wide, cold France ? But we shall see.

Adieu, my dearest love—remember Charles I. and Myrra. I have been already imagining how you will conduct some scenes. The second volume of St. Leon begins with this proud and true sentiment—" There is nothing which the human mind can conceive, which it may not execute." Shakspeare was only a human being.

Adieu till Thursday.—Your ever affectionate

P. B. S.

XXVII.—To T. L. Peacock.

Este, October 8, 1818.

My Dear P.—I have not written to you, I think, for six weeks. But I have been on the point of writing many times, and have often felt that I had many things to say. But I have not been without events to disturb and distract me, amongst which is the death of my little girl. She died of a disorder peculiar to the climate. We have all had bad spirits enough, and I, in addition, bad health. I *intend* to be better soon : there is no malady, bodily or mental, which does not either kill or is killed.

We left the Baths of Lucca, I think, the day after I wrote to you—on a visit to Venice—partly for the sake of seeing the city. We made a very delightful acquaintance there with a Mr. and Mrs. Hoppner, the gentleman an Englishman, and the lady a Swissesse, mild and beautiful, and unprejudiced, in the best sense of the word. The kind attentions of these people

made our short stay at Venice very pleasant. I saw Lord
Byron, and really hardly knew him again; he is changed into
the liveliest and happiest-looking man I ever met. He read me
the first canto of his "Don Juan"—a thing in the style of
Beppo, but infinitely better, and dedicated to Southey, in ten or
a dozen stanzas, more like a mixture of wormwood and verdi-
grease than satire. Venice is a wonderfully fine city. The
approach to it over the laguna, with its domes and turrets
glittering in a long line over the blue waves, is one of the finest
architectural delusions in the world. It seems to have—and
literally it has—its foundations in the sea. The silent streets
are paved with water, and you hear nothing but the dashing of
the oars, and the occasional cries of the gondolieri. I heard
nothing of Tasso. The gondolas themselves are things of a
most romantic and picturesque appearance; I can only compare
them to moths of which a coffin might have been the chrysalis.
They are hung with black, and painted black, and carpeted
with grey; they curl at the prow and stern, and at the former
there is a nondescript beak of shining steel, which glitters at the
end of its long black mass.

The Doge's palace, with its library, is a fine monument of
aristocratic power. I saw the dungeons, where these scoundrels
used to torment their victims. They are of three kinds—one
adjoining the place of trial, where the prisoners destined to
immediate execution were kept. I could not descend into them,
because the day on which I visited it was festa. Another under
the leads of the palace, where the sufferers were roasted to
death or madness by the ardours of an Italian sun: and others
called the Pozzi—or wells, deep underneath, and communicating
with those on the roof by secret passages—where the prisoners
were confined sometimes half up to their middles in stinking
water. When the French came here, they found only one old
man in the dungeons, and he could not speak. But Venice,
which was once a tyrant, is now the next worst thing, a slave;
for in fact it ceased to be free or worth our regret as a nation,
from the moment that the oligarchy usurped the rights of the
people. Yet, I do not imagine that it was ever so degraded as
it has been since the French, and especially the Austrian yoke.
The Austrians take sixty per cent. in taxes, and impose free
quarters on the inhabitants. A horde of German soldiers, as
vicious and more disgusting than the Venetians themselves,
insult these miserable people. I had no conception of the
excess to which avarice, cowardice, superstition, ignorance,
passionless lust, and all the inexpressible brutalities which

degrade human nature, could be carried, until I had passed a few days at Venice.

We have been living this last month near the little town from which I date this letter, in a very pleasant villa which has been lent to us, and we are now on the point of proceeding to Florence, Rome, and Naples—at which last city we shall spend the winter, and return northwards in the spring. Behind us here are the Euganean hills, not so beautiful as those of the Bagni di Lucca, with Arquà, where Petrarch's house and tomb are religiously preserved and visited. At the end of our garden is an extensive Gothic castle, now the habitation of owls and bats, where the Medici family resided before they came to Florence. We see before us the wide flat plains of Lombardy, in which we see the sun and moon rise and set, and the evening star, and all the golden magnificence of autumnal clouds. But I reserve wonder for Naples.

I have been writing—and indeed have just finished the first act of a lyric and classical drama, to be called "Prometheus Unbound." Will you tell me what there is in Cicero about a drama supposed to have been written by Æschylus under this title.

I ought to say that I have just read Malthus in a French translation. Malthus is a very clever man, and the world would be a great gainer if it would seriously take his lessons into consideration, if it were capable of attending seriously to anything but mischief—but what on earth does he mean by some of his inferences? Yours ever faithfully, P. B. S.

I will write again from Rome and Florence—in better spirits, and to more agreeable purpose, I hope. You saw those beautiful stanzas in the fourth canto about the Nymph Egeria. Well, I did not whisper a word about nympholepsy : I hope you acquit me—and I hope you will not carry delicacy so far as to let this suppress anything nympholeptic.

XXVIII.—To T. L. Peacock.

Ferrara, Nov. 8th, 1818.

My Dear P.—We left Este yesterday on our journey towards Naples. The roads were particularly bad ; we have, therefore, accomplished only two days' journey, of eighteen and twenty-four miles each, and you may imagine that our horses must be tolerably good ones, to drag our carriage, with five people and heavy luggage, through deep and clayey roads. The roads are, however, good during the rest of the way.

The country is flat, but intersected by lines of wood, trellised with vines, whose broad leaves are now stamped with the redness of their decay. Every here and there one sees people employed in agricultural labours, and the plough, the harrow, or the cart, drawn by long teams of milk-white or dove-coloured oxen of immense size and exquisite beauty. This, indeed, might be the country of Pasiphaes. In one farm-yard I was shown sixty-three of these lovely oxen, tied to their stalls, in excellent condition. A farm-yard in this part of Italy is somewhat different from one in England. First, the house, which is large and high, with strange-looking unpainted window-shutters, generally closed, and dreary beyond conception. The farm-yard and out-buildings, however, are usually in the neatest order. The threshing-floor is not under cover, but like that described in the Georgics, usually flattened by a broken column, and neither the mole, nor the toad, nor the ant, can find on its area a crevice for their dwelling. Around it, at this season, are piled the stacks of the leaves and stalks of Indian corn, which has lately been threshed and dried upon its surface. At a little distance are vast heaps of many-coloured zucche or pumpkins, some of enormous size, piled as winter food for the hogs. There are turkeys, too, and fowls wandering about, and two or three dogs, who bark with a sharp hylactism. The people who are occupied with the care of these things seem neither ill-clothed nor ill-fed, and the blunt incivility of their manners has an English air with it, very discouraging to those who are accustomed to the impudent and polished lying of the inhabitants of the cities. I should judge the agricultural resources of this country to be immense, since it can wear so flourishing an appearance, in spite of the enormous discouragements which the various tyranny of the governments inflicts on it. I ought to say that one of the farms belongs to a Jew banker at Venice, another Shylock.—We arrived late at the inn where I now write ; it was once the palace of a Venetian nobleman, and is now an excellent inn. To-morrow we are going to see the sights of Ferrara.

————

Nov. 9.

We have had heavy rain and thunder all night ; and the former still continuing, we went in the carriage about the town. We went first to look at the cathedral, but the beggars very soon made us sound a retreat ; so, whether, as it is said, there is a copy of a picture of Michael Angelo there or no, I cannot tell. At the public library we were more successful. This is, indeed, a magnificent establishment, containing, as they say, 160,000 volumes. We saw some illuminated manuscripts of church music, with verses of the psalms interlined between the square notes, each of which consisted of the most delicate tracery, in colours inconceivably vivid. They belonged to the neighbouring convent of Certosa, and are three or four hundred years old ; but their hues are as fresh as if they had been executed yesterday. The tomb of Ariosto occupies one end of the largest saloon of which the library is composed ; it is formed of various marbles, surmounted by an expressive bust of the poet, and subscribed with a few Latin verses, in a less miserable taste than those usually employed for similar purposes. But the most interesting exhibitions here, are the writings, etc., of Ariosto and Tasso, which are preserved, and were concealed from the undistinguishing depredations of the French with pious care. There is the arm-chair of Ariosto, an old plain wooden piece of furniture, the hard seat of which was once occupied by, but has now survived its cushion, as it has its master. I could fancy Ariosto sitting in it ; and the satires in his own handwriting which they unfold beside it, and the old bronze inkstand, loaded with figures, which belonged also to him, assists the willing delusion. This inkstand has an antique, rather than an ancient appearance. Three nymphs lean forth from the circumference, and on the top of the lid stands a cupid, winged and looking up, with a torch in one hand, his bow in the other, and his quiver beside him. A medal was bound round the skeleton of Ariosto, with his likeness impressed upon it. I cannot say I think it had much native expression ; but, perhaps, the artist was in fault. On the reverse is a hand, cutting with a pair of scissors the tongue from a serpent, upraised from the grass, with this legend—*Pro bono malum.* What this reverse of the boasted Christian maxim means, or how it applies to Ariosto, either as a satirist or a serious writer, I cannot exactly tell. The cicerone attempted to explain, and it is to his commentary that my bewildering is probably due—if, indeed, the meaning be very plain, as is possibly the case.

There is here a manuscript of the entire Gerusalemme Liberata, written by Tasso's own hand ; a manuscript of some poems, written in prison, to the Duke Alfonso ; and the satires of Ariosto, written also by his own hand ; and the Pastor Fido of Guarini. The Gerusalemme, though it had evidently been copied and recopied, is interlined, particularly towards the end, with numerous corrections. The hand-writing of Ariosto is a small, firm, and pointed character, expressing, as I should say, a strong and keen, but circumscribed energy of mind ; that of Tasso is large, free, and flowing, except that there is a checked expression in the midst of its flow, which brings the letters into a smaller compass than one expected from the beginning of the word. It is the symbol of an intense and earnest mind, exceeding at times its own depth, and admonished to return by the chillness of the waters of oblivion striking upon its adventurous feet. You know I always seek in what I see the manifestation of something beyond the present and tangible object ; and as we do not agree in physiognomy, so we may not agree now. But my business is to relate my own sensations, and not to attempt to inspire others with them. Some of the MSS. of Tasso were sonnets to his persecutor, which contain a great deal of what is called flattery. If Alfonso's ghost were asked how he felt those praises now, I wonder what he would say. But to me there is much more to pity than to condemn in these entreaties and praises of Tasso. It is as a bigot prays to and praises his god, whom he knows to be the most remorseless, capricious, and inflexible of tyrants, but whom he knows also to be omnipotent. Tasso's situation was widely different from that of any persecuted being of the present day ; for, from the depth of dungeons, public opinion might now at length be awakened to an echo that would startle the oppressor. But then there was no hope. There is something irresistibly pathetic to me in the sight of Tasso's own hand-writing, moulding expressions of adulation and entreaty to a deaf and stupid tyrant, in an age when the most heroic virtue would have exposed its possessor to hopeless persecution, and—such is the alliance between virtue and genius—which unoffending genius could not escape.

We went afterwards to see his prison in the hospital of Sant' Anna, and I enclose you a piece of the wood of the very door, which for seven years and three months divided this glorious being from the air and the light which had nourished in him those influences which he has communicated, through his poetry, to thousands. The dungeon is low and dark, and when I say that it is really a very decent dungeon, I speak as one who has seen the prisons in the doges' palace of Venice. But it is a horrible abode for the coarsest and meanest thing that ever wore the shape of man, much more for one of delicate susceptibilities and elevated fancies. It is low, and has a grated window, and being sunk some feet below the level of the earth,

97

is full of unwholesome damps. In the darkest corner is a mark in the wall where the chains were rivetted, which bound him hand and foot. After some time, at the instance of some Cardinal, his friend, the Duke allowed his victim a fire-place; the mark where it was walled up yet remains.

At the entrance of the Liceo, where the library is, we were met by a penitent; his form was completely enveloped in a ghost-like drapery of white flannel; his bare feet were sandalled; and there was a kind of net-work visor drawn over his eyes, so as entirely to conceal his face. I imagine that this man had been adjudged to suffer this penance for some crime known only to himself and his confessor, and this kind of exhibition is a striking instance of the power of the Catholic superstition over the human mind. He passed, rattling his wooden box for charity.*

Adieu.—You will hear from me again before I arrive at Naples.

Yours, ever sincerely,
P. B. S.

XXIX.—To T. L. Peacock.

Bologna, Monday, Nov. 9th, 1818.

My Dear P.—I have seen a quantity of things here—churches, palaces, statues, fountains, and pictures; and my brain is at this moment like a portfolio of an architect, or a print-shop, or a commonplace-book. I will try to recollect something of what I have seen; for, indeed, it requires, if it will obey, an act of volition. First, we went to the cathedral, which contains nothing remarkable, except a kind of shrine, or rather a marble canopy, loaded with sculptures, and supported on four marble columns. We went then to a palace—I am sure I forget the name of it—where we saw a large gallery of pictures. Of course, in a picture gallery you see three hundred pictures you forget, for one you remember. I remember, however, an interesting picture by Guido, of the Rape of Proserpine, in which Proserpine casts back her languid and half-unwilling eyes, as it were, to the flowers she had left ungathered in the fields of Enna. There was an exquisitely executed piece of

---

* These penitents ask alms, to be spent in masses for the souls in purgatory.—*M. S.*

Correggio, about four saints, one of whom seemed to have a pet dragon in a leash. I was told that it was the devil who was bound in that style—but who can make anything of four saints? For what can they be supposed to be about? There was one painting, indeed, by this master, Christ beautified, inexpressibly fine. It is a half figure, seated on a mass of clouds, tinged with an ethereal, rose-like lustre; the arms are expanded; the whole frame seems dilated with expression; the countenance is heavy, as it were, with the weight of the rapture of the spirit; the lips parted, but scarcely parted, with the breath of intense but regulated passion; the eyes are calm and benignant; the whole features harmonised in majesty and sweetness. The hair is parted on the forehead, and falls in heavy locks on each side. It is motionless, but seems as if the faintest breath would move it. The colouring, I suppose, must be very good, if I could remark and understand it. The sky is of a pale aerial orange, like the tints of latest sunset; it does not seem painted around and beyond the figure, but everything seems to have absorbed, and to have been penetrated by its hues. I do not think we saw any other of Correggio, but this specimen gives me a very exalted idea of his powers.

We went to see heaven knows how many more palaces— Ranuzzi, Marriscalchi, Aldobrandi. If you want Italian names for any purpose, here they are; I should be glad of them if I was writing a novel. I saw many more of Guido. One, a Samson drinking water out of an ass's jaw-bone, in the midst of the slaughtered Philistines. Why he is supposed to do this, God, who gave him this jaw-bone, alone knows—but certain it is, that the painting is a very fine one. The figure of Samson stands in strong relief in the foreground, coloured, as it were, in the hues of human life, and full of strength and elegance. Round him lie the Philistines in all the attitudes of death. One prone, with the slight convulsion of pain just passing from his forehead, whilst on his lips and chin death lies as heavy as sleep. Another leaning on his arm, with his hand, white and motionless, hanging out beyond. In the distance, more dead bodies; and, still further beyond, the blue sea and the blue mountains, and one white and tranquil sail.

There is a Murder of the Innocents, also, by Guido, finely coloured, with much fine expression—but the subject is very horrible, and it seemed deficient in strength—at least, you require the highest ideal energy, the most poetical and exalted conception of the subject, to reconcile you to such a contemplation. There was a Jesus Christ crucified, by the same, very fine. One gets tired, indeed, whatever may be the conception and execution of it, of seeing that monotonous and agonised form for ever exhibited in one prescriptive attitude of torture. But the Magdalen, clinging to the cross with the look of passive and gentle despair beaming from beneath her bright flaxen hair, and the figure of St. John, with his looks uplifted in passionate compassion ; his hands clasped, and his fingers twisting themselves together, as it were, with involuntary anguish ; his feet almost writhing up from the ground with the same sympathy ; and the whole of this arrayed in colours of a diviner nature, yet most like nature's self. Of the contemplation of this one would never weary.

There was a "Fortune," too, of Guido ; a piece of mere beauty. There was the figure of Fortune on a globe, eagerly proceeding onwards, and Love was trying to catch her back by the hair, and her face was half turned towards him ; her long chestnut hair was floating in the stream of the wind, and threw its shadow over her fair forehead. Her hazel eyes were fixed on her pursuer, with a meaning look of playfulness, and a light smile was hovering on her lips. The colours which arrayed her delicate limbs were ethereal and warm.

But, perhaps, the most interesting of all the pictures of Guido which I saw was a Madonna Lattante. She is leaning over her child, and the maternal feelings with which she is pervaded are shadowed forth on her soft and gentle countenance, and in her simple and affectionate gestures—there is what an unfeeling observer would call a dulness in the expression of her face ; her eyes are almost closed ; her lip depressed ; there is a serious, and even a heavy relaxation, as it were, of all the muscles which are called into action by ordinary emotions : but it is only as if the spirit of love, almost insupportable from its intensity, were brooding over and weighing down the soul, or whatever it is, without which the material frame is inanimate and inexpressive.

There is another painter here, called Franceschini, a Bolognese, who, though certainly very inferior to Guido, is yet a person of excellent powers. One entire church, that of Santa Catarina, is covered by his works. I do not know whether any of his pictures have ever been seen in England. His colouring is less warm than that of Guido, but nothing can be more clear and delicate ; it is as if he could have dipped his pencil in the hues of some serenest and star-shining twilight. His forms have the same delicacy and aerial loveliness ; their eyes are all bright with innocence and love ;

their lips scarce divided by some gentle and sweet emotion. His winged children are the loveliest ideal beings ever created by the human mind. These are generally, whether in the capacity of Cherubim or Cupid, accessories to the rest of the picture ; and the underplot of their lovely and infantine play is something almost pathetic, from the excess of its unpretending beauty. One of the best of his pieces is an Annunciation of the Virgin :—the Angel is beaming in beauty ; the Virgin, soft, retiring, and simple.

We saw, besides, one picture of Raphael—St. Cecilia : this is in another and higher style ; you forget that it is a picture as you look at it ; and yet it is most unlike any of those things which we call reality. It is of the inspired and ideal kind, and seems to have been conceived and executed in a similar state of feeling to that which produced among the ancients those perfect specimens of poetry and sculpture which are the baffling models of succeeding generations. There is a unity and a perfection in it of an incommunicable kind. The central figure, St. Cecilia, seems rapt in such inspiration as produced her image in the painter's mind ; her deep, dark, eloquent eyes lifted up ; her chesnut hair flung back from her forehead—she holds an organ in her hands—her countenance, as it were, calmed by the depth of its passion and rapture, and penetrated throughout with the warm and radiant light of life. She is listening to the music of heaven, and, as I imagine, has just ceased to sing, for the four figures that surround her evidently point, by their attitudes, towards her ; particularly St. John, who, with a tender yet impassioned gesture, bends his countenance towards her, languid with the depth of his emotion. At her feet lie various instruments of music, broken and unstrung. Of the colouring I do not speak ; it eclipses nature, yet it has all her truth and softness.

We saw some pictures of Domenichino, Caracci, Albano, Guercino, Elizabetta Sirani. The two former—remember, I do not pretend to taste—I cannot admire. Of the latter there are some beautiful Madonnas. There are several of Guercino, which they said were very fine. I dare say they were, for the strength and complication of his figures made my head turn round. One, indeed, was certainly powerful. It was the representation of the founder of the Carthusians exercising his austerities in the desert, with a youth as his attendant, kneeling beside him at an altar ; on another altar stood a skull and a crucifix ; and around were the rocks and the trees of the wilderness. I never saw such a figure as this fellow.

His face was wrinkled like a dried snake's skin, and drawn in long hard lines : his very hands were wrinkled. He looked like an animated mummy. He was clothed in a loose dress of death-coloured flannel, such as you might fancy a shroud might be, after it had wrapt a corpse a month or two. It had a yellow, putrified, ghastly hue, which it cast on all the objects around, so that the hands and face of the Carthusian and his companion were jaundiced by this sepulchral glimmer. Why write books against religion, when we may hang up such pictures ? But the world either will not or cannot see. The gloomy effect of this was softened, and, at the same time, its sublimity diminished, by the figure of the Virgin and Child in the sky, looking down with admiration on the monk, and a beautiful flying figure of an angel.

Enough of pictures. I saw the place where Guido and his mistress, Elizabetta Sirani, were buried. This lady was poisoned at the age of twenty-six, by another lover, a rejected one of course. Our guide said she was very ugly, and that we might see her portrait to-morrow.

Well, good-night, for the present. " To-morrow to fresh fields and pastures new."

November 16.

To-day we first went to see those divine pictures of Raffael and Guido again, and then rode up the mountains, behind this city, to visit a chapel dedicated to the Madonna. It made me melancholy to see that they had been varnishing and restoring some of these pictures, and that even some had been pierced by the French bayonets. These are symptoms of the mortality of man, and perhaps, few of his works are more evanescent than paintings. Sculpture retains its freshness for twenty centuries —the Apollo and the Venus are as they were. But books are perhaps the only productions of man coeval with the human race. Sophocles and Shakspeare can be produced and reproduced for ever. But how evanescent are paintings ! and must necessarily be. Those of Zeuxis and Apelles are no more ; and perhaps they bore the same relation to Homer and Æschylus, that those of Guido and Raffael bear to Dante and Petrarch. There is one refuge from the despondency of this contemplation. The material part, indeed, of their works must perish, but they survive in the mind of man, and the remembrances connected with them are transmitted from generation to generation. The poet embodies them in his creations ; the systems of philosophers are modelled to gentleness by their contemplation ;

opinion, that legislator, is infected with their influence ; men become better and wiser ; and the unseen seeds are perhaps thus sown, which shall produce a plant more excellent even than that from which they fell. But all this might as well be said or thought at Marlow as Bologna.

The chapel of the Madonna is a very pretty Corinthian building—very beautiful indeed. It commands a fine view of these fertile plains, the many-folded Apennines, and the city. I have just returned from a moonlight walk through Bologna. It is a city of colonnades, and the effect of moonlight is strikingly picturesque. There are two towers here—one 400 feet high— ugly things, built of brick, which lean both different ways ; and with the delusion of moonlight shadows, you might almost fancy that the city is rocked by an earthquake. They say they were built so on purpose ; but I observe in all the plain of Lombardy the church towers lean.

Adieu.—God grant you patience to read this long letter, and courage to support the expectation of the next. Pray part them from the *Cobbetts* on your breakfast table—they may fight it out in your mind.

Yours ever most sincerely,
P. B. S.

XXX.—To T. L. Peacock.

Rome, November 20th, 1818.

My Dear P.—Behold me in the capital of the vanished world! But I have seen nothing except St. Peter's and the Vatican, overlooking the city in the mist of distance, and the Dogana, where they took us to have our luggage examined, which is built between the ruins of a temple to Antoninus Pius. The Corinthian columns rise over the dwindled palaces of the modern town, and the wrought cornice is changed on one side, as it were, to masses of wave-worn precipices, which overhang you, far, far on high.

I take advantage of this rainy evening, and before Rome has effaced all other recollections, to endeavour to recall the vanished scenes through which we have passed. We left Bologna, I forget on what day, and passing by Rimini, Fano, and Foligno, along the Via Flaminia and Terni, have arrived at Rome after ten days' somewhat tedious, but most interesting journey. The most remarkable things we saw were the Roman excavations in the rock, and the great waterfall of Terni. Of course you have heard that there are a Roman bridge and a triumphal arch at Rimini, and in what excellent taste they are built. The bridge is not unlike the Strand bridge, but more bold in proportion, and of course infinitely smaller. From Fano we left the coast of the Adriatic, and entered the Apennines, following the course of the Metaurus, the banks of which were the scene of the defeat of Asdrubal : and it is said (you can refer to the book) that Livy has given a very exact and animated description of it. I forget all about it, but shall look as soon as our boxes are opened. Following the river, the vale contracts, the banks of the river become steep and rocky, the forests of oak and ilex which overhang its emerald-coloured stream, cling to their abrupt precipices. About four miles from Fossombrone, the river forces for itself a passage between the walls and toppling precipices of the loftiest Apennines, which are here rifted to their base, and undermined by the narrow and tumultuous torrent. It was a cloudy morning, and we had no conception of the scene that awaited us. Suddenly the low clouds were struck by the clear north wind, and like curtains of the finest gauze, removed one by one, were drawn from before the mountain, whose heaven-cleaving pinnacles and black crags overhanging one another, stood at length defined in the light of day. The road runs parallel to the river, at a considerable height, and is carried through the mountain by a vaulted cavern. The marks of the chisel of the legionaries of the Roman Consul are yet evident.

We passed on day after day, until we came to Spoleto, I think the most romantic city I ever saw. There is here an aqueduct of astonishing elevation, which unites two rocky mountains—there is the path of a torrent below, whitening the green dell with its broad and barren track of stones, and above there is a castle, apparently of great strength and of tremendous magnitude, which overhangs the city, and whose marble bastions are perpendicular with the precipice. I never saw a more impressive picture ; in which the shapes of nature are of the grandest order, but over which the creations of man, sublime from their antiquity and greatness, seem to predominate. The castle was built by Belisarius or Narses, I forget which, but was of that epoch.

From Spoleto we went to Terni, and saw the cataract of the Velino. The glaciers of Montanvert and the source of the Arveiron is the grandest spectacle I ever saw. This is the second. Imagine a river sixty feet in breath, with a vast volume of waters, the outlet of a great lake among the higher mountains, falling 300 feet into a sightless gulf of snow-white vapour, which bursts up for ever and for ever, from a circle of black crags, and thence leaping downwards, made five or six other cataracts, each fifty or a hundred feet high, which exhibit, on a smaller scale, and with beautiful and sublime variety, the same appearances. But words (and far less could painting) will not express it. Stand upon the brink of the platform of cliff, which is directly opposite. You see the ever-moving water stream down. It comes in thick and tawny folds, flaking off like solid snow gliding down a mountain. It does not seem hollow within, but without it is unequal, like the folding of linen thrown carelessly down ; your eye follows it, and it is lost below ; not in the black rocks which gird it around, but in its own foam and spray, in the cloud-like vapours boiling up from below, which is not like rain, nor mist, nor spray, nor foam, but water, in a shape wholly unlike anything I ever saw before. It is as white as snow, but thick and impenetrable to the eye. The very imagination is bewildered in it. A thunder comes up from the abyss wonderful to hear ; for, though it ever sounds, it is never the same, but, modulated by the changing motion, rises and falls intermittingly ; we passed half an hour in one spot looking at it, and thought but a few minutes had gone by. The surrounding scenery is, in its kind, the loveliest and most sublime that can be conceived. In our first walk we passed through some olive groves, of large and ancient trees, whose hoary and twisted trunks leaned in all directions. We then crossed a path of orange trees by the river side, laden with their golden fruit, and came to a forest of ilex of a large size, whose evergreen and acorn-bearing boughs were intertwined over our winding path. Around, hemming in the narrow vale, were pinnacles of lofty mountains of pyramidical rock clothed with all evergreen plants and trees ; the vast pine, whose feathery foliage trembled in the blue air, the ilex, that ancestral inhabitant of these mountains, the arbutus with its crimson-coloured fruit and glittering leaves. After an hour's walk, we came beneath the cataract of Terni, within the distance of half a mile ; nearer you cannot approach, for the Nar, which has here its confluence with the Velino, bars the passage. We then crossed the river formed by this confluence, over a narrow natural bridge of rock, and saw the cataract from the platform I first mentioned. We think of spending some time next year near this waterfall. The inn is very bad, or we should have stayed there longer.

We came from Terni last night to a place called Nepi, and to-day arrived at Rome across the much-belied Campagna di

Roma, a place I confess infinitely to my taste. It is a flattering picture of Bagshot Heath. But then there are the Apennines on one side, and Rome and St. Peter's on the other, and it is intersected by perpetual dells clothed with arbutus and ilex.

Adieu—very faithfully yours, P. B. S.

———

XXXI.—To T. L. PEACOCK.

Naples, December 22, 1818.

MY DEAR P.—I have received a letter from you here, dated November 1st; you see the reciprocation of letters from the term of our travels is more slow. I entirely agree with what you say about Childe Harold. The spirit in which it is written is, if insane, the most wicked and mischievous insanity that ever was given forth. It is a kind of obstinate and self-willed folly, in which he hardens himself. I remonstrated with him in vain on the tone of mind from which such a view of things alone arises. For its real root is very different from its apparent one. Nothing can be less sublime than the true source of these expressions of contempt and desperation. The fact is, that first, the Italian women with whom he associates, are perhaps the most contemptible of all who exist under the moon—the most ignorant, the most disgusting, the most bigoted; countesses (who) smell so strongly of garlic that an ordinary Englishman cannot approach them. Well, L. B. is familiar with the lowest sort of these women, the people his gondolieri pick up in the streets. He associates with wretches who seem almost to have lost the gait and physiognomy of man, and who do not scruple to avow practices which are not only not named, but I believe seldom even conceived in England. He says he disapproves, but he endures. He is heartily and deeply discontented with himself; and contemplating in the distorted mirror of his own thoughts the nature and the destiny of man, what can he behold but objects of contempt and despair? But that he is a great poet, I think the address to Ocean proves. And he has a certain degree of candour while you talk to him, but unfortunately it does not outlast your departure. No, I do not doubt, and, for his sake, I ought to hope, that his present career must end soon in some violent circumstance.

Since I last wrote to you, I have seen the ruins of Rome, the Vatican, St. Peter's, and all the miracles of ancient and modern art contained in that majestic city. The impression of it exceeds anything I have ever experienced in my travels. We stayed there only a week, intending to return at the end of February, and devote two or three months to its mines of inexhaustible contemplation, to which period I refer you for a minute account of it. We visited the Forum and the ruins of the Coliseum every day. The Coliseum is unlike any work of human hands I ever saw before. It is of enormous height and circuit, and the arches built of massy stones are piled on one another, and jut into the blue air, shattered into the forms of overhanging rocks. It has been changed by time into the image of an amphitheatre of rocky hills overgrown by the wild olive, the myrtle, and the fig-tree, and threaded by little paths, which wind among its ruined stairs and immeasurable galleries : the copsewood overshadows you as you wander through its labyrinths, and the wild weeds of this climate of flowers bloom under your feet. The arena is covered with grass, and pierces, like the skirts of a natural plain, the chasms of the broken arches around. But a small part of the exterior circumference remains—it is exquisitely light and beautiful ; and the effect of the perfection of its architecture, adorned with ranges of Corinthian pilasters, supporting a bold cornice, is such as to diminish the effect of its greatness. The interior is all ruin. I can scarcely believe that when encrusted with Dorian marble and ornamented by columns of Egyptian granite, its effect could have been so sublime and so impressive as in its present state. It is open to the sky, and it was the clear and sunny weather of the end of November in this climate when we visited it, day after day.

Near it is the arch of Constantine, cr rather the arch of Trajan ; for the servile and avaricious senate of degraded Rome ordered, that the monument of his predecessor should be demolished in order to dedicate one to the Christian reptile, who had crept among the blood of his murdered family to the supreme power. It is exquisitely beautiful and perfect. The Forum is a plain in the midst of Rome, a kind of desert full of heaps of stones and pits ; and though so near the habitations of men, is the most desolate place you can conceive. The ruins of temples stand in and around it, shattered columns and ranges of others complete, supporting cornices of exquisite workman- ship, and vast vaults of shattered domes distinct with regular compartments, once filled with sculptures of ivory or brass. The temples of Jupiter, and Concord, and Peace, and the Sun, and the Moon, and Vesta, are all within a short distance of this spot. Behold the wrecks of what a great nation once dedicated to the abstractions of the mind! Rome is a city, as it were, of the dead, or rather of those who cannot die, and who survive the puny generations which inhabit and pass over the spot which they have made sacred to eternity. In Rome, at least in the first enthusiasm of your recognition of ancient time, you see nothing of the Italians. The nature of the city assists the delusion, for its vast and antique walls describe a circumference of sixteen miles, and thus the population is thinly scattered over this space, nearly as great as London. Wide wild fields are enclosed within it, and there are grassy lanes and copses winding among the ruins, and a great green hill, lonely and bare, which overhangs the Tiber. The gardens of the modern palaces are like wild woods of cedar, and cypress, and pine, and the neglected walks are overgrown with weeds. The English burying-place is a green slope near the walls, under the pyramidal tomb of Cestius, and is, I think, the most beautiful and solemn cemetery I ever beheld. To see the sun shining on its bright grass, fresh, when we first visited it, with the autumnal dews, and hear the whispering of the wind among the leaves of the trees which have overgrown the tomb of Cestius, and the soil which is stirring in the sun-warm earth, and to mark the tombs, mostly of women and young people who were buried there, one might, if one were to die, desire the sleep they seem to sleep. Such is the human mind, and so it peoples with its wishes vacancy and oblivion.

I have told you little about Rome ; but I reserve the Pantheon, and St. Peter's, and the Vatican, and Raffael, for my return. About a fortnight ago I left Rome, and Mary and C—— followed in three days, for it was necessary to procure lodgings here without alighting at an inn. From my peculiar mode of travelling I saw little of the country, but could just observe that the wild beauty of the scenery and the barbarous ferocity of the inhabitants progressively increased. On entering Naples, the first circumstance that engaged my attention was an assassination. A youth ran out of a shop, pursued by a woman with a bludgeon, and a man armed with a knife. The man overtook him, and with one blow in the neck laid him dead in the road. On my expressing the emotions of horror and indignation which I felt, a Calabrian priest, who travelled with me, laughed heartily, and attempted to quiz me, as what the English call a flat. I never felt such an inclination to beat any one. Heaven knows I have little power, but he saw that I looked extremely displeased, and was silent. This same man, a fellow of gigantic strength and stature, had expressed the most frantic terror of robbers on the road ; he cried at the sight of my pistol, and it had been with great difficulty that the joint exertions of myself and the vetturino had quieted his hysterics.

But external nature in these delightful regions contrasts with and compensates for the deformity and degradation of humanity. We have a lodging divided from the sea by the royal gardens, and from our windows we see perpetually the blue waters of the bay, forever changing, yet forever the same, and encompassed by the mountainous island of Capreæ, the lofty peaks which overhang Salerno, and the woody hill of Posilipo, whose pro- montories hide from us Misenum and the lofty isle Inarime,* which, with its divided summit, forms the opposite horn of the bay. From the pleasant walks of the garden we see Vesuvius ; a smoke by day and a fire by night is seen upon its summit, and the glassy sea often reflects its light or shadow. The climate is delicious. We sit without a fire, with the windows open, and have almost all the productions of an English sum- mer. The weather is usually like what Wordsworth calls " the first fine day of March ;" sometimes very much warmer, though perhaps it wants that " each minute sweeter than before," which gives an intoxicating sweetness to the awakening of the earth from its winter's sleep in England. We have made two excursions, one to Baiæ and one to Vesuvius, and we pro- pose to visit, successively, the islands, Pæstum, Pompeii, and Beneventum.

We set off an hour after sunrise one radiant morning in a little boat ; there was not a cloud in the sky, nor a wave upon the sea, which was so translucent that you could see the hollow caverns clothed with the glaucous sea-moss, and the leaves and branches of those delicate weeds that pave the unequal bottom of the water. As noon approached, the heat, and especially the light, became intense. We passed Posilipo, and came first to the eastern point of the bay of Puzzoli, which is within the great bay of Naples, and which again incloses that of Baiæ. Here are lofty rocks and craggy islets, with arches and portals of precipice standing in the sea, and enormous caverns, which echoed faintly with the murmur of the languid tide. This is called La Scuola di Virgilio. We then went directly across to the promontory of Misenum, leaving the precipitous island of Nesida on the right. Here we were conducted to see the Mare Morto, and the Elysian fields ; the spot on which Virgil places

* The ancient name of Ischia.—*M. S.*

the scenery of the Sixth Æneid. Though extremely beautiful, as a lake, and woody hills, and this divine sky must make it, I confess my disappointment. The guide showed us an antique cemetery, where the niches used for placing the cinerary urns of the dead yet remain. We then coasted the bay of Baiæ to the left, in which we saw many picturesque and interesting ruins ; but I have to remark that we never disembarked but we were disappointed—while from the boat the effect of the scenery was inexpressibly delightful. The colours of the water and the air breathe over all things here the radiance of their own beauty. After passing the bay of Baiæ, and observing the ruins of its antique grandeur standing like rocks in the transparent sea under our boat, we landed to visit lake Avernus. We passed through the cavern of the Sibyl (not Virgil's Sybil) which pierces one of the hills which circumscribe the lake, and came to a calm and lovely basin of water, surrounded by dark woody hills, and profoundly solitary. Some vast ruins of the temple of Pluto stand on a lawny hill on one side of it, and are reflected in its windless mirror. It is far more beautiful than the Elysian fields—but there are all the materials for beauty in the latter, and the Avernus was once a chasm of deadly and pestilential vapours. About half a mile from Avernus, a high hill, called Monte Novo, was thrown up by volcanic fire.

Passing onward we came to Pozzoli, the ancient Dicæarchea, where there are the columns remaining of a temple to Serapis, and the wreck of an enormous amphitheatre, changed, like the Coliseum, into a natural hill of the overteeming vegetation. Here also is the Solfatara, of which there is a poetical description in the Civil War of Petronius, beginning—"Est locus," and in which the verses of the poet are infinitely finer than what he describes, for it is not a very curious place. After seeing these things we returned by moonlight to Naples in our boat. What colours there were in the sky, what radiance in the evening star, and how the moon was encompassed by a light unknown to our regions !

Our next excursion was to Vesuvius. We went to Resina in a carriage, where Mary and I mounted mules, and C—— was carried in a chair on the shoulders of four men, much like a member of parliament after he has gained his election, and looking, with less reason, quite as frightened. So we arrived at the hermitage of San Salvador, where an old hermit, belted with rope, set forth the plates for our refreshment.

Vesuvius is, after the Glaciers, the most impressive exhibition of the energies of nature I ever saw. It has not the immeasurable greatness, the overpowering magnificence, nor, above all, the radiant beauty of the glaciers ; but it has all their character of tremendous and irresistible strength. From Resina to the hermitage you wind up the mountain, and cross a vast stream of hardened lava, which is an actual image of the waves of the sea, changed into hard black stone by enchantment. The lines of the boiling flood seem to hang in the air, and it is difficult to believe that the billows which seem hurrying down upon you are not actually in motion. This plain was once a sea of liquid fire. From the hermitage we crossed another wast stream of lava, and then went on foot up the cone—this is the only part of the ascent in which there is any difficulty, and that difficulty has been much exaggerated. It is composed of rocks of lava, and declivities of ashes ; by ascending the former and descending the latter, there is very little fatigue. On the summit is a kind of irregular plain, the most horrible chaos that can be imagined ; riven into ghastly chasms, and heaped up with tumuli of great stones and cinders, and enormous rocks blackened and calcined, which had been thrown from the volcano upon one another in terrible confusion. In the midst stands the conical hill from which volumes of smoke, and the fountains of liquid fire, are rolled forth forever. The mountain is at present in a slight state of eruption ; and a thick heavy white smoke is perpetually rolled out, interrupted by enormous columns of an impenetrable black bituminous vapour, which is hurled up, fold after fold, into the sky with a deep hollow sound, and fiery stones are rained down from its darkness, and a black shower of ashes fell even where we sat. The lava, like the glacier, creeps on perpetually, with a crackling sound as of suppressed fire. There are several springs of lava ; and in one place it rushes precipitously over a high crag, rolling down the half-molten rocks and its own overhanging waves ; a cataract of quivering fire. We approached the extremity of one of the rivers of lava ; it is about twenty feet in breadth and ten in height ; and as the inclined plane was not rapid, its motion was very slow. We saw the masses of its dark exterior surface detach themselves as it moved, and betray the depth of the liquid flame. In the day the fire is but slightly seen ; you only observe a tremulous motion in the air, and streams and fountains of white sulphurous smoke.

At length we saw the sun sink between Capreæ and Inarime, and, as the darkness increased, the effect of the fire became more beautiful. We were, as it were, surrounded by streams and cataracts of the red and radiant fire ; and in the midst, from the column of bituminous smoke shot up into the air, fell the vast masses of rock, white with the light of their intense heat, leaving behind them through the dark vapour trains of splendour. We descended by torch-light, and I should have enjoyed the scenery on my return, but they conducted me, I know not how, to the hermitage in a state of intense bodily suffering, the worst effect of which was spoiling the pleasure of Mary and C——. Our guides on the occasion were complete savages. You have no idea of the horrible cries which they suddenly utter, no one knows why; the clamour, the vociferation, the tumult. C—— in her palanquin suffered most from it; and when I had gone on before, they threatened to leave her in the middle of the road, which they would have done had not my Italian servant promised them a beating, after which they became quiet. Nothing, however, can be more picturesque than the gestures and the physiognomies of these savage people. And when, in the darkness of night, they unexpectedly begin to sing in chorus some fragments of their wild but sweet national music, the effect is exceedingly fine.

Since I wrote this, I have seen the museum of this city. Such statues! There is a Venus; an ideal shape of the most winning loveliness. A Bacchus, more sublime than any living being. A Satyr, making love to a youth: in which the expressed life of the sculpture, and the inconceivable beauty of the form of the youth, overcome one's repugnance to the subject. There are multitudes of wonderfully fine statues found in Herculaneum and Pompeii. We are going to see Pompeii the first day that the sea is waveless. Herculaneum is almost filled up; no more excavations are made; the king bought the ground and built a palace upon it.

You don't see much of Hunt. I wish you could contrive to see him when you go to town, and ask him what he means to answer to Lord Byron's invitation. He has now an opportunity, if he likes, of seeing Italy. What do you think of joining his party, and paying us a visit next year; I mean as soon as the reign of winter is dissolved? Write to me your thoughts upon this. I cannot express to you the pleasure it would give me to welcome such a party.

I have depression enough of spirits and not good health, though I believe the warm air of Naples does me good. We see absolutely no one here.

Adieu, my dear P——.
Affectionately your friend,
P. B. S.

XXXII.—To T. L. Peacock.

Naples, Jan. 26th, 1819.

My Dear P.—Your two letters arrived within a few days of each other, one being directed to Naples, and the other to Livorno. They are more welcome visitors to me than mine can be to you. I writing as from sepulchres, you from the habitations of men yet unburied ; though the sexton, Castlereagh, after having dug their grave, stands with his spade in his hand, evidently doubting whether he will not be forced to occupy it himself. Your news about the bank-note trials is excellent good. Do I not recognise in it the influence of Cobbett ? You don't tell me what occupies Parliament. I know you will laugh at my demand, and assure me that it is indifferent. Your pamphlet I want exceedingly to see. Your calculations in the letter are clear, but require much oral explanation. You know I am an infernal arithmetician. If none but me had contemplated "lucentemque globum lunæ, Titaniaque astra," the world would yet have doubted whether they were many hundred feet higher than the mountain tops.

In my accounts of pictures and things, I am more pleased to interest you than the many ; and this is fortunate, because, in the first place, I have no idea of attempting the latter, and if I did attempt it, I should assuredly fail. A perception of the beautiful characterises those who differ from ordinary men, and those who can perceive it would not buy enough to pay the printer. Besides, I keep no journal, and the only records of my voyage will be the letters I send you. The bodily fatigue of standing for hours in galleries exhausts me ; I believe that I don't see half that I ought, on that account. And then we know nobody ; and the common Italians are so sullen and stupid, it's impossible to get information from them. At Rome, where the people seem superior to any in Italy, I cannot fail to stumble on something more. O, if I had health, and strength, and equal spirits, what boundless intellectual improvement might I not gather in this wonderful country ! At present I write little else but poetry, and little of that. My first act of Prometheus is complete, and I think you would like it. I consider poetry very subordinate to moral and political science, and if I were well, certainly I would aspire to the latter; for I can conceive a great work, embodying the discoveries of all ages, and harmonising the contending creeds by which mankind have been ruled. Far from me is such an attempt, and I shall be content, by

98

exercising my fancy, to amuse myself, and perhaps some others, and cast what weight I can into the scale of that balance, which the Giant of Arthegall holds.

Since you last heard from me, we have been to see Pompeii, and are waiting now for the return of spring weather, to visit, first, Pæstum, and then the islands; after which we shall return to Rome. I was astonished at the remains of this city; I had no conception of anything so perfect yet remaining. My idea of the mode of its destruction was this:—First, an earthquake shattered it, and unroofed almost all its temples, and split its columns; then a rain of light small pumice-stones fell; then torrents of boiling water, mixed with ashes, filled up all its crevices. A wide, flat hill, from which the city was excavated, is now covered by thick woods, and you see the tombs and the theatres, the temples and the houses, surrounded by the uninhabited wilderness. We entered the town from the side towards the sea, and first saw two theatres; one more magnificent than the other, strewn with the ruins of the white marble which formed their seats and cornices, wrought with deep, bold sculpture. In the front, between the stage and the seats, is the circular space, occasionally occupied by the chorus. The stage is very narrow, but long, and divided from this space by a narrow enclosure parallel to it, I suppose for the orchestra. On each side are the consuls' boxes, and below, in the theatre at Herculaneum, were found two equestrian statues of admirable workmanship, occupying the same place as the great bronze lamps did at Drury Lane. The smallest of the theatres is said to have been comic, though I should doubt. From both you see, as you sit on the seats, a prospect of the most wonderful beauty.

You then pass through the ancient streets; they are very narrow, and the houses rather small, but all constructed on an admirable plan, especially for this climate. The rooms are built round a court, or sometimes two, according to the extent of the house. In the midst is a fountain, sometimes surrounded with a portico, supported on fluted columns of white stucco; the floor is paved with mosaic, sometimes wrought in imitation of vine leaves, sometimes in quaint figures, and more or less beautiful, according to the rank of the inhabitant. There were paintings on all, but most of them have been removed to decorate the royal museums. Little winged figures, and small ornaments of exquisite elegance, yet remain. There is an ideal life in the forms of these paintings of an incomparable loveliness, though most are evidently the work of very inferior artists. It

seems as if, from the atmosphere of mental beauty which surrounded them, every human being caught a splendour not his
own. In one house you see how the bed-rooms were managed :
—a small sofa was built up, where the cushions were placed ;
two pictures, one representing Diana and Endymion, the other
Venus and Mars, decorate the chamber ; and a little niche,
which contains the statue of a domestic god. The floor is composed of a rich mosaic of the rarest marbles, agate, jasper, and
porphyry ; it looks to the marble fountain and the snow-white
columns, whose entablatures strew the floor of the portico they
supported. The houses have only one storey, and the apartments, though not large, are very lofty. A great advantage
results from this, wholly unknown in our cities. The public
buildings, whose ruins are now forests, as it were, of white fluted
columns, and which then supported entablatures, loaded with
sculptures, were seen on all sides over the roofs of the houses.
This was the excellence of the ancients. Their private expenses
were comparatively moderate ; the dwelling of one of the chief
senators of Pompeii is elegant indeed, and adorned with most
beautiful specimens of art, but small. But their public buildings
are everywhere marked by the bold and grand designs of an
unsparing magnificence. In the little town of Pompeii, (it contained about twenty thousand inhabitants,) it is wonderful to see
the number and the grandeur of their public buildings. Another
advantage, too, is that, in the present case, the glorious scenery
around is not shut out, and that, unlike the inhabitants of the
Cimmerian ravines of modern cities, the ancient Pompeians
could contemplate the clouds and the lamps of heaven ; could
see the moon rise high behind Vesuvius, and the sun set in the
sea, tremulous with an atmosphere of golden vapour, between
Inarime and Misenum.

We next saw the temples. Of the temple of Æsculapius
little remains but an altar of black stone, adorned with a cornice
imitating the scales of a serpent. His statue, in terra-cotta,
was found in the cell. The temple of Isis is more perfect. It
is surrounded by a portico of fluted columns, and in the area
around it are two altars, and many ceppi for statues ; and a
little chapel of white stucco, as hard as stone, of the most
exquisite proportion ; its panels are adorned with figures in
bas-relief, slightly indicated, but of a workmanship the most
delicate and perfect that can be conceived. They are Egyptian
subjects, executed by a Greek artist, who has harmonised all the
unnatural extravagances of the original conception into the
supernatural loveliness of his country's genius. They scarcely

touch the ground with their feet, and their wind-uplifted robes seem in the place of wings. The temple in the midst raised on a high platform, and approached by steps, was decorated with exquisite paintings, some of which we saw in the museum at Portici. It is small, of the same materials as the chapel, with a pavement of mòsaic, and fluted Ionic columns of white stucco, so white that it dazzles you to lock at it.

Thence through other porticos and labyrinths of walls and columns (for I cannot hope to detail everything to you), we came to the Forum. This is a large square, surrounded by lofty porticos of fluted columns, some broken, some entire, their entablatures strewed under them. The temple of Jupiter, of Venus, and another temple, the Tribunal, and the Hall of Public Justice, with their forests of lofty columns, surround the Forum. Two pedestals or altars of an enormous size (for, whether they supported equestrian statues, or were the altars of the temple of Venus, before which they stand, the guide could not tell), occupy the lower end of the Forum. At the upper end, supported on an elevated platform, stands the temple of Jupiter. Under the colonnade of its portico we sate, and pulled out our oranges, and figs, and bread, and medlars (sorry fare, you will say), and rested to eat. Here was a magnificent spectacle. Above and between the multitudinous shafts of the sun-shining columns was seen the sea, reflecting the purple heaven of noon above it, and supporting, as it were, on its line the dark lofty mountains of Sorrento, of a blue inexpressibly deep, and tinged towards their summits with streaks of new-fallen snow. Between was one small green island. To the right was Capreæ, Inarime, Prochyta, and Misenum. Behind was the single summit of Vesuvius, rolling forth volumes of thick white smoke, whose foam-like column was sometimes darted into the clear dark sky, and fell in little streaks along the wind. Between Vesuvius and the nearer mountains, as through a chasm, was seen the main line of the loftiest Apennines, to the east. The day was radiant and warm. Every now and then we heard the subterranean thunder of Vesuvius ; its distant deep peals seemed to shake the very air and light of day, which interpenetrated our frames, with the sullen and tremendous sound. This sound was what the Greeks beheld (Pompeii, you know, was a Greek city). They lived in harmony with nature ; and the interstices of their incomparable columns were portals, as it were, to admit the spirit of beauty which animates this glorious universe to visit those whom it inspired. If such is Pompeii, what was Athens ? What scene was exhibited from the Acropolis, the Parthenon, and the temples of Hercules, and Theseus, and the Winds? The islands and the Ægean sea, the mountains of Argolis, and the peaks of Pindus and Olympus, and the darkness of the Bœotian forests interspersed?

From the Forum we went to another public place; a triangular portico, half enclosing the ruins of an enormous temple, It is built on the edge of the hill overlooking the sea. That black point is the temple. In the apex of the triangle stands an altar and a fountain, and before the altar once stood the statue of the builder of the portico. Returning hence, and following the consular road, we came to the eastern gate of the city. The walls are of enormous strength, and inclose a space of three miles. On each side of the road beyond the gate are built the tombs. How unlike ours! They seem not so much hiding-places for that which must decay, as voluptuous chambers for immortal spirits. They are of marble, radiantly white; and two, especially beautiful, are loaded with exquisite bas-reliefs. On the stucco-wall that incloses them are little emblematic figures, of a relief exceedingly low, of dead and dying animals, and little winged genii, and female forms bending in groups in some funereal office. The higher reliefs represent, one a nautical subject, and the other a Bacchanalian one. Within the cell stand the cinerary urns, sometimes one, sometimes more. It is said that paintings were found within; which are now, as has been everything moveable in Pompeii, removed, and scattered about in royal museums. These tombs were the most impressive things of all. The wild woods surround them on either side; and along the broad stones of the paved road which divides them, you hear the late leaves of autumn shiver and rustle in the stream of the inconstant wind, as it were, like the step of ghosts. The radiance and magnificence of these dwellings of the dead, the white freshness of the scarcely finished marble, the impassioned or imaginative life of the figures which adorn them, contrast strangely with the simplicity of the houses of those who were living when Vesuvius overwhelmed them.

I have forgotten the amphitheatre, which is of great magnitude, though much inferior to the Coliseum. I now understand why the Greeks were such great poets; and, above all, I can account, it seems to me, for the harmony, the unity, the perfection, the uniform excellence, of all their works of art. They lived in a perpetual commerce with external nature, and nourished themselves upon the spirit of its forms. Their theatres were all open to the mountains and the sky. Their columns, the ideal types of a sacred forest, with its roof of interwoven tracery, admitted the light and wind ; the odour and the freshness of the country penetrated the cities. Their temples were mostly upaithric ; and the flying clouds, the stars, or the deep sky, were seen above. O, but for that series of wretched wars which terminated in the Roman conquest of the world ; but for the Christian religion, which put the finishing stroke on the ancient system ; but for those changes that conducted Athens to its ruin—to what an eminence might not humanity have arrived !

In a short time I hope to tell you something of the museum of this city.

You see how ill I follow the maxim of Horace, at least in its literal sense : "nil admirari"—which I should say, "properes est una "—to prevent there ever being anything admirable in the world. Fortunately Plato is of my opinion ; and I had rather err with Plato than be right with Horace.

At this moment I received your letter, indicating that you are removing to London. I am very much interested in the subject of this change, and beg you would write me all the particulars of it. You will be able now to give me perhaps a closer insight into the politics of the times than was permitted you at Marlow. Of H—— I have a very slight opinion. There are rumours here of a revolution in Spain. A ship came in twelve days from Catalonia, and brought a report that the king was massacred ; that eighteen thousand insurgents surrounded Madrid ; but that before the popular party gained head enough, seven thousand were murdered by the Inquisition. Perhaps you know all by this time. The old king of Spain is dead here. Cobbett is a fine ὑμενοποιος—does his influence increase or diminish ? What a pity that so powerful a genius should be combined with the most odious moral qualities.

We have reports here of a change in the English ministry—to what does it amount ? for, besides my national interest in it, I am on the watch to vindicate my most sacred rights, invaded by the chancery court.

I suppose now we shall not see you in Italy this spring, whether Hunt comes or not. It's probable I shall hear nothing from him for some months, particularly if he does not come. Give me *ses nouvelles.*

I am under an English surgeon here, who says I have a disease of the liver, which he will cure. We keep horses, as this kind of exercise is absolutely essential to my health. Elise*

* A Swiss girl whom we had engaged as nursery-maid two years before, at Geneva.—*M. S.*

has just married our Italian servant, and has quitted us ; the man was a great rascal, and cheated enormously : this event was very much against our advice.

I have scarcely been out since I wrote last.

Adieu !—Yours most faithfully,

P. B. S.

XXXIII.—To T. L. Peacock.

Naples, February 25th, 1819.

My Dear Peacock—I am much interested to hear your progress in the object of your removal to London. There is no person in the world who would more sincerely rejoice in any good that might befall you than I should.

We are on the point of quitting Naples for Rome. The scenery which surrounds this city is more delightful than any within the immediate reach of civilized man. I do not think I have mentioned to you the Lago d'Agnano and the Caccia d'Ischieri, and I have since seen what obscures those lovely forms in my memory. They are both the craters of extinguished volcanos, and Nature has thrown forth forests of oak and ilex, and spread mossy lawns and clear lakes over the dead or sleeping fire. The first is a scene of a wider and milder character, with soft sloping, wooded hills, and grassy declivities declining to the lake, and cultivated plains of vines woven upon poplar trees, bounded by the theatre of hills. Innumerable wild water-birds, quite tame, inhabit this place. The other is a royal chace, is surrounded by steep and lofty hills, and only accessible through a wide gate of massy oak, from the vestibule of which the spectacle of precipitous hills, hemming in a narrow and circular vale, is suddenly disclosed. The hills are covered with thick woods of ilex, myrtle, and laurustinus ; the polished leaves of the ilex, as they wave in their multitudes under the partial blasts which rush through the chasms of the vale, glitter above the dark masses of foliage below, like the white foam of waves upon a deep blue sea. The plain so surrounded is at most three miles in circumference. It is occupied partly by a lake, with bold shores wooded by evergreens, and interrupted by a sylvan promonotry of the wild forest, whose mossy boughs overhang its expanse, of a silent and purple darkness, like an Italian midnight ; and partly by the forest itself, of all gigantic trees, but the oak especially, whose jagged boughs, now leafless, are hoary with thick lichens, and loaded with the massy and deep foliage of the ivy. The effect of the dark eminences that surround this plain, seen through the boughs, is of an enchanting solemnity. (There we saw in one instance wild boars and a deer, and in another—a spectacle little suited to the antique and Latonian nature of the place—King Ferdinand in a winter enclosure, watching to shoot wild boars.) The underwood was principally evergreen, all lovely kinds of fern and furze ; the cytisus, a delicate kind of furze with a pretty yellow blossom, the myrtle, and the myrica. The willow trees had just begun to put forth their green and golden buds, and gleamed like points of lambent fire among the wintry forest. The Grotta del Cane, too, we saw, because other people see it ; but would not allow the dogs to be exhibited in torture for our curiosity. The poor little animals stood moving their tails in a slow and dismal manner, as if perfectly resigned to their condition—a cur-like emblem of voluntary servitude. The effect of the vapour, which extinguishes a torch, is to cause suffocation at last, through a process which makes the lungs feel as if they were torn by sharp points within. So a surgeon told us, who tried the experiment on himself.

There was a Greek city, sixty miles to the south of Naples, called Posidonia, now Pesto, where there still subsist three temples of Etruscan * architecture, one almost perfect. From this city we have just returned. The weather was most unfavourable for our expedition. After two months of cloudless serenity, it began raining cats and dogs. The first night we slept at Salerno, a large city situate in the recess of a deep bay ; surrounded with stupendous mountains of the same name. A few miles from Torre del Greco we entered on the pass of the mountains, which is a line dividing the isthmus of those enormous piles of rock which compose the southern boundary of the bay of Naples, and the northern one of that of Salerno. On one side is a lofty conical hill, crowned with the turrets of a ruined castle, and cut into platforms for cultivation ; at least every ravine and glen, whose precipitous sides admitted of other vegetation but that of the rock-rooted ilex : on the other, the aethereal snowy crags of an immense mountain, whose terrible lineaments were at intervals concealed or disclosed by volumes of dense clouds, rolling under the tempest. Half a mile from this spot, between orange and lemon groves of a lovely village, suspended as it were on an amphitheatral

* The architecture is Doric.—*T. L. P.*

precipice, whose golden globes contrasted with the white walls and dark green leaves which they almost outnumbered, shone the sea. A burst of the declining sunlight illumined it. The road led along the brink of the precipice towards Salerno. Nothing could be more glorious than the scene. The immense mountains covered with the rare and divine vegetation of this climate, with many-folding vales, and deep dark recesses, which the fancy scarcely could penetrate, descended from their snowy summits precipitously to the sea. Before us was Salerno, built into a declining plain, between the mountains and the sea. Beyond, the other shore of sky-cleaving mountains, then dim with the mist of tempest. Underneath, from the base of the precipice where the road conducted, rocky promontories jutted into the sea, covered with olive and ilex woods, or with the ruined battlements of some Norman or Saracen fortress. We slept at Salerno, and the next morning before daybreak proceeded to Posidonia. The night had been tempestuous, and our way lay by the sea sand. It was utterly dark, except when the long line of wave burst, with a sound like thunder, beneath the starless sky, and cast up a kind of mist of cold white lustre. When morning came, we found ourselves travelling in a wide desert plain, perpetually interrupted by wild irregular glens, and bounded on all sides by the Apennines and the sea. Sometimes it was covered with forest, sometimes dotted with underwood, or mere tufts of fern and furze, and the wintry dry tendrils of creeping plants. I have never, but in the Alps, seen an amphitheatre of mountains so magnificent. After travelling fifteen miles we came to a river, the bridge of which had been broken, and which was so swollen that the ferry would not take the carriage across. We had, therefore, to walk seven miles of a muddy road, which led to the ancient city across the desolate Maremma. The air was scented with the sweet smell of violets of an extraordinary size and beauty. At length we saw the sublime and massy colonnades, skirting the horizon of the wilderness. We entered by the ancient gate, which is now no more than a chasm in the rock-like wall. Deeply sunk in the ground beside it, were the ruins of a sepulchre, which the ancients were in the custom of building beside the public way. The first temple, which is the smallest, consists of an outer range of columns, quite perfect, and supporting a perfect architrave and two shattered frontispieces.* The proportions

* The three temples are amphiprostyle ; that is, they have two prospects or fronts, each of six columns in the two first, and of nine in the Basilica. See Major's *Ruins of Paestum.* 1768.—*T. L. P.*

are extremely massy, and the architecture entirely unornamented and simple. These columns do not seem more than forty feet high,* but the perfect proportions diminish the apprehension of their magnitude ; it seems as if inequality and irregularity of form were requisite to force on us the relative idea of greatness. The scene from between the columns of the temple, consists on one side of the sea, to which the gentle hill on which it is built slopes, and on the other, of the grand amphitheatre of the loftiest Apennines, dark purple mountains, crowned with snow and intercepted there by long bars of hard and leaden-coloured cloud. The effect of the jagged outline of mountains, through groups of enormous columns on one side, and on the other the level horizon of the sea, is inexpressibly grand. The second temple is much larger, and also more perfect. Beside the outer range of columns, it contains an interior range of column above column, and the ruins of a wall, which was the screen of the penetralia. With little diversity of ornament, the order of architecture is similar to that of the first temple. The columns in all are fluted, and built of a porous volcanic stone, which time has dyed with a rich and yellow colour. The columns are one-third larger, and like that of the first, diminish from the base to the capital, so that, but for the chastening effect of their admirable proportions, their magnitude would, from the delusion of perspective, seem greater, not less, than it is ; though perhaps we ought to say, not that this symmetry diminishes your apprehension of their magnitude, but that it overpowers the idea of relative greatness, by establishing within itself a system of relations, destructive of your idea of its relation with other objects, on which our ideas of size depend. The third temple is what they call a Basilica ; three columns alone remain of the interior range ; the exterior is perfect, but that the cornice and frieze in many places have fallen. This temple covers more ground than either of the others, but its columns are of an intermediate magnitude between those of the second and the first.

We only contemplated these sublime monuments for two hours, and of course could only bring away so imperfect a conception of them, as is the shadow of some half-remembered dream.

---

* The height of the columns is respectively 18 feet 6 inches, and 28 feet 5 inches and 6½ lines, in the two first temples ; and 21 feet 6 inches in the Basilica. This shows the justice of the remarks on the difference of real and apparent magnitude.—*T. L. P.*

The royal collection of paintings in this city is sufficiently miserable. Perhaps the most remarkable is the original studio by Michael Angelo of the " Day of Judgment," which is painted in *fresco* on the Sixtine chapel of the Vatican. It is there so defaced as to be wholly indistinguishable. I cannot but think the genius of this artist highly overrated. He has not only no temperance, no modesty, no feeling for the just boundaries of art (and in these respects an admirable genius may err), but he has no sense of beauty, and to want this is to want the sense of the creative power of mind. What is terror without a contrast with, and a connexion with, loveliness. How well Dante understood this secret—Dante, with whom this artist has been so presumptuously compared ! What a thing his " Moses " is ; how distorted from all that is natural and majestic. . . . In the picture to which I allude, God is leaning out of heaven. The Holy Ghost, in the shape of a dove, is under him. Under the Holy Ghost stands Jesus Christ, in an attitude of haranguing the assembly. This figure, which his subject, or rather the view which it became him to take of it, ought to have modelled of a calm, severe, awe-inspiring majesty, is in the attitude of commonplace resentment. On one side of this figure are the elect ; on the other, the host of heaven ; they ought to have been what the Christians call *glorified bodies*, floating onward, and radiant with that everlasting light (I speak in the spirit of their faith), which had consumed their mortal veil. They are in fact very ordinary people. Below is the ideal purgatory, I imagine, in mid air, in the shapes of spirits, some of whom demons are dragging down, others falling as it were by their own weight, others half-suspended in that Mahomet-coffin-kind of attitude which most moderate Christians, I believe, expect to assume. Every step towards hell approximates to the region of the artist's exclusive power. There is great imagination in many of the situations of these unfortunate spirits. But hell and death are his real sphere. The bottom of the picture is divided by a lofty rock, in which there is a cavern whose entrance is thronged by devils, some coming in with spirits, some going out for prey. The blood-red light of the fiery abyss glows through their dark forms. On one side, are the devils in all hideous forms, struggling with the damned, who have received their sentence, and are chained in all forms of agony by knotted serpents, and writhing on the crags in every variety of torture. On the other, are the dead, coming out of their graves—horrible forms. Such is the famous " Day of Judgment" of Michael Angelo ; a kind of *Titus Andronicus* in painting, but the author surely no Shakspeare. The other paintings are one or two of Raphael or his pupils, very sweet and lovely. A "Danäe" of Titian, a picture, the softest and most voluptuous form, with languid and uplifted eyes, and warm yet passive limbs. A "Maddelena," by Guido, with dark brown hair, and dark brown eyes, and an earnest, soft, melancholy look. And some excellent pictures, in point of execution, by Annibal Caracci. None others worth a second look. Of the gallery of statues I cannot speak. They require a volume, not a letter. Still less what can I do at Rome?

I have just seen the *Quarterly* for September, not from my own box. I suppose there is no chance now of the organization of a review! This is a great pity. The *Quarterly* is undoubtedly conducted with talent, great talent, and affords a dreadful preponderance against the cause of improvement. If a band of staunch reformers, resolute and skilful, were united in so close and constant a league as that in which interest and fanaticism have bound the members of that literary coalition!

Adieu. Address your next letter to Rome, whence you shall hear from me soon again. M. and C. unite with me in the very kindest remembrances.—Most faithfully yours,

P. B. S.

A doctor here has been messing me, and I believe has done me an important benefit. One of his pretty schemes has been putting caustic on my side. You may guess how much quiet I have had since it was laid on.

XXXIV.—To T. L. P.

Rome, March 23rd, 1819.

MY DEAR P.—I wrote to you the day before our departure from Naples. We came by slow journeys, with our own horses, to Rome, resting one day at Mola di Gaeta, at the inn called Villa di Cicerone, from being built on the ruins of his Villa, whose immense substructions overhang the sea, and are scattered among the orange-groves. Nothing can be lovelier than the scene from the terraces of the inn. On one side precipitous mountains, whose bases slope into an inclined plane of olive and orange copses—the latter forming, as it were, an emerald sky of leaves, starred with innumerable globes of their ripening fruit, whose rich splendour contrasted with the deep green foliage ; on the other the sea—bounded on one side by the antique town of Gaeta, and the other by what appears to be an island, the promontory of Circe. From Gaeta to Terracina the whole scenery is of the most sublime character. At Terracina, precipitous conical crags of immense height shoot into the sky and overhang the sea. At Albano, we arrived again in sight of Rome. Arches after arches in unending lines stretching across the uninhabited wilderness, the blue defined line of the mountains seen between them ; masses of nameless ruin standing like rocks out of the plain ; and the plain itself, with its billowy and unequal surface, announced the neighbourhood of Rome. And what shall I say to you of Rome? If I speak of the inanimate ruins, the rude stones piled upon stones, which are the sepulchres of the fame of those who once arrayed them with the beauty which has faded, will you believe me insensible to the vital, the almost breathing creations of genius yet subsisting in their perfection ? What has become, you will ask, of the Appollo, the Gladiator, the Venus of the Capitol ? What of the Apollo di Belvedere, the Laocoön ? What of Raffael and Guido ? These things are best spoken of when the mind has drunk in the spirit of their forms ; and little indeed can I, who must devote no more than a few months to the contemplation of them, hope to know or feel of their profound beauty.

I think I told you of the Coliseum, and its impressions on me on my first visit to this city. The next most considerable relic of antiquity, considered as a ruin, is the Thermæ of Caracalla. These consist of six enormous chambers, above 200 feet in height, and each enclosing a vast space like that of a field. There are, in addition, a number of towers and labyrinthine recesses, hidden and woven over by the wild growth of weeds and ivy. Never was any desolation more sublime and lovely. The perpendicular wall of ruin is cloven into steep ravines filled up with flowering shrubs, whose thick twisted roots are knotted in the rifts of the stones. At every step the aerial pinnacles of shattered stone group into new combinations of effect, and tower above the lofty yet level walls, as the distant mountains change their aspect to one travelling rapidly along the plain. The perpendicular walls resemble nothing more than that cliff of Bisham wood, that is overgrown with wood, and yet is stony and precipitous—you know the one I mean ; not the chalk-pit, but the spot that has the pretty copse of fir-trees and privet-bushes at its base, and where H—— and I scrambled up, and you, to my infinite discontent, would go home. These walls surround green and level spaces of lawn, on which some elms have grown, and which are interspersed towards their skirts by masses of the fallen ruin, overtwined with the broad leaves of the creeping weeds. The blue sky canopies it, and is as the everlasting roof of these enormous halls.

But the most interesting effect remains. In one of the buttresses, that supports an immense and lofty arch, "which bridges the very winds of heaven," are the crumbling remains of an antique winding staircase, whose sides are open in many places to the precipice. This you ascend, and arrive on the summit of these piles. There grow on every side thick entangled wildernesses of myrtle, and the myrletus, and bay, and the flowering laurestinus, whose white blossoms are just developed, the white fig, and a thousand nameless plants sown by the wandering winds. These woods are intersected on every side by paths, like sheep-tracks through the copse-wood of steep mountains, which wind to every part of the immense labyrinth. From the midst rise those pinnacles and masses, themselves like mountains, which have been seen from below. In one place you wind along a narrow strip of weed-grown ruin : on one side is the immensity of earth and sky, on the other a narrow chasm, which is bounded by an arch of enormous size, fringed by the many-coloured foliage and blossoms, and supporting a lofty and irregular pyramid, over-grown like itself with the all-prevailing vegetation. Around rise other crags and other peaks, all arrayed, and the deformity of their vast desolation softened down, by the undecaying investiture of nature. Come to Rome. It is a scene by which expression is overpowered ; which words cannot convey. Still further, winding up one half of the shattered pyramids, by the path through the blooming copse-wood, you come to a little mossy lawn, surrounded by the wild shrubs ; it is overgrown with anemonies, wall-flowers, and violets, whose stalks pierce the starry moss, and with radiant blue flowers, whose names I know not, and which scatter through the air the divinest odour, which, as you recline under the shade of the ruin, produces sensations of voluptuous faint-ness, like the combinations of sweet music. The paths still wind on, threading the perplexed windings, other labyrinths, other lawns, and deep dells of wood, and lofty rocks, and terrific chasms. When I tell you that these ruins cover several acres, and that the paths above penetrate at least half their extent, your imagination will fill up all that I am unable to express of this astonishing scene.

I speak of these things not in the order in which I visited

them, but in that of the impression which they made on me, or perhaps chance directs. The ruins of the ancient Forum are so far fortunate that they have not been walled up in the modern city. They stand in an open, lonesome place, bounded on one side by the modern city, and the other by the Palatine Mount, covered with shapeless masses of ruin. The tourists tell you all about these things, and I am afraid of stumbling on their language when I enumerate what is so well known. There remain eight granite columns of the Ionic order, with their entablature, of the temple of Concord, founded by Camillus. I fear that the immense expanse demanded by these columns forbids us to hope that they are the remains of any edifice dedicated by that most perfect and virtuous of men. It is supposed to have been repaired under the Eastern Emperors; alas, what a contrast of recollections! Near them stand those Corinthian fluted columns, which supported the angle of a temple; the architrave and entablature are worked with delicate sculpture. Beyond, to the south, is another solitary column; and still more distant, three more, supporting the wreck of an entablature. Descending from the Capitol to the Forum, is the triumphal arch of Septimius Severus, less perfect than that of Constantine, though from its proportions and magnitude a most impressive monument. That of Constantine, or rather of Titus (for the relief and sculpture, and even the colossal images of Dacian captives, were torn by a decree of the senate from an arch dedicated to the latter, to adorn that of this stupid and wicked monster, Constantine, one of whose chief merits consists in establishing a religion, the destroyer of those arts which would have rendered so base a spoliation unnecessary), is the most perfect. It is an admirable work of art. It is built of the finest marble, and the outline of the reliefs is in many parts as perfect as if just finished. Four Corinthian fluted columns support, on each side, a bold entablature, whose bases are loaded with reliefs of captives in every attitude of humiliation and slavery. The compartments above express, in bolder relief, the enjoyment of success; the conqueror on his throne, or in his chariot, or nodding over the crushed multitudes, who writhe under his horses' hoofs, as those below express the torture and abjectness of defeat. There are three arches, whose roofs are panneled with fretwork, and their sides adorned with similar reliefs. The keystone of these arches is supported each by two winged figures of Victory, whose hair floats on the wind of their own speed, and whose arms are outstretched, bearing trophies, as if impatient to meet.

They look, as it were, borne from the subject extremities of the earth, on the breath which is the exhalation of that battle and desolation, which it is their mission to commemorate. Never were monuments so completely fitted to the purpose for which they were designed, of expressing that mixture of energy and error which is called a triumph.

I walk forth in the purple and golden light of an Italian evening, and return by star or moonlight, through this scene. The elms are just budding, and the warm spring winds bring unknown odours, all sweet from the country. I see the radiant Orion through the mighty columns of the temple of Concord, and the mellow fading light softens down the modern buildings of the capitol, the only ones that interfere with the sublime desolation of the scene. On the steps of the capitol itself, stand two colossal statues of Castor and Pollux, each with his horse, finely executed, though far inferior to those of Monte Cavallo, the cast of one of which you know we saw together in London. This walk is close to our lodging, and this is my evening walk.

What shall I say of the modern city? Rome is yet the capital of the world. It is a city of palaces and temples, more glorious than those which any other city contains, and of ruins more glorious than they. Seen from any of the eminences that surround it, it exhibits domes beyond domes, and palaces, and colonnades interminably, even to the horizon ; interspersed with patches of desert, and mighty ruins which stand girt by their own desolation, in the midst of the fanes of living religions and the habitations of living men, in sublime loneliness. St. Peter's is, as you have heard, the loftiest building in Europe. Externally it is inferior in architectural beauty to St Paul's, though not wholly devoid of it ; internally it exhibits littleness on a large scale, and is in every respect opposed to antique taste. You know my propensity to admire ; and I tried to persuade myself out of this opinion—in vain ; the more I see of the interior of St. Peter's, the less impression as a whole does it produce on me. I cannot even think it lofty, though its dome is considerably higher than any hill within fifty miles of London ; and when one reflects, it is an astonishing monument of the daring energy of man. Its colonnade is wonderfully fine, and there are two fountains, which rise in spire-like columns of water to an immense height in the sky, and falling on the porphyry vases from which they spring, fill the whole air with a radiant mist, which at noon is thronged with innumerable rainbows. In the midst stands an obelisk. In front is the palace-like façade of St. Peter's, certainly magnificent ; and there is produced, on the whole, an architectural combination unequalled in the world. But the dome of the temple is concealed, except at a very great distance, by the façade and the inferior part of the building, and that diabolical contrivance they call an attic.

The effect of the Pantheon is totally the reverse of that of St. Peter's. Though not a fourth part of the size, it is, as it were, the visible image of the universe ; in the perfection of its proportions, as when you regard the unmeasured dome of heaven, the idea of magnitude is swallowed up and lost. It is open to the sky, and its wide dome is lighted by the ever-changing illumination of the air. The clouds of noon fly over it, and at night the keen stars are seen through the azure darkness, hanging immoveably, or driving after the driving moon among the clouds. We visited it by moonlight ; it is supported by sixteen columns, fluted and Corinthian, of a certain rare and beautiful yellow marble, exquisitely polished, called here *giallo antico*. Above these are the niches for the statues of the twelve gods. This is the only defect of this sublime temple ; there ought to have been no interval between the commencement of the dome and the cornice, supported by the columns. Thus there would have been no diversion from the magnificent simplicity of its form. This improvement is alone wanting to have completed the unity of the idea.

The fountains of Rome are, in themselves, magnificent combinations of art, such as alone it were worth coming to see. That in the Piazza Navona, a large square, is composed of enormous fragments of rock, piled on each other, and penetrated as by caverns. This mass supports an Egyptian obelisk of immense height. On the four corners of the rock recline, in different attitudes, colossal figures representing the four divisions of the globe. The water bursts from the crevices beneath them. They are sculptured with great spirit ; one impatiently tearing a veil from his eyes ; another with his hands stretched upwards. The Fontana di Trevi is the most celebrated, and is rather a waterfall than a fountain ; gushing out from masses of rock, with a gigantic figure of Neptune ; and below are two river gods, checking two winged horses, struggling up from among the rocks and waters. The whole is not ill conceived nor executed ; but you know not how delicate the imagination becomes by dieting with antiquity day after day ! The only things that sustain the comparison are Raffael, Guido, and Salvator Rosa.

The fountain on the Quirinal, or rather the group formed by the statues, obelisk, and the fountain, is, however, the most admirable of all. From the Piazza Quirinale, or rather Monte Cavallo, you see the boundless ocean of domes, spires, and columns, which is the City, Rome. On a pedestal of white marble rises an obelisk of red granite, piercing the blue sky. Before it is a vast basin of porphyry, in the midst of which rises a column of the purest water, which collects into itself all the overhanging colours of the sky, and breaks them into a thousand prismatic hues and graduated shadows—they fall together with its dashing water-drops into the outer basin. The elevated situation of this fountain produces, I imagine, this effect of colour. On each side, on an elevated pedestal, stand the statues of Castor and Pollux, each in the act of taming his horse ; which are said, but I believe wholly without authority, to be the work of Phidias and Praxiteles. These figures combine the irresistible energy with the sublime and perfect loveliness supposed to have belonged to their divine nature. The reins no longer exist, but the position of their hands and the sustained and calm command of their regard, seem to require no mechanical aid to enforce obedience. The countenances at so great a height are scarcely visible, and I have a better idea of that of which we saw a cast together in London, than of the other. But the sublime and living majesty of their limbs and mien, the nervous and fiery animation of the horses they restrain, seen in the blue sky of Italy, and overlooking the city of Rome, surrounded by the light and the music of that crystalline fountain, no cast can communicate.

These figures were found at the Baths of Constantine ; but, of course, are of remote antiquity. I do not acquiesce however in the practice of attributing to Phidias, or Praxiteles, or Scopas, or some great master, any admirable work that may be found. We find little of what remained, and perhaps the works of these were such as greatly surpassed all that we conceive of most perfect and admirable in what little has escaped the *deluge*. If I am too jealous of the honour of the Greeks, our masters and creators, the gods whom we should worship,— pardon me.

I have said what I feel without entering into any critical discussions of the *ruins* of Rome, and the mere outside of this inexhaustible mine of thought and feeling. Hobhouse, Eustace, and Forsyth, will tell all the shew-knowledge about it,—" the common stuff of the earth." By-the-bye, Forsyth is worth reading, as I judge from a chapter or two I have seen. I cannot get the book here.

I ought to have observed that the central arch of the

triumphal Arch of Titus yet subsists, more perfect in its proportions, they say, than any of a later date. This I did not
remark. The figures of Victory, with unfolded wings, and each
spurning back a globe with outstretched feet, are, perhaps, more
beautiful than those on either of the others. Their lips are
parted : a delicate mode of indicating the fervour of their desire
to arrive at the destined resting-place, and to express the eager
respiration of their speed. Indeed, so essential to beauty were
the forms expressive of the exercise of the imagination and the
affections considered by *Greek* artists, that no ideal figure of
antiquity, not destined to some representation directly exclusive
of such a character, is to be found with closed lips. Within
this arch are two panneled alto relievos, one representing a
train of people bearing in procession the instruments of Jewish
worship, among which is the holy candlestick with seven
branches ; on the other, Titus standing on a quadriga, with a
winged Victory. The grouping of the horses, and the beauty,
correctness, and energy of their delineation, is remarkable,
though they are much destroyed.

XXXV.—To **T. L. P.**

Rome, April 6th, 1819.

MY DEAR P.—I sent you yesterday a long letter, all about
antique Rome, which you had better keep for some leisure day.
I received yours, and one of Hunt's, yesterday.—So, you know
the B——s ? I could not help considering Mrs. B., when I
knew her, as the most admirable specimen of a human being I
had ever seen. Nothing earthly ever appeared to be more perfect than her character and manners. It is improbable that I
shall ever meet again the person whom I so much esteemed,
and still admire. I wish, however, that when you see her, you
would tell her that I have not forgotten her, nor any of the
amiable circle once assembled round her ; and that I desire
such remembrances to her as an exile and a *Pariah* may be permitted to address to an acknowledged member of the community
of mankind. I hear they dined at your lodgings. But no men
tion of A—— and his wife—where were they ? C——, though
so young when I saw her, gave indications of her mother's
excellences ; and, certainly less fascinat n g, is, I doubt not,
equally amiable, and more sincere. It was hardly possible
for a person of the extreme subtlety and delicacy of Mrs. B——'s
understanding and affections, to be quite sincere and constant.

I am all anxiety about your I. H. affair. There are few who will feel more hearty satisfaction at your success, in this or any other enterprise, than I shall. Pray let me have the earliest intelligence.

When shall I return to England? The Pythia has ascended the tripod, but she replies not. Our present plans—and I know not what can induce us to alter them—lead us back to Naples in a month or six weeks, where it is almost decided that we should remain until the commencement of 1820. You may imagine, when we receive such letters as yours and Hunt's, what this resolution costs us—but these are not our only communications from England. My health is materially better. My spirits, not the most brilliant in the world; but that we attribute to our solitary situation, and, though happy, how should I be lively? We see something of Italian society indeed. The Romans please me much, especially the women, who, though totally devoid of every kind of information, or culture of the imagination, or affections, or understanding—and, in this respect, a kind of gentle savages—yet contrive to be interesting. Their extreme innocence and naïveté, the freedom and gentleness of their manners; the total absence of affectation, makes an intercourse with them very like an intercourse with uncorrupted children, whom they resemble in loveliness as well as simplicity. I have seen two women in society here of the highest beauty; their brows and lips, and the moulding of the face modelled with sculptural exactness, and the dark luxuriance of their hair floating over their fine complexions; and the lips—you must hear the commonplaces which escape from them, before they cease to be dangerous. The only inferior part are the eyes, which, though good and gentle, want the mazy depth of colour behind colour, with which the intellectual women of England and Germany entangle the heart in soul-inwoven labyrinths.

This is holy-week, and Rome is quite full. The Emperor of Austria is here, and Maria Louisa is coming. On their journey through the other cities of Italy, she was greeted with loud acclamations, and *vivas* of Napoleon. Idiots and slaves! Like the frogs in the fable, because they are discontented with the log, they call upon the stork, who devours them. Great festas, and magnificent funzioni here—we cannot get tickets to all. There are five thousand strangers in Rome, and only room for five hundred, at the celebration of the famous Miserere, in the Sixtine chapel, the only thing I regret we shall not be present at. After all, Rome is eternal; and were all that *is* extinguished, that which *has been*, the ruins and the sculptures, would remain, and Raffael and Guido be alone regretted.

In the Square of St. Peter's there are about three hundred fettered criminals at work, hoeing out the weeds that grow between the stones of the pavement. Their legs are heavily ironed, and some are chained two by two. They sit in long rows, hoeing out the weeds, dressed in parti-coloured clothes. Near them sit or saunter groups of soldiers, armed with loaded muskets. The iron discord of those innumerable chains clanks up into the sonorous air, and produces, contrasted with the musical dashing of the fountains, and the deep azure beauty of the sky, and the magnificence of the architecture around, a conflict of sensations allied to madness. It is the emblem of Italy—moral degradation contrasted with the glory of nature and the arts.

We see no English society here; it is not probable that we would if we desired it, and I am certain that we should find it unsupportable. The manners of the rich English are wholly unsupportable, and they assume pretensions which they would not venture upon in their own country. I am yet ignorant of the event of Hobhouse's election. I saw the last numbers were—Lamb, 4200; and Hobhouse, 3900—14th day. There is little hope. That mischievous Cobbett has divided and weakened the interests of the popular party, so that the factions that prey upon our country have been able to coalesce to its exclusion. The N——s you have not seen. I am curious to know what kind of a girl Octavia becomes; she promised well. Tell H—— his Melpomene is in the Vatican, and that her attitude and drapery surpass, if possible, the graces of her countenance.

My " Prometheus Unbound " is just finished, and in a month or two I shall send it. It is a drama, with characters and mechanism of a kind yet unattempted; and I think the execution is better than any of my former attempts. By-the-bye, have you seen Ollier? I never hear from him, and am ignorant whether some verses I sent him from Naples, entitled, I think, " Lines on the Euganean hills," have reached him in safety or not. As to the Reviews, I suppose there is nothing but abuse; and this is not hearty or sincere enough to amuse me. As to the poem now printing,* I lay no stress on it one way or the other. The concluding lines are natural.

I believe, my dear P., that you wish us to come back to

* Rosalind and Helen.

England. How is it possible? Health, competence, tranquillity —all these Italy permits, and England takes away. I am regarded by all who know or hear of me, except, I think, on the whole, five individuals, as a rare prodigy of crime and pollution, whose look even might infect. This is a large computation, and I don't think I could mention more than three. Such is the spirit of the English abroad as well as at home.

Few compensate, indeed, for all the rest, and if I were *alone* I should laugh ; or if I were rich enough to do all things, which I shall never be. Pity me for my absence from those social enjoyments which England might afford me, and which I know so well how to appreciate. Still I shall return some fine morning, out of pure weakness of heart.

My dear P., most faithfully yours,

P. B. SHELLEY.

XXXVI.—TO MR. AND MRS. GISBORNE.

(LEGHORN.)

Rome, April 6th, 1819.

MY DEAR FRIENDS—A combination of circumstances, which Mary will explain to you, leads us back to Naples in June, or rather the end of May, where we shall remain until the ensuing winter. We shall take a house at Portici or Castel a Mare, until late in the autumn.

The object of this letter is to ask you to spend this period with us. There is no society which we have regretted or desired so much as yours, and in our solitude the benefit of your concession would be greater than I can express. What is a sail to Naples? It is the season of tranquil weather and prosperous winds. If I knew the magic that lay in any given form of words, I would employ them to persuade ; but I fear that all I can say is, as you know with truth, we desire that you would come—we wish to see you. You came to see Mary at Lucca, directly I had departed to Venice. It is not our custom, when we can help it, any more than it is yours, to divide our pleasures.

What shall I say to entice you? We shall have a piano, and some books, and—little else, besides ourselves. But what will be most inviting to you, you will give much, though you may receive but little, pleasure.

But whilst I write this with more desire than hope, yet some of that, perhaps the project may fall into your designs. It is intolerable to think of your being buried at Livorno. The success assured by Mr. Reveley's talents requires another scene. You may have decided to take this summer to consider—and why not with us at Naples, rather than at Livorno?

I could address with respect to Naples, the words of Polypheme in Theocritus, to all the friends I wish to see, and you especially :

'Εξένθοις, Γαλάτεια, καὶ ἐξενθοῖσα λάθοιο,
"Ωσπερ ἐγὼ νῦν ὧδε καθήμενος, οἴκαδ' ἀπενθεῖν.*

Most sincerely yours,
P. B. SHELLEY.

XXXVII.—To T. L. P.

Rome, June 8th, 1819.

MY DEAR FRIEND—Yesterday, after an illness of only a few days, my little William died. There was no hope from the moment of the attack. You will be kind enough to tell all my friends, so that I need not write to them. It is a great exertion to me to write this, and it seems to me as if, hunted by calamity as I have been, that I should never recover any cheerfulness again.

If the things Mary desired to be sent to Naples have not been shipped, send them to Livorno.

We leave this city for Livorno to-morrow morning, where we have written to take lodgings for a month. I will then write again.   Yours ever affectionately,
P. B. SHELLEY.

XXXVIII.—To T. L. P.

Livorno, June 20th, 1819.

MY DEAR PEACOCK—Our melancholy journey finishes at this town, but we retrace our steps to Florence, where, as I imagine, we shall remain some months. O that I could

* Come, O Galatea ; and having come, forget, as do I, now sitting here, to return home.—*M. S.*

return to England !   How heavy a weight when misfortune
is added to exile, and solitude, as if the measure were not full,
heaped high on both.   O that I could return to England ;
I hear you say, "Desire never fails to generate capacity."   Ah !
but that ever-present Malthus, Necessity, has convinced Desire
that even though it generated capacity, its offspring must
starve.   Enough of melancholy !   *Nightmare Abbey*, though
no cure, is a palliative.   I have just received the parcel which
contained it, and at the same time the *Examiners*, by the
way of Malta.   I am delighted with *Nightmare Abbey*.   I
think Scythrop a character admirably conceived and executed ;
and I know not how to praise sufficiently the lightness,
chastity, and strength of the language of the whole.   It
perhaps exceeds all your works in this.   The catastrophe is
excellent.   I suppose the moral is contained in what Falstaff
says—"For God's sake, talk like a man of this world ; " and
yet, looking deeper into it, is not the misdirected enthusiasm
of Scythrop what J. C. calls the " salt of the earth ? "   My
friends the Gisbornes here admire and delight in it exceedingly.
I think I told you that they (especially the lady) are
people of high cultivation.   She is a woman of profound
accomplishments and the most refined taste.

Cobbett still more and more delights me, with all my horror
of the sanguinary commonplaces of his creed.   His design
to overthrow bank notes by forgery is very comic.   One of the
volumes of Birbeck interested me exceedingly.   The letters I
think stupid, but suppose that they are useful.

I do not, as usual, give you an account of my journey,
for I had neither the health nor the spirit to take notes.
My health was greatly improving, when watching and anxiety
cast me into a relapse.   The doctors (I put little faith in the
best) tell me I must spend the winter in Africa or Spain.   I
shall of course prefer the latter, if I choose either.

Are you married, or why do I not hear from you ?   *That*
were a good reason.

M. and C. unite with me in kindest remembrances to
you, and in congratulations, if she exist, to the new married
lady.

When shall I see you again ?—Ever yours, most faithfully,
                                                    P. B. S.

Pray do not forget Mary's things.
I have not heard from you since the middle of April.

XXXIX.—To T. L. Peacock.

Livorno, July 6, 1819.

My Dear Peacock—I have lost some letters, and, in all probability, at least one from you, as I can account in no other manner for not having heard from you since March 26th. We have changed our design of going to Florence immediately, and are now established for three months in a little country house in a pretty verdant scene near Livorno.

I have a study here in a tower, something like Scythrop's, where I am just beginning to recover the faculties of reading and writing. My health, whenever no Libecchio blows, improves. From my tower I see the sea, with its islands, Gorgona, Capraja, Elba, and Corsica, on one side, and the Apennines on the other. Milly surprised us the other day by first discovering a comet, on which we have been speculating. She may "make a stir, like a great astronomer."*

The direct purpose of this letter, however, is to ask you about the box which I requested you to send to me to Naples. If it has been sent, let me entreat you (for really it is of the most serious consequence to us) to write to me by return of post, stating the name of the ship, the bill of lading, etc., so that I may get it without difficulty. If it has not been sent, do me the favour to send it instantly, direct to Livorno. If you have not the time, you can ask Hogg. If you cannot get the things from Mrs. Hunt (a possible case), send those you were to buy, and the things from Furnival,† alone. You can add what books you think fit. The last parcel I have received from you is that of last September.

All good wishes, and many hopes that you have already that

> * Eyes of some men travel far
> For the finding of a star :
> Up and down the heavens they go,
> Men that make a mighty rout :
> I'm as great as they, I trow,
> Since the day I found thee out,
> Little flower ! I'll make a stir,
> Like a great astronomer.
> —Wordsworth.—*To the Little Celandine.*

† A surgeon at Egham, in whom Shelley had great confidence.— *T. L. P.*

success on which there will be no congratulations more cordial than those you will receive from me.

Ever most sincerely yours,
P. B. SHELLEY.

I shall receive your letter, if written by return of post, in thirty days : a distance less formidable than Rome or Naples.

XL.—To T. L. PEACOCK.

Livorno, July, 1819.

MY DEAR P.—We still remain, and shall remain nearly two months longer at Livorno. Our house is a melancholy one,* and only cheered by letters from England. I got your note, in which you speak of three letters having been sent to Naples, which I have written for. I have heard also from H——, who confirms the news of your success, an intelligence most grateful to me.

The object of the present letter is to ask a favour of you. I have written a tragedy, on the subject of a story well known in Italy, and, in my conception, eminently dramatic. I have taken some pains to make my play fit for representation, and those who have already seen it judge favourably. It is written without any of the peculiar feelings and opinions which characterise my other compositions ; I having attended simply to the impartial development of such characters, as it is probable the persons represented really were, together with the greatest degree of popular effect to be produced by such a development. I send you a translation of the Italian manuscript on which my play is founded, the chief subject of which I have touched very delicately ; for my principal doubt, as to whether it would succeed as an acting play, hangs entirely on the question, as to whether such a thing as incest in this shape, however treated, would be admitted on the stage. I think, however, it will form no objection : considering, first, that the facts are matter of history ; and, secondly, the peculiar delicacy with which I have treated it.

I am exceedingly interested in the question of whether this attempt of mine will succeed or no. I am strongly inclined to the affirmative at present, founding my hopes on this, that, as a composition, it is certainly not inferior to any

* We had lost our eldest, and at that time, only child, the preceding month at Rome.—*M. S.*

of the modern plays that have been acted, with the exception of " Remorse ; " that the interests of its plot is incredibly greater and more real ; and that there is nothing beyond what the multitude are contented to believe that they can understand, either in imagery, opinion, or sentiment. I wish to preserve a complete incognito, and can trust to you, that whatever else you do, you will at least favour me on this point. Indeed this is essential, deeply essential to its success. After it had been acted, and successfully (could I hope such a thing), I would own it if I pleased, and use the celebrity it might acquire to my own purposes.

What I want you to do is, to procure for me its presentation at Covent Garden. The principal character, Beatrice, is precisely fitted for Miss O'Neil, and it might even seem written for her, (God forbid that I should ever see her play it—it would tear my nerves to pieces,) and, in all respects, it is fitted only for Covent Garden. The chief male character, I confess, I should be very unwilling that any one but Kean should play—that is impossible, and I must be contented with an inferior actor. I think you know some of the people of that theatre, or, at least, some one who knows them ; and when you have read the play, you may say enough, perhaps, to induce them not to reject it without consideration— but of this, perhaps, I may judge from the tragedies which they have accepted, there is no danger at any rate.

Write to me as soon as you can on this subject, because it is necessary that I should present it, or, if rejected by the theatre, print it this coming season ; lest somebody else should get hold of it, as the story, which now only exists in manuscript, begins to be generally known among the English. The translation which I send you is to be prefixed to the play, together with a print of Beatrice. I have a copy of her picture by Guido, now in the Colonna palace at Rome—the most beautiful creature you can conceive.

Of course, you will not show the manuscript to any one—and write to me by return of post, at which time the play will be ready to be sent.

I expect soon to write again, and it shall be a less selfish letter. As to Ollier, I don't know what has been published, or what has arrived at his hands.—My " Prometheus," though ready, I do not send till I know more.

Ever yours, most faithfully,
P. B. S.

XLI.—To Leigh Hunt.

Livorno, August 15th, 1819.

MY DEAR FRIEND—How good of you to write to us so often, and such kind letters !   But it is like lending to a beggar. What can I offer in return ?

Though surrounded by suffering and disquietude, and, latterly, almost overcome by our strange misfortune,* I have not been idle.   My "Prometheus" is finished, and I am also on the eve of completing another work,† totally different from anything you might consider that I should write ; of a more popular kind ; and, if anything of mine could deserve attention, of higher claims.   "Be innocent of the knowledge, dearest chuck, till thou approve the performance."

I send you a little poem‡ to give to Ollier for publication, but *without my name.*   P. will correct the proofs.   I wrote it with the idea of offering it to the "Examiner," but I find it is too long.   It was composed last year at Este ; two of the characters you will recognise ; and the third is also in some degree a painting from nature, but, with respect to time and place, ideal. You will find the little piece, I think, in some degree consistent with your own ideas of the manner in which poetry ought to be written.   I have employed a certain familiar style of language to express the actual way in which people talk with each other, whom education and a certain refinement of sentiment have placed above the use of vulgar idioms.   I use the word *vulgar* in its most extensive sense.   The vulgarity of rank and fashion is as gross in its way as that of poverty, and its cant terms equally expressive of bare conceptions, and therefore equally unfit for poetry.   Not that the familiar style is to be admitted in the treatment of a subject wholly ideal, or in that part of any subject which relates to common life, where the passion, exceeding a certain limit, touches the boundaries of that which is ideal.   Strong passion expresses itself in metaphor, borrowed from objects alike remote or near, and casts over all the shadow of its own greatness.   But what am I about? If *you* grandmother sucks eggs, was it I who taught her ?

If *you* would really correct the proof, I need not trouble P., who, I suppose, has enough.   Can you take it as a compliment that I prefer to trouble you ?

* The sudden death of William Shelley, then our only child, which happened in Rome, 6th June, 1819.—*M. S.*
† The Cenci.   ‡ Julian and Maddalo.

I do not particularly wish this poem to be known as mine ;
but, at all events, I would not put my name to it. I leave you
to judge whether it is best to throw it into the fire, or to publish
it. So much for self—*self,* that burr that will stick to one. Your
kind expressions about my Eclogue gave me great pleasure ;
indeed, my great stimulus in writing, is to have the approbation
of those who feel kindly towards me. The rest is mere duty.
I am also delighted to hear that you think of us and form
fancies about us. We cannot yet come home.

Most affectionately yours,
P. B. SHELLEY.

XLII.—To T. L. PEACOCK.

Livorno, August (probably 22nd), 1819.

MY DEAR PEACOCK—I ought first to say, that I have not
yet received one of your letters from Naples ; but your present
letter tells me all that I could desire to hear.

My employments are these : I awaken usually at seven; read
half-an-hour ; then get up ; breakfast ; after breakfast ascend
my tower, and read or write until two. Then we dine. After
dinner I read Dante with Mary, gossip a little, eat grapes and
figs, sometimes walk, though seldom, and at half-past five pay a
visit to Mrs. Gisborne, who reads Spanish with me until near
seven. We then come for Mary, and stroll about till supper
time. Mrs. Gisborne is a sufficiently amiable and very
accomplished woman ; she is δημοκρατικη and αθεη—how far she
may be φιλανθρωπη I don't know, for she is the antipodes of
enthusiasm. Her husband, a man with little thin lips, receding forehead, and a prodigious nose, is an [   ] bore. His
nose is something quite Slawkenbergian—it weighs on the
imagination to look at it. It is that sort of nose which trans-
forms all the g's its wearer utters into k's. It is a nose once
seen never to be forgotten, and which requires the utmost
stretch of Christian charity to forgive. I, you know, have a
little turn-up nose ; Hogg has a large hook one ; but add them
both together, square them, cube them, you will have but a faint
idea of the nose to which I refer.

I most devoutly wish I were living near London. I do not
think I shall settle so far off as Richmond ; and to inhabit any
intermediate spot on the Thames would be to expose myself to
the river damps ; not to mention that it is not much to my taste.
My inclinations point to Hampstead ; but I do not know

whether I should not make up my mind to something more completely suburban. What are mountains, trees, heaths, or even the glorious and ever-beautiful sky, with such sunsets as I have seen at Hampstead, to friends? Social enjoyment, in some form or other, is the alpha and the omega of existence. All that I see in Italy—and from my tower window I now see the magnificent peaks of the Apennine half enclosing the plain —is nothing ; it dwindles into smoke in the mind, when I think of some familiar forms of scenery, little perhaps in themselves, over which old remembrances have thrown a delightful colour. How we prize what we despised when present ! The ghosts of our dead associations rise and haunt us, in revenge for our having let them starve, and abandoned them to perish.

You don't tell me if you see the B——'s ; nor are they included in the list of the *conviti* at the monthly symposium. I will attend it in imagination.

One thing, I own, I am curious about ; and in the chance of the letters not coming from Naples, pray tell me. What is it you do at the India House? Hunt writes, and says you have got a *situation* in the India House : Hogg that you have an *honourable employment :* Godwin writes to Mary that you have got *so much or so much :* but nothing of what you do. The devil take these general terms. Not content with having driven all poetry out of the world, at length they make war on their own allies ; nay, on their very parents, dry facts. If it had not been the age of generalities, any one of these people would have told me what you did.

I have been much better these last three weeks. My work on the Cenci, which was done in two months, was a fine anti-dote to nervous medicines, and kept up, I think, the pain in my side, as sticks do a fire. Since then, I have materially im-proved. I do not walk enough. C., who is sometimes my companion, does not dress in exactly the right time. I have no stimulus to walk. Now, I go sometimes to Livorno on business; and that does me good.

England seems to be in a very disturbed state, if we may judge from some Paris papers. I suspect it is rather exag-gerated. But the change should commence among the higher orders, or anarchy will only be the last flash before despotism.

I have been reading Calderon in Spanish. A kind of Shak-speare is this Calderon ; and I have some thoughts, if I find that I cannot do anything better, of translating some of his plays.

The *Examiners* I receive. Hunt, as a political writer,

pleases me more and more. Adieu. M. and C. send their best remembrances.

Your most faithful friend,   P. B. SHELLEY.

Pray send me some books, and Clare would take it as a great favour if you would send her *music books.*

XLIII.—TO LEIGH HUNT.

Livorno, Sept. 3, 1819.

MY DEAR FRIEND—At length has arrived Ollier's parcel, and with it the portrait. What a delightful present ! It is almost yourself, and we sat talking with it, and of it, all the evening. It is a great pleasure to us to possess it, a pleasure in time of need, coming to us when there are few others. How we wish it were you, and not your picture ! How I wish we were with you !

This parcel, you know, and all its letters, are now a year old —some older. There are all kinds of dates, from March to August, and "your date," to use Shakspeare's expression, "is better in a pie or a pudding, than in your letter."—"Virginity," Parolles says, but letters are the same thing in another shape.

With it came, too, Lamb's works. I have looked at none of the other books yet. What a lovely thing is his " Rosamund Gray ! " How much knowledge of the sweetest and deepest parts of our nature in it ! When I think of such a mind as Lamb's—when I see how unnoticed remain things of such exquisite and complete perfection, what should I hope for myself, if I had not higher objects in view than fame ?

I have seen too little of Italy, and of pictures. Perhaps P. has shown you some of my letters to him. But at Rome I was very ill, seldom able to go out without a carriage : and though I kept horses for two months there, yet there is so much to see ! Perhaps I attended more to sculpture than painting, its forms being more easily intelligible than that of the latter. Yet, I saw the famous works of Raffaele, whom I agree with the whole world in thinking the finest painter. Why, I can tell you another time. With respect to Michael Angelo I dissent, and think with astonishment and indignation of the common notion that he equals, and in some respects, exceeds Raffaele. He seems to me to have no sense of moral dignity and love-liness ; and the energy for which he has been so much praised, appears to me to be a certain rude, external, mechanical quality, in comparison with anything possessed by Raffaele, or even much inferior artists. His famous painting in the Sixtine Chapel seems to me deficient in beauty and majesty, both in the conception and the execution. He has been called the Dante of painting ; but if we find some of the gross and strong outlines which are employed in the most distasteful passages of the " Inferno," where shall we find *your* Francesca —where the spirit coming over the sea in a boat, like Mars rising from the vapours of the horizon—where Matilda gathering flowers, and all the exquisite tenderness, and sensibility, and ideal beauty, in which Dante excelled all poets except Shakspeare ?

As to Michael Angelo's *Moses*—but you have a cast of that in England. I write these things, heaven knows why !

I have written something and finished it, different from anything else, and a new attempt for me ; and I mean to dedicate it to you. I should not have done so without your approbation, but I asked your picture last night, and it smiled assent. If I did not think it in some degree worthy of you, I would not make you a public offering of it. I expect to have to write to you soon about it. If Ollier is not turned Jew, Christian, or become infected with *the Murrain,* he will publish it. Don't let him be frightened, for it is nothing which, by any courtesy of language, can be termed either moral or immoral.

Mary has written to Marianne for a parcel, in which I beg you will make Ollier enclose what you know would most interest me—your " Calendar," (a sweet extract from which I saw in the Examiner,) and the other poems belonging to you ; and, for some friends of mine, my Eclogue. This parcel, which must be sent instantly, will reach me by October, but don't trust letters to it, except just a line or so. When you write, write by the post.

Ever your affectionate,   P. B. S.

My love to Marianne and Bessy, and Thornton too, and Percy, etc., and if you could imagine any way in which I could be useful to them here, tell me. I will enquire about the Italian chalk. You have no idea of the pleasure this portrait gives us.

XLIV.—TO C. OLLIER.

Leghorn, September 6th, 1819.

DEAR SIR—I received your packet with Hunt's picture about a fortnight ago ; and your letter with Nos. 1, 2, and 3 yesterday, but not No. 4, which is probably lost or mislaid, through the extreme irregularity of the Italian post.

The ill account you give of the success of my poetical attempts, sufficiently accounts for your silence ; but I believe that the truth is, I write less for the public than for myself. Considering that perhaps the parcel will be another year on its voyage, I rather wish, if this letter arrives in time, that you would send the *Quarterly's* article by the post, and the rest of the *Review* in the parcel. Of course, it gives me a certain degree of pleasure to know that any one likes my writings ; but it is objection and enmity alone that rouses my *curiosity.* My *Prometheus,* which has been long finished, is now being transcribed, and will soon be forwarded to you for publication. It is, in my judgment, of a higher character than anything I have yet attempted, and is perhaps less an imitation of anything that has gone before it. I shall also send you another work, calculated to produce a very popular effect, and totally in a different style from anything I have yet composed. This will be sent already printed. The *Prometheus* you will be so good as to print as usual. . . .

In the *Rosalind and Helen,* I see there are some few errors, which are so much the worse because they are errors in the sense. If there should be any danger of a second edition, I will correct them.

I have read your *Altham,* and Keats's poem, and Lamb's works. For the second in this list, much praise is due to me for having read it, the author's intention appearing to be that no person should possibly get to the end of it. Yet it is full of some of the highest and the finest gleams of poetry ; indeed, everything seems to be viewed by the mind of a poet which is described in it. I think, if he had printed about fifty pages of fragments from it, I should have been led to admire Keats as a poet more than I ought, of which there is now no danger. In *Altham* you have surprised and delighted me. It is a natural story, most unaffectedly told ; and, what is more, told in a strain of very pure and powerful English, which is a very rare merit. You seem to have studied our language to some purpose ; but I suppose I ought to have waited for *Inesilla.*

The same day that your letter came, came the news of the Manchester work, and the torrent of my indignation has not yet done boiling in my veins. I wait anxiously to hear how the country will express its sense of this bloody, murderous oppression of its destroyers. " Something must be done. What, yet I know not."

In your parcel (which I pray you to send in some safe manner, forwarding to me the bill of lading, etc., in a regular mercantile way, so that my parcel may come in six weeks, not twelve months) send me Jones's Greek Grammar and some sealing-wax.

Whenever I publish, send copies of my books to the following people from me :—

Mr. Hunt,	Mr. Godwin,	Mr. Hogg,
Mr. Peacock,	Mr. Keats,	Mr. Thomas Moore,
Mr. Horace Smith,	Lord Byron (at Murray's).	

Yours, obliged and faithful,

PERCY B. SHELLEY.

XLV.—TO T. L. PEACOCK.

Livorno, September 9th, 1816.

MY DEAR PEACOCK—I send you the tragedy.* You will see that the subject has not been treated as you suggested, and why it was not susceptible of such treatment. In fact, it was then already printing when I received your letter, and it has been treated in such a manner that I do not see how the subject forms an objection. You know *Œdipus* is performed on the fastidious French stage, a play much more broad than this. I confess I have some hopes, and some friends here persuade me that they are not unfounded.

Many thanks for your attention in sending the papers which contain the terrible and important news of Manchester. These are, as it were, the distant thunders of the terrible storm which is approaching. The tyrants here, as in the French Revolution, have first shed blood. May their execrable lessons not be learnt with equal facility! Pray let me have the *earliest* political news which you consider of importance at this crisis.

Yours ever most faithfully, P. B. S.

XLVI.—TO T. L. PEACOCK.

Leghorn, September 21st, 1819.

MY DEAR PEACOCK—You will have received a short letter sent with the tragedy, and the tragedy itself by this time. I am, you may believe, anxious to hear what you think of it, and how the manager talks about it. I have printed in Italy 250 copies,

* The *Cenci.*

because it costs, with all duties and freightage, about half what it would cost in London, and these copies will be sent by sea. My other reason was a belief that the seeing it in print would enable the people at the theatre to judge more easily. Since I last wrote to you Mr. Gisborne is gone to England for the purpose of obtaining a situation for Henry Reveley. I have given him a letter to you, and you would oblige me by showing what civilities you can, and by forwarding his views, either by advice or recommendation, as you may find opportunity. Henry is a most amiable person, and has great talents as a mechanic and engineer. Mr. Gisborne is a man who knows I cannot tell how many languages, and has read almost all the books you can think of ; but all that they contain seems to be to his mind what water is to a sieve. His liberal opinions are all the reflections of Mrs. G.'s, a very amiable, accomplished, and completely unprejudiced woman.

Charles Clairmont is now with us on his way to Vienna. He has spent a year or more in Spain, where he has learnt Spanish, and I make him read Spanish all day long. It is a most powerful and expressive language, and I have already learnt sufficient to read with great ease their poet Calderon. I have read about twelve of his plays. Some of them certainly deserve to be ranked among the grandest and most perfect productions of the human mind. He exceeds all modern dramatists, with the exception of Shakspeare, whom he resembles, however, in the depth of thought and subtlety of imagination of his writings, and in the rare power of interweaving delicate and powerful comic traits with the most tragical situations, without diminishing their interest. I rate him far above Beaumont and Fletcher.

I have received all the papers you sent me, and the *Examiners* regularly, perfumed with muriatic acid. What an infernal business this of Manchester ! What is to be done ? Something assuredly. H. Hunt has behaved, I think, with great spirit and coolness in the whole affair.

I have sent you my *Prometheus*, which I do not wish to be sent to Ollier for publication until I write to that effect. Mr. Gisborne will bring it, as also some volumes of Spenser, and the two last of Herodotus and *Paradise Lost*, which may be put up with the others.

If my play should be accepted, don't you think it would excite some interest, and take off the unexpected horror of the story, by showing that the events are real, if it could be made to appear in some paper in some form ?

You will hear from me again shortly, as I send you by

sea the *Cencis* printed, which you will be good enough to
keep. Adieu.

Yours most faithfully,

P. B. SHELLEY.

XLVII.—TO LEIGH HUNT.

Livorno, Sept. 27th, 1819.

MY DEAR FRIEND—We are now on the point of leaving
this place for Florence, where we have taken pleasant apartments for six months, which brings us to the 1st of April, the
season at which new flowers and new thoughts spring forth upon
the earth and in the mind. What is then our destination is yet
undecided. I have not seen Florence, except as one sees the
outside of the streets ; but its *physiognomy* indicates it to be a
city which, though the ghost of a republic, yet possesses most
amiable qualities. I wish you could meet us there in the spring,
and we would try to muster up a "lièta brigata," which, leaving
behind them the pestilence of remembered misfortunes, might
act over again the pleasures of the Interlocutors in Boccaccio.
I have been lately reading this most divine writer. He is,
in a high sense of the word, a poet, and his language has
the rhythm and harmony of verse. I think him not equal
certainly to Dante or Petrarch, but far superior to Tasso
and Ariosto, the children of a later and of a colder day. I
consider the three first as the productions of the vigour of
the infancy of a new nation—as rivulets from the same spring
as that which fed the greatness of the republics of Florence
and Pisa, and which checked the influence of the German
emperors ; and from which, through obscurer channels, Raffaele
and Michael Angelo drew the light and the harmony of their
inspiration. When the second-rate poets of Italy wrote,
the corrupting blight of tyranny was already hanging on
every bud of genius. Energy, and simplicity, and unity of
of idea, were no more. In vain do we seek in the finest
passages of Ariosto and Tasso, any expression which at all
approaches in this respect to those of Dante and Petrarch.
How much do I admire Boccaccio ! What descriptions of
nature are those in his little introductions to every new day !
It is the morning of life stripped of that mist of familiarity
which makes it obscure to us. Boccaccio seems to me to
have possessed a deep sense of the fair ideal of human life,

considered in its social relations. His more serious theories of love agree especially with mine. He often expresses things lightly too, which have serious meanings of a very beautiful kind. He is a moral casuist, the opposite of the Christian, stoical, ready-made, and worldly system of morals. Do you remember one little remark, or rather maxim of his, which might do some good to the common narrow-minded conceptions of love,—" Bocca bacciata non perde ventura ; anzi rinnuova, come fa la luna ? "

We expect Mary to be confined towards the end of October. The birth of a child will probably retrieve her from some part of her present melancholy depression.

It would give me much pleasure to know Mr. Lloyd. Do you know, when I was in Cumberland, I got Southey to borrow a copy of Berkeley from him, and I remember observing some pencil notes in it, probably written by Lloyd, which I thought particularly acute. One, especially, struck me as being the assertion of a doctrine, of which even then I had long been persuaded, and on which I had founded much of my persuasions, as regarded the imagined cause of the universe—" Mind cannot create, it can only perceive." Ask him if he remembers having written it. Of Lamb you know my opinion, and you can bear witness to the regret which I felt, when I learned that the calumny of an enemy had deprived me of his society whilst in England.—Ollier told me that the Quarterly are going to review me. I suppose it will be a pretty   , and as I am acquiring a taste for humour and drollery, I confess I am curious to see it. I have sent my " Prometheus Unbound " to P. ; if you ask him for it he will show it you. I think it will please you.

Whilst I went to Florence, Mary wrote, but I did not see her letter.—Well, good b'ye. Next Monday I shall write to you from Florence. Love to all.

Most affectionately your friend,

P. B. S.

———

XLVIII.—To Mrs. Gisborne.

Florence, October 13th or 14th, 1819.

My Dear Friend—The regret we feel at our absence from you persuades me that it is a state which cannot last, and which, so long as it must last, will be interrupted by some intervals, one of which is destined to be, your all coming to visit us here. Poor Oscar! I feel a kind of remorse to think of the unequal love with which two animated beings regard each other, when I experience no such sensations for him, as those which he manifested for us. His importunate regret is, however, a type of ours, as regards you. Our memory—if you will accept so humble a metaphor—is for ever scratching at the door of your absence.

About Henry and the steam-engine.* I am in torture until this money comes from London, though I am sure that it will and must come; unless, indeed, my banker has broke, and then it will be my loss, not Henry's—a little delay will mend the matter. I would then write instantly to London an effectual letter, and by return of post all would be set right—it would then be a thing easily set straight—but if it were not, you know me too well not to know that there is no personal suffering, or degradation, or toil, or anything that can be named, with which I do not feel myself bound to support this enterprise of Henry. But all this rhodomontade only shows how correct Mr. Bielby's advice was, about the discipline necessary for my imagination. No doubt that all will go on with mercantile and commonplace exactness, and that you will be spared the suffering, and I the virtue, incident to some untoward event.

I am anxious to hear of Mr. Gisborne's return, and I anticipate the surprise and pleasure with which he will learn that a resolution has been taken which leaves you nothing to regret in that event. It is with unspeakable satisfaction that I reflect that my entreaties and persuasions overcame your scruples on this point, and that whatever advantage shall accrue from it will belong to you, whilst any reproach due to the imprudence of such an enterprise must rest on me. I shall thus share the pleasure of success, and bear the blame and loss, (if such a thing were possible,) of a reverse; and what more can a man, who is a friend to another, desire for himself? Let us believe in a kind of optimism, in which we are our own gods. It is best that Mr. Gisborne should have returned; it is best that I should have over-persuaded you and Henry; it is best that you should all live together, without any more solitary

---

* Shelley set on foot the building of a steam-boat, to ply between Marseilles, Genoa, and Leghorn. Such an enterprise promised fortune to his friend who undertook to build it, and the anticipation filled him with delight. Unfortunately, an unforeseen complication of circumstances caused the design to be abandoned, when already far advanced towards completion.—*M. S.*

attempts ; it is best that this one attempt should have been made, otherwise, perhaps, one thing which is best might not have occurred ; and it is best that we should think all this for the best, even though it is not ; because Hope, as Coleridge says, is a solemn duty, which we owe alike to ourselves and to the world—a worship to the spirit of good within, which requires, before it sends that inspiration forth, which impresses its likeness upon all that it creates, devoted and disinterested homage.

A different scene is this from that in which you made the chief character of our changing drama. We see no one, as usual. Madame M—— is quiet, and we only meet her now and then, by chance. Her daughter, not so fair, but I fear as cold, as the snowy Florimel in Spenser, is in and out of love with C—— as the winds happen to blow ; and C——, who, at the moment I happen to write, is in a high state of transitory contentment, is setting off to Vienna in a day or two.

My £100, from what mistake remains to be explained, has not yet arrived, and the banker here is going to advance me £50, on my bill at three months—all additional facilitation, should any such be needed, for the steam-boat. I have yet seen little of Florence. The gallery I have a design of studying piece-meal ; one of my chief objects in Italy being the observing in statuary and painting the degree in which, and the rules according to which, that ideal beauty, of which we have so intense yet so obscure an apprehension, is realised in external forms.

Adieu.—I am anxious for Henry's first letter. Give to him and take to yourself those sentiments, whatever they may be, with which you know that I cannot cease to regard you.

Most faithfully and affectionately yours,

P. B. S.

I had forgotten to say that I should be very much obliged to you, if you would contrive to send The Cenci, which are at the printer's, to England, by the next ship. I forgot it in the hurry of departure.—I have just heard from P., saying, that he don't think that my tragedy will do, and that he don't much like it. But I ought to say, to blunt the edge of his criticism, that he is a nursling of the exact and superficial school in poetry.

If Mr. G. is returned, send the " Prometheus " with them.

XLIX.—To C. Ollier.

Florence, Oct. 15, 1819.

Dear Sir,
The droll remarks of the *Quarterly,* and Hunt s kind defence, arrived as safe as such poison, and safer than such an antidote, usually do.

I am on the point of sending to you 250 copies of a work which I have printed in Italy ; which you will have to pay four or five pounds duty upon, on my account. Hunt will tell you the *kind of thing* it is, and in the course of the winter I shall send directions for its publication, *until the arrival of which directions, I request that you would have the kindness not* to open the box, *or, if by necessity it is opened, to abstain from observing yourself, or permitting others to observe, what it contains.** I trust this confidently to you, it being of consequence. Meanwhile, assure yourself that this work has no reference, direct or indirect, to politics, or religion, or personal satire, and that this precaution is merely literary.

The *Prometheus,* a poem in my best style, whatever that may amount to, will arrive with it, but in MS., which you can print and publish in the season. It is the most perfect of my productions.

Southey wrote the article in question, I am well aware. Observe the impudence of the man in speaking of himself. The only remark worth notice in this piece is the assertion that I imitate Wordsworth. It may as well be said that Lord Byron imitates Wordsworth, or that Wordsworth imitates Lord Byron, both being great poets, and deriving from the new springs of thought and feeling, which the great events of our age have exposed to view, a similar tone of sentiment, imagery, and expression. A certain similarity all the best writers of any particular age inevitably are marked with, from the spirit of that age acting on all. This I had explained in my Preface, which the writer was too disingenuous to advert to. As to the other trash, and particularly that lame attack on my personal character, which was meant so ill, and which I am not the man to feel, 'tis all nothing. I am glad, with respect to that part of it which alludes to Hunt, that it should so have happened that I dedicate, as you will see, a work which has all the capacities for being popular to that excellent person. I was amused, too, with the finale ; it is like the end of the first act of an opera,

* The italics are Shelley's own.—*L. S.*

when that tremendous concordant discord sets up from the
orchestra, and everybody talks and sings at once. It describes
the result of my battle with their Omnipotent God ; his pulling
me under the sea by the hair of my head, like Pharaoh ; my
calling out like the devil who was *game* to the last; swearing
and cursing in all comic and horrid oaths, like a French postillion
on Mount Cenis ; entreating everybody to drown themselves ;
pretending not to be drowned myself when I *am* drowned ; and,
lastly, *being* drowned.*

You would do me a particular kindness if you would call on
Hunt, and ask him when my parcel went, the name of the ship,
and the name of the captain, and whether he has any bill of
lading, which, if he has, you would oblige me by sending,
together with the rest of the information, by return of post,
addressed to the Post Office, Florence.

Yours very sincerely,

P. B. SHELLEY.

L.—TO HENRY REVELEY.

Florence, Oct. 28, 1819.

MY DEAR HENRY—So it seems *I* am to begin the correspondence, though I have more to ask than to tell.

You know our bargain ; you are to write me *uncorrected*
letters, just as the words come, so let me have them—I like coin
from the mint—though it may be a little rough at the edges ;—
clipping is penal according to our statute.

In the first place, listen to a reproach ; you ought to have
sent me an acknowledgment of my last billet. I am very
happy to hear from Mr. Gisborne, and he knows well enough
how to interest me himself, not to need to rob me of an occasion
of hearing from you. Let you and I try if we cannot be as
punctual and business-like as the best of them. But no clipping
and coining, if you please.

Now take this that I say in a light just so serious as not to
give you pain. In fact, my dear fellow, my motive for soliciting
your correspondence, and that flowing from your own mind, and
clothed in your own words, is, that you may begin to accustom
to discipline yourself in the only practice of life in which you
appear deficient. You know that you are writing to a person
persuaded of all the confidence and respect due to your powers

* Shelley's frequent allusions to his being drowned are very
singular.—*L. S.*

in those branches of science to which you have addicted yourself ; and you will not permit a false shame with regard to the mere mechanical arrangement of words to overbalance the advantage arising from the free communication of ideas. Thus you will become day by day more skilful in the management of that instrument of their communication, on which the attainment of a person's just rank in society depends. Do not think me arrogant. There are subjects of the highest importance in which you are far better qualified to instruct me, than I am qualified to instruct you on this subject.

Well, how goes on all ? The boilers, the keel of the boat, and the cylinder, and all the other elements of that soul which is to guide our "monstruo de fuego y agua" over the sea ? Let me hear news of their birth, and how they thrive after they are born. And is the money arrived at Mr. Webb's ? Send me an account of the number of crowns you realise ; as I think we had better, since it is a transaction in this country, keep our accounts in money of this country.

We have rains enough to set the mills going, which are essential to your great iron bar.   I suppose it is at present either made or making.

My health is better so long as the scirocco blows, and, but for my daily expectation of Mary's confinement, I should have been half tempted to have come to see you. As it is, I shall wait till the boat is finished. On the subject of your actual and your expected progress, you will certainly allow me to hear from you.

Give my kindest regards to your mother and Mr. Gisborne—tell the latter, whose billet I have neglected to answer, that I did so, under the idea of addressing him in a post or two on a subject which gives me considerable anxiety about you all.   I mean the continuance of your property in the British funds at this crisis of approaching revolution.   It is the business of a friend to say what he thinks without fear of giving offence ; and, if I were not a friend, argument is worth its market-price anywhere.

Believe me, my dear Henry,

Your very faithful friend,

P. B. S.

LI.—To Mr. and Mrs. Gisborne.

Florence, Oct. 28, 1819.

My Dear Friends—I receive this morning the strange and unexpected news, that my bill of £200 has been returned to Mr.

Webb protested. Ultimately this can be nothing but delay, as I have only drawn from my banker's hands so much as to leave them still in possession of £80, and this I positively know, and can prove by documents. By return of post, for I have not only written to my banker, but to private friends, no doubt Henry will be enabled to proceed. Let him meanwhile do all that can be done.

Meanwhile, to save time, could not money be obtained temporarily, at Livorno, from Mr. W——, or Mr. G——, or any of your acquaintance, on my bills at three or six months, indorsed by Mr. Gisborne and Henry, so that he may go on with his work ? If a month is of consequence, think of this.

Be of good cheer, Madonna mia, all will go well. The inclosed is for Henry, and was written before this news, as he will see ; but it does not, strange as it is, abate one atom of my cheer.

Accept, dear Mr. G., my best regards.

Yours faithfully,

P. B. S.

LII.—TO MR. AND MRS. GISBORNE.

Florence, Nov. 6, 1819.

MY DEAR FRIENDS—I have just finished a letter of five sheets on Carlile's affair, and am in hourly expectation of Mary's confinement : you will imagine an excuse for my silence.

I forbear to address you, as I had designed, on the subject of your income as a public creditor of the English government, as it seems you have not the exclusive management of your funds ; and the peculiar circumstances of the delusion are such that none but a very few persons will ever be brought to see its instability but by the experience of loss. If I were to convince you, Henry would probably be unable to convince his uncle. In vindication, however, of what I have already said, allow me to turn your ·attention to England at this *hour*.

In order to meet the national expenses, or rather that some approach towards meeting them might seem to be made, a tax of £3,000,000 was imposed. The first consequence of this has been a *defalcation* in the revenue at the rate of £3,600,000 a-year. Were the country in the most tranquil and prosperous state, the minister, in such a condition of affairs, must reduce the interest of the national debt, or add to it ; a process which would only insure the greater ultimate reduction of the interest.

But the people are nearly in a state of insurrection, and the least unpopular noblemen perceive the necessity of conducting a spirit, which it is no longer possible to oppose. For submitting to this necessity—which, be assured, the haughty aristocrats unwillingly did—Lord Fitzwilliam has been degraded from his situation of Lord-Lieutenant. An additional army of 11,500 men has received orders to be organised. Everything is preparing for a bloody struggle, in which, if the ministers succeed, they will assuredly diminish the interest of the national debt, for no combination of the heaviest tyranny can raise the taxes for its payment. If the people conquer, the public creditor will equally suffer; for it is monstrous to imagine that they will submit to the perpetual inheritance of a double aristocracy. They will perhaps find some crown and church lands, and appropriate the tithes to make a kind of compensation to the public creditor. They will confiscate the estates of their political enemies. But all this will not pay a tenth part of their debt. The existing government, atrocious as it is, is the surest party to which a public creditor may attach himself. He may reason that *it may last my time*, though in the event the ruin is more complete than in the case of a popular revolution. I know you too well to believe you capable of arguing in this manner; I only reason on how things stand.

Your income may be reduced from £210 to £150, and then £100, and then, by the issue of immense quantities of paper to save the immediate cause of one of the conflicting parties, to any value however small ; or the source of it may be cut off at once. The ministers had, I doubt not, long since determined to establish an arbitrary government ; and if they had not determined so, they have now entangled themselves in that consequence of their instinct as rulers, and if they recede they must perish. They are, however, not receding, and we are on the eve of great actions.

Kindest regards to Henry. I hope he is not stopped for want of money, as I shall assuredly send him what he wants in a month from the date of my last letter. I received his letter from Pistoia, and have no other criticism to make on it, except the severest—that it is too short. How goes on Portuguese—and Theocritus ? I have deserted the odorous gardens of literature, to journey across the great sandy desert of politics ; not, as you may imagine, without the hope of finding some enchanted paradise. In all probability, I shall be overwhelmed by one of the tempestuous columns which are forever traversing, with the speed of a storm, and the confusion of a chaos, that pathless wilderness. You meanwhile will be lamenting in some happy oasis that I do not return. This is out-Calderonizing Muley. We have had lightning and rain here in plenty. I like the Cascini very much, where I often walk alone, watching the leaves, and the rising and falling of the Arno. I am full of all kinds of literary plans.

Meanwhile, all yours most faithfully,
P. B. S.

LIII.—To Leigh Hunt.

Firenze, Nov. 13, 1819.

MY DEAR FRIEND—Yesterday morning Mary brought me a little boy. She suffered but two hours' pain, and is now so well that it seems a wonder that she stays in bed. The babe is also quite well, and has begun to suck. You may imagine that this is a great relief and a great comfort to me amongst all my misfortunes, past, present, and to come.

Since I last wrote to you, some circumstances have occurred not necessary to explain by letter, which makes my pecuniary condition a very painful one. The physicians absolutely forbid my travelling to England in the winter, but I shall probably pay you a visit in the spring. With what pleasure, among all the other sources of regret and discomfort with which England abounds for me, do I *think* of looking on the original of that kind and earnest face, which is now opposite Mary's bed. It will be the only thing which Mary will envy me, or will need to envy me, in that journey, for I shall come alone. Shaking hands with you is worth all the trouble ; the rest is clear loss.

I will tell you more about myself and my pursuits in my next letter.

Kind love to Marianne, Bessy, and all the children. Poor Mary begins (for the first time) to look a little consoled ; for we have spent, as you may imagine, a miserable five months.

Good-bye, my dear Hunt.

Your affectionate friend,
P. B. S.

I have had no letter from you *for a month.*

LIV.—To Mrs. Gisborne.

Florence, Nov. 16, 1819.

Madonna—I have been lately voyaging in a sea without my pilot, and although my sail has often been torn, my boat become leaky, and the log lost, I have yet sailed in a kind of way from island to island ; some of craggy and mountainous magnificence, some clothed with moss and flowers, and radiant with fountains, some barren deserts. *I have been reading Calderon without you.* I have read the "Cisma de Ingalaterra," the "Cabellos de Absolom," and three or four others. These pieces, inferior to those we read, at least to the "Principe Constante," in the splendour of particular passages, are perhaps superior in their satisfying completeness. The Cabellos de Absolom is full of the deepest and tenderest touches of nature. Nothing can be more pathetically conceived than the character of old David, and the tender and impartial love, overcoming all insults and all crimes, with which he regards his conflicting and disobedient sons. The incest scene. of Amnon and Tamar is perfectly tremendous. Well may Calderon say in the person of the former :—

> Si sangre sin fuego hiere,
> que fara sangre con fuego ?

Incest is, like many other incorrect things, a very poetical circumstance. It may be the excess of love or hate. It may be the defiance of everything for the sake of another, which clothes itself in the glory of the highest heroism ; or it may be that cynical rage which, confounding the good and the bad in existing opinions, breaks through them for the purpose of rioting in selfishness and antipathy. Calderon, following the Jewish historians, has represented Amnon's action in the basest point of view—he is a prejudiced savage, acting what he abhors, and abhorring that which is the unwilling party to his crime.

Adieu. Madonna, yours truly,　　　　　P. B. S.

I transcribe you a passage from the Cisma de Ingalaterra—spoken by "Carlos, Embaxador de Francia, enamorado de Ana Bolena." Is there anything in Petrarch finer than the second stanza ?*

> * Porque apenas el Sol se coronaba
> de nueva luz en la estacion primeva,
> quando yo en sus umbrales adoraba
> segundo Sol en abreviada esfera ;

LV.—To John Gisborne.

My Dear Sir,—I envy you the first reading of Theocritus.
Were not the Greeks a glorious people? What is there, as Job
says of the Leviathan, like unto them? If the army of Nicias
had not been defeated under the walls of Syracuse ; if the
Athenians had, acquiring Sicily, held the balance between
Rome and Carthage, sent garrisons to the Greek colonies in the
south of Italy, Rome might have been all that its intellectual
condition entitled it to be, a tributary, not the conqueror of
Greece ; the Macedonian power would never have attained to
the dictatorship of the civilised states of the world. Who
knows whether, under the steady progress which philosophy
and social institutions would have made, (for, in the age to
which I refer, their progress was both rapid and secure) among

> la noche apenas trémula baxaba,
> à solos mis deseos lisonjera,
> quando un jardin, republica de flores,
> era tercero fiel de mis amores.
>
> Alli, el silencio de la noche fria,
> el jazmin, que en las redes se enlazava,
> el cristal de la fuente que corria,
> el arroyo que á solas murmurava,
> El viento que en las hojas se movia,
> el Aura que en las flores respirava ;
> todo era amor' ; què mucho, si en tal calma,
> aves, fuentes, ·y flores tienen alma !
>
> No has visto providente y officiosa,
> mover el ayre iluminada aveja,
> que hasta beber la purpura á la rosa
> ya se acerca cobarde, y ya se alexa ?
> No has visto enamorada mariposa,
> dar cercos á la luz, hasta que dexa,
> en monumento facil abrasadas
> las alas de color tornasoladas ?
>
> Assi mi amor, cobarde muchos dias,
> tornos hizo á la rosa y á la llama ;
> temor che ha sido entre cenizas frias,
> tantas vezes llorado de quien ama ;
> pero el amor, que vence con porfias,
> y la ocasion, que con disculpas llama,
> me animaron, y aveja y mariposa
> quemè las alas, y llegué á la rosa.

a people of the most perfect physical organization, whether the Christian religion would have arisen, or the barbarians have overwhelmed the wrecks of civilisation which had survived the conquest and tyranny of the Romans? What then should we have been? As it is, all of us who are worth anything, spend our manhood in unlearning the follies, or expiating the mistakes, of our youth. We are stuffed full of prejudices ; and our natural passions are so managed, that if we restrain them we grow intolerant and precise, because we restrain them not according to reason, but according to error ; and if we do not restrain them, we do all sorts of mischief to ourselves and others. Our imagination and understanding are alike subjected to rules the most absurd ;—so much for Theocritus and the Greeks.

In spite of all your arguments, I wish your money were out of the funds. This middle course which you speak of, and which may probably have place, will amount to your losing not all your income, nor retaining all, but have the half taken away. I feel intimately persuaded, whatever political forms may have place in England, that no party can continue many years, perhaps not many months, in the administration, without diminishing the interest of the national debt.—And once having commenced—and having done so safely—where will it end?

Give Henry my kindest thanks for his most interesting letter, and bid him expect one from me by the next post.

Mary and the babe continue well.—Last night we had a magnificent thunder storm, with claps that shook the house like an earthquake. Both Mary and C——— unite with me in kindest remembrances to all.

Most faithfully yours obliged,
P. B. S.

Florence, Nov. 16th, 1819.

LVI.—To a Lady.

[*Exact date unknown.*]

" It is probable that you will be earnest to employ the sacred talisman of language. To acquire these you are now necessitated to sacrifice many hours of the time, when, instead of being conversant with particles and verbs, your nature incites you to contemplation and inquiry concerning the objects which they conceal. You desire to enjoy the beauties of eloquence and poetry—to sympathise in the original language with the institutors and martyrs of ancient freedom. The generous and inspiriting examples of philosophy and virtue, you desire intimately to know and feel ; not as mere facts detailing names, and dates, and motions of the human body, but clothed in the very language of the actors,—that language dictated by and expressive of the passions and principles that governed their conduct. Facts are not what we want to know in poetry, in history, in the lives of individual men, in satire, or panegyric. They are the mere divisions, the arbitrary points on which we hang, and to which we refer those delicate and evanescent hues of mind, which language delights and instructs us in precise proportion as it expresses. What is a translation of Homer into English? A person who is ignorant of Greek, need only look at *Paradise Lost*, or the tragedy of *Lear* translated into French, to obtain an analogical conception of its worthless and miserable inadequacy. Tacitus, or Livius, or Herodotus, are equally undelightful and uninstructive in translation. You require to know and to be intimate with those persons who have acted a distinguished part to benefit, to enlighten, or even to pervert and injure humankind. Before you can do this, four years are yet to be consumed in the discipline of the ancient languages, and those of modern Europe, which you only imperfectly know, and which conceal from your intimacy such names as Ariosto, Tasso, Petrarch, and Macchiavelli ; or Goethe, Schiller, Wieland, etc. The French language you, like every other respectable woman, already know ; and if the great name of Rousseau did not redeem it, it would have been perhaps as well that you had remained entirely ignorant of it."

LVII.—To Henry Reveley.

Florence, Nov. 17th, 1819.

My Dear Henry—I was exceedingly interested by your letter, and I cannot but thank you for overcoming the inaptitude of a long disuse at my request, for my pleasure. It is a great thing done, the successful casting of the cylinder—may it be a happy auspice for what is to follow ! I hope, in a few posts, to remit the necessary money for the completion. Meanwhile, are not those portions of the work which can be done without expense, saving time in their progress? Do you think you lose much money or time by this delay?

All that you say of the alteration in the form of the boat strikes me, though one of the multitude in this respect, as improvement. I long to get aboard her, and be an unworthy partaker in the glory of the astonishment of the Livornese, when she returns from her cruise round Melloria. When do you think she will be fit for sea?

Your volcanic description of the birth of the cylinder is very characteristic of you, and of it.* One might imagine God, when he made the earth, and saw the granite mountains and flinty promontories flow into their craggy forms, and the splendour of their fusion filling millions of miles of the void space, like the tail of a comet, so looking, so delighting in his work. God sees his machine spinning round the sun, and delights in its success, and has taken out patents to supply all the suns in space with the same manufacture. Your boat will be to the ocean of water, what this earth is to the ocean of ether—a prosperous and swift voyager.

When shall we see you all? *You* not, I suppose, till your boat is ready to sail—and then, if not before, I must, of course, come to Livorno. Our plans for the winter are yet scarcely defined; they tend towards our spending February and March at Pisa, where our communications will not be so distant, nor so epistolary. C—— left us a week ago, not without many lamentations, as all true lovers pay on such occasions. He is to write me an account of the *Trieste* steam-boat, which I will transmit to you.

Mrs. Shelley and Miss C—— return you their kindest salutations, with interest.

Most affectionately yours,
P. B. S.

* I insert the extract alluded to from Mr. Reveley's letter:—

"*Friday*, 12*th Nov.*

"The event is now past—both the steam cylinder and air-pump were cast at three o'clock this afternoon. At two o'clock this morning I repaired to the mill to see that the preliminary operations, upon which the ultimate success of a *fount* greatly depends, were conducted with proper attention. The moulds are buried in a pit, made close, before the mouth of the furnace, so that the melted metal, when the plug is driven in, may run easily into them, and fill up the vacant space left between the core and the shell, in order to form the desired cylinders. The fire was lighted in the furnace at nine, and in three hours the metal was fused. At three o'clock it was ready to cast, the fusion

LVIII.—To Leigh Hunt.

Florence, Nov. 23, 1819.

My Dear Hunt—*Why* don't you write to us ? I was preparing to send you something for your " Indicator," but I have
been a drone instead of a bee in this business, thinking that perhaps, as you did not acknowledge any of my late enclosures, it
would not be welcome to you, whatever I might send.

What a state England is in! But you will never write
politics. I don't wonder ; but I wish, then, that you would
write a paper in the " Examiner " on the actual state of the
country, and what, under all circumstances of the conflicting
passions and interests of men, we are to expect. Not what we
ought to expect, nor what, if so and so were to happen, we
might expect ;—but what, as things are, there is reason to
believe will come ;—and send it me for my information. Every
word a man has to say is valuable to the public now ; and thus
you will at once gratify your friend, nay, instruct, and either
exhilarate him, or force him to be resigned, and awaken the
minds of the people.

I have no spirits to write what I do not know whether you
will care much about ; I know well that if I were in great
misery, poverty, etc., you would think of nothing else but how
to amuse and relieve me. You omit me if I am prosperous.

I could laugh, if I found a joke, in order to put you in good-

being remarkably rapid, owing to the perfection of the furnace. The
metal was also heated to an extreme degree, boiling with fury, and
seeming to dance with the pleasure of running into its proper form.
The plug was struck, and a massy stream of a bluish dazzling whiteness
filled the moulds in the twinkling of a shooting star. The castings will
not be cool enough to be drawn up till to-morrow afternoon ; but, to
judge from all appearances, I expect them to be perfect."

" *Saturday*, 13*th Nov.*

" They have been excavated and drawn up. I have examined them
and found them really perfect ; they are massive and strong to bear any
usage and sea-water, *in sæcula sæculorum.* I am now going on gently
with the brass-work, which does not require any immediate expenses,
and which I attend to entirely myself. I have no workmen about me
at present.

" With kindest salutations to Mrs. Shelley and Miss C.,

" I remain, most truly,

" Your obliged friend and devoted servant,

" Henry W. Reveley."

—*M. S.*

humour with me after my scolding ; in good-humour enough to write to us. . . . Affectionate love to and from all. This ought not only to be the *Vale* of a letter, but a superscription over the gate of life.

Your sincere friend,
P. B. SHELLEY.

I send you a *sonnet.* I don't expect you to publish it, but you may show it to whom you please.

LIX.—TO LEIGH HUNT.

Florence, November, 1819.

MY DEAR FRIEND—Two letters, both bearing date Oct. 20, arrive on the same day ; one is always glad of twins.

We hear of a box arrived at Genoa with books and clothes ; it must be yours. Meanwhile the babe is wrapt in flannel petticoats, and we get on with him as we can. He is small, healthy, and pretty. Mary is recovering rapidly. Marianne, I hope, is quite well.

You do not tell me whether you have received my lines on the Manchester affair. They are of the exoteric species, and are meant, not for the "Indicator," but the "Examiner." I would send for the former, if you like, some letters on such subjects of art as suggest themselves in Italy. Perhaps I will, at a venture, send you a specimen of what I mean next post. I enclose you in this a piece for the "Examiner," or let it share the fate, whatever that fate may be, of the "Masque of Anarchy."*

I am sorry to hear that you have employed yourself in translating the "Aminta," though I doubt not it will be a just and beautiful translation. You ought to write Amintas. You ought to exercise your fancy in the perpetual creation of new forms of gentleness and beauty.

With respect to translation, even *I* will not be seduced by it ; although the Greek plays, and some of the ideal dramas of Calderon, (with which I have lately, and with inexpressible wonder and delight, become acquainted) are perpetually tempting me to throw over their perfect and glowing forms the grey veil of my own words. And you know me too well to suspect

* Peter Bell the Third.—*M. S.*

that I refrain from a belief that what I could substitute for them
would deserve the regret which yours would, if suppressed. I
have confidence in my moral sense alone ; but that is a kind of
originality. I have only translated the Cyclops of Euripides,
when I could absolutely do nothing else ; and the Symposium
of Plato, which is the delight and astonishment of all who read
it ; I mean the original, or so much of the original as is seen in
my translation, not the translation itself.

I think I have had an accession of strength since my residence
in Italy, though the disease itself in the side, whatever it may
be, is not subdued. Some day we shall all return from Italy.
I fear that in England things will be carried violently by the
rulers, and they will not have learned to yield in time to the
spirit of the age. The great thing to do is to hold the balance
between popular impatience and tyrannical obstinacy ; to incul-
cate with fervour both the right of resistance and the duty of
forbearance. You know my principles incite me to take all the
good I can get in politics, for ever aspiring to something more.
I am one of those whom nothing will fully satisfy, but who are
ready to be partially satisfied in all that is practicable. We
shall see.

Give Bessy a thousand thanks from me for writing out in that
pretty neat hand your kind and powerful defence. Ask what
she would like best from Italian land. We mean to bring you
all something ; and Mary and I have been wondering what it
shall be. Do you, each of you, choose.

Adieu, my dear friend,
Yours affectionately ever,
P. B. S.

LX.—From Shelley to Mr. Ollier.

Florence, December 15th, 1819.

DEAR SIR—Pray, give Mr. Procter my best thanks for his
polite attention. I read the article you enclosed with the
pleasure which every one feels, of course, when they are praised
or defended ; though the praise would have given me more
pleasure if it had been less excessive. I am glad, however, to
see the *Quarterly* cut up, and that by one of their own people.
Poor Southey has enough to endure. Do you know, I think
the article in *Blackwood* could not have been written by a
favourer of Government and a religionist. I don't believe any

such one could sincerely like my writings. After all, is it not some friend in disguise, and don't you know who wrote it?

There is one very droll thing in the *Quarterly.* They say that "my chariot-wheels are broken." Heaven forbid! My chariot, you may tell them, was built by one of the best makers in Bond Street, and it has gone several thousand miles in perfect security. What a comical thing it would be to make the following advertisement :—"A report having prevailed, in consequence of some insinuations in the *Quarterly Review,* that Mr. Shelley's chariot wheels are broken, Mr. Charters, of Bond Street, begs to assure the public that they, after having carried him through Italy, France, and Switzerland, still continue in excellent repair."

When the box comes, you may write a note to Mr. Peacock ; or it would be better to call on him, and ask if *my tragedy is accepted?* If not, publish what you find in the box. I think it will succeed as a publication. Let *Prometheus* be printed without delay. You will receive the additions, which Mrs. S. is now transcribing, in a few days. It has already been read to many persons. My *Prometheus* is the best thing I ever wrote.

Pray, what have you done with *Peter Bell?* Ask Mr. Hunt for it, and for some other poems of a similar character I sent him to give you to publish. I think *Peter* not bad in his way ; but perhaps no one will believe in anything in the shape of a joke from me.

Of course with my next box you will send me the *Dramatic Sketches.** I have only seen the extracts in the *Examiner.* They have some passages painfully beautiful. When I consider the vivid energy to which the minds of men are awakened in this age of ours, ought I not to congratulate myself that I am a contemporary with names which are great, or will be great, or ought to be great?

Have you seen my poem, *Julian and Maddalo?* Suppose you print that in the manner of Hunt's *Hero and Leander;* for I mean to write three other poems, the scenes of which will be laid at Rome, Florence, and Naples, but the subjects of which will be all drawn from dreadful or beautiful realities, as that of this was.

If I have health—but I will neither boast nor promise. I am preparing an octavo on reform—a commonplace kind of book— which, now that I see the passion of party will postpone the great struggle till another year, I shall not trouble myself to

* By B. W. Procter—(Barry Cornwall).

finish for this season. I intend it to be an instructive and readable book, appealing from the passions to the reason of men.

Yours very sincerely,
P. B. S.

LXI.—To HENRY REVELEY.

Florence, 18*th Dec.*, 1819.

MY DEAR HENRY—You see, as I said, it only amounts to delay, all this abominable entanglement. I send you 484 dollars, or ordinary francesconi, I suppose, but you will tell me what you receive in Tuscan money, if they are not—the produce of £100. So my heart is a little lightened, which, I assure you, was heavy enough until this moment, on your account. I write to Messrs. Ward to pay you.

I have received no satisfactory letter from my bankers, but I must expect it every week—or, at least, in a month from this date, when I will not fail to transmit you the remainder of what may be necessary.

Everybody here is talking of a steam-ship which is building at Leghorn ; one person said, as if he knew the whole affair, that he was waiting in Tuscany to take his departure to Naples in it. Your name has not, to my knowledge, been mentioned. I think you would do well to encourage this publicity.

I have better health than I have known for a long time—ready for any stormy cruise. When will the ship be ready to sail ? We have been feeding ourselves with the hope that Mr. Gisborne and your mother would have paid us their promised visit. I did not even hope, perhaps not even wish, that you should, until the engine is finished. My regret at this failure has several times impelled me to go to Leghorn—but I have always resisted the temptation. Ask them, entreat them, from me, to appoint some early day. We have a bed and room, and everything prepared.

I write in great haste, as you may see. Ever believe me, my dear Henry, your attached friend,

P. B. S.

LXII.—To Mr. and Mrs. Gisborne.

Florence, Dec. 23rd, 1819.

My Dear Friends—I suffered more pain than it would be manly to confess, or than you can easily conceive, from that wretched uncertainty about the money. At last, however, it is certain that you will encounter no further check in the receiving supplies, and a weight is taken from my spirits, which, in spite of many other causes of discomfort, makes itself known to have been a heavy load, by the lightness which I now feel in writing to you.

So the steam-boat will take three months to finish? The vernal equinox will be over by that time, and the early wakening of the year have paved the Mediterranean with calm. Among other circumstances to regret in this delay, it is so far well that our first cruise will be made in serene weather.

I send you enclosed a mandate for 396 francesconi, which is what M. Torlonia incorrectly designates a hundred pounds—but as we count in the money of the country, that need make no difference to us.

I have just finished an additional act to " Prometheus," which Mary is now transcribing, and which will be enclosed for your inspection before it is transmitted to the bookseller. I am engaged in a political work—I am busy enough, and if the faculties of my mind were not imprisoned within a mind, whose bars are daily cares and vulgar difficulties, I might yet do something—but as it is——

Mary is well—but for this affair in London I think her spirits would be good. What shall I—what can I—what ought I to do? You cannot picture to yourself my perplexity.

Adieu, my dear friends.

Ever yours, faithfully attached,
P. B. S.

LXIII.—To C. Ollier.

Pisa, Jan. 20th, 1820.

Dear Sir—I send you the *Witch of Atlas*, a fanciful poem, which, if its merit be measured by the labour which it cost, is worth nothing ; and the errata of *Prometheus*, which I ought to have sent long since—a formidable list, as you will see.

I have lately, and but lately, received Mr. Gisborne's parcel, with reviews, etc. I request you to convey to Mr. Procter my thanks for the present of his works, as well as for the pleasure which I received from the perusal, especially of the *Dramatic Sketches.*

The reviews of my *Cenci* (though some of them, and especially that marked " John Scott," are written with great malignity) on the whole give me as much encouragement as a person of my habits of thinking is capable of receiving from such a source, which is, inasmuch as they coincide with, and confirm, my own decisions. My next attempt (if I should write more) will be a drama, in the composition of which I shall attend to the advice of my critics, to a certain degree. But I doubt whether I *shall* write more. I could be content either with the Hell or the Paradise of poetry; but the torments of its purgatory vex me, without exciting my powers sufficiently to put an end to the vexation.

I have also to thank *you* for the present of one or two of your publications. I am enchanted with your *Literary Miscellany*, although the last article it contains has excited my polemical faculties so violently, that the moment I get rid of my ophthalmia, I mean to set about an answer to it, which I will send to you, if you please. It is very clever, but, I think, very false.* Who is your commentator on the German Drama? He is a powerful thinker, though I differ from him *toto cœlo* about the Devils of Dante and Milton. If you know him personally, pray ask him from me what he means by receiving the *spirit into me;*† and (if really it is any good) how one is to get at it. I was immeasurably amused by the quotation from Schlegel about the way in which the popular faith is destroyed—first the Devil, then the Holy Ghost, then God the Father. I had written a Lucianic essay to prove the same thing. There are two beautiful stories, too, in this *Miscellany*. It pleased me altogether infinitely. I was also much pleased with the *Retrospective Review*—that is, with all the quotations from old books in it ; but it is very ill executed.

---

* The article (which was written by Mr. Peacock) was an Essay on Poetry, which the writer regarded as a worn-out delusion of barbarous times. —*L. S.*

† The writer was the late Archdeacon Hare, who, despite his orthodoxy, was a great admirer of Shelley's genius. He contended that Milton erred in making the Devil a majestical being, and hoped that Shelley would in time humble his soul, and "receive the spirit into him."—*L. S.*

When the spirit moves you, write and give me an account of the ill success of my verses.

Who wrote the review in your publication of my *Cenci?* It was written in a friendly spirit, and, if you know the author, I wish you would tell him from me how much obliged I am to him for this spirit, more gratifying to me than any literary laud.

Dear Sir,

Yours very truly,

P. B. S.

_____

LXIV.—TO JOHN GISBORNE.

MY DEAR SIR—We have suddenly taken the determination to avail ourselves of this lovely weather to approach you as far as Pisa. I need not assure you—unless my malady should violently return—you will see me at Leghorn.

We *embark;* and I promise myself the delight of the sky, the water, and the mountains. I must suffer at any rate, but I expect to suffer less in a boat than in a carriage. I have many things to say, which let me reserve till we meet.

I sympathise in all your good news, as I have done in your ill. Let Henry take care of himself, and not, desiring to combine too many advantages, check the progress of his recovery, the greatest of all.

Remember me affectionately to him and to Mrs. Gisborne, and accept for yourself my unalterable sentiments of regard. Meanwhile, *consider well your plans*, which I only half understand.

Ever most faithfully yours,

P. B. SHELLEY.

Florence, 25th Jan., 1820.

_____

LXV.—TO MR. AND MRS. GISBORNE.

Pisa, 9th Feb., 1820.

PRAY let us see you soon, or our threat may cost both us and you something—a visit to Livorno. The stage direction on the present occasion is, (exit Moonshine) and enter Wall; or rather four walls, who surround and take prisoners the Galan and Dama.

Seriously, pray do not disappoint us. We shall watch the sky, and the death of the scirocco must be the birth of your ˉrrival.

Mary and I are going to study mathematics. We design to take the most compendious, yet certain methods of arriving at the great results. We believe that your right-angled Triangle will contain the solution of the problem of how to proceed.

Do not write, but *come.* Mary is too idle to write, but all that she has to say is *come.* She joins with me in condemning the moonlight plan. Indeed we ought not to be so selfish as to allow you to come at all, if it is to cost you all the fatigue and annoyance of returning the same night. But it will not be—so adieu.

LXVI.—TO C. OLLIER.

Pisa, March 6th, 1820.

DEAR SIR—I do not hear that you have received *Prometheus* and the *Cenci ;* I therefore think it safest to tell you how and when to get them if you have not yet done so.

Give the bill of lading Mr. Gisborne sent you to a broker in the City, whom you employ to get the package, and to pay the duty on the unbound books. The ship sailed in the middle of December, and will assuredly have arrived long before now.

Prometheus Unbound, I must tell you, is my favourite poem ; I charge you, therefore, specially to pet him and feed him with fine ink and good paper. *Cenci* is written for the multitude, and ought to sell well. I think, if I may judge by its merits, the *Prometheus* cannot sell beyond twenty copies. I hear nothing either from Hunt, or you, or any one. If you condescend to write to me, mention something about Keats.

Allow me particularly to request you to send copies of whatever I publish to Horace Smith.

Maybe you will see me in the summer ; but in that case I shall certainly return to this "Paradise of Exiles" by the ensuing winter.

If any of the Reviews abuse me, cut them out and send them. If they praise, you need not trouble yourself. I feel ashamed if I could believe that I should deserve the latter ; the former, I flatter myself, is no more than a just tribute. If Hunt praises me, send it, because that is of another character of thing.

Dear Sir, yours very truly,
PERCY B. SHELLEY.

LXVII.—To C. Ollier.

Pisa, March 13th, 1820.

Dear Sir,
I am anxious to hear that you have received the parcel from Leghorn, and to learn what you are doing with the *Prometheus.* If it can be done without great difficulty, I should be very glad that the *revised* sheets might be sent by the post to me at Leghorn. It might be divided into four partitions, sending me four or five sheets at once.

My friends here have great hopes that the *Cenci* will succeed as a publication. It was refused at Drury Lane,* although expressly written for theatrical exhibition, on a plea of the story being too horrible. I believe it singularly fitted for the stage.

Let me request you to give me frequent notice of my *literary interests* also.

I am, dear Sir,
Your very obliged servant,
Percy B. Shelley.

I hope you are not implicated in the late plot.† Not having heard from Hunt, I am afraid that he, at least, has something to do with it. It is well known, since the time of Jaffier, that a conspirator has no time to think about his friends.

LXVIII.—To Mr. and Mrs. Gisborne.

Pisa, April 23, 1820.

My Dear Friends—We are much pained to hear of the illness you all seem to have been suffering, and still more at the apparent dejection of your last letter. We are in daily expectation this lovely weather of seeing you, and I think the change of air and scene might be good for your health and spirits, even if *we* cannot enliven you. I shall have some business at Livorno soon ; and I thought of coming to fetch you, but I have changed my plan, and mean to return with you, that I may save myself two journeys.

I have been thinking, and talking, and reading Agriculture

* This is apparently a slip of the pen for Covent Garden.—*L. S.*
† The Cato Street Conspiracy.—*L. S.*

this last week. But I am very anxious to see you, especially now as instead of six hours, you give us thirty-six, or perhaps more. I shall hear of the steam-engine, and you will hear of *our* plans when we meet, which will be in so short a time, that I neither inquire nor communiate.

Ever affectionately yours,
P. B. SHELLEY.

LXIX.—To C. OLLIER.

Pisa, May 14*th,* 1820.

DEAR SIR,

I reply to your letter by return of post, to confirm what I said in a former letter respecting a new edition of the *Cenci,* which ought by all means to be instantly urged forward.

I see by your account that I have been greatly mistaken in my calculations of the *profit* of my writings. As to the trifle due to me, it may as well remain in your hands.

As to the printing of the *Prometheus,* be it as you will. But, in this case, I shall repose or trust in your care respecting the correction of the press ; especially in the lyrical parts, where a minute error would be of much consequence. Mr. Gisborne will revise it ; he heard it recited, and will therefore more readily seize any error.

If I had even intended to publish *Julian and Maddalo* with my name, yet I would not print it with *Prometheus.* It would not harmonize. It is an attempt in a different style, in which I am not yet sure of myself—a *sermo pedestris* way of treating human nature, quite opposed to the idealisms of that drama. If you print *Julian and Maddalo,* I wish it to be printed in some unostentatious form, accompanied with the fragment of *Athanase,* and exactly in the manner in which I sent it ; and I particularly desire that my name be not annexed to the first edition of it, in any case.

If *Peter Bell* be printed (you can best judge if it will sell or no, and there would be no other reason for printing such a trifle), attend, I pray you, particularly to completely concealing the author ; and for Emma read Betty, as the name of Peter's sister. Emma, I recollect, is the real name of the sister of a great poet who might be mistaken for Peter. I ought to say that I send you poems in a few posts, to print at the end of *Prometheus,* better fitted for that purpose than any in your possession.

Keats, I hope, is going to show himself a great poet ; like the sun, to burst through the clouds, which, though dyed in the finest colours of the air, obscured his rising. The Gisbornes will bring me from you copies of whatever may be published when they leave England.

Dear Sir,
Yours faithfully,
P. B. SHELLEY.

———

LXX.—To T. L. PEACOCK.

Pisa, May, 1820.

MY DEAR PEACOCK—I congratulate you most sincerely on your choice and on your marriage. . . . I was very much amused by your laconic account of the affair. It is altogether extremely like the *dénouement* of one of your own novels, and as such serves to a theory I once imagined, that in everything any man ever wrote, spoke, acted, or imagined, is contained, as it were, on allegorical idea of his own future life, as the acorn contains the oak.

But not to ascend in my balloon. I have written to ask him to pay me a visit, and though I had no hope of success, I commissioned him to endeavour to bring *you.* This becomes still more improbable from your news ; but I need not say that your amiable mountaineer would make you still more welcome. My friends, the Gisbornes, are now really on their way to London, where they propose to stay only six weeks. I think you will like Mrs. Gisborne. Henry is an excellent fellow, but not very communicative. If you find anything in the shape of dulness or otherwise to endure in Mr. Gisborne, endure it for the lady's sake and mine ; but for Heaven's sake ! do not let him know that I think him stupid. Indeed, perhaps I do him an injustice.* Hogg will find it very agreeable (if he postpones his visit so long, or if he visits me at all) to join them on their return. I wish you, and Hogg, and Hunt, and—I know not who besides— would come and spend some months with me together in this wonderful land.

---

* I think he did. I found Mr. Gisborne an agreeable and well-informed man. He and his amiable and accomplished wife have long been dead. I should not have printed what Shelley says of him if any person were living whom the remembrance could annoy.—*T. L. P.*

We know little of England here. I take in Galignani's paper, which is filled with extracts from the *Courier*, and from those accounts it appears probable that there is but little unanimity in the mass of the people ; with on the one side the success of ministers, and on the other the exasperation of the poor.

I see my tragedy has been republished in Paris ; if that is the case, it ought to sell in London ; but I hear nothing from Ollier.

I have suffered extremely this winter ; but I feel myself most materially better at the return of spring. I am on the whole greatly benefited by my residence in Italy, and but for certain moral causes should probably have been enabled to re-establish my system completely. Believe me, my dear Peacock, yours very sincerely,

P. B. S.

Pray make my best regards acceptable to your new companion.

LXXI.—To John Gisborne,

(LONDON.)

Pisa, May 26th, 1820.

My Dear Friends—I write to you thus early, because I have determined to accept of your kind offer about the correction of "Prometheus." The bookseller makes difficulties about sending the proofs to me, and to whom else can I so well entrust what I am so much interested in having done well; and to whom would I prefer to owe the recollection of an additional kindness done to me? I enclose you two little papers of corrections and additions ;—I do not think you will find any difficulty in interpolating them into their proper places.

Well, how do you like London, and your journey ; the Alps in their beauty and their eternity ; Paris in its slight and transitory colours ; and the wearisome plains of France—and the *moral* people with whom you drank tea last night? Above all, *how* are you? And of the last question, believe me, we are anxiously waiting for a reply—until which I will say nothing, nor ask anything. I rely on the journal with as much security as if it were already written.

I am just returned from a visit to Leghorn, Casciano, and our old fortress at Sant' Elmo. I bought the vases you saw for about twenty sequins less than Micale asked, and had them packed up, and, by the polite assistance of your friend, Mr. Guebhard, sent them on board. I found your Giuseppe very useful in all this business. He got me tea and breakfast, and I slept in your house, and departed early the next morning for Casciano. Everything seems in excellent order at Casa Ricci —garden, pigeons, tables, chairs, and beds. As I did not find my bed sealed up, I left it as I found it. What a glorious prospect you had from the windows of Sant' Elmo! The enormous chain of the Apennines, with its many-folded ridges, islanded in the misty distance of the air ; the sea, so immensely distant, appearing as at your feet ; and the pro- digious expanse of the plain of Pisa, and the dark green marshes lessened almost to a strip by the height of the blue mountains overhanging them. Then the wild and unreclaimed fertility of the foreground, and the chestnut trees, whose vivid foliage made a sort of resting-place to the sense before it darted itself to the jagged horizon of this prospect. I was altogether delighted. I had a respite from my nervous symptoms, which was compensated to me by a violent cold in the head. There was a tradition about you at Sant' Elmo—*An English family that had lived here in the time of the French.* The doctor, too, at the Bagni, knew you. The house is in a most dilapidated condition, but I suppose all that is curable.

We go to the Bagni* next month—but still direct to Pisa as safest. I shall write to you the *ultimates* of my commission in my next letter. I am undergoing a course of the Pisan baths, on which I lay no singular stress—but they soothe. I ought to have peace of mind, leisure, tranquillity ; this I expect soon. Our anxiety about Godwin is very great, and any information that you could give a day or two earlier than he might, respecting any decisive event in his law-suit, would be a great relief. Your impressions about Godwin, (I speak especially to Madonna mia, who had known him before), will especially interest me. You know that added years only add to my admiration of his intellectual powers, and even the moral resources of his character. Of my other friends I say nothing. To see Hunt is to like him; and there is one other recommenda- tion which he has to you, he is my friend. To know H——, if any one can know him, is to know something very unlike, and inexpressibly superior, to the great mass of men.

Will Henry write me an adamantine letter, flowing not like

* Baths of natural warm spring, distant four miles from Pisa, and called indifferently Bagni di Pisa, and Bagni di San Giuliano.—*M. S.*

the words of Sophocles, with honey, but molten brass and iron, and bristling with wheels and teeth? I saw his steam-boat asleep under the walls. I was afraid to waken it, and ask it whether it was dreaming of him, for the same reason that I would have refrained from awakening Ariadne, after Theseus had left her—unless I had been Bacchus.

Affectionately and anxiously yours,.

P. B. S.

LXXII.—To Mr. and Mrs. Gisborne,

(LONDON.)

My Dear Friends—I am to a certain degree indifferent as to the reply to our last proposal, and, therefore, will not allude to it. Permit me only on subjects of this nature to express one sentiment, which you would have given me credit for, even if not expressed. Let no considerations of *my* interest, or any retrospect to the source from which the funds were supplied, modify your decision as to returning and pursuing or abandoning the adventure of the steam-engine. My object was solely your true advantage, and it is when I am baffled of this, by any attention to a mere form, that I shall be ill-requited. Nay, more, I think it for your interest, should you obtain almost whatever situation for Henry, to accept Clementi's proposal, and remain in England ;—not without accepting it, for it does no more than balance the difference of expense between Italy and London ; and if you have any trust in the justice of my moral sense, and believe that in what concerns true honour and virtuous conduct in life, I am an experienced counsellor, you will not hesitate—these things being equal—to accept this proposal. The opposition I made, while you were in Italy, to the abandonment of the steam-boat project, was founded, you well know, on the motives which have influenced everything that ever has guided, or ever will guide anything that I can do or say respecting you. I thought it against Henry's interest. I think it now against his interest that he and you should abandon your prospects in England. As to us—we are uncertain people, who are chased by the spirits of our destiny from purpose to purpose, like clouds by the wind.

There is one thing more to be said. If you decide to remain in England, assuredly it would be foolish to return. Your journey would cost you between £100 and £200, a sum far greater than you could expect to save by the increased price by which you would sell your things. Remit the matter to me, and I will cast off my habitual character, and attend to the minutest points. With Mr. G——'s, devil take his name, I can't write it, —you know who's, assistance, all this might be accomplished in such a manner as to save a very considerable sum. Though I shall suffer from your decision in the proportion as your society is delightful to me, I cannot forbear expressing my persuasion, that the time, the expense, and the trouble of returning to Italy, if your ultimate decision be to settle in London, ought all to be spared. A year, a month, a week, at Henry's age, and with his purposes, ought not to be unemployed. It was the depth with which I felt this truth, which impelled me to incite him to this adventure of the steam-boat.

LXXIII.—To T. L. PEACOCK.

Leghorn, July 12th, 1820.

MY DEAR PEACOCK—I remember you said that when —— married you were afraid you would see or hear but little of him. " There are two voices," says Wordsworth, " one of the mountains and one of the sea, each a mighty voice." So you have two wives—one of the mountains, all of whose claims I perfectly admit, whose displeasure I deprecate, and from whom I feel assured that I have nothing to fear : the other of the sea, perhaps, makes you write so much, that you have not a scrawl to spare. I make bold to write to you on the news that you are correcting my *Prometheus,* for which I return thanks. I hear of you from Mr. Gisborne, but from you I do not hear.

Nothing, I think, shows the generous gullibility of the English nation more than their having adopted her Sacred Majesty a͏ʳ the heroine of the day, in spite of all their prejudices and bigotry. I, for my part, of course wish no harm to happen to her, even if she has, as I firmly believe, amused herself in a manner rather indecorous with any courier or baron. But I cannot help adverting to it as one of the absurdities of royalty, that a vulgar woman, with all those low tastes which prejudice considers as vices, and a person whose habits and manners every one would shun in private life, without any redeeming virtues, should be turned into a heroine because she is a queen, or, as a collateral reason, because her husband is a king ; and he, no less than his ministers, are so odious that everything, however disgusting, which is opposed to them, is admirable. The Paris paper, which I take in, copied some excellent remarks from the *Examiner* about it.

We are just now occupying the Gisbornes' house at Leghorn, and I have turned Mr. Reveley's workshop into my study. The Libecchio here howls like a chorus of fiends all day, and the weather is just pleasant,—not at all hot, the days being very misty, and the nights divinely serene. I have been reading with much pleasure the Greek romances. The best of them is the pastoral of Longus : but they are all very entertaining, and would be delightful if they were less rhetorical and ornate. I am translating in *ottava rima* the *Hymn to Mercury* of Homer. Of course my stanza precludes a literal translation. My next effort will be, that it should be legible—a quality much to be desired in translations.

I am told that the magazines, etc., blaspheme me at a great rate. I wonder why I write verses, for nobody reads them. It is a kind of disorder, for which the regular practitioners prescribe what is called a torrent of abuse ; but I fear that can hardly be considered as a specific.

I enclose two additional poems, to be added to those printed at the end of *Prometheus :* and I send them to you, for fear Ollier might not know what to do in case he objected to some expressions in the fifteenth and sixteenth stanzas ;* and that you would do me the favour to insert an asterisk or asterisks, with as little expense to the sense as may be. The other poem I send to you, not to make two letters. I want Jones's *Greek Grammar* very much for Mary, who is deep in Greek. I thought of sending for it in sheets by the post ; but as I find it would cost as much as a parcel, I would rather have a parcel, including it and some other books, which you would do me a great favour by sending by the first ship. Never send us more reviews than two back on any of Lord Byron's works, as we get them here.—Believe me, my dear Peacock,

Sincerely and affectionately yours,

P. B. S.

Jones's *Greek Grammar ;* Schrevelii *Lexicon ;* The *Greek Exercises ; Melincourt,* and *Headlong Hall ;* papers, *Indicators,* and whatever else you may think interesting. Godwin's *Answer to Malthus,* if out.

* These were the 15th and 16th stanzas of the *Ode to Liberty.—T. L. P.*

LXXIV.—To Mrs. Shelley,

(LEGHORN.)

MY DEAR LOVE—I believe I shall have taken a very pleasant and spacious apartment at the Bagni for three months. It is as all the others are—dear. I shall give forty or forty-five sequins for the three months, but as yet I do not know which. I could get others something cheaper, and a great deal worse; but if we would write, it is requisite to have space.

To-morrow evening, or the following morning, you will probably see me. T—— is planning a journey to England to secure his property in the event of a revolution, which, he is persuaded, is on the eve of exploding. I neither believe that, nor do I fear that the consequences will be so immediately destructive to the existing forms of social order. Money will be delayed, and the exchange reduced very low, and my annuity and Mrs. M.'s, on account of these being *money*, will be in some danger; but land is quite safe. Besides, it will not be so rapid. Let us hope we shall have a reform. T—— will be lulled into security, while the slow progress of things is still flowing on, after this affair of the Queen may appear to be blown over. There are bad news from Palermo: the soldiers resisted the people, and a terrible slaughter, amounting, it is said, to four thousand men, ensued. The event, however, was as it should be. Sicily, like Naples, is free. By the brief and partial accounts of the Florence paper, it appears that the enthusiasm of the people was prodigious, and that the women fought from the houses, raining down boiling oil on the assailants.

I am promised a bill on Vienna on the 5th, the day on which my note will be paid, and the day on which I purpose to leave Leghorn. Mrs. M. is very unhappy at the idea of T.'s going to England, though she seems to feel the necessity of it. Some time or other he must go to settle his affairs, and they seem to agree that this is the best opportunity. *I* have no thought of leaving Italy. The best thing we can do is to save money, and, if things take a decided turn, (which I am convinced they will at last, but not perhaps for two or three years,) it will be time for me to assert my rights, and preserve my annuity. Meanwhile, another event may decide us. Kiss sweet babe, and kiss yourself for me—I love you affectionately.

P. B. S.

Casa Silva,
Sunday morning, 23rd *July,* 1820.

I have taken the house for forty sequins for three months—a good bargain, and a very good house as things go—this is about thirteen sequins a-month. To-morrow I go to look over the inventory ; expect me therefore on Tuesday morning.

Sunday evening.

LXXV.—To Mrs. Shelley,

(bagni di san giuliano.)

I am afraid, my dearest, that I shall not be able to be with you so soon as to-morrow evening, though I shall use every exertion. Del Rosso I have not seen, nor shall until this evening. Jackson I have, and he is to drink tea with us this evening, and bring the *Constitutionnel*.

You will have seen the papers, but I doubt that they will not contain the latest and most important news. It is certain, by private letters from merchants, that a serious insurrection has broken out at Paris, and the *reports* last night are, that an attack made by the populace on the Tuileries still continued when the last accounts came away. At Naples the constitutional party have declared to the Austrian minister, that if the Emperor should make war on them, their first action would be to put to death *all* the members of the royal family—a necessary and most just measure, when the forces of the combatants, as well as the merits of their respective causes, are so unequal. That kings should be everywhere the hostages for liberty were admirable.

What will become of the Gisbornes, or of the English at Paris ? How soon will England itself, and perhaps Italy, be caught by the sacred fire ? And what, to come from the solar system to a grain of sand, *shall we do ?*

Kiss babe for me, and your own self. I am somewhat better, but my side still vexes me—a little.

Your affectionate S.

[Leghorn], Casa Ricci, Sept. 1st, 1820.

LXXVI.—To James Ollier.

Pisa, November 10th, 1820.

Dear Sir—Mr. Gisborne has sent me a copy of the *Prometheus*, which is certainly most beautifully printed. It is to be regretted that the errors of the press are so numerous, and in many respects so destructive of the sense of a species of poetry which, I fear, even without this disadvantage, very few will understand or like. I shall send you the list of *errata* in a day or two.

I send some poems to be added to the pamphlet of *Julian and Maddalo.* I think you have some other smaller poems belonging to that collection, and I believe you know that I do not wish my name to be printed on the title-page, though I have no objection to my being known as the author.

I enclose also another poem, which I do not wish to be printed with *Julian and Maddalo*, but at the end of the second edition of the *Cenci*, or of any other of my writings to which my name is affixed, if any other should at present have arrived at a second edition, which I do not expect. I have a purpose in this arrangement, and have marked the poem I mean by a cross.

I can sympathise too feelingly in your brother's misfortune.* It has been my hard fate also to watch the gradual death of a beloved child, and to survive him. Present my respects to your brother.

My friend Captain Medwin is with me, and has shown me a poem on Indian hunting, which he has sent you to publish. It is certainly a very elegant and classical composition, and, even if it does not belong to the highest style of poetry, I should be surprised if it did not succeed. May I challenge your kindness to do what you can for it?

You will hear from me again in a post or two. The *Julian and Maddalo*, and the accompanying poems, are all my saddest verses raked up into one heap. I mean to mingle more smiles with my tears in future.

Your obedient servant,
P. B. SHELLEY.

LXXVII.—To T. L. P.

Pisa, November (probably 15th), 1820.

MY DEAR PEACOCK—I delayed to answer your last letter, because I was waiting for something to say : at least something that should be likely to be interesting to you. The box

* Chas. Ollier had just lost a daughter.—*L. S.*

containing my books, and consequently your Essay against the cultivation of poetry, has not arrived ; my wonder, meanwhile, in what manner you support such a heresy in this matter-of-fact and money-loving age, holds me in suspense. Thank you for your kindness in correcting *Prometheus*, which I am afraid gave you a great deal of trouble. Among the modern things which have reached me is a volume of poems by Keats : in other respects insignificant enough, but containing the fragment of a poem called *Hyperion*. I dare say you have not time to read it ; but it is certainly an astonishing piece of writing, and gives me a conception of Keats which I confess I had not before.

I hear from Mr. Gisborne that you are surrounded with papers—a chaos of which you are the god ; a sepulchre which encloses in a dormant state the chrysalis of the Pavonian Psyche. May you start into life some day, and give us another *Melincourt*. Your *Melincourt* is exceedingly admired, and I think much more so than any of your other writings. In this respect the world judges rightly. There is more of the true spirit, and an object less indefinite, than in either *Headlong Hall* or Scythrop.

I am, speaking literally, infirm of purpose. I have great designs, and feeble hopes of accomplishing them. I read books, and, though I am ignorant enough, they seem to teach me nothing. To be sure, the reception the public have given me might go far enough to damp any man's enthusiasm. They teach you, it may be said, only what is true. Very true, I doubt not, and the more true the less agreeable. I can compare my experience in this respect to nothing but a series of wet blankets. I have been reading nothing but Greek and Spanish. Plato and Calderon have been my gods. A schoolfellow of mine from India is staying with me, and we are beginning Arabic together. Mary is writing a novel, illustrative of the manners of the Middle Ages in Italy, which she has raked out of fifty old books. I promise myself success from it ; and certainly, if what is wholly original will succeed, I shall not be disappointed.

Adieu. *In publica commoda peccem, si longo sermone.*

Ever faithfully yours,

P. B. SHELLEY

LXXVIII.—To the Editor of the " Quarterly Review."

Sir—Should you cast your eye on the signature of this letter
before your read the contents, you might imagine that they
related to a slanderous paper which appeared in your Review
some time since. I never notice annonymous attacks. The
wretch who wrote it has doubtless the additional reward of a
consciousness of his motives, besides the thirty guineas a sheet,
or whatever it is that you pay him. Of course you cannot be
answerable for all the writings which you edit, and *I* certainly
bear you no ill-will for having edited the abuse to which I
allude—indeed, I was too much amused by being compared to
Pharaoh, not readily to forgive editor, printer, publisher, stitcher,
or any one, except the despicable writer, connected with something so exquisitely entertaining. Seriously speaking, I am not
in the habit of permitting myself to be disturbed by what is said
or written of me, though, I dare say, I may be condemned
sometimes justly enough. But I feel, in respect to the writer in
question, that " I am there sitting, where he durst not soar."
    The case is different with the unfortunate subject of this
letter, the author of Endymion, to whose feelings and situation
I entreat you to allow me to call your attention. I write considerably in the dark ; but if it is Mr. Gifford that I am
addressing, I am persuaded that in an appeal to his humanity
and justice, he will acknowledge the *fas ab hoste doceri.* I am
aware that the first duty of a Reviewer is towards the public,
and I am willing to confess that the Endymion is a poem
considerably defective, and that, perhaps, it deserved as much
censure as the pages of your Review record against it ; but, not
to mention that there is certain contemptuousness of phraseology
from which it is difficult for a critic to abstain, in the review of
Endymion, I do not think that the writer has given it its due
praise. Surely the poem, with all its faults, is a very remarkable production for a man of Keats's age, and the promise of
ultimate excellence is such as has rarely been afforded even by
such as has afterwards attained high literary eminence. Look
at book ii., line 833, etc., and book iii., line 113 to 120—read
down that page, and then again from line 193. I could cite
many other passages, to convince you that it deserved milder
usage. Why it should have been reviewed at all, excepting for
the purpose of bringing its excellences into notice, I cannot
conceive, for it was very little read, and there was no danger

that it should become a model to the age of that false taste, with which I confess that it is replenished.

Poor Keats was thrown into a dreadful state of mind by this review, which, I am persuaded, was not written with any intention of producing the effect, to which it has, at least, greatly contributed, of embittering his existence, and inducing a disease from which there are now but faint hopes of his recovery. The first effects are described to me to have resembled insanity, and it was by assiduous watching that he was restrained from effecting purposes of suicide. The agony of his sufferings at length produced the rupture of a blood-vessel in the lungs, and the usual process of consumption appears to have begun. He is coming to pay me a visit in Italy; but I fear that unless his mind can be kept tranquil, little is to be hoped from the mere influence of climate.

But let me not extort anything from your pity. I have just seen a second volume, published by him evidently in careless despair. I have desired my bookseller to send you a copy, and allow me to solicit your special attention to the fragment of a poem entitled "Hyperion," the composition of which was checked by the Review in question. The great proportion of this piece is surely in the very highest style of poetry. I speak impartially, for the canons of taste to which Keats has conformed in his other compositions are the very reverse of my own. I leave you to judge for yourself : it would be an insult to you to suppose that from motives, however honourable, you would lend yourself to a deception of the public.

.   .   .   .   .

(*This letter was never sent.*)

LXXIX.—To JOHN GISBORNE,

(AT LEGHORN.)

Pisa, oggi, (November, 1820.)

MY DEAR SIR—I send you the Phædon and Tacitus. I congratulate you on your conquest of the Iliad. You must have been astonished at the perpetually increasing magnificence of the last seven books. Homer there truly begins to be himself. The battle of the Scamander, the funeral of Patroclus, and the high and solemn close of the whole bloody tale in tenderness and inexpiable sorrow, are wrought in a manner incomparable with anything of the same kind. The Odyssey is sweet, but there is nothing like this.

I am bathing myself in the light and odour of the flowery and starry Autos. I have read them all more than once. Henry will tell you how much I am in love with Pacchiani. I suffer from my disease considerably. Henry will also tell you how much, and how whimsically, he alarmed me last night.

My kindest remembrances to Mrs. Gisborne, and best wishes for your health and happiness.

Faithfully yours,
P, B. S.

I have a new Calderon coming from Paris.

———

LXXX.—To T. L. P.

Pisa, February 15*th,* 1821.

MY DEAR PEACOCK—The last letter I received from you, nearly four months from the date thereof, reached me by the boxes which the Gisbornes sent by sea. I am happy to learn that you continue in good external and internal preservation. I received at the same time your printed denunciations against general, and your written ones against particular poetry; and I agree with you as decidedly in the latter as I differ in the former. The man whose critical gall is not stirred up by such rhymes as ——'s, may safely be conjectured to possess no gall at all. The world is pale with the sickness of such stuff. At the same time, your anathemas against poetry itself excited me to a sacred rage, or *cacoëthes scribendi* of vindicating the insulted Muses. I had the greatest possible desire to break a lance with you, within the lists of a magazine, in honour of my mistress Urania; but God willed that I should be too lazy, and wrested the victory from your hope: since first having unhorsed poetry, and the universal sense of the wisest in all ages, an easy conquest would have remained to you in me, the knight of the shield of shadow and the lance of gossamere. Besides, I was at that moment reading Plato's *Ion,* which I recommend you to reconsider. Perhaps in the comparison of Platonic and Malthusian doctrines, the *mavis errare* of Cicero is a justifiable argument; but I have a whole quiver of arguments on such a subject.

Have you seen Godwin's answer to the apostle of the rich? And what do you think of it? It has not yet reached me, nor has your box, of which I am in daily expectation.

We are now in the crisis and point of expectation in Italy. The Neapolitan and Austrian armies are rapidly approaching each other, and every day the news of a battle may be expected. The former have advanced into the Ecclesiastical States, and taken hostages from Rome, to assure themselves of the neutrality of that power, and appear determined to try their strength in open battle. I need not tell you how little chance there is that the new and undisciplined levies of Naples should stand against a superior force of veteran troops. But the birth of liberty in nations abounds in reversals of the ordinary laws of calculation : the defeat of the Austrians would be the signal of insurrection throughout all Italy.

I am devising literary plans of some magnitude. But nothing is more difficult and unwelcome than to write without a confidence of finding readers ; and if my plan of the *Cenci* found none or few, I despair of ever producing anything that shall merit them.

Among your anathemas of the modern attempts in poetry, do you include Keats's *Hyperion?* I think it very fine. His other poems are worth little ; but if the *Hyperion* be not grand poetry, none has been produced by our contemporaries.

I suppose *you* are writing nothing but Indian laws, etc. I have but a faint idea of your occupation ; but I suppose it has something to do with pen and ink.

Mary desires to be kindly remembered to you ; and I remain, my dear Peacock, yours very faithfully,

P. B. SHELLEY.

LXXXI.—TO C. OLLIER.

Pisa, Feb. 16th, 1821.

DEAR SIR,
    I send you three poems—*Ode to Naples,* a sonnet, and a longer piece, entitled *Epipsychidion.* The two former are my own; and you will be so obliging as to take the first opportunity of publishing according to your own discretion.

The longer poem, I desire, should not be considered as my own; indeed, in a certain sense, it is a production of a portion of me already dead; and in this sense the advertisement is no fiction.* It is to be published simply for the esoteric few; and I make its author a secret, to avoid the malignity of those who turn sweet food into poison; transforming all they touch into the corruption of their own natures. My wish with respect to it is, that it should be printed immediately in the simplest form, and merely one hundred copies: those who are capable of judging and feeling rightly with respect to a composition of so abstruse a nature, certainly do not arrive at that number— among those, at least, who would ever be excited to read an obscure and anonymous production; and it would give me no pleasure that the vulgar should read it. If you have any book-selling reason against publishing so small a number as a hundred, merely, distribute copies among those to whom you think the poetry would afford any pleasure, and send me, as soon as you can, a copy by the post. I have written it so as to give very little trouble, I hope, to the printer, or to the person who revises. I would be much obliged to you if you would take this office on yourself.

Is there any expectation of a second edition of the *Revolt of Islam?* I have many corrections to make in it, and one part will be wholly remodelled. I am employed in high and new designs in verse; but they are the labours of years, perhaps.

We expect here every day the news of a battle between the armies of Austria and Naples. The latter have advanced upon Rome; and the first affair will probably take place in the Ecclesiastical States. You may imagine the expectation of all here.

Pray send me news of my intellectual children. For *Prometheus,* I expect and desire no great sale. The *Cenci* ought to have been popular.

I remain, dear Sir,
Your very obedient servant,
PERCY B. SHELLEY.

* In his preface he speaks of the poem as having been written by a person who "died at Florence, as he was preparing for a voyage to one of the wildest of the Sporades, which he had bought, and where it was his hope to have realized a scheme of life suited, perhaps, to that happier and better world of which he is now an inhabitant, but hardly practicable in this." The preface is signed " S."—*L. S.*

LXXXII.—To C. Ollier.

Pisa, Feb. 22*nd,* 1821.

DEAR SIR—Peacock's essay is at Florence at present.   I have sent for it, and will transmit to you my paper [on Poetry] as soon as it is written, which will be in a very few days.   Nevertheless, I should be sorry that you delayed your magazine through any dependence on me.   I will not accept anything for this paper, as I had determined to write it, and promised it you, before I heard of your liberal arrangements ; but perhaps in future, if I think I have any thoughts worth publishing, I shall be glad to contribute to your magazine on those terms.   Meanwhile, you are perfectly at liberty to publish the *Ode to Naples,* the sonnet, or any short piece you may have of mine.

I suppose *Julian and Maddalo* is published.   If not, do not add the *Witch of Atlas* to that peculiar piece of writing ; you may put my name to the *Witch of Atlas,* as usual.   The piece I last sent you, I wish, as I think I told you, to be printed immediately, and that anonymously.   I should be very glad to receive a few copies of it by the box, but I am unwilling that it should be any longer delayed.

I doubt about *Charles the First;* but, if I do write it, it shall be the birth of severe and high feelings.   You are very welcome to it, on the terms you mention, and, when once I see and feel that I can write it, it is already written.*   My thoughts aspire to a production of a far higher character ; but the execution of it will require some years.   I write what I write chiefly to inquire, by the reception which my writings meet with, how far I am fit for so great a task, or not.   And I am afraid that your account will not present me with a very flattering result in this particular.

You may expect to hear from me within a week, with the answer to Peacock.   I shall endeavour to treat the subject in its elements, and unveil the inmost idol of the error.

If any Review of note abuses me excessively, or the contrary, be so kind as to send it me by post.

If not too late, pray send me by the box the following books :—The most copious and correct history of the discoveries of Geology.   If one publication does not appear to contain what I require, send me two or three.   A history of the late war in Spain ; I think one has been written by Southey.   Major *Somebody's* account of the siege of Zaragosa ; it is a little pamphlet.

* The play was never finished.—ED.

Burnet's *History of his Own Times;* and the *Old English Drama*, 3 vols.

Excuse my horrible pens, ink, and paper. I can get no pen that will mark ; or, if you will not excuse them, send me out some English ones.

I am delighted to hear of Procter's success, and hope that he will proceed gathering laurels. Pray tell me how the *Prometheus Unbound* was received.

Dear Sir,
Your very obliged servant,
PERCY B. SHELLEY.

LXXXIII.—TO C. OLLIER.

Pisa, March 20th, 1821.

DEAR SIR,
I send you the *Defence of Poetry*, Part I. It is transcribed, I hope, legibly.

I have written nothing which I do not think necessary to the subject. Of course, if any expressions should strike you as too unpopular, I give you the power of omitting them; but I trust you will, if possible, refrain from exercising it. In fact, I hope that I have treated the question with that temper and spirit as to silence cavil. I propose to add two other parts in two succeeding Miscellanies. It is to be understood that, although you may omit, you do not alter or add.

Pray let me hear from you soon.

Dear Sir,
Yours very sincerely,
P. B. S.

LXXXIV.—TO T. L. P.

Pisa, March 21st, 1821.

MY DEAR PEACOCK—I dispatch by this post the first part of an essay, intended to consist of three parts, which I design for an antidote to your *Four Ages of Poetry*.* You will see that I have taken a more general view of what is poetry than

---

* The "Four Ages of Poetry" here alluded to was published in Ollier's *Literary Miscellany*. Shelley wrote the "Defence of Poetry" as an answer to it ; and as he wrote it, it contained many

you have, and will perhaps agree with several of my positions,
without considering your own touched. But read and judge;
and do not let us imitate the great founders of the picturesque,
Price and Payne Knight, who, like two ill-trained beagles,
began snarling at each other when they could not catch the
hare.

I hear the welcome news of a box from England announced
by Mr. Gisborne. How much new poetry does it contain?
The Bavii and Mævii of the day are fertile; and I wish those
who honour me with boxes would read and inwardly digest
your *Four Ages of Poetry;* for I had much rather, for my
own private reading, receive political, geological, and moral
treatises, than this stuff in *terza, ottava,* and *tremillesima rima,*
whose earthly baseness has attracted the lightning of your
undiscriminating censure upon the temple of immortal song.
These verses enrage me far more than those of Codrus did
Juvenal, and with better reason. Juvenal need not have been
stunned, unless he had liked it; but my boxes are packed with
this trash, to the exclusion of better matter. But your box will
make amends.

We are surrounded here in Pisa by revolutionary volcanos,
which as yet give more light than heat: the lava has not yet
reached Tuscany. But the news in the papers will tell you
far more than it is prudent for me to say; and for this once I
will observe your rule of political silence. The Austrians wish
that the Neapolitans and Piedmontese would do the same.

We have seen a few more people than usual this winter,
and have made a very interesting acquaintance with a Greek
Prince, perfectly acquainted with ancient literature, and full of
enthusiasm for the liberties and improvement of his country.
Mary has been a Greek student several months, and is reading
Antigone with our turbaned friend, who in return is taught
English. C. has passed the carnival at Florence, and has

allusions to the article and its author, such as "If I know the knight
by the device of his shield, I have only to inscribe Cassandra,
Antigone, or Alcestis on mine to blunt the point of his spear;" taking
one instance of a favourite character from each of the three great Greek
tragedians. All these allusions were struck out by Mr. John Hunt
when he prepared the paper for publication in the *Liberal.* The
demise of that periodical prevented the publication, and Mrs. Shelley
subsequently printed it from Mr. Hunt's *rifacciamento,* as she received
it. The paper as it now stands is a defence without an attack.
Shelley intended this paper to be in three parts, but the other two
were not written.—*T. L. P.*

338

LETTERS.

been præternaturally gay. I have had a severe ophthalmia, and have read or written little this winter ; and have made acquaintance in an obscure convent with the only Italian for whom I ever felt any interest.*

I want you to do something for me : that is, to get me two pounds' worth of Tassi's gems, in Leicester Square, the prettiest according to your taste ; among them, the head of Alexander ; and to get me two seals engraved and set, one smaller, and the other handsomer : the device a dove with outspread wings, and this motto round it :

Μάντις εἰμ' ἐσθγῶν ἀγώνων.

LXXXV.—To Henry Reveley.

My Dear Henry—Our ducking last night has added fire, instead of quenching the nautical ardour which produced it ; and I consider it a good omen in any enterprise, that it begins in evil ; as being more or less probable that it will end in good. I hope *you* have not suffered from it. I am rather feverish, but very well as to the side, whence I expected the worst consequences. I send you directions for the complete equipment of our boat, since you have so kindly promised to undertake it. In putting into execution, a little more or less expense in so trifling an affair is to be disregarded. I need not say that the approaching season invites expedition. You can put her in hand immediately, and write the day on which we may come for her.

We expect with impatience the arrival of our false friends, who have so long cheated us with delay ; and Mary unites with me in desiring, that, as *you* participated equally in the crime, you should not be omitted in the expiation.

All good be with you.—Adieu. Yours faithfully,   S.

Williams desires to be kindly remembered to you, and begs to present his compliments to Mr. and Mrs. G——, and—heaven knows what.

Pisa, Tuesday, 1 o'clock, 17th April, 1821.

* Lady Emilia Viviani, the subject of his *Epipsychidion.*

LXXXVI.—To HENRY REVELEY.

Pisa, April 19*th.*

MY DEAR HENRY—The rullock, or place for the oar, ought not to be placed where the oar-pins are now, but ought to be nearer to the mast ; as near as possible, indeed, so that the rower has room to sit.   In addition let a false keel be made in this shape, so as to be four inches deep at the stern, and to decrease towards the prow.   It may be as thin as you please.

Tell Mr. and Mrs. G—— that I have read the Numancia, and after wading through the singular stupidity of the first act, began to be greatly delighted, and, at length, interested in a very high degree, by the power of the writer in awakening pity and admiration, in which I hardly know by whom he is excelled. There is little, I allow, in a strict sense, to be called *poetry* in this play ; but the command of language, and the harmony of versification, is so great as to deceive one into an idea that it is poetry.

Adieu.—We shall see you soon.

Yours ever truly,   S.

LXXXVII.—To MR. AND MRS. GISBORNE.

Bagni, Tuesday Evening
(*June* 5*th,* 1821).

MY DEAR FRIENDS—We anxiously expect your arrival at the Baths ; but as I am persuaded that you will spend as much time with us as you can save from your necessary occupations before your departure, I will forbear to vex you with impor- tunity.   My health does not permit me to spend many hours from home.   I have been engaged these last days in composing a poem on the death of Keats, which will shortly be finished ; and I anticipate the pleasure of reading it to you, as some of the very few persons who will be interested in it and understand it. It is a highly-wrought *piece of art*, and perhaps better, in point of composition, than anything I have written.

I have obtained a purchaser for some of the articles of your three lists, a catalogue of which I subjoin.   I shall do my utmost to get more ; could you not send me a complete list of your *furniture*, as I have had inquiries made about chests of drawers, etc.

My unfortunate box! it contained a chaos of the elements of "Charles I." If the idea of the *creator* had been packed up with them, it would have shared the same fate ; and that, I am afraid, has undergone another sort of shipwreck.

Very faithfully and affectionately yours,   S.

LXXXVIII.—To C. Ollier.

Pisa, June 8th, 1821.

Dear Sir,

You may announce for publication a poem entitled *Adonais.* It is a lament on the death of poor Keats, with some interposed stabs on the assassins of his peace and of his fame ; and will be preceded by a criticism on *Hyperion,* asserting the due claims which that fragment gives him to the rank which I have assigned him. My poem is finished, and consists of about forty Spenser stanzas. I shall send it you, either printed at Pisa, or transcribed in such a manner as it shall be difficult for the reviser to leave such errors as *assist* the obscurity of the *Prometheus.* But, in case I send it printed, it will be merely that mistakes may be avoided; [so] that I shall only have a few copies struck off in the cheapest manner.

If you have interest enough in the subject, I could wish that you inquired of some of the friends and relations of Keats respecting the circumstances of his death, and could transmit me any information you may be able to collect, and especially as to the degree in which, as I am assured, the brutal attack in the *Quarterly Review* excited the disease by which he perished.

I have received no answer to my last letter to you. Have you received my contribution to your magazine?

Dear Sir,
Yours very sincerely,
P. B. Shelley.

LXXXIX.—To John Gisborne.

My Dear Friend—I have received the heart-rending account of the closing scene of the great genius whom envy and ingratitude scourged out of the world. I do not think that if I had seen it before, I could have composed my poem. The enthusiasm of the imagination would have overpowered the sentiment.

As it is, I have finished my Elegy ; and this day I send it to the press at Pisa. You shall have a copy the moment it is completed. I think it will please you. I have dipped my pen in consuming fire for his destroyers; otherwise the style is calm and solemn.

Pray, when shall we see you? Or are the streams of Helicon less salutary than sea-bathing for the nerves? Give us as much as you can before you go to England, and rather divide the term than not come soon.

Mrs. —— wishes that none of the books, desk, etc., should be packed up with the piano; but that they should be sent, one by one, by Pepi. Address them to *me* at her house. She desired me to have them addressed to *me*, why I know not.

A droll circumstance has occurred. Queen Mab, a poem written by me when very young, in the most furious style, with long notes against Jesus Christ, and God the Father, and the king, and bishops, and marriage, and the devil knows what, is just published by one of the low booksellers in the Strand, against my wish and consent, and all the people are at logger-heads about it. H. S. gives me this account. You may imagine how much I am amused. For the sake of a dignified appearance, however, and really because I wish to protest against all the bad poetry in it, I have given orders to say that it is all done against my desire, and have directed my attorney to apply to Chancery for an injunction, which he will not get.

I am pretty ill, I thank you, just now ; but I hope you are better.

Most affectionately yours,   P. B. S.

Pisa. Saturday, June 16th, 1821.)

XC.—To The "Examiner."

June 22nd, 1821.

"A POEM, entitled *Queen Mab*, was written by me at the age of eighteen—I dare say, in a sufficiently intemperate spirit. I have not seen this production for several years : I doubt not but that it is perfectly worthless in point of literary composition ; and that, in all that concerns moral and political speculation, as well as in the subtler discriminations of metaphysical and religious doctrine, it is still more crude and immature. I am a devoted enemy to religious, political, and domestic oppression ; and I regret this publication, not so much from literary vanity, as because I fear it is better fitted to injure than to serve the sacred cause of freedom." . . .

―――

XCI.—To Mr. and Mrs. Gisborne.

Bagni, Friday Night
(July 13th, 1821).

My Dear Friends—I have been expecting every day a writ to attend at your court at Guebhard's, whence you know it is settled that I should conduct you hither to spend your last days in Italy. A thousand thanks for your maps ; in return for which I send you the only copy of "Adonais" the printer has yet delivered. I wish I could say, as Glaucus could, in the exchange for the arms of Diomed,—ἐκατόμβιοι ἐννεαβοίων.

I will only remind you of "Faust ;" my desire for the conclusion of which is only exceeded by my desire to welcome you. Do you observe any traces of him in the poem I send you? Poets—the best of them, are a very cameleonic race; they take the colour not only of what they feed on, but of the very leaves under which they pass.

Mary is just on the verge of finishing her novel; but it cannot be in time for you to take to England.—Farewell.

Most faithfully yours,
P. B. S.

―――

XCII.—To Mrs. and Mrs Gisborne.

My Dearest Friends—I am fully repaid for the painful emotions from which some verses of my poem sprang, by your sympathy and approbation—which is all the reward I expect— and as much as I desire. It is not for me to judge whether, in the high praise your feelings assign me, you are right or wrong. The poet and the man are two different natures ; though they exist together, they may be unconscious of each other, and incapable of deciding on each other's powers and efforts by any reflex act. The decision of the cause, whether or no *I* am a poet, is removed from the present time to the hour when our posterity shall assemble ; but the court is a very severe one, and I fear that the verdict will be, " Guilty—death !"

I shall be with you on the first summons. I hope that the time you have reserved for us, "this bank and shoal of time," is not so short as you once talked of.

In haste, most affectionately yours,

P. B. S.

Bagni, July 19*th.*

XCIII.—TO MRS SHELLEY,

(BAGNI DI PISA).

Tuesday, Lione Bianco, Florence
(*August* 1*st*, 1821).

MY DEAREST LOVE—I shall not return this evening; nor, unless I have better success, to-morrow. I have seen many houses, but very few within the compass of our powers; and, even in those which seem to suit, nothing is more difficult than to bring the proprietors to terms. I congratulate myself on having taken the season in time, as there is great expectation of Florence being full next winter. I shall do my utmost to return to-morrow evening. You may expect me about ten or eleven o'clock, as I shall purposely be late, to spare myself the excessive heat.

The Gisbornes (four o'clock, Tuesday,) are just set out in a diligence-and-four, for Bologna. They have promised to write from Paris. I spent three hours this morning principally in the contemplation of the Niobe, and of a favourite Apollo; all worldly thoughts and cares seem to vanish from before the sublime emotions such spectacles create; and I am deeply impressed with the great difference of happiness enjoyed by those who live at a distance from these incarnations of all that the finest minds have conceived of beauty, and those who can resort to their company at pleasure. What should we think if we were forbidden to read the great writers who have left us their works? And yet to be forbidden to live at Florence or Rome, is an evil of the same kind, of scarcely less magnitude.

I am delighted to hear that the W.'s are with you. I am convinced that Williams must persevere in the use of the doccia. Give my most affectionate remembrances to them. I shall know all the houses in Florence, and can give W. a good account of them all. You have not sent my passport, and I must get home as I can. I suppose you did not receive my note.

I grudge my sequins for a carriage ; but I have suffered from the sun and the fatigue, and dare not expose myself to that which is necessary for house-hunting.

Kiss little babe, and how is he ? but I hope to see him fast asleep to-morrow night. And pray, dearest Mary, have some of your novel prepared for my return.

Your ever affectionate   S.

XCIV.—TO MRS. SHELLEY,

(BAGNI DI PISA.)

Bologna, Agosto 6.

DEAREST MINE—I am at Bologna, and the caravella is ordered for Ravenna. I have been detained, by having made an embarrassing and inexplicable arrangement, more than twelve hours ; or I should have arrived at Bologna last night instead of this morning.

Though I have travelled all night at the rate of two miles and a-half an hour, in a little open calesso, I am perfectly well in health. One would think that I were the spaniel of Destiny, for the more she knocks about me, the more I fawn on her. I had an overturn about day-break ; the old horse stumbled, and threw me and the fat vetturino into a slope of meadow, over the hedge. My angular figure stuck where it was pitched ; but my vetturino's spherical form rolled fairly to the bottom of the hill, and that with so few symptoms of reluctance in the life that animated it, that my ridicule (for it was the drollest sight in the world) was suppressed by my fear that the poor devil had been hurt. But he was very well, and we continued our journey with great success.

My love to the Williams's. Kiss my pretty ones, and accept an affectionate one for yourself from me. The chaise waits. I will write the first night from Ravenna at length.

Yours ever,   S.

XCV.—TO MRS. SHELLEY.

Ravenna, August 7, 1821.

MY DEAREST MARY—I arrived last night at ten o'clock, and sate up talking with Lord Byron until five this morning. I then went to sleep, and now awake at eleven, and having despatched my breakfast as quick as possible, mean to devote the interval until twelve, when the post departs, to you.

Lord Byron is very well, and was delighted to see me. He has in fact completely recovered his health, and lives a life totally the reverse of that which he led at Venice. He has a permanent sort of liaison with Contessa Guiccioli, who is now at Florence, and seems from her letters to be a very amiable woman. She is waiting there until something shall be decided as to their emigration to Switzerland or stay in Italy ; which is yet undetermined on either side. She was compelled to escape from the Papal territory in great haste, as measures had already been taken to place her in a convent, where she would have been unrelentingly confined for life. The oppression of the marriage contract, as existing in the laws and opinions of Italy, though less frequently exercised, is far severer than that of England. I tremble to think of what poor Emilia is destined to.

Lord Byron had almost destroyed himself in Venice : his state of debility was such that he was unable to digest any food, he was consumed by hectic fever, and would speedily have perished, but for this attachment, which has reclaimed him from the excesses into which he threw himself from carelessness and pride, rather than taste. Poor fellow ! he is now quite well, and immersed in politics and literature. He has given me a number of the most interesting details on the former subject, but we will not speak of them in a letter. Fletcher is here, and as if like a shadow, he waxed and waned with the substance of his master : Fletcher also has recovered his good looks, and from amidst the unseasonable grey hairs, a fresh harvest of flaxen locks put forth.

We talked a great deal of poetry, and such matters last night ; and as usual differed, and I think more than ever. He affects to patronise a system of criticism fit for the production of mediocrity, and although all his fine poems and passages have been produced in defiance of this system, yet I recognise the pernicious effects of it in the Doge of Venice ; and it will cramp and limit his future efforts however great they may be, unless he gets rid of it. I have read only parts of it, or rather he himself read them to me, and gave me the plan of the whole.

Lord Byron has also told me of a circumstance that shocks me exceedingly ; because it exhibits a degree of desperate and wicked malice for which I am at a loss to account. When I hear such things my patience and my philosophy are put to a severe proof, whilst I refrain from seeking out some obscure

hiding-place, where the countenance of man may never meet
me more. . . . .

. . . . Imagine my despair of good, imagine how it is
possible that one of so weak and sensitive a nature as mine can
run further the gauntlet through this hellish society of men.
You should write to the Hoppners a letter refuting the charge,
in case you believe, and know, and can prove that it is false ;
stating the grounds and proofs of your belief. I need not
dictate what you should say ; nor, I hope, inspire you with
warmth to rebut a charge, which you only can effectually rebut.
If you will send the letter to me here, I will forward it to the
Hoppners. Lord Byron is not up, I do not know the Hoppners'
address, and I am anxious not to lose a post.

XCVI.—To Mrs. Shelley.

Thursday, 8th August.

My Dearest Mary—I wrote to you yesterday, and I begin
another letter to-day, without knowing exactly when I can send
it, as I am told the post only goes once a-week. I dare say the
subject of the latter half of my letter gave you pain, but it was
necessary to look the affair in the face, and the only satisfactory
answer to the calumny must be given by you, and could be
given by you alone. This is evidently the source of the violent
denunciations of the Literary Gazette, in themselves contemptible
enough, and only to be regarded as effects, which show us their
cause, which, until we put off our mortal nature, we never
despise—that is, the belief of persons who have known and seen
you, that you are guilty of crimes.

.　　　　.　　　　.　　　　.　　　　.　　　　.

After having sent my letter to the post yesterday, I went to
see some of the antiquities of this place ; which appear to be
remarkable. This city was once of vast extent, and the traces
of its remains are to be found more than four miles from the
gate of the modern town. The sea, which once came close to
it, has now retired to the distance of four miles, leaving a melancholy extent of marshes, interspersed with patches of cultivation,
and towards the seashore with pine forests, which have followed
the retrocession of the Adriatic, and the roots of which are
actually washed by its waves. The level of the sea and of this
tract of country correspond so nearly, that a ditch dug to a few

feet in depth, is immediately filled up with sea water. All the ancient buildings have been choked up to the height of from five to twenty feet by the deposit of the sea, and of the inundations, which are frequent in the winter. I went in L. B.'s carriage, first to the Chiesa San Vitale, which is certainly one of the most ancient churches in Italy. It is a rotunda, supported upon buttresses and pilasters of white marble ; the ill effect of which is somewhat relieved by an interior row of columns. The dome is very high and narrow. The whole church, in spite of the elevation of the soil, is very high for its breadth, and is of a very peculiar and striking construction. In the section of one of the large tables of marble with which the church is lined, they showed me the *perfect figure*, as perfect as if it had been painted, of a Capuchin friar, which resulted merely from the shadings and the position of the stains in the marble. This is what may be called a pure anticipated cognition of a Capuchin.

I then went to the tomb of Theodosius, which has now been dedicated to the Virgin, without, however, any change in its original appearance. It is about a mile from the present city. This building is more than half overwhelmed by the elevated soil, although a portion of the lower storey has been excavated, and is filled with brackish and stinking waters, and a sort of vaporous darkness, and troops of prodigious frogs. It is a remarkable piece of architecture, and without belonging to a period when the ancient taste yet survived, bears, nevertheless, a certain impression of that taste. It consists of two stories ; the lower supported on Doric arches and pilasters, and a simple entablature. The other circular within, and polygonal outside, and roofed with one single mass of ponderous stone, for it is evidently one, and Heaven alone knows how they contrived to lift it to that height. It is a sort of flattish dome, rough-wrought within by the chisel, from which the Northern conquerors tore the plates of silver that adorned it, and polished without, with things like handles appended to it, which were also wrought out of the solid stone, and to which I suppose the ropes were applied to draw it up. You ascend externally into the second storey by a flight of stone steps, which are modern.

The next place I went to, was a church called *la chiesa di Sant' Appollinare*, which is a Basilica, and built by one, I forget whom, of the Christian Emperors ; it is a long church, with a roof like a barn, and supported by twenty-four columns of the finest marble, with an altar of jasper, and four columns of jasper, and giallo antico, supporting the roof of the tabernacle, which are said to be of immense value. It is something like that church (I forget the name of it) we saw at Rome, fuore delle mura.* I suppose the Emperor stole these columns, which seem not at all to belong to the place they occupy. Within the city, near the church of San Vitale, there is to be seen the tomb of the Empress Galla Placidia, daughter of Theodosius the Great, together with those of her husband Constantius, her brother Honorius, and her son Valentinian—all Emperors. The tombs are massy cases of marble, adorned with rude and taste-less sculpture of lambs, and other Christian emblems, with scarcely a trace of the antique. It seems to have been one of the first effects of the Christian religion to destroy the power of producing beauty in art. These tombs are placed in a sort of vaulted chamber, wrought over with rude mosaic, which is said to have been built in 1300. I have yet seen no more of Ravenna.

Friday.

We ride out in the evening, through the pine forests which divide this city from the sea. Our way of life is this, and I have accommodated myself to it without much difficulty :—L. B. gets up at two, breakfasts; we talk, read, etc., until six; then we ride, and dine at eight ; and after dinner sit talking till four or five in the morning. I get up at twelve, and am now devoting in the interval between my rising and his, to you.

L. B. is greatly improved in every respect. In genius, in temper, in moral views, in health, in happiness. The connexion with la Guiccioli has been an inestimable benefit to him. He lives in considerable splendour, but within his income, which is now about £4000 a-year; £100 of which he devotes to purposes of charity. He has had mischievous passions, but these he seems to have subdued, and he is becoming what he should be, a virtuous man. The interest which he took in the politics of Italy, and the actions he performed in consequence of it, are subjects not fit to be *written,* but are such as will delight and surprise you. He is not yet decided to go to Switzerland—a place, indeed, little fitted for him : the gossip and the cabals of those anglicised coteries would torment him, as they did before, and might exasperate him into a relapse of libertinism, which he says he plunged into not from taste, but despair. La Guic-cioli and her brother (who is L. B.'s friend and confidant, and acquiesces perfectly in her connexion with him,) wish to go to

---

* San Paolo fuore delle mura—burnt down, and its beautiful columns calcined by the fire, in 1823—now rebuilt.—*M. S.*

Switzerland ; as L. B. says, merely from the novelty of the pleasure of travelling. L. B. prefers Tuscany or Lucca, and is trying to persuade them to adopt his views. He has made *me* write a long letter to her to engage her to remain—an odd thing enough for an utter stranger to write on subjects of the utmost delicacy to his friend's mistress. But it seems destined that I am always to have some active part in every body's affairs whom I approach. I have set down, in lame Italian, the strongest reasons I can think of against the Swiss emigration— to tell you truth, I should be very glad to accept, as my fee, his establishment in Tuscany. Ravenna is a miserable place ; the people are barbarous and wild, and their language the most infernal patois that you can imagine. He would be, in every respect, better among the Tuscans. I am afraid he would not like Florence, on account of the English there. There is Lucca, Florence, Pisa, Siena, and I think nothing more. What think you of Prato, or Pistoia, for him ?—no Englishman approaches those towns ; but I am afraid no house could be found good enough for him in that region.

He has read to me one of the unpublished cantos of Don Juan, which is astonishingly fine. It sets him not only above, but far above, all the poets of the day—every word is stamped with immortality. I despair of rivalling Lord Byron, as well I may, and there is no other with whom it is worth contending. This canto is in the style, but totally, and sustained with incredible ease and power, like the end of the second canto. There is not a word which the most rigid asserter of the dignity of human nature would desire to be cancelled. It fulfils, in a certain degree, what I have long preached of producing—something wholly new and relative to the age, and yet surpassingly beautiful. It may be vanity, but I think I see the trace of my earnest exhortations to him to create something wholly new. He has finished his *life* up to the present time, and given it to Moore, with liberty for Moore to sell it for the best price he can get, with condition that the bookseller should publish it after his death. Moore has sold it to Murray for *two thousand pounds.* I have spoken to him of Hunt, but not with a direct view of demanding a contribution ; and, though I am sure that if asked it would not be refused—yet there is something in me that makes it impossible. Lord Byron and I are excellent friends, and were I reduced to poverty, or were I a writer who had no claims to a higher station than I possess—or did I possess a higher than I deserve, we should appear in all things as such, and I would freely ask him any favour. Such is not the case. The demon of mistrust and pride lurks between two persons in our situation, poisoning the freedom of our inter-course. This is a tax, and a heavy one, which we must pay for being human. I think the fault is not on my side, nor is it likely, I being the weaker. I hope that in the next world these things will be better managed. What is passing in the heart of another, rarely escapes the observation of one who is a strict anatomist of his own.

Write to me at Florence, where I shall remain a day at least, and send me letters, or news of letters. How is my little dar-ling? And how are you, and how do you get on with your book? Be severe in your corrections, and expect severity from me, your sincere admirer. I flatter myself you have composed something unequalled in its kind, and that, not content with the honours of your birth and your hereditary aristocracy, you will add still higher renown to your name. Expect me at the end of my appointed time. I do not think I shall be detained. Is C. with you, or is she coming? Have you heard anything of my poor Emilia, from whom I got a letter the day of my de-parture, saying, that her marriage was deferred for a *very short* time, on account of the illness of her sposo? How are the Williams's, and Williams especially? Give my very kindest love to them.

Lord B. has here splendid apartments in the house of his mistress's husband, who is one of the richest men in Italy. *She* is divorced, with an allowance of 1200 crowns a-year, a miser-able pittance from a man who has 120,000 a-year.—Here are two monkeys, five cats, eight dogs, and ten horses, all of whom, (except the horses), walk about the house like the masters of it. *Tita* the Venetian is here, and operates as my valet ; a fine fellow, with a prodigious black beard, and who has stabbed two or three people, and is one of the most good-natured looking fellows I ever saw.

We have good rumours of the Greeks here, and a Russian war. I hardly wish the Russians to take any part in it. My maxim is with Æschylus :—τὸ δυσσεβὲς—μετὰ μὲν πλείονα τίκτει, σφετέρα δείκοτα γεννᾷ. There is a Greek exercise for you. How should slaves produce anything but tyranny—even as the seed produces the plant ?

Adieu, dear Mary.
Yours affectionately,   S.

XCVII.—To T. L. P.

Ravenna, August (probably 10th), 1821.

MY DEAR PEACOCK—I received your last letter just as I was setting off from the Bagni on a visit to Lord Byron at this place. Many thanks for all your kind attention to my accursed affairs. . . .

I have sent you by the Gisbornes a copy of the *Elegy on Keats.* The subject, I know, will not please you ; but the composition of the poetry, and the taste in which it is written, I do not think bad. You and the enlightened public will judge. Lord Byron is in excellent cue both of health and spirits. He has got rid of all those melancholy and degrading habits which he indulged at Venice. He lives with one woman, a lady of rank here, to whom he is attached, and who is attached to him, and is in every respect an altered man. He has written three more cantos of *Don Juan.* I have yet only heard the fifth, and I think that every word of it is pregnant with immortality. I have not seen his late plays, except *Marino Faleiro,* which is very well, but not so transcendently fine as *Don Juan.* Lord Byron gets up at two. I get up, quite contrary to my usual custom, but one must sleep or die, like Southey's sea-snake in Kehama, at twelve. After breakfast, we sit talking till six. From six to eight we gallop through the pine forests which divide Ravenna from the sea ; then come home and dine, and sit up gossiping till six in the morning. I do not think this will kill me in a week or fortnight, but I shall not try it longer. Lord B.'s establishment consists, besides servants, of ten horses, eight enormous dogs, three monkies, five cats, an eagle, a crow, and a falcon ; and all these, except the horses, walk about the house, which every now and then resounds with their unarbitrated quarrels, as if they were the masters of it. Lord B. thinks you wrote a pamphlet signed *John Bull ;* he says he knew it by the style resembling *Melincourt,* of which he is a great admirer. I read it, and assured him that it could not possibly be yours. I write nothing, and probably shall write no more. It offends me to see my name classed among those who have no name. If I cannot be something better, I had rather be nothing. My motive was never the infirm desire of fame ; and if I should continue an author, I feel that I should desire it. This cup is justly given to one only of an age ; indeed, participation would make it worthless : and unfortunate they who seek it and find it not.

I congratulate you—I hope I ought to do so—on your expected stranger.   He is introduced into a rough world.

Ever most faithfully yours,

P. B. S.

———

XCVIII.—TO MRS. SHELLEY.

Saturday—Ravenna.

MY DEAR MARY—You will be surprised to hear that L. B. has decided upon coming to *Pisa*, in case he shall be able, with my assistance, to prevail upon his mistress to remain in Italy, of which I think there is little doubt.   He wishes for a large and magnificent house, but he has furniture of his own, which he would send from Ravenna.   Inquire if any of the large palaces are to be let.   We discussed Prato, Pistoia, Lucca, etc., but they would not suit him so well as Pisa, to which, indeed, he shows a decided preference.   So let it be !   Florence he objects to, on account of the prodigious influx of English.

I don't think this circumstance ought to make any difference in our own plans with respect to this winter in Florence, because we could easily reassume our station with the spring, at Pugnano or the baths, in order to enjoy the society of the noble lord. But do you consider this point, and write to me your full opinion, at the Florence post-office.

I suffer much to-day from the pain in my side, brought on, I believe, by this accursed water.   In other respects, I am pretty well, and my spirits are much improved ; they had been improving, indeed, before I left the baths, after the deep dejection of the early part of the year.

I am reading " Anastasius."   One would think that L. B. had taken his idea of the three last cantos of Don Juan from this book.   That, of course, has nothing to do with the merit of this latter, poetry having nothing to do with the invention of facts. It is a very powerful, and very entertaining novel, and a faithful picture, they say, of modern Greek manners.   I have read L. B.'s Letter to Bowles : some good things—but he ought not to write prose criticism.

You will receive a long letter, sent with some of L. B.'s, express to Florence.   I write this in haste.

Yours most affectionately,   S.

———

XCIX.—To Mrs. Shelley.

Ravenna, 15th Aug., 1821.

. . . . . .

I went the other day to see Allegra at her convent, and stayed with her about three hours. She is grown tall and slight for her age, and her face is somewhat altered. The traits have become more delicate, and she is much paler, probably from the effect of improper food. She yet retains the beauty of her deep blue eyes and of her mouth, but she has a contemplative seriousness which, mixed with her excessive vivacity, which has not yet deserted her, has a very peculiar effect in a child. She is under very strict discipline as may be observed from the immediate obedience she accords to the will of her attendants. This seems contrary to her nature, but I do not think it has been obtained at the expense of much severity. Her hair, scarcely darker than it was, is beautifully profuse, and hangs in large curls on her neck. She was prettily dressed in white muslin, and an apron of black silk, with trousers. Her light and airy figure and her graceful motions were a striking contrast to the other children there. She seemed a thing of a finer and a higher order. At first she was very shy, but after a little caressing, and especially after I had given her a gold chain which I had bought at Ravenna for her, she grew more familiar, and led me all over the garden, and all over the convent, running and skipping so fast that I could hardly keep up with her. She showed me her little bed, and the chair where she sat at dinner, and the carozzina in which she and her favourite companions drew each other along a walk in the garden. I had brought her a basket of sweetmeats, and before eating any of them she gave her companions and each of the nuns a portion. This is not much like the old Allegra. I asked her what I should say from her to her mama, and she said :—

"Che mi manda un bacio e un bel vestituro."

"E come vuoi il vestituro sia fatto?"

"Tutto di seta e d'oro," was her reply.

Her predominant foible seems the love of distinction and vanity, and this is a plant which produces good or evil according to the gardener's skill. I then asked what I should say to papa? "Che venga farmi un visitino e che porta seco la *mammina.*" Before I went away she made me run all over the convent, like a mad thing. The nuns, who were half in bed, were ordered to hide themselves, and on returning Allegra began ringing the bell which calls the nuns to assemble. The tocsin of the convent sounded, and it required all the efforts of the prioress to prevent the spouses of God from rendering themselves, dressed or undressed, to the accustomed signal. Nobody scolded her for these *scappature*, so I suppose she is well treated, so far as temper is concerned. Her intellect is not much cultivated. She knows certain *orazioni* by heart, and talks and dreams of *Paradiso* and all sorts of things, and has a prodigious list of saints, and is always talking of the Bambino. This will do her no harm, but the idea of bringing up so sweet a creature in the midst of such trash till sixteen !

C.—To Mrs. Shelley.

Ravenna, Tuesday, August 15*th*, 1821.

My Dearest Love—I accept your kind present of your picture, and wish you would get it prettily framed for me. I will wear, for your sake, upon my heart this image which is ever present to my mind.

I have only two minutes to write, the post is just setting off. I shall leave this place on Thursday or Friday morning. You would forgive me for my longer stay, if you knew the fighting I have had to make it so short. I need not say where my own feelings impel me.

It still remains fixed that L. B. should come to Tuscany, and, if possible, Pisa ; but more of that to-morrow.

Your faithful and affectionate   S.

CI.—To Mrs. Shelley.

Wednesday, Ravenna.

My Dearest Love—I write, though I doubt whether I shall not arrive before this letter ; as the post only leaves Ravenna once a week, on Saturdays, and as I hope to set out to-morrow evening by the courier. But as I must necessarily stay a day at Florence, and as the natural incidents of travelling may prevent me from taking my intended advantage of the couriers, it is probable that this letter will arrive first. Besides, as I will explain, I am not *yet* quite my own master. But that by and bye. I do not think it necessary to tell you of my impatience to return to you and my little darling, or the disappointment with which I have prolonged my absence from you. I am happy to think that you are not quite alone.

Lord Byron is still decided upon Tuscany : and such is his impatience, that he has desired me—as if I should not arrive in time—to write to you to inquire for the best unfurnished palace in Pisa, and to enter upon a treaty for it. It is better not to be on the Lung' Arno ; but, in fact, there is no such hurry, and as I shall see you so soon it is not worth while to trouble yourself about it.

I told you I had written by L. B.'s desire to la Guiccioli, to dissuade her and her family from Switzerland. Her answer is this moment arrived, and my representation seems to have reconciled them to the unfitness of that step. At the conclusion of a letter, full of all the fine things she says she has heard of me, is this request, which I transcribe ;—"*Signore—la vostra bontà mi fa ardita di chiedervi un favore—me lo accorderete voi ? Non partite da Ravenna senza Milord.*" Of course, being now, by all the laws of knighthood, captive to a lady's request, I shall only be at liberty on *my parole*, until Lord Byron is settled at Pisa. I shall reply, of course, that the *boon* is granted, and that if her lover is reluctant to quit Ravenna, after I have made arrangements for receiving him at Pisa, I am bound to place myself in the same situation as now, to assail him with importunities to rejoin her. Of this there is, fortunately, no need ; and I need not tell you there is no fear that this chivalric submission of mine to the great general laws of antique courtesy, against which I never rebel, and which is my religion, should interfere with my quick returning, and long remaining with you, dear girl.

I have seen Dante's tomb, and worshipped the sacred spot. The building and its accessories are comparatively modern, but, the urn itself, and the tablet of marble, with his portrait in relief, are evidently of equal antiquity with his death. The countenance has all the marks of being taken from his own ; the lines are strongly marked, far more than the portraits, which, however, it resembles ; except, indeed, the eye, which is half closed, and reminded me of Pacchiani. It was probably taken after death. I saw the library, and some specimens of the earliest illuminated printing from the press of *Faust.* They are on vellum, and of an execution little inferior to that of the present day.

We ride out every evening as usual, and practice pistol-shooting at a pumpkin ; and I am not sorry to observe, that I approach towards my noble friend's exactness of aim. The water here is villainous, and I have suffered tortures ; but I now drink nothing but alcalescent water, and am much relieved. I have the greatest trouble to get away ; and L. B., as a reason for my stay, has urged, that, without either me or the Guiccioli, he will certainly fall into his old habits. I then talk, and he listens to reason ; and I earnestly hope that he is too well aware of the terrible and degrading consequences of his former mode of life, to be in danger from the short interval of temptation that will be left him. L. B. speaks with great kindness and interest of you, and seems to wish to see you.

Thursday, Ravenna.

I HAVE received your letter with that to Mrs. Hoppner. I do not wonder, my dearest friend, that you should have been moved. I was at first, but speedily regained the indifference which the opinion of anything, or anybody, except our own consciousness, amply merits ; and day by day shall more receive from me. I have not recopied your letter ; such a measure would destroy its authenticity, but have given it to Lord Byron, who has engaged to send it with his own comments to the Hoppners. People do not hesitate, it seems, to make themselves panders and accomplices to slander, for the Hoppners had exacted from Lord Byron that these accusations should be concealed from *me*. Lord Byron is not a man to keep a secret, good or bad ; but in openly confessing that he has not done so, he must observe a certain delicacy, and therefore wished to send the letter himself, and indeed this adds weight to your representations. Have you seen the article in the Literary Gazette on me ? They evidently allude to some story of this kind—however cautious the Hoppners have been in preventing the calumniated person from asserting his justification, you know too much of the world not to be certain that this was the utmost limit of their caution. So much for nothing.

Lord Byron is immediately coming to Pisa. He will set off the moment I can get him a house. Who would have imagined this ? Our first thought ought to be ——, our second our own plans. The hesitation in your letter about Florence has communicated itself to me ; although I hardly see what we can do about Horace Smith, to whom our attentions are so due, and would be so useful. If I do not arrive before this long scrawl, write something to Florence to decide me. I shall certainly, not without strong reasons, at present *sign* the agreement for the old codger's house; although the extreme beauty and fitness of the place, should we decide on Florence, might well overbalance the objection of your deaf visitor. One thing—with Lord Byron and the people we know at Pisa, we should have a security and protection, which seems to be more questionable at Florence. But I do not think that this consideration ought to weigh. What think you of remaining at Pisa? The Williams's would probably be induced to stay there if we did ; Hunt would certainly stay, at least this winter, near us, should he emigrate at all ; Lord Byron and his Italian friends would remain quietly there ; and Lord Byron has certainly a great regard for us—the regard of such a man is worth—*some* of the tribute we must pay to the base passions of humanity in any intercourse with those within their circle ; he is better worth it than those on whom we bestow it from mere custom. The —— are there, and as far as solid affairs are concerned, are my friends. . . . At Pisa I need not distil my water—if I *can* distil it anywhere. Last winter I suffered less from my painful disorder than the winter I spent at Florence. The arguments for Florence you know, and they are very weighty; judge (*I know you like the job*,) which scale is overbalanced.

My greatest content would be utterly to desert all human society. I would retire with you and our child to a solitary island in the sea, would built a boat, and shut upon my retreat the floodgates of the world. I would read no reviews, and talk with no authors. If I dared trust my imagination, it would tell me that there are one or two chosen companions besides yourself whom I should desire. But to this I would not listen —where two or three are gathered together, the devil is among them. And good, far more than evil impulses, love, far more than hatred, has been to me, except as you have been its object, the source of all sorts of mischief. So on this plan, I would be *alone*, and would devote, either to oblivion or to future generations, the overflowings of a mind which, timely withdrawn from the contagion, should be kept fit for no baser object. But this it does not appear that we shall do.

The other side of the alternative (for a medium ought not to be adopted) is to form for ourselves a society of our own class, as much as possible in intellect, or in feelings ; and to connect ourselves with the interests of that society. Our roots never struck so deeply as at Pisa, and the transplanted tree flourishes not. People who lead the lives which we led until last winter, are like a family of Wahabee Arabs, pitching their tent in the midst of London. We must do one thing or the other—for yourself, for our child, for our existence. The calumnies, the sources of which are probably deeper than we perceive, have ultimately, for object, the depriving us of the means of security and subsistence. You will easily perceive the gradations by which calumny proceeds to pretext, pretext to persecution, and persecution to the ban of fire and water. It is for this, and not because this or that fool, or the whole court of fools, curse and rail, that calumny is worth refuting or chastising.

———

CII.—To Leigh Hunt.

Pisa, August 26th, 1821.

My Dearest Friend—Since I last wrote to you, I have been on a visit to Lord Byron at Ravenna. The result of this visit was a determination, on his part, to come and live at Pisa ; and I have taken the finest palace on the Lung' Arno for him. But the material part of my visit consists in a message which he desires me to give you, and which, I think, ought to add to your determination—for such a one I hope you have formed, of restoring your shattered health and spirits by a migration to these " regions mild of calm and serene air."

He proposes that you should come and go shares with him and me, in a periodical work, to be conducted here ; in which each of the contracting parties should publish all their original compositions, and share the profits. He proposed it to Moore, but for some reason it was never brought to bear. There can be no doubt that the *profits* of any scheme in which you and Lord Byron engage, must, from various, yet co-operating reasons, be very great. As for myself, I am, for the present, only a sort of link between you and him, until you can know each other, and effectuate the arrangement ; since (to entrust you with a secret which, for your sake, I withhold from Lord Byron) nothing would induce me to share in the profits, and still less, in the borrowed splendour of such a patnership. You and he, in different manners, would be equal, and would bring, in a different manner, but in the same proportion, equal stocks of reputation and success. Do not let my frankness with you, nor my belief that you deserve it more than Lord Byron, have the effect of deterring you from assuming a station in modern literature, which the universal voice of my contemporaries forbids me either to stoop or to aspire to. I am, and I desire to be, nothing.

I did not ask Lord Byron to assist me in sending a remittance for your journey; because there are men, however excellent, from whom we would never receive an obligation, in the worldly sense of the word; and I am as jealous for my friend as for myself; but I suppose that I shall at last make up an impudent face, and ask Horace Smith to add to the many obligations he has conferred on me. I know I need only ask.

I think I have never told you how very much I like your "Amyntas;" it almost reconciles me to translations. In another sense I still demur. You might have written another such poem as the "Nymphs," with no great access of efforts. I am full of thoughts and plans, and should do something, if the feeble and irritable frame which incloses it was willing to obey the spirit. I fancy that then I should do great things. Before this you will have seen "Adonais." Lord Byron, I suppose from modesty, on account of his being mentioned in it, did not say a word of "Adonais," though he was loud in his praise of "Prometheus," and, what you will not agree with him in, censure of "the Cenci." Certainly, if "Marino Faliero" is a drama, "the Cenci" is not—but that between ourselves. Lord Byron is reformed, as far as gallantry goes, and lives with a beautiful and sentimental Italian lady, who is as much attached to him as may be. I trust greatly to his intercourse with you, for his creed to become as pure as he thinks his conduct is. He has many generous and exalted qualities, but the canker of aristocracy wants to be cut out.

.   .   .   .

CIII.—To Horace Smith.

Pisa, Sept. 14*th*, 1821.

My Dear Smith—I cannot express the pain and disappointment with which I learn the change in your plans, no less than the afflicting cause of it. Florence will no longer have any attractions for me this winter, and I shall contentedly sit down in this humdrum Pisa, and refer to hope and to chance the pleasure I had expected from your society this winter. What shall I do with your packages, which have now, I believe, all arrived at Guebhard's at Leghorn? Is it not possible that a favourable change in Mrs. Smith's health might produce a corresponding change in your determinations, and would it, or would it not, be premature to forward the packages to your present residence, or to London? I will pay every possible attention to your instructions in this regard.

I had marked down several houses in Florence, and one especially on the Arno, a most lovely place, though they asked rather more than perhaps you would have chosen to pay—yet nothing approaching to an English price.—I do not yet entirely give you up.—Indeed, I should be sorry not to hope that Mrs. Smith's state of health would not soon become such, as to remove your principal objection to this delightful climate. I have not, with the exception of three or four days, suffered in the least from the heat this year. Though, it is but fair to confess, that my temperament approaches to that of the salamander.

We expect Lord Byron here in about a fortnight. I have just taken the finest palace in Pisa for him, and his luggage, and his horses, and all his train, are, I believe, already on their way hither. I dare say you have heard of the life he led at Venice, rivalling the wise Solomon almost, in the number of his concubines. Well, he is now quite reformed, and is leading a most sober and decent life, as cavaliere servente to a very pretty Italian woman, who has already arrived at Pisa, with her father and her brother (such are the manners of Italy), as the jackals of the lion. He is occupied in forming a new drama, and, with views which I doubt not will expand as he proceeds, is determined to write a series of plays, in which he will follow the French tragedians and Alfieri, rather than those of England and Spain, and produce something new, at least, to England. This seems to me the wrong road ; but genius like his is destined to lead and not to follow. He will shake off his shackles as he finds they cramp him. I believe he will produce something very great ; and that familiarity with the dramatic power of human nature, will soon enable him to soften down the severe and unharmonising traits of his " Marino Faliero." I think you know Lord Byron personally, or is it your brother? If the latter, I know that he wished particularly to be introduced to you, and that he will sympathise, in some degree, in this great disappointment which I feel in the change, or, as I yet hope, in the prorogation of your plans.

I am glad you like " Adonais," and, particularly, that you do not think it metaphysical, which I was afraid it was. I was resolved to pay some tribute of sympathy to the unhonoured dead, but I wrote, as usual, with a total ignorance of the effect that I should produce.—I have not yet seen your pastoral drama ; if you have a copy, could you favour me with it ? It will be six months before I shall receive it from England. I have heard it spoken of with high praise, and I have the greatest curiosity to see it.

The Gisbornes promised to buy me some books in Paris, and I had asked you to be kind enough to advance them what they might want to pay for them. I cannot conceive why they did not execute this little commission for me, as they knew how very much I wished to receive these books by the same conveyance as the filtering-stone. Dare I ask you to do me the favour to buy them ? *A complete edition of the works of Calderon,* and the French translation of Kant, a German Faust, and to add the Nympholept ?—I am indifferent as to a little more or less expense, so that I may have them immediately. I will send you an order on Paris for the amount, together with the thirty-two francs you were kind enough to pay for me.

All public attention is now centred on the wonderful revolution in Greece. I dare not, after the events of last winter, hope that slaves can become freemen so cheaply ; yet I know one Greek of the highest qualities, both of courage and conduct, the Prince Mavrocordato, and if the rest be like him, all will go well.—The news of this moment is, that the Russian army has orders to advance.

Mrs. S. unites with me in the most heartfelt regret. And I remain, my dear Smith,

Most faithfully yours,   P. B. S.

If you happen to have brought a copy of Clarke's edition of Queen Mab for me, I should like very well to see it.—I really hardly know what this poem is about. I am afraid it is rather rough.

CIV.—To C. Ollier.

Pisa, September 25th, 1821.

Dear Sir,

It will give me great pleasure if I can arrange the affair of Mrs. Shelley's novel with you to her and your satisfaction. She has a specific purpose in the sum which she instructed me to require ; and although this purpose could not be answered without ready money, yet I should find means to answer her wishes in that point, if you could make it convenient to pay one-third at Christmas, and give bills for the other two-thirds at twelve and eighteen months. It would give me peculiar satisfaction that you, rather than any other person, should be the publisher of this work ; it is the product of no slight labour, and, I flatter myself, of no common talent. I doubt it will give no less credit than it will receive from your names. I trust you know me too well to believe that my judgment deliberately given in testimony of the value of any production is influenced by motives of interest or partiality.

The romance is called *Castruccio, Prince of Lucca,* and is founded (not upon the novel of Macchiavelli under that name, which substitutes a childish fiction for the far more romantic truth of history, but) upon the actual story of his life. He was a person who, from an exile and an adventurer, after having served in the wars of England and Flanders in the reign of our Edward the Second, returned to his native city, and, liberating it from its tyrants, became himself its tyrant, and died in the full splendour of his dominion, which he had extended over the half of Tuscany. He was a little Napoleon, and, with a dukedom instead of an empire for his theatre, brought upon the same all the passions and the errors of his antitype. The chief interest of this romance rests upon Euthanasia, his betrothed bride, whose love for him is only equalled by her enthusiasm for the liberty of the republic of Florence, which is in some sort her country, and for that of Italy, to which Castruccio is a devoted enemy, being an ally of the party of the Emperor. This character is a masterpiece ; and the key-stone of the drama, which is built up with admirable art, is the conflict between these passions and these principles. Euthanasia, the last survivor of a noble house, is a feudal countess, and her castle is the scene of the exhibition of the knightly manners of the time. The character of Beatrice, the prophetess, can only be done justice to in the very language of the author. I know nothing in Walter Scott's novels which at all approaches to the beauty and sublimity of this—creation, I may almost say, for it is perfectly original ; and, although founded upon the ideas and manners of the age which is represented, is wholly without a similitude in any fiction I ever read. Beatrice is in love with Castruccio, and dies ; for the romance, although interspersed with much lighter matter, is deeply tragic, and the shades darken and gather as the catastrophe approaches. All the manners, customs, opinions, of the age are introduced ; the superstitions, the heresies, and the religious persecutions are displayed ; the minutest circumstance of Italian manners in that age is not omitted ; and the whole seems to me to constitute a living and a moving picture of an age almost forgotten. The author visited the scenery which she describes in person ; and one or two of the inferior characters are drawn from her own observation of the Italians, for the national character shows itself still in certain instances under the same forms as it wore in the time of Dante.* The novel consists, as I told you before, of three volumes, each at least equal to one of the *Tales of my Landlord,* and they will be very soon ready to be sent. In case you should accept the present offer, I will make one observation which I consider of essential importance. It ought to be printed in half volumes at a time, and sent to the author for her last corrections by the post. It may be printed on thin paper like that of this letter, and the expense shall fall upon me. Lord Byron has his works sent in this manner ; and no person, who has either fame to lose or money to win, ought to publish in any other manner.

By-the-bye, how do I stand with regard to these two great objects of human pursuit ? I *once* sought something nobler and better than either ; but I might as well have reached at the moon, and now, finding that I have grasped the air, I should not be sorry to know what substantial sum, especially of the former, is in your hands on my account. The gods have made the reviewers the almoners of this worldly dross, and I think I must write an ode to flatter them to give me some ; if I would not that they put me off with a bill on posterity, which, when my ghost shall present, the answer will be—" no effects."

Charles the First is conceived, but not born. Unless I am sure of making something good, the play will not be written. Pride, that ruined Satan, will kill *Charles the First,* for his midwife would be only *less than him whom thunder has made greater.* I am full of great plans ; and, if I should tell you them, I should add to the list of these riddles.

* The book here alluded to was ultimately published under the title of *Valperga.* Mrs. Shelley received £400 for the copyright ; and this sum was generously devoted to the relief of Godwin's pecuniary difficulties. In a letter to Mrs. Gisborne, dated June 30th, 1821, Mrs. Shelley says that she first formed the conception at Marlow ; that this took a more definite shape at Naples ; that the work was delayed several times ; and that it was " a child of a mighty slow growth." It was also, she says, a work of labour, as she had read and consulted a great many books.—*L. S.*

I have not seen Mr. Procter's *Mirandola.* Send it me in the box, and pray send me the box immediately. It is of the utmost consequence ; and, as you are so obliging as to say you will not neglect my commissions, pray send this without delay. I hope it *is* sent, indeed, and that you have recollected to send me several copies of *Prometheus,* the *Revolt of Islam,* and the *Cenci,* etc., as I requested you. Is there any chance of a second edition of the *Revolt of Islam?* I could materially improve that poem on revision. The *Adonais,* in spite of its mysticism, is the least imperfect of my compositions, and, as the image of my regret and honour for poor Keats, I wish it to be so. I shall write to you, probably, by next post on the subject of that poem, and should have sent the promised criticism for the second edition, had I not mislaid, and in vain sought for, the volume that contains *Hyperion.* Pray give me notice against what time you want the second part of my *Defence of Poetry.* I give you this Defence, and you may do what you will with it.

Pray give me an immediate answer about the novel.

I am, my dear Sir,
Your very obliged servant,
Percy B. Shelley.

I ought to tell you that the novel has not the smallest tincture of any peculiar theories in politics or religion.

CV.—To John Gisborne.

Pisa, October 22, 1821.

My Dear Gisborne—At length the post brings a welcome letter from you, and I am pleased to be assured of your health and safe arrival. I expect with interest and anxiety the intelligence of your progress in England, and how far the advantages there compensate the loss of Italy. I hear from Hunt that he is determined on emigration, and if I thought the letter would arrive in time, I should beg you to suggest some advice to him. But you ought to be incapable of forgiving me in the fact of depriving England of what it must lose when Hunt departs.

Did I tell you that Lord Byron comes to settle at Pisa, and that he has a plan of writing a periodical work in connection with Hunt? His house, Madame Felichi's, is already taken and fitted up for him, and he has been expected every day these six weeks. La Guiccioli, who awaits him impatiently, is a very pretty, sentimental, innocent Italian, who has sacrificed an immense fortune for the sake of Lord Byron, and who, if I know anything of my friend, of her and of human nature, will hereafter have plenty of leisure and opportunity to repent her rashness. Lord Byron is, however, quite cured of his gross habits, as far as habits ; the perverse ideas on which they were formed are not yet eradicated.

We have furnished a house at Pisa, and mean to make it our head-quarters. I shall get all my books out, and entrench myself like a spider in a web. If you can assist P. in sending them to Leghorn, you would do me an especial favour ; but do not buy me Calderon, Faust, or Kant, as H. S. promises to send them me from Paris, where I suppose you had not time to procure them. Any other books you or Henry think would accord with my design, Ollier will furnish you with.

I should like very much to hear what is said of my " Adonais," and you would oblige me by cutting out, or making Ollier cut out, any respectable criticism on it and sending it me ; you know I do not mind a crown or two in postage. The Epipsychidion is a mystery ; as to real flesh and blood, you know that I do not deal in those articles ; you might as well go to a gin-shop for a leg of mutton, as expect anything human or earthly from me. I desired Ollier not to circulate this piece except to the συνετοί, and even they, it seems, are inclined to approximate me to the circle of a servant girl and her sweetheart. But I intend to write a Symposium of my own to set all this right.

I am just finishing a dramatic poem, called Hellas, upon the contest now raging in Greece—a sort of imitation of the Persæ of Æschylus, full of lyrical poetry. I try to be what I might have been, but am not successful. I find that (I dare say I shall quote wrong,)

> " Den herrlichsten, den sich der Geist emprängt
> Drängt immer fremd und fremder Stoff sich an."

The Edinburgh Review lies. Godwin's answer to Malthus is victorious and decisive ; and that it should not be generally acknowledged as such, is full of evidence of the influence of successful evil and tyranny. What Godwin is, compared to Plato and Lord Bacon, we well know ; but compared with these miserable sciolists, he is a vulture to a worm.

I read the Greek dramatists and Plato for ever. You are right about Antigone ; how sublime a picture of a woman ! and what think you of the choruses, and especially the lyrical complaints of the godlike victim ? and the menaces of Tiresias, and their rapid fulfilment? Some of us have, in a prior existence, been in love with an Antigone, and that makes us find no full content in any mortal tie. As to books, I advise you to live near the British Museum, and read there. I have read, since I saw you, the "Jungfrau von Orleans" of Schiller,—a fine play, if the fifth act did not fall off. Some Greeks, escaped from the defeat in Wallachia, have passed through Pisa to re-embark at Leghorn for the Morea; and the Tuscan Government allowed them, during their stay and passage, three lire each per day and their lodging; that is good. Remember me and Mary most kindly to Mrs. Gisborne and Henry, and believe me,

Yours most affectionately,

P. B. S.

CVI.—To C. Ollier.

Pisa, Nov. 11th, 1821.

Dear Sir—I send you the drama of *Hellas*, relying on your assurance that you will be good enough to pay immediate attention to my literary requests. What little interest this poem may ever excite, depends upon its immediate publication; I entreat you, therefore, to have the goodness to send the MS. instantly to a printer, and the moment you get a proof despatch it to me by the post. The whole might be sent at once. Lord Byron has his poem sent to him in this manner, and I cannot see that the inferiority in the composition of a poem can affect the powers of a printer in the matter of despatch, etc. If any passages should alarm you in the notes, you are at liberty to suppress them; the poem contains nothing of a tendency to danger.

Do not forget my other questions. I am especially curious to hear the fate of *Adonais.* I confess I should be surprised if *that* poem were born to an immortality of oblivion.

Within a few days I may have to write to you on a subject of greater interest. Meanwhile, I rely on your kindness for carrying my present request into immediate effect.

Dear Sir,

Your very faithful servant,

Percy B. Shelley.

I need not impress on you the propriety of giving a speedy answer to Mrs. S.'s proposal. Her volumes are now ready for the press. The *Ode to Napoleon* to print at the end.

CVII.—TO JOSEPH SEVERN.

Pisa, November 29th, 1821.

DEAR SIR—I send you the elegy on poor Keats—and I wish it were better worth your acceptance. You will see, by the preface, that is was written before I could obtain any particular account of his last moments ; all that I still know, was communicated to me by a friend who had derived his information from Colonel Finch ; I have ventured to express, as I felt, the respect and admiration which *your* conduct towards him demands.

In spite of his transcendent genius, Keats never was, nor ever will be, a popular poet ; and the total neglect and obscurity in which the astonishing remnants of his mind still lie, was hardly to be dissipated by a writer, who, however he may differ from Keats in more important qualities, at least resembles him in that accidental one, a want of popularity.

I have little hope, therefore, that the poem I send you will excite any attention, nor do I feel assured that a critical notice of his writings would find a single reader. But for these considerations, it had been my intention to have collected the remnants of his compositions, and to have published them with a life and criticism.—Has he left any poems or writings of whatsoever kind, and in whose possession are they ? Perhaps you would oblige me by information on this point.

Many thanks for the picture you promised me : I shall consider it among the most sacred relics of the past.

For my part, I little expected, when I last saw Keats at my friend Leigh Hunt's, that I should survive him.

Should you ever pass through Pisa, I hope to have the pleasure of seeing you, and of cultivating an acquaintance into something pleasant, begun under such melancholy auspices.

Accept, my dear sir, the assurances of my sincere esteem, and believe me,

Your most sincere and faithful servant,
PERCY B. SHELLEY.

Do you know Leigh Hunt? I expect him and his family *here* every day.

CVIII.—To T. L. Peacock.

Pisa. January (probably 11th), 1822.

MY DEAR PEACOCK—I am still at Pisa, where I have at length fitted up some rooms at the top of a lofty palace that overlooks the city and the surrounding region, and have collected books and plants about me, and established myself for some indefinite time, which, if I read the future, will not be short. I wish you to send my books by the very first opportunity, and I expect in them a great augmentation of comfort. Lord Byron is established here, and we are constant companions. No small relief this, after the dreary solitude of the understanding and the imagination in which we pass the first years of our expatriation, yoked to all sorts of miseries and discomforts. Of course you have seen his last volume, and if you before thought him a great poet, what is your opinion now that you have read *Cain?* The *Foscari* and *Sardanapalus* I have not seen ; but as they are in the style of his later writings, I doubt not they are very fine. We expect Hunt here every day, and remain in great anxiety on account of the heavy gales which he must have encountered at Christmas. Lord Byron has fitted up the lower apartments of his palace for him, and Hunt will be agreeably surprised to find a commodious lodging prepared for him after the fatigues and dangers of his passage. I have been long idle, and, as far as writing goes, despondent ; but I am now engaged on *Charles the first,* and a devil of a nut it is to crack.

M. and C., who is not with us just at present, are well, and so is our little boy, the image of poor William. We live, as usual, tranquilly. I get up, or at least wake, early; read and write till two; dine; go to Lord B.'s, and ride, or play at billiards, as the weather permits ; and sacrifice the evening either to light books or whoever happens to drop in. Our furniture, which is very neat, cost fewer shillings than that at Marlow did pounds sterling ; and our windows are full of plants, which turn the sunny winter into spring. My health is better—my cares are lighter ; and although nothing will cure the consumption of my purse, yet it drags on a sort of life in death, very like its master, and seems, like Fortunatus's, always empty yet never quite exhausted. You will have seen my *Adonais,* and perhaps my *Hellas,* and I think, whatever you may think of the subject, the composition of the first poem will not wholly displease you. I wish I had something better to do than furnish this jingling food for the hunger of oblivion, called verse, but I have not; and since you give me no encouragement about India,* I cannot hope to have.

How is your little star, and the heaven which contains the milky way in which it glimmers?

Adieu—Yours ever, most truly,   S.

CIX.—To Horace Smith.

Pisa, 25th January, 1822.

My Dear Smith—I have delayed this fortnight answering your kind letter because I was in treaty for a *Calderon*, which at last I have succeeded in procuring at a tolerably moderate price. All the other books you mention I should be glad to have ; together with whatever others might fall in your way that you might think interesting.

Will you not think my exactions upon your kindness interminable if I ask you to execute another commission for me? It is to buy a good pedal harp, without great ornament or any appendage that would unnecessarily increase the expense— but good ; nor should I object to its being second-hand, if that were equally compatible with its being despatched immediately. Together with the harp I should wish for five or six napoleons' worth of harp music, at your discretion. I do not know the price of harps at Paris, but I suppose that from seventy to eighty guineas would cover it, and I trust to your accustomed kindness, as I want it for a present, to make the immediate advance, as if I were to delay, the grace of my compliment would be lost. Do not take much trouble about it, but simply take what you find, if you are so exceedingly kind as to oblige me. It had better be sent by Marseilles, through some merchant or in any other manner you think best, addressed to me at Messrs. Guebhard and Co., merchants, Leghorn ; the books may be sent together with it.

Our party at Pisa is the same as when I wrote last. Lord Byron unites us at a weekly dinner, when my nerves are generally shaken to pieces by sitting up contemplating the rest making themselves vats of claret, etc., till three o'clock in the

---

* He had expressed a desire to be employed politically at the court of a native prince, and I had told him that such employment was restricted to the regular service of the East India Company.— *T. L. P.*

morning.   We regret *your* absence exceedingly, and Lord
Byron has desired me to convey his best remembrances to you.
I imagine it is *you*, and not your brother, for whom they are
intended.   Hunt was expected, and Lord Byron had fitted up a
part of his palace for his accommodation, when we heard that
the late violent storms had forced him to put back ; and that
nothing could induce Marianne to put to sea again.   This, for
many reasons that I cannot now explain, has produced a chaos
of perplexities. . . .   The reviews and journals, they say,
continue to attack me, but I value neither the fame they can
give nor the fame they can take away, therefore blessed be the
name of the reviews.

Pray, if possible, let the " Nympholept " be included in the
package.

Believe me, my dear Smith,
Your most obliged and affectionate friend,
P. B. SHELLEY.

CX.—TO JOHN GISBORNE.

Pisa, April 10, 1822.

MY DEAR GISBORNE—I have received Hellas, which is
prettily printed, and with fewer mistakes than any poem I ever
published.   Am I to thank you for the revision of the press ? or
who acted as midwife to this last of my orphans, introducing it
to oblivion, and me to my accustomed failure ?   May the cause
it celebrates be more fortunate than either !   Tell me how you
like Hellas, and give me your opinion freely.   It was written
without much care, and in one of those few moments of
enthusiasm which now seldom visit me, and which make me
pay dear for their visits.   I know what to think of Adonais, but
what to think of those who confound it with the many bad
poems of the day, I know not.

I have been reading over and over again Faust, and always
with sensations which no other composition excites.   It deepens
the gloom and augments the rapidity of ideas, and would
therefore seem to me an unfit study for any person who is a prey
to the reproaches of memory, and the delusions of an imagination
not to be restrained.   And yet the pleasure of sympathising
with emotions known only to few, although they derive their sole
charm from despair, and the scorn of the narrow good we can
attain in our present state, seems more than to ease the pain
which belongs to them.   Perhaps all discontent with the *less* (to

use a Platonic sophism,) supposes the sense of a just claim to the *greater*, and that we admirers of Faust are on the right road to Paradise. Such a supposition is not more absurd, and is certainly less demoniacal, than that of Wordsworth, where he says—

"This earth,
Which is the world of all of us, and where
We find our happiness, or not at all."

As if, after sixty years' suffering here, we were to be roasted alive for sixty million more in hell, or charitably annihilated by a *coup de grâce* of the bungler who brought us into existence at first !

Have you read Calderon's *Magico Prodigioso?* I find a striking singularity between Faust and this drama, and if I were to acknowledge Coleridge's distinction, should say Goethe was the *greatest* philosopher, and Calderon the *greatest* poet. *Cyprian* evidently furnished the *germ* of Faust, as Faust may furnish the germ of other poems ; although it is as different from it in structure and plan as the acorn from the oak. I have — imagine my presumption—translated several scenes from both, as the basis of a paper for our journal. I am well content with those from Calderon, which in fact gave me very little trouble ; but those from Faust—I feel how imperfect a representation, even with all the licence I assume to figure to myself how Goethe would have written in English, my words convey. No one but Coleridge is capable of this work.

We have seen here a translation of some scenes, and indeed the most remarkable ones, accompanying those astonishing etchings which have been published in England from a German master. It is not bad—and faithful enough—but how weak ! how incompetent to represent Faust ! I have only attempted the scenes omitted in this translation, and would send you that of the *Walpurgisnacht*, if I thought Ollier would place the postage to my account. What etchings those are ! I am never satiated with looking at them ; and, I fear, it is the only sort of translation of which Faust is susceptible. I never perfectly understood the Hartz Mountain scene, until I saw the etching ; and then, Margaret in the summer-house with Faust ! The artist makes one envy his happiness that he can sketch such things with calmness, which I only dared look upon once, and which made my brain swim round only to touch the leaf on the opposite side of which I knew that it was figured. Whether it is that the artist has surpassed Faust, or that the pencil surpasses language in some subjects, I know not, or that I am more affected by a visible image, but the etching certainly excited me far more than the poem it illustrated. Do you remember the fifty-fourth letter of the first part of the " Nouvelle Héloïse ?" Goethe, in a subsequent scene, evidently had that letter in his mind, and this etching is an idealism of it. So much for the world of shadows !

What think you of Lord Byron's last volume ? In my opinion it contains finer poetry than has appeared in England since the publication of Paradise Regained. Cain is apocalyptic—it is a revelation not before communicated to man. I write nothing but by fits. I have done some of Charles I. ; but although the poetry succeeded very well, I cannot seize on the conception of the subject as a whole, and seldom now touch the canvas. You know I don't think much about Reviews, nor of the fame they give, nor that they take away. It is absurd in any Review to criticise Adonais, and still more to pretend that the verses are bad. Prometheus was never intended for more than five or six persons.

And how are you getting on ? Do your plans still want success ? Do you regret Italy ? or any thing that Italy contains ? And in case of an entire failure in your expectations, do you think of returning here ? You see the first blow has been made at funded property:—do you intend to confide and invite a second ? You would already have saved something per cent., if you had invested your property in Tuscan land. The next best thing would be to invest it in English, and reside upon it. I tremble for the consequences, to you personally, from a prolonged confidence in the funds. Justice, policy, the hopes of the nation and renewed institutions, demand your ruin, and I, for one, cannot bring myself to desire what is in itself desirable, till you are free. You see how liberal I am of advice ; but you know the motives that suggest it. What is Henry about, and how are his prospects ? Tell him that some adventurers are engaged upon a steam-boat at Leghorn, to make the *trajet* we projected. I hope he is charitable enough to pray that they may succeed better than we did.

Remember me most affectionately to Mrs. Gisborne, to whom, as well as to yourself, I consider that this letter is written. How is she, and how are you all in health ? And pray tell me, what are your plans of life, and how Henry succeeds, and whether he is married or not ? How can I send you such small sums as you may want for postages, etc., for I do not mean to tax with my unreasonable letters both your purse and your patience? We go this summer to Spezzia; but direct as ever to Pisa,—Mrs. —— will forward our letters. If you see anything which you think would particularly interest me, pray make Ollier pay for sending it out by post. Give my best and affectionate regards to H——, to whom I do not write at present, imagining that you will give him a piece of this letter.

Ever most faithfully yours,   P. B. S.

———

CXI.—To Horatio Smith.

Pisa, April 11th, 1822.

MY DEAR SMITH.—I have, as yet, received neither the . . ., nor his metaphysical companions—*Time, my Lord, has a wallet on his back,* and I suppose he has bagged them by the way. As he has had a good deal of *alms* for oblivion out of me, I think he might as well have favoured me this once; I have, indeed, just dropped another mite into his treasury, called *Hellas,* which I know not how to send to you; but I dare say, some fury of the Hades of authors will bring one to Paris. It is a poem written on the Greek cause last summer—a sort of lyrical, dramatic, nondescript piece of business.

You will have heard of a *row* we have had here, which, I dare say, will grow to a serious size before it arrives at Paris. It was, in fact, a trifling piece of business enough, arising from an insult of a drunken dragoon, offered to one of our party, and only serious, because one of Lord B.'s servants wounded the fellow dangerously with a pitchfork. He is now, however, recovering, and the echo of the affair will be heard long after the original report has ceased.

Lord Byron has read me one or two letters of Moore to him,* in which Moore speaks with great kindness of me; and of course I cannot but feel flattered by the approbation of a man, my inferiority to whom I am proud to acknowledge.—Amongst other things, however, Moore, after giving Lord B. much good advice about public opinion, etc., seems to deprecate MY influence on his mind, on the subject of religion, and to attribute the tone assumed in "Cain" to my suggestions. Moore cautions him against my influence on this particular, with the most friendly zeal; and it is plain that his motive springs from a desire of

* For Mr. Moore's account of this incident, and his own feelings and opinions on the subject—those imputed to him by Shelley being purely conjectural—see Moore's Life of Byron, Vol. II. p. 584, first edition. —*M. S.*

benefiting Lord B., without degrading me. I think you know Moore. Pray assure him that I have not the smallest influence over Lord Byron, in this particular, and if I had, I certainly should employ it to eradicate from his great mind the delusions of Christianity, which, in spite of his reason, seem perpetually to recur, and to lay in ambush for the hours of sickness and distress. "Cain" was *conceived* many years ago, and begun before I saw him last year at Ravenna. How happy should I not be to attribute to myself, however indirectly, any participation in that immortal work!—I differ with Moore in thinking Christianity useful to the world ; no man of sense can think it true ; and the alliance of the monstrous superstitions of the popular worship with the pure doctrines of the Theism of such a man as Moore, turns to the profit of the former, and makes the latter the fountain of its own pollution. I agree with him, that the doctrines of the French, and Material Philosophy, are as false as they are pernicious ; but still they are better than Christianity, inasmuch as anarchy is better than despotism ; for this reason, that the former is for a season, and the latter is eternal. My admiration of the character, no less than of the genius of Moore, makes me rather wish that he should not have an ill opinion of me.

Where are you? We settle this summer near Spezzia ; Lord Byron at Leghorn. May not I hope to see you, even for a trip in Italy? I hope your wife and little ones are well. Mine grows a fine boy, and is quite well.

I have contrived to get my musical coals at Newcastle itself.— My dear Smith, believe me,

Faithfully yours,　　　　　P. B. S.

CXII.—To Mrs. Shelley,

(at spezzia.)

Lerici, Sunday, April 28th, 1822.

Dearest Mary—I am this moment arrived at Lerici, where I am necessarily detained, waiting the furniture, which left Pisa last night at midnight ; and as the sea has been calm, and the wind fair, I may expect them every moment. It would not do to leave affairs here in an *impiccio*, great as is my anxiety to see you.—How are you, my best love? How have you sustained the trials of the journey? Answer me this question, and how my little babe and Clare are.

Now to business :—Is the Magni House taken ? if not, pray occupy yourself instantly in finishing the affair, even if you are obliged to go to Sarzana, and send a messenger to me to tell me of your success. I, of course, cannot leave Lerici, to which place the boats (for we were obliged to take two), are directed. But *you* can come over in the same boat that brings this letter, and return in the evening.

I ought to say that I do not think that there is accommodation for you all at this inn ; and that, even if there were, you would be better off at Spezzia ; but if the Magni House is taken, then there is no possible reason why you should not take a row over in the boat that will bring this—but don't keep the men long. I am anxious to hear from you on every account.

Ever yours, S.

CXIII.—To Horatio Smith,

(VERSAILLES.)

Lerici, May, 1822.

MY DEAR SMITH—It is some time since I have heard from you ; are you still at Versailles ? Do you still cling to France, and prefer the arts and conveniences of that over-civilised country to the beautiful nature and mighty remains of Italy ? As to me, like Anacreon's swallow, I have left my Nile, and have taken up my summer quarters here, in a lonely house, close by the sea-side, surrounded by the soft and sublime scenery of the gulf of Spezzia. I do not write ; I have lived too long near Lord Byron, and the sun has extinguished the glow-worm ; for I cannot hope, with St. John, that "*the light came into the world, and the world knew it not.*"

The object of my present letter is, however, a request, and as it concerns that most odious of all subjects, money, I will put it in the shortest shape—Godwin's law-suit, he tells us, is decided against him ; and he is adjudged to pay £400. He writes, of course, to his daughter in the greatest distress : but we have no money except our income, nor any means of procuring it. My wife has sent him her novel, which is now finished, the copyright of which will probably bring him £300 or £400—as Ollier offered the former sum for it, but as he required a considerable delay for the payment, she rejected his offer. Now, what I wish to know is, whether you could with convenience lend me the £400 which you once dedicated to this service, and allow Godwin to have it, under the precautions and stipulations which I formerly annexed to its employment. You could not obviously allow this money to lie idle waiting for this event, without interest. I forgot this part of the business till this instant, and now I reflect that I ought to have assured you of the regular payment of interest, which I omitted to mention, considering it a matter of course.

I can easily imagine that circumstances may have arisen to make this loan inconvenient or impossible.—In any case, believe me,

My dear Smith,

Yours very gratefully and faithfully,

P. B. SHELLEY.

———

CXIV.—TO HORATIO SMITH.

Lerici, June 29th, 1822.

MY DEAR SMITH.—Pray thank Moore for his obliging message. I wish I could as easily convey my sense of his genius and character. I should have written to him on the subject of my late letter, but that I doubted how far I was justified in doing so; although, indeed, Lord Byron made no secret of his communication to me. It seems to me that things have now arrived at such a crisis as requires every man plainly to utter his sentiments on the inefficacy of the existing religion, no less than political systems, for restraining and guiding mankind. Let us see the truth, whatever that may be. The destiny of man can scarcely be so degraded, that he was born only to die; and if such should be the case, delusions, especially the gross and preposterous ones of the existing religion, can scarcely be supposed to exalt it. If every man said what he thought, it could not subsist a day. But all, more or less, subdue themselves to the element that surrounds them, and contribute to the evils they lament by the hypocrisy that springs from them.

England appears to be in a desperate condition, Ireland still worse; and no class of those who subsist on the public labour will be persuaded that *their* claims on it must be diminished. But the government must content itself with less in taxes, the landholder must submit to receive less rent, and the fundholder a diminished interest, or they will all get nothing. I once thought to study these affairs, and write or act in them. I am glad that my good genius said, *refrain.* I see little public virtue, and I foresee that the contest will be one of blood and gold, two elements which however much to my taste in my pockets and my veins, I have an objection to out of them.

Lord Byron continues at Leghorn, and has just received from Genoa a most beautiful little yacht, which he caused to be built there. He has written two new cantos of Don Juan, but I have not seen them. I have just received a letter from Hunt, who has arrived at Genoa. As soon as I hear that he has sailed, I shall weigh anchor in my little schooner, and give him chase to Leghorn, when I must occupy myself in some arrangements for him with Lord Byron. Between ourselves, I greatly fear that this alliance will not succeed ; for I, who could never have been regarded as more than the link of the two thunderbolts, cannot now consent to be even that ; and how long the alliance may continue, I will not prophesy. Pray do not hint my doubts on the subject to any one, or they might do harm to Hunt ; and they *may* be groundless.

I still inhabit this divine bay, reading Spanish dramas, and sailing, and listening to the most enchanting music. We have some friends on a visit to us, and my only regret is that the summer must ever pass, or that Mary has not the same pre-dilection for this place that I have, which would induce me never to shift my quarters.

Farewell.—Believe me ever your affectionate friend,

P. B. SHELLEY.

CXV.—TO MRS. WILLIAMS,

(CASA MAGNI.)

Pisa, July 4, 1822.

YOU will probably see Williams before I can disentangle myself from the affairs with which I am now surrounded. I return to Leghorn to-night, and shall urge him to sail with the first fair wind, without expecting me. I have thus the pleasure of contributing to your happiness when deprived of every other, and of leaving you no other subject of regret, but the absence of one scarcely worth regretting. I fear you are solitary and melancholy at Villa Magni, and, in the intervals of the greater and more serious distress in which I am compelled to sym-pathise here, I figure to myself the countenance which had been the source of such consolation to me, shadowed by a veil of sorrow.

How soon those hours passed, and how slowly they return, to pass so soon again, perhaps for ever, in which we have lived

together so intimately, so happily ! Adieu, my dearest friend !
I only write these lines for the pleasure of tracing what will
meet your eyes.　Mary will tell you all the news.

S.

CXVI.—To Mrs. Shelley,

(casa magni.)

Pisa, July 4, 1822.

My Dearest Mary—I have received both your letters, and
shall attend to the instructions they convey.　I did not think of
buying the Bolivar ; Lord B. wishes to sell her, but I imagine
would prefer ready money.　I have as yet made no inquiries
about houses near Pugnano—I have no moment of time to spare
from Hunt's affairs ; I am detained unwillingly here, and you
will probably see Williams in the boat before me,—but that will
be decided to-morrow.

Things are in the worst possible situation with respect to poor
Hunt.　I find Marianne in a desperate state of health, and on
our arrival at Pisa sent for Vaccà.　He decides that her case is
hopeless, and that although it will be lingering, must inevitably
end fatally.　This decision he thought proper to communicate
to Hunt ; indicating at the same time, with great judgment and
precision, the treatment necessary to be observed for availing
himself of the chance of his being deceived.　This intelligence
has extinguished the last spark of poor Hunt's spirits, low
enough before.　The children are well and much improved.

Lord Byron is at this moment on the point of leaving Tuscany.
The Gambas have been exiled, and he declares his intention of
following their fortunes.　His first idea was to sail to America,
which was changed to Switzerland, then to Genoa, and last to
Lucca.　Everybody is in despair and everything in confusion.
Trelawny was on the point of sailing to Genoa for the purpose
of transporting the Bolivar overland to the lake of Geneva, and
had already whispered in my ear his desire that I should not
influence Lord Byron against this terrestrial navigation.　He
next received *orders* to weigh anchor and set sail for Lerici.
He is now without instructions, moody and disappointed.　But
it is the worst for poor Hunt, unless the present storm should
blow over.　He places his whole dependence upon the scheme
of a journal, for which every arrangement has been made.
Lord Byron must of course furnish the requisite funds at
present, as I cannot ; but he seems inclined to depart without

the necessary explanations and arrangements due to such a situation as Hunt's. These, in spite of delicacy, I must procure ; he offers him the copyright of the Vision of Judgment for the first number. This offer, if sincere, is *more* than enough to set up the journal, and, if sincere, will set everything right.

How are you, my best Mary ? Write especially how is your health and how your spirits are, and whether you are not more reconciled to staying at Lerici, at least during the summer.

You have no idea how I am hurried and occupied ; I have not a moment's leisure, but will write by next post. Ever, dearest Mary, Yours affectionately, S.

I have found the translation of the Symposium.

APPENDIX.

———◆———

EARLY PROSE WRITINGS.

LIMITS of space have made it impossible to give representative excerpts from all Shelley's early prose writings, as was originally intended, and only three will be found represented here accordingly. As it may be useful for purposes of reference to have a full list of the early writings, however, we append one giving the titles in the order in which they were published :—

THE NECESSITY OF ATHEISM; Oxford, 1811.

AN ADDRESS TO THE IRISH PEOPLE; Dublin, 1812.

PROPOSALS FOR AN ASSOCIATION of those Philanthropists, who, convinced of the inadequacy of the moral and political state of Ireland to produce benefits which are nevertheless attainable, are willing to unite to accomplish its regeneration; Dublin, 1812.

DECLARATION OF RIGHTS; Dublin, 1812.

LETTER TO LORD ELLENBOROUGH; [Printed at Barnstaple] 1812.

A VINDICATION OF NATURAL DIET; London, 1813.

A REFUTATION OF DEISM ; London, 1814.

A PROPOSAL FOR PUTTING REFORM TO THE VOTE throughout the Kingdom, by the Hermit of Marlow ; London, 1817.

"WE PITY THE PLUMAGE, BUT FORGET THE DYING BIRD." An Address to the People, on the Death of the Princess Charlotte, by the Hermit of Marlow; London, 1817.

═══════════

Excerpts from

AN ADDRESS TO THE IRISH PEOPLE.

DUBLIN, 1812.

•   •   •   •   •   •

I LOOK upon the Catholic Emancipation, and the restoration of the liberties and happiness of Ireland, so far as they are compatible with the English Constitution, as great and important events. I hope to see them soon. But if all ended here, it would give me little pleasure —I should still see thousands miserable and wicked, things would still be wrong. I regard, then, the accomplishment of these things as the road to a greater reform—that reform after which virtue and wisdom shall have conquered pain and vice. When no Government will be wanted, but that of your neighbour's opinion.—I look to these things with hope and pleasure, because I consider that they will certainly happen, and because men will not then be wicked and miserable. But I do not consider that they will or can immediately happen; their arrival will be gradual, and it all depends upon yourselves how soon or how late these great changes will happen. If all of you to-morrow were virtuous and wise, Government, which to-day is a safe-guard, would then become a tyranny. But I cannot expect a rapid change. Many are obstinate and determined in their vice, whose selfishness makes them think only of their own good, when, in fact, the best way even to bring that about, is to make others happy. I do not wish to see things changed now, because it cannot be done without violence, and we may assure ourselves that none of us are fit for any change hovever good, if we condescend to employ force in a cause which we think right. Force makes the side that employs it directly wrong, and as much as we may pity we cannot approve the headstrong and intolerant zeal of its adherents.

Can you conceive, O Irishmen! a happy state of society—conceive men of every way of thinking living together like brothers. The descendant of the greatest Prince would there be entitled to no more respect than the son of a peasant. There would be no pomp and no parade, but that which the rich now keep to themselves, would then be distributed among the people. None would be in magnificence, but the superfluities then taken from the rich would be sufficient, when spread abroad, to make every one comfortable.—No lover would then be false to his mistress, no mistress would desert her lover. No friend would play false, no rents, no debts, no taxes, no frauds of any kind would disturb the general happiness: good as they would be, wise as they would be, they would be daily getting better and wiser. No beggars would exist, nor any of those wretched women, who are now reduced to a state of the most horrible misery and vice, by men whose wealth makes them villainous and hardened. No thieves or murderers, because poverty would never drive men to take away comforts from another, when he had enough for himself. Vice and misery, pomp and poverty, power and obedience, would then be banished altogether.—It is for such a state as this, Irishmen, that I exhort you to prepare.

* * * * * * * *

I have purposely avoided any lengthened discussion on those griev-ances to which your hearts are from custom, and the immediate interest of the circumstances, probably most alive at present. I have not however wholly neglected them. Most of all have I insisted on their instant palliation and ultimate removal; nor have I omitted a consideration of the means which I deem most effectual for the accom-plishment of this great end. How far you will consider the former worthy of your adoption, so far shall I deem the latter probable and interesting to the lovers of human kind. And I have opened to your view a new scene—does not your heart bound at the bare possibility of your posterity possessing that liberty and happiness of which during ours lives powerful exertions and habitual abstinence may give us a foretaste. Oh ! if your hearts do not vibrate at such as this ; then ye are dead and cold—ye are not men.

I now come to the application of my principles, the conclusion of my address ; and O Irishmen, whatever conduct ye may feel yourselves bound to pursue, the path which duty points to, lies before me clear and unobscured. Dangers may lurk around it, but they are not the dangers which lie beneath the footsteps of the hypocrite or temporizer.

For I have not presented to you the picture of happiness on which my fancy doats as an uncertain meteor to mislead honourable enthusiasm, or blindfold the judgment which makes virtue useful. I have not proposed crude schemes, which I should be imcompetent to mature, or desired to excite in you any virulence against the abuses of political institution ; where I have had occasion to point them out I have recommended moderation whilst yet I have earnestly insisted upon energy and perseverance ; I have spoken of peace, yet declared that resistance is laudable ; but the intellectual resistance which I recommend, I deem essential to the introduction of the millenium of virtue, whose period every one can, so far as he is concerned, forward by his own proper power. I have not attempted to shew, that the Catholic claims or the claims of the people, to a full representation in Parliament, or any of those claims to real rights, which I have insisted upon as introductory to the ultimate claim of *all*, to universal happiness, freedom, and equality ; I have not attempted, I say, to shew that these can be granted consistently with the spirit of the English Constitution :* this is a point which I do not feel myself inclined to discuss, and which I consider foreign to my object. But I have shewn that these claims have for their basis, truth and justice, which are immutable, and which in the ruin of Governments shall rise like a Phœnix from their ashes.

.   .   .   .   .   ,   .

* Note.—The excellence of the Constitution of Great Britain, appears to me, to be its indefiniteness and versatility, whereby it may be unresistingly accommodated to the progression of wisdom and virtue. Such accommodation I desire ; but I wish for the cause before the effect.

DECLARATION OF RIGHTS.

1. GOVERNMENT has no rights ; it is a delegation from several individuals for the purpose of securing their own. It is therefore just, only so far as it exists by their consent, useful only so far as it operates to their well-being.

2. If these individuals think that the form of government which they or their forefathers constituted is ill adapted to produce their happiness, they have a right to change it.

3. Government is devised for the security of Rights. The rights of man are liberty, and an equal participation of the commonage of Nature.

4. As the benefit of the governed is, or ought to be, the origin of government, no men can have any authority that does not expressly emanate from *their* will.

5. Though all governments are not so bad as that of Turkey, yet none are so good as they might be. The majority of every country have a right to perfect their government. The minority should not disturb them; they ought to secede, and form their own system in their own way.

6. All have a right to an equal share in the benefits and burdens of Government. Any disabilities for opinion imply, by their existence, bare-faced tyranny on the side of Government, ignorant slavishness on the side of the governed.

7. The rights of man, in the present state of society, are only to be secured by some degree of coercion to be exercised on their violator. The sufferer has a right that the degree of coercion employed be as slight as possible.

8. It may be considered as a plain proof of the hollowness of any proposition if power be used to enforce instead of reason to persuade its admission. Government is never supported by fraud until it cannot be supported by reason.

9. No man has a right to disturb the public peace by personally resisting the execution of a law, however bad. He ought to acquiesce, using at the same time the utmost powers of his reason to promote its repeal.

10. A man must have a right to act in a certain manner, before it can be his duty. He may, before he ought.

11. A man has a right to think as his reason directs; it is a duty he owes to himself to think with freedom, that he may act from conviction.

12. A man has a right to unrestricted liberty of discussion. Falsehood is a scorpion that will sting itself to death.

13. A man has not only a right to express his thoughts, but it is his duty to do so.

14. No law has a right to discourage the practice of truth. A man ought to speak the truth on every occasion. A duty can never be criminal; what is not criminal cannot be injurious.

15. Law cannot make what is in its nature virtuous or innocent to be criminal, any more than it can make what is criminal to be innocent. Government cannot make a law; it can only pronounce that which was the law before its organization; viz., the moral result of the imperishable relations of things.

16. The present generation cannot bind their posterity: the few cannot promise for the many.

17. No man has a right to do an evil thing that good may come.

18. Expediency is inadmissible in morals. Politics are only sound when conducted on principles of morality : they are, in fact, the morals of nations.

19. Man has no right to kill his brother. It is no excuse that he does so in uniform : he only adds the infamy of servitude to the crime of murder.

20. Man, whatever be his country, has the same rights in one place as another—the rights of universal citizenship.

21. The government of a country ought to be perfectly indifferent to every opinion. Religious differences, the bloodiest and most rancorous of all, spring from partiality.

22. A delegation of individuals, for the purpose of securing their rights, can have no undelegated power of restraining the expression of their opinion.

23. Belief is involuntary; nothing involuntary is meritorious or reprehensible. A man ought not to be considered worse or better for his belief.

24. A Christian, a Deist, a Turk, and a Jew, have equal rights: they are men and brethren.

25. If a person's religious ideas correspond not with your own, love him nevertheless. How different would yours have been had the chance of birth placed you in Tartary or India !

26. Those who believe that Heaven is, what earth has been, a monopoly in the hands of a favoured few, would do well to reconsider their opinion ; if they find that it came from their priest or their grandmother, they could not do better than reject it.

27. No man has a right to be respected for any other possessions but those of virtue and talents. Titles are tinsel, power a corruptor, glory a bubble, and excessive wealth a libel on its possessor.

28. No man has a right to monopolise more than he can enjoy ; what the rich give to the poor, whilst millions are starving, is not a perfect favour, but an imperfect right.

29. Every man has a right to a certain degree of leisure and liberty, because it is his duty to attain a certain degree of knowledge. He may, before he ought.

30. Sobriety of body and mind is necessary to those who would be free ; because, without sobriety, a high sense of philanthropy cannot actuate the heart, nor cool and determined courage execute its dictates.

31. The only use of government is to repress the vices of man. If man were to-day sinless, to-morrow he would have a right to demand that government and all its evils should cease.

Man ! thou whose rights are here declared, be no longer forgetful of the loftiness of thy destination. Think of thy rights, of those possessions which will give thee virtue and wisdom, by which thou mayest arrive at happiness and freedom. They are declared to thee by one who knows thy dignity, for every hour does his heart swell with honourable pride in the contemplation of what thou mayest attain—by one who is not forgetful of thy degeneracy, for every moment brings home to him the bitter conviction of what thou art.

Awake!—arise!—or be for ever fallen.

LETTER TO LORD ELLENBOROUGH.

My Lord—As the station to which you have been called by your country is important, so much the more awful is your responsibility, so much the more does it become you to watch lest you inadvertently punish the virtuous and reward the vicious.

You preside over a Court which is instituted for the suppression of crime, and to whose authority the people submit on no other conditions than that its decrees should be conformable to justice.

If it should be demonstrated that a judge had condemned an innocent man, the bare existence of laws in conformity to which the accused is punished would but little extenuate his offence. The inquisitor, when he burns an obstinate heretic, may set up a similar plea; yet few are sufficiently blinded by intolerance to acknowledge its validity. It will less avail such a judge to assert the policy of punishing one who has committed no crime. Policy and morality ought to be deemed synonymous in a court of justice, and he whose conduct has been regulated by the latter principle, is not justly amenable to any penal law for a supposed violation of the former. It is true, my Lord, laws exist which suffice to screen you from the animadversion of any constituted power, in consequence of the un-merited sentence which you have passed upon Mr. Eaton; but there are no laws which screen you from the reproof of a nation's disgust, none which ward off the just judgment of posterity, if that posterity will deign to recollect you.

But what right do you punish Mr. Eaton? What but antiquated precedents, gathered from times of priestly and tyrannical domination, can be adduced in palliation of an outrage so insulting to humanity and justice? Whom has he injured? What crime has he committed? Wherefore may he not walk abroad like other men, and follow his accustomed pursuits? What end is proposed in confining this man, charged with the commission of no dishonourable action? Wherefore did his aggressor avail himself of popular prejudice, and return no answer but one of commonplace contempt to a defence of plain and simple sincerity? Lastly, when the prejudices of the jury as Christians, were strongly and unfairly inflamed* against this injured man,

* See the Attorney-General's Speech.—(S.)

as a Deist, wherefore did not you, my Lord, check such unconstitutional pleading, and desire the jury to pronounce the accused innocent or criminal* without reference to the particular faith which he professed ?

In the name of justice, what answer is there to these questions ? The answer which Heathen Athens made to Socrates is the same with which Christian England must attempt to silence the advocates of this injured man. "He has questioned established opinions." Alas ! the crime of inquiry is one which religion never has forgiven. Implicit faith and fearless inquiry have in all ages been irreconcileable enemies. Unrestrained philosophy has in every age opposed itself to the reveries of credulity and fanaticism. The truths of astronomy demonstrated by Newton have superseded astrology ; since the modern discoveries in chemistry, the philosopher's stone has been deemed attainable. Miracles of every kind have become rare in proportion to the hidden principles which those who study nature have developed. That which is false will ultimately be controverted by its own falsehood. That which is true needs but publicity to be acknowledged. It is ever a proof that the falsehood of a proposition is felt by those who use power and coercion, not reasoning and persuasion, to procure its admission. Falsehood skulks in holes and corners, "it lets I dare not wait upon I would, like the poor cat in the adage," except when it has power, and then, as it was a coward, it is a tyrant ; but the eagle-eye of truth darts thro' the undazzling sunbeam of the immutable and just, gathering there wherewith to vivify and illuminate a universe !

Wherefore, I repeat, is Mr. Eaton punished ? Because he is a Deist. And what are you, my Lord ? A Christian. Ha, then ! the mask has fallen off ; you persecute him because his faith differs from yours. You copy the persecutors of Christianity in your actions, and are an additional proof that your religion is as bloody, barbarous, and intolerant as theirs. If some Deistical bigot in power (supposing such a character for the sake of illustration) should in dark and barbarous ages, have enacted a statute making the profession of Christianity criminal ; if you, my Lord, were a Christian bookseller, and Mr. Eaton a Judge, those arguments which you consider adequate to justify yourself for the sentence you have passed must likewise suffice, in the suppositionary case, to justify Mr. Eaton in sentencing you to Newgate and the pillory for being a Christian. Whence is any right derived, but that which power confers, for persecution ? Do you think to convert Mr. Eaton to your religion by embittering his existence ? You might force him by torture to profess your tenets, but he could not believe them, except you should make them credible, which perhaps exceeds your power. Do you think to please the God you worship by this exhibition of your zeal ? If so, the Demon to whom

---

* By Mr. Fox's bill (1791) juries are, in cases of libel, judges both of the law and the fact.—(S.)

some nations offer human hecatombs is less barbarous than the Deity of civilised society.

You consider man as an accountable being—but he can only be accountable for those actions which are influenced by his will.

Belief and disbelief are utterly distinct from and unconnected with volition. They are the apprehension of the agreement or disagreement of the ideas which compose any proposition. Belief is an involuntary operation of the mind, and, like other passions, its intensity is purely proportionate to the degrees of excitement. Volition is essential to merit or demerit. How, then, can merit or demerit be attached to what is distinct from that faculty of the mind whose presence is essential to their being? I am aware that religion is founded on the voluntariness of belief, as it makes it a subject of regard and punishment; but before we extinguish the steady ray of reason and common sense, it is fit that we should discover, which we cannot do without their assistance, whether or no there be any other which may suffice to guide us through the labyrinth of life.

If the law *de hæretico comburendo* had not been formally repealed, I conceive that, from the promise held out by your Lordship's zeal, we need not despair of beholding the flames of persecution rekindled in Smithfield. Even now the lash that drove Descartes and Voltaire from their native country, the chains which bound Galileo, the flames which burned Vanini, again resound :— And where? in a nation that presumptuously calls itself the sanctuary of freedom. Under a government which, whilst it infringes the very right of thought and speech, boasts of permitting the liberty of the press, a man is pilloried and imprisoned because he is a Deist, and no one raises his voice in the indignation of outraged humanity. Does the Christian God, whom his followers eulogize as the Deity of humility and peace—He, the regenerator of the world, the meek reformer—authorise one man to rise against another, and, because lictors are at his beck, to chain and torture him as an Infidel?

When the Apostles went abroad to convert the nations, were they enjoined to stab and poison all who disbelieved the divinity of Christ's mission ; assuredly, they would have been no more justifiable in this case than he is at present who puts into execution the law which inflicts pillory and imprisonment on the Deist.

Has not Mr. Eaton an equal right to call your Lordship an Infidel as you have to imprison him for promulgating a different doctrine from that which you profess? What do I say? Has he not even a stronger plea? The word *Infidel* can only mean anything when applied to a person who professes that which he disbelieves. The test of truth is an undivided reliance on its inclusive powers ; the test of conscious falsehood is the variety of the forms under which it presents itself, and its tendency towards employing whatever coercive means may be within its command, in order to procure the admission of what is unsusceptible of support from reason or persuasion. A dispassionate observer would feel himself more powerfully interested in favor of a man, who, depending on the truth of his opinions, simply stated his reasons for entertaining them, than in that of his aggressor, who, daringly avowing his unwillingness or incapacity to answer them by argument, proceeded to repress the energies and break the spirit of their promulgator by that torture and imprisonment whose infliction he could command.

I hesitate not to affirm that the opinions which Mr. Eaton sustained, when undergoing that mockery of a trial, at which your Lordship presided, appear to me more true and good than those of his accuser; but were they false as the visions of a Calvinist, it still would be the duty of those who love liberty and virtue to raise their voice indignantly against a reviving system of persecution—against the coercively repressing any opinion, which, if false, needs but the opposition of truth; which, if true, in spite of force must ultimately prevail.

Mr. Eaton asserted that the scriptures were, from beginning to end, a fable and imposture,* that the Apostles were liars and deceivers. He denied the miracle, the resurrection, and ascension of Jesus Christ. He did so: and the Attorney-General denied the proposition which he asserted, and asserted that which he denied. What singular conclusion is deducible from this fact? None, but that the Attorney-General and Mr. Eaton sustained two opposite opinions. The Attorney-General puts some obsolete and tyrannical laws in force against Mr. Eaton, because he publishes a book tending to prove that certain supernatural events, which are supposed to have taken place eighteen centuries ago, in a remote corner of the world, did not actually take place. But how is the truth or falsehood of the facts in dispute relevant to the merit or demerit attachable to the advocates of the two opinions? No man is accountable for his belief, because no man is capable of directing it. Mr. Eaton is therefore totally blameless. What are we to think of the justice of a sentence which punishes an individual against whom it is not even attempted to attach the slightest stain of criminality?

It is asserted that Mr. Eaton's opinions are calculated to subvert morality. How? What moral truth is spoken of with irreverence or ridicule in the book which he published? Morality, or the duty of a man and citizen, is founded on the relations which arise from the association of human beings, and which vary with the circumstances produced by the different states of this association. This duty, in similar situations, must be precisely the same in all ages and nations. The opinion contrary to this has arisen from a supposition that the will of God is the source or criterion of morality. It is plain that the utmost exertion of Omnipotence could not cause that to be virtuous which actually is vicious. An all-powerful Demon might, indubitably, annex punishments to virtue and rewards to vice, but could not by these means effect the slightest change in their abstract and immutable

* See the Attorney-General's Speech.—(S.)

natures. Omnipotence could vary, by a providential interposition, the relations of human society; in this latter case, what before was virtuous would become vicious, according to the necessary and natural result of the alteration; but the abstract natures of the opposite principles would have sustained not the slightest change. For instance, the punishment with which society restrains the robber, the assassin, and the ravisher, is just, laudable, and requisite. We admire and respect the institutions which curb those who would defeat the ends for which society was established; but, should a precisely similar coercion be exercised against one merely who expressed his disbelief of a system admitted by those entrusted with the executive power, using at the same time no methods of promulgation but those afforded by reason, certainly this coercion would be eminently inhuman and immoral; and the supposition that any revelation from an unknown power avails to palliate a persecution so senseless, unprovoked, and indefensible, is at once to destroy the barrier which reason places between vice and virtue, and leave to unprincipled fanaticism a plea whereby it may excuse every act of frenzy which its own wild passions, and the inspirations of the Deity, have engendered.

Moral qualities are such as only a human being can possess. To attribute them to the Spirit of the Universe, or to suppose that it is capable of altering them, is to degrade God into man, and to annex to this incomprehensible Being qualities incompatible with any *possible definition of its nature*. It may be here objected :—Ought not the Creator to possess the perfections of the creature ? No. To attribute to God the moral qualities of man, is to suppose him susceptible of passions, which, arising out of corporeal organisation, it is plain that a pure Spirit cannot possess. A bear is not perfect except he is rough, a tiger is not perfect if he be not voracious, an elephant is not perfect if otherwise than docile. How *deep* an argument must not that be which proves that the Deity is as rough as a bear, as voracious as a tiger, and as docile as an elephant. But even suppose, with the vulgar, that God is a venerable old man, seated on a throne of clouds, his breast the theatre of various passions analogous to those of humanity, his will changeable and uncertain as that of an earthly king; still, goodness and justice are qualities seldom nominally denied him, and it will be admitted that he disapproves of any action incompatible with those qualities. Persecution for opinion is unjust. With what consistency, then, can the worshippers of a Deity whose benevolence they boast embitter the existence of their fellow being, because his ideas of that Deity are different from those which they entertain ? Alas ! there is no consistency in those persecutors who worship a benevolent Deity; those who worship a Demon would alone act consonantly to these principles by imprisoning and torturing in his name.

Persecution is the only name applicable to punishment inflicted on an individual in consequence of his opinions. What end is persecution designed to answer ? Can it convince him whom it injures ? Can it prove to the people the falsehood of his opinions ? It may make *him* a hypocrite, and *them* cowards; but bad means can promote no good end. The unprejudiced mind looks with suspicion on a doctrine that needs the sustaining hand of power.

Socrates was poisoned because he dared to combat the degrading superstitions in which his countrymen were educated. Not long after his death Athens recognised the injustice of his sentence ; his accuser, Melitus, was condemned, and Socrates became a demigod.

Jesus Christ was crucified because he attempted to supersede the ritual of Moses with regulations more moral and humane—his very judge made public acknowledgment of his innocence, but a bigoted and ignorant mob demanded the deed of horror—Barabbas the murderer and traitor was released. The meek reformer Jesus was immolated to the sanguinary Deity of the Jews. Time rolled on, time changed the situations, and with them the opinions of men.

The vulgar, ever in extremes, became persuaded the crucifixion of Jesus was a supernatural event. Testimonies of miracles, so frequent in unenlightened ages, were not wanting to prove that he was something divine. This belief, rolling through the lapse of ages, met with the reveries of Plato and the reasonings of Aristotle, and acquired force and extent, until the divinity of Jesus became a dogma, which to dispute was death, which to doubt was infamy.

Christianity is now the established religion : he who attempts to impugn it, must be contented to behold murderers and traitors take precedence of him in public opinion ; though, if his genius be equal to his courage, and assisted by a peculiar coalition of circumstances, future ages may exalt him to a divinity, and persecute others in his name, as he was persecuted in the name of his predecessors in the homage of the world.

The same means that have supported every other popular belief, have supported Christianity. War, imprisonment, murder, and falsehood ; deeds of unexampled and incomparable atrocity have made it what it is. We derive from our ancestors a belief thus fostered and supported : we quarrel, persecute, and hate for its maintenance. Does not analogy favour the opinion that, as, like other systems, Christianity has arisen and augmented, so like them it will decay and perish ; that, as violence, darkness, and deceit, not reasoning and persuasion, have procured its admission among mankind, so, when enthusiasm has subsided, and time, that infallible controverter of false opinions, has involved its pretended evidences in the darkness of antiquity, it will become obsolete ; that Milton's poem alone will give permanency to the remembrance of its absurdities ; and that men will laugh as heartily at grace, faith, redemption, and original sin, as they now do at the metamorphoses of Jupiter, the miracles of Romish saints, the efficacy of witchcraft, and the appearance of departed spirits.

Had the Christian Religion commenced and continued by the mere force of reasoning and persuasion, by its self-evidence, excellence and fitness, the preceding analogy would be inadmissible. We should never speculate on the future obsoleteness of a system perfectly conformable to nature and reason : it would endure so long as they endured ; it would be a truth as indisputable as the light of the sun, the criminality of murder, and other facts, physical and moral, which, depending on our organisation and relative situations, must remain acknowledged as satisfactory, so long as man is man. It is an incontrovertible fact, the consideration of which ought to repress the hasty conclusions of credulity, or moderate its obstinacy in maintaining them, that, had the Jews not been a barbarous and fanatical race of men, had even the resolution of Pontius Pilate been equal to his candour, the Christian Religion never could have prevailed, it could not even have existed. Man ! the very existence of whose most cherished opinions depends from a thread so feeble, arises out of a source so equivocal, learn at least humility ; own at least that it is possible for thyself also to have been seduced by education and circumstance into the admission of tenets destitute of rational proof, and the truth of which has not yet been satisfactorily demonstrated. Acknowledge at least that the falsehood of thy brother's opinions is no sufficient reason for his meriting thy hatred. What ! because a fellow being disputes the reasonableness of thy faith, wilt thou punish him with torture and imprisonment ? If persecution for religious opinions were admitted by the moralist, how wide a door would not be open by which convulsionists of every kind might make inroads on the peace of society ! How many deeds of barbarism and blood would not receive a sanction ! But I will demand, if that man is not rather entitled to the respect than the discountenance of society, who, by disputing a received doctrine, either proves its falsehood and inutility (thereby aiming at the abolition of what is false and useless), or gives to its adherents an opportunity of establishing its excellence and truth. Surely this can be no crime. Surely the individual who devotes his time to fearless and unrestricted inquiry into the grand questions arising out of our moral nature ought rather to receive the patronage, than encounter the vengeance, of an enlightened legislature. I would have you to know, my Lord, that fetters of iron cannot bind or subdue the soul of virtue. From the damps and solitude of its dungeon it ascends, free and undaunted, whither thine, from the pompous seat of judgment, dare not soar. I do not warn you to beware lest your profession as a Christian should make you forget that you are a man ; but I warn you against festinating that period, which, under the present coercive system, is too rapidly maturing, when the seats of justice shall be the seats of venality and slavishness, and the cells of Newgate become the abode of all that is honourable and true.

I mean not to compare Mr. Eaton with Socrates or Jesus ; he is a man of blameless and respectable character ; he is a citizen unimpeached with crime ; if, therefore, his rights as a citizen and a man have been infringed, they have been infringed by illegal and immoral violence. But I will assert that, should a second Jesus arise among men ; should such a one as Socrates again enlighten the earth ; lengthened imprisonment and infamous punishment (according to the regimen of persecution revived by your Lordship) would effect what hemlock and the cross have heretofore effected, and the stain on the national character, like that on Athens and Judea, would remain indelible, but by the destruction of the history in which it is recorded. When the Christian Religion shall have faded from the earth, when its memory like that of Polytheism now shall remain, but remain only as the subject of ridicule and wonder, indignant posterity would attach immortal infamy to such an outrage ; like the murder of Socrates, it would secure the execration of every age.

The horrible and wide-wasting enormities, which gleam like comets through the darkness of gothic and superstitious ages, are regarded by the moralist as no more than the necessary effect of known causes ; but, when an enlightened age and nation signalises itself by a deed becoming none but barbarians and fanatics, philosophy itself is even induced to doubt whether human nature will ever emerge from the pettishness and imbecility of its childhood. The system of persecution, at whose new birth, you, my Lord, are one of the presiding midwives, is not more impotent and wicked than inconsistent. The press is loaded with what are called (ironically, I should conceive) *proofs* of the Christian religion : these books are replete with invective and calumny against infidels ; they presuppose that he who rejects Christianity must be utterly divested of reason and feeling ; they advance the most unsupported assertions, and take as first principles the most revolting dogmas. The inferences drawn from these assumed premises are imposingly logical and correct ; but, if a foundation is weak, no architect is needed to foretell the instability of the superstructure. If the truth of Christianity is not disputable, for what purpose are these books written ? If there are sufficient to prove it, what further need of controversy ? *If God has spoken, why is the universe not convinced ?* If the Christian religion needs deeper learning, more painful investigation to establish its genuineness, wherefore attempt to accomplish that by force, which the human mind can alone effect with satisfaction to itself ? If, lastly, its truth *cannot* be demonstrated, wherefore impotently attempt to snatch from God the government of his creation, and impiously assert that the Spirit of Benevolence has left that knowledge most essential to the well-being of man, the only one which, since its promulgation, has been the subject of unceasing cavil, the causes of irreconcileable hatred ? Either the Christian religion is true, or it is not. If true it comes from God, and its authenticity can admit of doubt and dispute no further than its Omnipotent Author is willing to allow. If true it admits of rational proof, and is capable of being placed equally beyond controversy, as the principles which have been established concerning matter and mind, by Locke and Newton ; and in proportion to the usefulness of the fact in dispute, so must it be supposed that a benevolent being is anxious to procure the diffusion of its knowledge on the earth,—If false, surely no enlightened legislature would punish the reasoner, who opposes a system so much the more fatal and pernicious as it is extensively admitted; so much the more productive of absurd and ruinous consequences, as it is entwined by education, with the prejudices and affections of the human heart, in the shape of a popular belief.

Let us suppose that some half-witted philosopher should assert that the earth was the centre of the universe, or that idea could enter the human mind independently of sensation or reflexion. This man would assert what is demonstrably incorrect; he would promulgate a false opinion. Yet, would he therefore deserve pillory and imprisonment? By no means; probably few would discharge more correctly the duties of a citizen and a man. I admit that the case above stated is not precisely in point. The thinking part of the community has not received as indisputable the truth of Christianity, as they have that of the Newtonian system. A very large portion of society, and that powerfully and extensively connected, derives its sole emolument from the belief of Christianity, as a popular faith.

To torture and imprison the asserter of a dogma, however ridiculous and false, is highly barbarous and impolitic. How, then, does not the cruelty of persecution, become aggravated when it is directed against the opposer of an opinion *yet under dispute*, and which men of unrivalled acquirements, penetrating genius, and stainless virtue, have spent, and at last sacrificed, their lives in combating!

The time is rapidly approaching, I hope that you, my Lord, may live to behold its arrival, when the Mahometan, the Jew, the Christian, the Deist, and the Atheist, will live together in one community, equally sharing the benefits which arise from its association, and united in the bonds of charity and brotherly love. My Lord, you have condemned an innocent man : no crime was imputed to him— and you sentenced him to torture and imprisonment. I have not addressed this letter to you with the hope of convincing you that you have acted wrong. The most unprincipled and barbarous of men are not unprepared with sophisms to prove that they would have acted in no other manner, and to show that vice is virtue. But I raise my solitary voice to express my disapprobation, so far as it goes, of the cruel and unjust sentence you passed upon Mr. Eaton—to assert, so far as I am capable of influencing, those rights of humanity which you have wantonly and unlawfully infringed.

My Lord,
Yours, &c.